Interpreting Japanese Society

The contributors to this new edition of *Interpreting Japanese Society* have all spent long periods living and working in Japan and they cover such areas as religion, ritual, leisure, family and social relations. Many of the chapters also examine local perceptions of time and space, thus offering invaluable keys to understanding and interpreting indigenous ways of thinking not easily accessible to outsiders with more superficial experience. New topics for this edition include an original interpretation of the sinister Aum Shinrikyo, a Japanese view of Western philosophy, an account of hi-tech computerized healers and an explanation of ghost marriages.

This new, updated and revitalized edition of a classic work demonstrates the depth and quality of an anthropological approach to the study of the people who inhabit Japan. It also shows the important contribution research in such a rapidly changing industrialized nation can make to the subject of anthropology.

Joy Hendry is Professor of Social Anthropology at Oxford Brookes University. She has twenty-five years' experience specializing in the study of Japan and is the author of *Understanding Japanese Society* and *Wrapping Culture*.

Interpreting Japanese Society

Anthropological approaches

Edited by Joy Hendry

Second edition

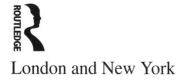

London and New York

First edition published 1986 by JASO

Second edition published 1998 by Routledge
11 New Fetter Lane, London EC4P 4EE

Simultaneously published in the USA and Canada
by Routledge
29 West 35th Street, New York, NY 10001

Typeset in Times by Keystroke, Jacaranda Lodge, Wolverhampton
Printed and bound in Great Britain by TJ International Ltd, Padstow, Cornwall

British Library Cataloguing in Publication Data
A catalogue record for this book is available from the British Library

Library of Congress Cataloging in Publication Data
A catalogue record for this book has been requested

ISBN 0–415–17267–5 (hbk)
ISBN 0–415–17268–3 (pbk)

Contents

Illustrations

FIGURES

TABLES

Contributors

Jane M. Bachnik is Professor of Anthropology at the Ministry of Education, National Institute of Multi-media Education, Chiba, Japan. Interests include: the family, the organization of self and social order, and internet usage, all in contemporary Japan, and pedagogy for cross-cultural teaching and learning. Publications: *Situated Meaning: Inside and Outside in Japanese Self, Society and Language* (1994), *Family, Self and Society in Contemporary Japan* (in press) and *A Pedagogy for Cross-Cultural Teaching and Learning* (in press).

Patrick Beillevaire is an anthropologist and historian, chargé de recherche at the Centre National de la Recherche Scientifique, and a member of the Centre de Recherche sur le Japon of the Ecole des Hautes Etudes en Sciences Sociales (Paris); his current areas of research are nineteenth-century Okinawan history, and the comparative study of rituals in the Ryūkyūs.

Eyal Ben-Ari is Associate Professor in the Department of Sociology and Anthropology of the Hebrew University of Jerusalem. His most recent books include *Body Projects in Japanese Childcare: Culture, Organization and Emotions in a Preschool* (1996) and *Japanese Childcare: An Interpretive Study of Organization and Culture* (1997). He has carried out fieldwork on Japanese white collar suburbs, Japanese kindergartens and the Japanese community in Singapore.

Augustin Berque is Director of the Centre de Recherche sur le Japon of the Ecole des Hautes Etudes en Sciences Sociales (Paris). His recent books include *Les Raisons du Paysage: De la Chine Antique aux Environnements de Synthèse* (1995), *Nihon no Fūdosei* (1995), *Être humains sur la Terre: Principes d'éthique de l'ecoumène* (1996). He is also editor of the *Dictionnaire de la Civilisation Japonaise* (1994). *Nature, Artifice and Japanese Culture* is a recent translation of his work into English (1997).

Laurence Caillet is Full Professor in the Department of Ethnology, Comparative Sociology, Prehistory and Ethnomusicology at the University of Paris-X Nanterre. Her interests include Japanese folklore, history of Japanese anthropology, fictive kinship, and worldview in contemporary urban Japanese society. She has published *Syncrétisme au Japon, O-Mizutori: le ritual de l'eau* *de Jouvence* (1981), *Fêtes et Rites des 4 Saisons au Japan* (1981), *La Maison Yamazaki* (1991), and *The House of Yamazaki* (1994).

Thomas Crump, following his first visit in 1980, has produced numerous publications relating to Japan, including two books, *The Death of an Emperor* (1990) and *The Japanese Numbers Game* (1992). Having retired from teaching anthropology at the University of Amsterdam in 1994, he still continues with research and fieldwork in Japan, relating particularly to the place of animals in Japanese culture.

Roger Goodman is University Lecturer in the Social Anthropology of Japan and a Fellow of St Antony's College, University of Oxford specializing on Japanese education and social welfare. He is the author of *Japan's International Youth* (1990) and co-editor and author of *Ideology and Practice in Modern Japan* (1992), *Case Studies on Human Rights in Japan* (1996) and *In Search of the East Asian Welfare State* (1998).

David C. Lewis is an anthropological consultant for a number of charitable organizations, in addition to being a freelance writer and lecturer. He is also a Research Associate of the Mongolia and Inner Asia Studies Unit at the University of Cambridge. One of his books, *The Unseen Face of Japan* (1993), contains material based on his anthropological studies of contemporary religious practices, beliefs and experiences in two neighbourhoods of a Japanese city.

Sepp Linhart is Professor of Japanese studies at Vienna University, Austria, specializing in the sociology and social history of modern Japan. His research is mainly on work and leisure, on the history of entertainment and on old age in Japan. His English-language publications include, as co-editor, *Japanese Biographies: Life Histories, Life Cycles, Life Stages* (1992) and *Aging: Asian Concepts and Experiences Past and Present* (1997). In spring 1998 his mono-graph *A Cultural History of the Ken Game* will be published in Japanese.

Dolores P. Martinez is a Lecturer at the School of Oriental and African Studies, University of London. Her fieldwork was on *abalone* (awabi) divers (the famous *ama*) in Mie-ken and her interests include popular culture, maritime anthro-pology, tourism and Japanese religion. She is co-editor, with Jan van Bremen, of *Ceremony and Ritual in Japan: Religious Practices in an Industrialised Society* (1995) and editor of *The Worlds of Japanese Popular Culture* (1998).

Kazuto Matsunaga is Professor of Social Anthropology and Folklore at Fukuoka University, Japan, specializing in comparative studies of the symbolism of the right and of the left. He is the author of *Symbolism of the Left Hand* (1995, in Japanese), and a number of research papers, such as 'Funeral Practices at Isen-cho, Tokunoshima, Kagoshima prefecture' (1996, in Japanese), and 'The Cultural Meaning of Reversal in Japanese Folk Beliefs' (1997, in Japanese).

Brian Moeran is a social anthropologist who has spent more than a dozen years living in Japan. His current interests are in Asian advertising, media and consumer culture and he is the author of numerous books, including *Women, Media and Consumption in Japan* (edited with Lise Skov), *A Japanese Advertising Agency: An Anthropology of Media and Markets*, and *Folk Art Potters of Japan*.

Okpyo Moon is Professor of Anthropology, Academy of Korean Studies. She gained a D.Phil at the University of Oxford, and is the author of *From Paddy Field to Ski Slope: The Revitalisation of a Japanese Village* (1989), 'Marketing Nature in Rural Japan' in P. Asquith and A. Kalland (eds) *Japanese Images of Nature: Cultural Perspectives* (1996) and 'Tourism and Cultural Development: Japanese and Korean Contexts' in Y. Shinji *et al. Tourism and Cultural Development in Asia and Oceania* (1997).

Mary Picone is Maître de Conférence at the Ecole des Hautes Etudes en Sciences Sociales (Paris), and a member of the Centre de Recherche sur le Japon.

James Valentine is Lecturer in the Department of Applied Social Science at the University of Stirling. His current research focuses on representations of marginalised sexuality, disability and ethnicity in Japanese culture. He co-edited *Unwrapping Japan* (1990), and his recent publications include 'Skirting and Suiting Stereotypes: Representations of Marginalised Sexualities in Japan' in *Theory, Culture and Society* (1997), and 'Pots and Pans: Identification of Queer Japanese in Terms of Discrimination' in A. Livia and K. Hall (eds) *Queerly Phrased* (1997).

Jan van Bremen is a cultural anthropologist and intellectual historian at Leiden University, interested in ceremony and ritual and the history and theory of anthropology and folklore studies. He is co-editor, with D.P. Martinez, of *Ceremony and Ritual in Japan: Religious Practices in an Industrialised Society* (1994), and, with Akitoshi Shimizu, of *Anthropology and Colonialism in Asia* (1998).

Teigo Yoshida is Emeritus Professor of Cultural Anthropology, University of Tokyo, specializing in Japanese village society, folk beliefs, rituals and religion. He is the author of *Nihon no Tsukimono* (1972) and *Shūkyō Jinruigaku* (1984), and editor of *Gyōson no Shakai-jinruigakuteki Kenkyū* (1979). His English papers include 'Mystical Retribution, Spirit Possession and Social Structure in a Japanese Village', *Ethnology* VI, 3 (1967) and 'Stranger as God: The Place of the Outsider in Japanese Folk Religion', *Ethnology* XX, 2 (1981).

Foreword to second edition

While the high quality of the original edition of *Interpreting Japanese Society* has been proven to specialist readers, this welcome new edition promises to make it accessible to the wider audience it deserves. Many original articles have been revised and updated, new ones added, and chapters reorganized around the thematic focus of space and time.

The book covers an impressive variety of topics and approaches, offering a good many conceptual slices of Japanese culture and society. Chapters address cosmology, rituals, village and new town, tradition and change, tourism, hi-tech healers, drinking parties, amusement quarters, child adoption and dance. Some authors pay more attention to Japanese modes of logical reasoning, knowing and believing, while others focus on behaviour, activities, social interaction and organization. (To a limited extent this contrast may correspond with differences between British and continental European scholarship.) Some are rigorous in text analysis; others present field-based ethnographies where one sees and hears live Japanese persons. Some chapters concentrate more on theoretical issues, and others more on empirical generalizations. By pointing up these differences I do not mean to pigeonhole any of the authors, only to show the range of relative emphases. I should stress that every chapter is theoretically guided, reflecting editor Joy Hendry's anthropological commitment to universalism.

Diversity is one of the book's great strengths. Not only does it appeal to heterogeneous domains and levels of audience interest, it also offers in a single volume a comprehensive spectrum of Japan as a complex society. An even greater strength lies in the way that all the chapters, variable as they are, are coherently organized around the central theme of space and time. This is the kind of textbook instructors look for when teaching graduate or upper-level undergraduate courses about Japan, or social/cultural anthropology in general. Not just a textbook, this should also serve as a research guide for specialists.

The ultimate merit of a book stems from its authors, and here we have a roster of prominent and solid scholars, well established in Japanese studies, anthropology, and related disciplines. Written largely by European authors, this collection is likely to stimulate American readers with new insights and to re-sensitize them to the epistemological problems of studying other cultures.

Finally, this volume attests to the editor's remarkable skill, her open-minded and level-headed judgement over where Japanese studies should be going, and her organizational leadership. Joy Hendry has played a key role in establishing the anthropology of Japan in Britain and continental Europe. At the same time, she continues to be a productive scholar whose work enjoys international repute. The great respect Hendry's colleagues have for her no doubt motivated their acceptance of her editorial agenda. Congratulations, Joy.

Takie Sugiyama
Lebra,
University of Hawaii

Acknowledgements

In bringing out the second edition of this book, I would like to thank again those who assisted in the preparation of the first, and above all Jonathan Webber, who took responsibility for many details of which I became fully aware only as I prepared the second edition alone. The voluntary staff of the *Journal of the Anthropological Society of Oxford*, in particular Bob Parkin, helped immeasurably to get the first edition under way, and I am especially glad that we can include D. P. Martinez and Roger Goodman, who as students did the copy editing and wrote the index respectively, this time as fully fledged contributors. I would like once again to acknowledge the hospitality of the Nissan Institute, largely through its Director, Professor Arthur Stockwin, for the conference on which the original book was based and for the invaluable practical help at that time of Roger Goodman, Brian Moeran, Mary Picone, Arne Røkkum, Valerie Saunders, Michael Shackleton, and Professor and Mrs Teigo Yoshida. Nick Allen, Noriaki Hashimoto, Yoko Hirose, James McMullen, Chihoko Moran, Brian Powell, Irene Powell and Ann Waswo all assisted at various stages in the initial editorial process. I would like to thank the many users of the original book for their encouragement to bring out another version, especially the reviewers and anonymous readers, of whom one, Takie Sugiyama Lebra, revealed herself and kindly agreed to write the Foreword to this new edition. I must also commend Vicky Smith and James Whiting at Routledge who have been wonderful pillars of support as we have dealt with new, revised and old papers all in the same volume.

We were initially supported financially by the Japan Foundation Endowment Committee and the Nissan benefaction to Oxford University. On the technical side, Stephen Ashworth, who typeset the first volume at the Oxford University Computing Service, must be thanked for retrieving the original papers and supplying them on disk ten years after the event, and Gerry Black, of Oxford Brookes University, for helping me to grapple with their unfamiliar format. The maps were produced by Chris Topley at the Department of Geology and Physical Sciences, Oxford Brookes University. For permissions, thanks to Kodansha Ltd of Tokyo for allowing us to publish (on page 92) a modified version of the diagram that first appeared in a work by Nakane Chie in 1972; Arnold Hodder Headline for the reproduction of Augustin Berque's paper which first appeared in the journal *Ecumene*, and the Catholic University of America Press for allowing us to use a revised version of a paper by Eyal Ben-Ari which originally appeared in *Anthropological Quarterly*. I would like to thank Kazuto Matsunaga and James Valentine for supplying the photographs which appear in the new text, and Jan van Bremen for obtaining permission from Fujita Shōichi to use the photograph reproduced in chapter 7. Responsibility for the content, opinions and conclusions expressed in the papers that follow lies solely, however, with the individual authors and not, of course, with the institutions and persons mentioned above who have so generously supported this project.

J. H.
Oxford, June 1997

Note on the text

Following the pattern set with the first edition of this book, with a mixture of approaches perhaps characterizing the joint editorship of one anthropologist specializing in Japanese studies and the other an anthropologist with only a general interest in the subject of Japan, we have, for example (with the exception of the maps), used macrons where they occur in Japanese personal names, place names and particular terms referred to – but not for Tokyo, Kyoto, etc. (more properly Tōkyō, Kyōtō), on the grounds that such names are to be considered as part of the English-language cultural domain. Similarly, we have followed the Japanese naming practice of putting the family name first, but with certain exceptions, that is, the names of those individuals (the two Japanese contributors to this book are a nice case in point) who have identified themselves as being equally content with the usual English style. However, all Japanese authors mentioned in lists of references are supplied with a comma after the family name, following Western practice.

COVER PHOTOGRAPH

The cover photograph on the paperback edition of the book shows some of the dancers discussed and analysed in chapter 17 by James Valentine (photo: Jim Holmes/Axiom).

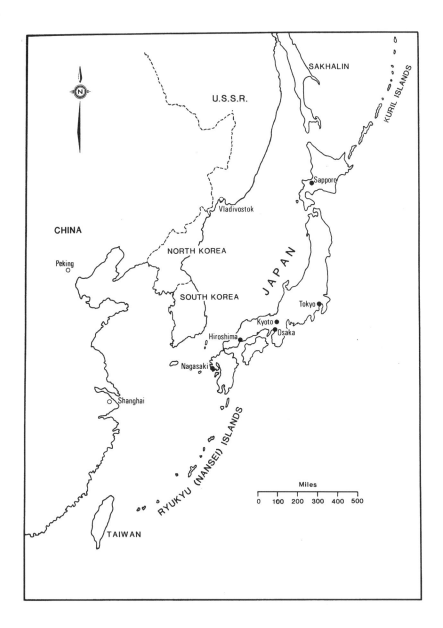

Map 1 Japan

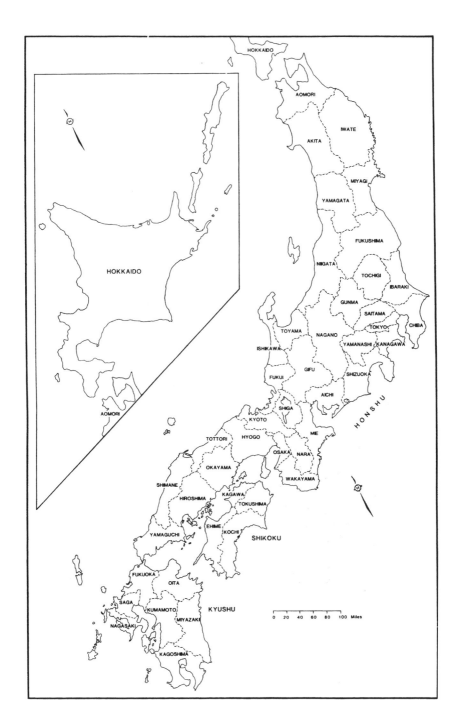

Map 2 Japan: prefectures (excluding Ryūkyū Islands)

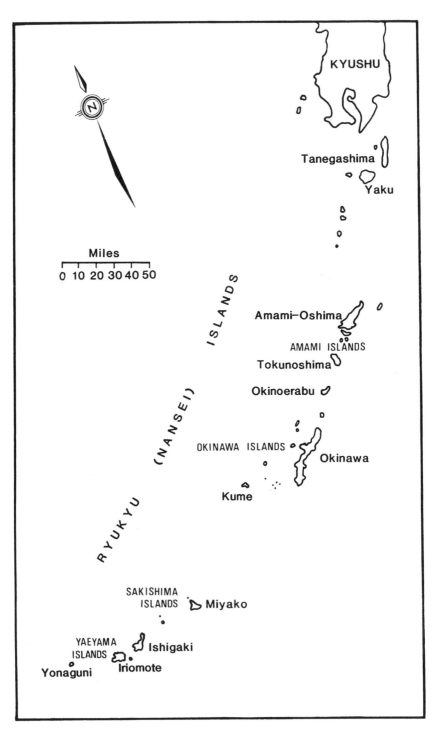

Map 3 Ryūkyū (Nansei) Islands: Japan's South-western Archipelago

Introduction

The contribution of social anthropology to Japanese studies

Joy Hendry

It gives me great pleasure to be able to introduce a second edition of *Interpreting Japanese Society*. The original version of this book was published as a record of the founding meeting of the Japan Anthropology Workshop (JAWS), a tentative gathering, almost as if to assess the wider strength of my own conviction that anthropology, and in particular social anthropology, had something important and interesting to offer to the more established field of Japanese Studies. It was published as an occasional paper of the *Journal of the Anthropological Society of Oxford* (*JASO*), and, as such, it was not as widely available as it might have been had we approached a commercial publisher.

Nevertheless, the book became something of a classic, a useful resource for teaching and research over ten years later, with several of the original chapters still the most authoritative contributions in their particular areas. The Japan Anthropology Workshop has, of course, grown beyond all initial expectations, and the value of anthropology to Japanese Studies is now well founded. I will always be grateful for the initial support of *JASO* editor Jonathan Webber, who was joint editor of the first edition. Although his interests have moved on and he is no longer co-editor, he has backed my resolve to bring out the second edition.

Anthropology has also moved on since I wrote the initial Introduction, and there has been much soul searching, especially amongst practitioners and critics in the United States, about its value in a postmodern world. My original Introduction laid out some of the characteristics of social anthropology, particularly in its European context, in an effort to convince sceptical Japanese Studies scholars of its value. I stand by the value, but perhaps now I can also offer the excellent Japanese material contained within these covers as an example of the continuing contribution that the subject of anthropology can make in a country at the cutting edge of high technology.

At the time of the first publication of this book, analysis of industrialized societies like Japan was quite limited, and the Introduction opened by explaining a growing interest in Japan among European scholars trained in social anthropology and other related fields, but geographically isolated from one another. It bemoaned a lack of opportunity for such scholars to share ideas, and the book was a first attempt to establish cooperation between us, and with our Japanese counterparts, for the future.

Since then, so much has been published in the field that Jan van Bremen has felt unable succinctly to update the original second chapter of the book, which was entitled, 'The post-1945 Anthropology of Japan'. Instead, he has made a new contribution, based on the work of Japanese anthropologists, which he did not include before, and to this I will return, but I would like to refer briefly here to the now quite numerous publications associated with meetings of the Japan Anthropology Workshop. Papers from the second meeting, held in conjunction with the European Association for Japanese Studies, were published in *Contemporary European Writing on Japan: Scholarly Views from Eastern and Western Europe* (Nish 1987). The fruits of our next solo meeting became *Unwrapping Japan* (Ben-Ari *et al.* 1990), which sought to emphasize the value of Japan to the study of anthropology, and whose deliberations were cited as a good example of collaboration between Japanese and foreign anthropologists (Yoshida 1987). The next gathering addressed the subject of *Ideology and Practice* (Goodman and Refsing 1992), and the following one *Ceremony and Ritual in Japan* (van Bremen and Martinez 1995).

Each of these publications continued the pattern, established in the first edition of *Interpreting Japanese Society*, of drawing on predominantly European and Japanese scholarship, and while *JAWS* has now matured into a more international organization (see, for example, Asquith and Kalland 1997; Ashkenazy and Clammer, forthcoming), this second edition will allow a wider audience access to some of the best early Japanese/European collaboration. Indeed, this was a quality of the book cited by both the anonymous readers engaged by Routledge to justify its reworking, and our hope is that it can thereby contribute to a rounder view of Japan than is currently evident in the rather closed American literature.

In the first edition we acknowledged our debt to the longer-established practice of cultural anthropology in Japan and the United States, which provided us with inspiration and background to prepare us for fieldwork, and to the personal help given to us in Japan. We also drew attention to some of the distinct philosophical traditions developed in Europe, perhaps most notably in British social anthropology, where different theoretical approaches had led us to ask different questions. It was evident from the contributions that we claimed no great unity, and there was of course considerable transatlantic influence and communication, but one aim of the book was to give an airing to European traditions somewhat different from those current in America.

This theme continues in the second edition where we have retained all our original contributors, and added two who were associated, as students, with the first conference. Of these, twelve are European, two are Japanese, one Korean, one self-styled 'Middle-Eastern' and two American, though all with considerable European training or influence, and they have all incorporated European approaches into their studies of Japan. A majority of the original contributors have retained their chapters, though several have been revised and updated, but four have chosen to replace their original chapters with newer work. The chapter contributed by Jan van Bremen, together with that of one of our new contributors, Roger Goodman, have inspired a new section on kinship and social relations.

One of the reasons why social anthropology had not previously figured very largely in Japanese Studies was because of its earlier emphasis on the study of pre-literate peoples, especially those with whom the rest of the world had had little communication. This fact influenced some of the negative Japanese reaction to *The Chrysanthemum and the Sword*, the best-selling anthropological treatise by Ruth Benedict commissioned by the US Office of War Information. In this Introduction I am going to suggest, however, that this background gives us a particular advantage in looking at the specific case of Japan. At the same time, it will also be possible to outline some of the approaches shared by the contributors to this volume.

To start with the most general and uncontroversial of our common features, all the contributors to this book talk about Japan on the basis of experience gained through fieldwork, albeit in many cases in addition to considerable library research. Ideally fieldwork involves participant observation. The researcher lives, as far as is possible, a life identical with the people he or she is interested in. In other words, as outsiders we try to live as a Japanese person might, and, most importantly, to see the world through Japanese eyes. We aim to gain an inside view of Japan and to understand the categories of the Japanese language, not as dictionary translations of English, French or German, but as Japanese concepts, related to other Japanese concepts, and forming part of *a* Japanese – not *the* Japanese – view of the world. For, in a complex society, there will be a number of different world-views, although some features may be shared, and even our Japanese contributors have chosen to examine worlds distinct from their own.

In this volume we have chosen to focus, among other things, on notions of time and space. These are culturally variable concepts and therefore need to be interpreted in a Japanese context. It might be thought that time and space are universal aspects of the world, valid in the same way for every society. Anthropologists have shown that this is not the case and that there is surprisingly wide variation in the way in which different societies measure time and comprehend space. By understanding the way in which these notions work in a particular society, it is possible to gain considerable insight into some of the central preoccupations and ways of thinking of the people being studied.

Berque's original chapter exemplified this approach in a consideration of Japanese perceptions of nature and its relation to space, but his work has developed (see, for example, Berque 1997), and he has submitted a newer piece which demonstrates the use of anthropology to examine considerations of space in the writing of the Japanese philosopher Watsuji Tetsuro in a European context. Ben-Ari's new chapter approaches the subject from a bottom-up perspective, examining various perceptions of 'place' among people living in and around the newly created community where he carried out fieldwork. He draws on recent anthropological theory as he examines the implications of these perceptions for action and 'contested' expressions of identity. The chapter submitted by our other new contributor, D. P. Martinez, examines the ritual expression of spatial boundaries through wider changes over time.

Beillevaire and Caillet have kept their original chapters, both also concerned with ritual, the former in the Ryūkyū Islands, where a relationship is demonstrated between space and 'temporality' or 'being in time', while the latter discusses the perception of time in the Japanese ritual year. This incorporates three different calendrical systems, two imported from outside Japan. Crump considers Japanese conceptions of numbers and cosmos, which he compares with traditional Pythagorean views. He has revised his chapter in the light of subsequent work for this new edition, and includes interesting references to the use of computer technology for determining one's fate according to ancient ideas.

Bachnik's chapter, which discusses the importance of the environment or context involving notions of time and space in the expression of the relational nature of the self in Japan, has been moved to the new section on kinship and social relations, as has the chapter by Moon, which has been revised to incorporate new theory and data gathered on return visits she has made to the field. The two new chapters in this section are concerned with practical consequences of deep-rooted ideas about the importance of continuity through time in family lines. Goodman uses his understanding of this principle, which affects both the running of children's homes and the traditional Japanese attitudes towards adoption, to explain why Western models of adoption and fostering for the welfare of a child have failed to make much impact in Japan. Van Bremen, on the other hand, considers new forms of death rites which have been found in twentieth-century Japan, notably a variety which involves ghost marriage to ensure the correct progress of the departed in their spiritual life.

In this second edition, the themes of time and space run through all the sections, at the suggestion of one of our anonymous readers, and Valentine's chapter, which was originally in the first section, has been moved to the last one, which takes up the theme of leisure. His concern is still with the spatial and temporal features of dance in Japan, but he has expanded the methodological aspects of his chapter, giving more emphasis to the ways in which dance performances can act as models of and for social reality but also examining the way social observers construct models of these models.

It might be commented that a native Japanese is in a better position to elucidate concepts such as time and space in their own language, but this leads to a second characteristic feature of social anthropology. We tend to look at societies other than our own, even in the countries where we have been brought up. This is the crux of the matter, for the values and categories we are taught as children become natural to us, unquestioned unless we move away. In looking at our own societies, we run the risk of taking for granted things which are in fact culturally relative. After all, time and space are things with which we are exceedingly bound up, and the same may be said for the subjects of the second section, namely, religion, science and cosmology.

Here, for example, the chapters by Picone and Lewis touch on topics such as illness and death, which can be highly emotive in one's own society; the anthropologist as outsider may be in a position to take a more dispassionate view, although van Bremen's new chapter challenges this assertion by drawing on much Japanese work on the subject of death. Once we have moved out of our own milieu for a period, it becomes easier to stand outside when we return, but by and large it is thought to be difficult to become detached enough to make a useful social anthropological analysis of the precise area to which we initially belonged.[1] We tend to follow Rousseau's maxim, reiterated by Lévi-Strauss (1966: 247), that to know Man one has to view him from a distance.

There is, of course, a problem with similarities between the societies of the observer and the observed, which may nevertheless be very different from other societies. We may well be more likely to note down, or just to find more interesting, differences between our host culture and that of our upbringing, as I have discovered in comparing Kim's account, from a Korean point of view, of some phenomena that I have also described elsewhere from my English one.

Since the first edition of this book, Harumi Befu and Josef Kreiner have held a conference to consider the extent to which the countries of origin of anthropologists affected their interpretations of Japan (Befu and Kreiner 1992). This followed up on an issue of concern in Britain at the time of the first edition, discussed in a volume addressing the subject of semantic anthropology, where it was argued that our explanations as anthropologists are 'as semantically engulfing as are those of the people we seek to explain; how unwittingly we impose shapes on the ethnographic data we claim to extract from other societies'.[2] I argued, then, that at the level of cultural background, at least, we had in this volume a splendid forum for the minimization of the problem, for the reports came from observers from no fewer than ten different nations, each with a different, though no doubt in many cases related, set of 'cultural baggage' to apply to the study of Japan.

There has been much discussion along these lines in the intervening period, already referred to above and now known as the 'writing culture' debate, but I would like to confine my comments again to the fact that both writers and subjects hail from industrialized societies. This brought up a two-way benefit of our particular field, for Japan was at the time the one highly industrialized society which had a very different cultural background from most other such societies. Within our own communities, then, we could provide detailed information to make possible an assessment of the numerous figures published comparing 'industrialized societies' as if this quality automatically gave them all sorts of other comparable features. We were well qualified, I suggested, to enter into the debate about the usefulness of 'convergence theory',[3] the assumption that the more industrialized or 'modern' we get, the more alike our social life would become – or, to put it in the more stark and sarcastic terms used by Collick, that 'modernization' is a 'sort of escalator leading from "traditional" to "modern" society – and that the differences between societies are simply the result of their different positions on this escalator' (1981: 9–10).

In the original volume, the chapters by Lewis and Picone presented evidence which challenged the theory that secularization accompanies industrialization, examining instead new features of religious behaviour that emerged in an urban context. Lewis discerned the importance of 'pseudo-scientific' explanations for traditional ideas, and his revised chapter includes an interesting new interpretation of the sinister and destructive Aum sect which was blamed for the poisoning of commuters on the Tokyo underground. Picone's new chapter addresses the roles of 'alternative' or spiritual healers, and points out that the legitimization they offer may be through association or affiliation with scientific and academic bodies, as well as religious ones. Van Bremen's new chapter documents an increase in rites associated with spiritual welfare in the twentieth century, and Martinez's chapter addresses the question of belief in the face of outside analysis of ritual.

Moon's chapter still considers the relationship between economic development and social change in a specific community, providing data which also challenge the common view of modernization as a unilineal transformation of societies. She in fact found more traditional patterns of social organization in a group with greater economic development than in one with very little change in the economic sphere, and this trend continues. Ben-Ari's chapter examines in detail all the 'complexity and contestation' of place-making in a newly built, mixed community which, he argues, is not only of the type now occupied by around one-third of the Japanese population, but also an important location of debates about middle-class ideology. He tackles head-on the problems of studying community in a complex differentiated world, but warns against overlooking 'enduring coordinates in the way Japanese conceptualize their communities'.

From our participant point of view, we have access to information about Japanese society which explains the way in which superficially 'Western' institutions work in practice in the Japanese case. Thus, within the social sciences we can complement the work of sociologists, economists and political scientists by operating at a grassroots level. Anthropologists usually seek out small groups to study so that they can get to know all the members well – and they spend long periods of time with the same people. They are thus in a position to distinguish what people do from what they say they do, and what they say they should do. Moeran's analysis of the importance of drinking sessions for local political behaviour is a particularly good example, since the Japanese political system appears superficially similar to those of other industrialized countries on which it was originally based.

One of the chief aims, at least of British social anthropological work, has been a holistic approach, which implies that one needs to evaluate all things within their social context. Several chapters in this book illustrate the value of this approach. Valentine's examination of elements of Japanese dance in their wider context is a good example, as is Linhart's interpretation of modern *sakariba* as a response to the pressures of urban life, this being the culmination of a consideration of this phenomenon in its historical context. Crump, too, relates the Japanese concern with numbers to the 'exigencies of Japanese life', illustrating how traditional symbols continue to be adapted to modern needs.

An interesting question here is whether this 'holistic' and 'contextual' approach helps us to understand a people who describe themselves in precisely these words – holistic and contextual – in contributions to the *Nihonjinron* literature (i.e., Japanese theories about what it is that makes them uniquely Japanese). Kumon Shumpei exemplifies this style of writing (in English) when he contrasts the Japanese cognitive process, which he describes as 'analytical', i.e., going from a whole to its parts, with a Western one which he sees as 'comprehensive', i.e., proceeding from individual elements to a larger whole. This he illustrates by comparing a Japanese expression of understanding, *wakatta*, which literally translates as 'divided', with a Western expression 'to comprehend' which implies the opposite (1982: 8–9). This is part of the evidence adduced to support his notion of Japanese as 'holists'. Further examples include an intriguing suggestion that Japanese word order follows a similarly analytic course which may be represented as '(S,v,p)' where S denotes a system, v a variable within that system, and p the value the variable takes in the specific case being discussed (ibid.: 13–14). This scheme seems to apply particularly to sentences with both *wa* and *ga* in them, where the word followed by *ga* may be seen as a variable of the word followed by *wa*.

The part of Kumon's argument which characterizes Japanese as contextualists contrasts the notion not only with that of 'individualist', but also with that of 'collectivist', according to a distinction made by Yoshida Tamito. Put succinctly, the contextualist retains a personal identity, which the collectivist probably loses, but this personal identity is virtually inseparable from the contextual identity. Thus, the individual changes, like the Greek god Proteus, depending on the context he is in or the people he is with. Kumon goes on to explain that a contextual, when separated from or not in a context, is like an amoeba and has no definite shape. However, once he joins a context, his shape is determined.[4]

Kumon gives as examples of contexts for self-realization the *sō*, *nakama* and *uchi*, 'inside' groups to which a Japanese individual may belong. The existence and importance of such groups for Japanese people have been pointed out by many observers, including anthropologists. Indeed, the so-called 'group model' of Japanese society has been a target for some criticism. Befu, for example, points out the common failure of commentators on Japanese society to distinguish between the group model as an ideological statement and the group model as a proposition about actual behaviour (1980: 36). He suggests that the emphasis on the group model is related to the contrast it provides with the individualistic nature of the societies of the observers concerned and, for Japanese commentators, the harmonious and unique picture it presents of Japanese society (ibid.: 38–43).[5] Bachnik's chapter in this volume points out the slippage here between a 'group model' and 'groupism' in her discussion of the more general problems of distinguishing between models and human practice.

The criticism of the group model is part of a wider criticism of the idea that any one model can be used to explain a complex society like that of Japan, with the implied assumption that there is one, homogeneous Japanese people about whom all sorts of statements can be made (see, for example, Sugimoto and Mouer 1981: 3). Sugimoto and Mouer suggest that this so-called holistic approach was initiated by Ruth Benedict's experience, previous to working on the Japanese, with the small-scale societies which formed the more traditional subject-matter of, in her case, cultural anthropology (ibid.: 5).

In my view, there is a problem here about the various uses of the term 'holistic'.

There is a great deal of difference between looking at social phenomena in their context, seeing them as part of a 'whole', as anthropologists do, and suggesting that the whole of a nation like Japan is made up of homogeneous parts. Kumon's use of the term would seem to add yet another dimension to its meaning, although I think his notion is closer to the former type than it is to the latter. Moreover, his argument about 'contexts' actually encourages a more microscopic view.

His argument is also concerned with cognitive processes which are learned along with language, not necessarily implying any more homogeneity than that of sharing modes of communication (including language, symbolism, etc.). In this respect, several of our chapters operate on the same level, particularly those which are concerned with notions of time and space; and Valentine's examination of dance as a cultural document is an example of a different order. On the other hand, some of the chapters, such as those of Beillevaire, Matsunaga, van Bremen and Yoshida demonstrate meticulous attention to regional variation in conceptions of cosmology. Nevertheless, Yoshida makes the important point that these regional studies should not lose sight of the more global perspective which emphasizes similarities between cultures.

It is important, then, not to confuse the self-analysis of *Nihonjinron* with anthropological description. The very existence of the *Nihonjinron* debate is itself ethnographically important, as Befu has shown (1984), and it presents a problem to the outside observer to decide whether or not it is possible to use the same criteria for analysis as these Japanese writers use themselves. For their type of approach diverges from the ultimate aim of anthropology in that they appear to seek to demonstrate Japan's uniqueness by comparison with unspecified amorphous outsiders – usually deemed Western – whereas anthropology seeks (if not always successfully) to find some universal principles by which all human societies can be described, and thus sets out to describe any particular society in relation to those principles. In other words, one tries to avoid explaining Japanese society in one's own terms, or solely in Japanese terms, but rather aims to apply value-free criteria as far as possible. Bachnik's carefully argued chapter illustrates both the complexities involved and the success with which such an exercise can be accomplished.

Thus, Moeran is able to compare the behaviour of his Japanese potters with that of Maoris of New Zealand, in the light of general theories about political oratory in 'traditional' societies; and Yoshida can interpret the dual sovereignty and complementary protection between brothers and sisters found in the Amami and Okinawan islands as a case of the classification of powers comparable with the situation found in ancient India and among the Meru of east Africa. Matsunaga's chapter contributes to the abundant material on the propensity of people to make classificatory distinctions between left and right; van Bremen refers to general theory on death rites; and Martinez comments on the question of belief. The last two chapters also make valuable references to Japan's Asian context.

Nakane Chie's work has been classed with *Nihonjinron* (see, for example, Hata and Smith 1983), but her *Japanese Society* (1973) is also clearly based on theories of social anthropological analysis. I think much of the criticism of this book stems from a lack of understanding of the social anthropological approach, or, more precisely, of the difference between a French structural approach and the previous structural functionalism of Radcliffe-Brown (see, for example, Hata and Smith 1983: 367). The 'model' presented in *Japanese Society* is not meant to explain all behaviour everywhere in Japan, but rather to elucidate an underlying structure, another kind of language, which is quite different, since once such a structure is identified, variations and transformations are only to be expected. Nakane's *Kinship and Economic Organisation in Rural Japan* (1967) well illustrates her awareness of such variations.

One of the problems of anthropology and its 'holistic' tradition is that one needs to define a small enough 'whole' with which to work. In this sense, one may return to Kumon briefly and note that the Japanese 'contexts' provide ideal manageable groups for anthropological investigation. The long-term nature of many such groups makes possible the type of face-to-face interaction which characterizes the small-scale societies on which anthropologists are trained. It is obviously not a 'small-scale' quality of Japanese society which makes it directly comparable with societies in Africa, New Guinea and South America. It is partly, I would argue, the way in which it has skilfully maintained face-to-face groups within the complex, industrialized nation it has become. This makes possible a kind of analysis now rather less applicable to studies of, for example, European communities.[6]

It is as difficult to describe succinctly what are the qualities of such face-to-face groups as it is to explain briefly what is social anthropology. In the space available here I can make only a few summary remarks, but I hope they will communicate the essence of the matter. One of the striking characteristics would seem to be the effectiveness of diffuse sanctions as a means of social control. In societies with no written laws or courts of any kind, or without even a centralized political system, some kind of order is nevertheless maintained in everyday life. Members of such societies share a system of values, a set of norms about how to behave in their relations with one another; and for the most part they live within the limits of each other's expectations. It is one of the interests of the anthropologist to try to ascertain the social mechanisms which underlie such order, and these vary widely from place to place.

It is sometimes useful to look at the sanctions which come into play when someone does step out of line, or to see what happens when a dispute arises. In such a society there are, nevertheless, various institutionalized ways of dealing with recalcitrants, but these may take the form of quite spontaneous reactions on the part of the people around at the time, including gossip, ridicule and informal ostracism. There may also be notions of what we would class as supernatural retribution, so that illness and accidents may be interpreted as punishments for some misdemeanour. Evans-Pritchard's (1937) convincing arguments for the role of notions of witchcraft as a means of social control amongst the Azande people of the Sudan provide but one concrete example. Such explanations are not unknown in Japan, as is evident in the chapters by Lewis, Picone and van Bremen.

However, it is not the particular mechanisms which are of interest here, but the general principle that people living in face-to-face groups are constrained by the experience to behave in a way which is acceptable to other members of their group. In a complex society, an individual has the ultimate option of moving away from a group which he or she finds intolerable, but the more involved one becomes in a group the harder it is to break the bonds. Where the importance of belonging to such a group is fostered from an early age,[7] as in the case of Japan, this is sometimes almost impossible.

Thus, even in a country where there is a legal system it is useful to be able to analyse other mechanisms of social control, especially where there is plenty of evidence to suggest that the legal system is in fact rather little used, and avoided wherever possible. These mechanisms will vary from group to group, but my own research (Hendry 1986) would suggest that Japanese education inculcates in children a predisposition to respond to diffuse sanctions and pressures associated with identification with a particular group.

A similar argument could be put forward about politics and decision-making. A training in social anthropology provides one with a certain amount of knowledge about how decisions are made in politically acephalous societies, with no system of leadership immediately recognizable from a Western point of view. I suggest that this can be quite useful when one is confronted with the emphasis on consensus and unanimity which is found in Japanese ideology. When a vote produces 100 per cent agreement, as was the case in elections in the village where I worked, one needs to look elsewhere to see how decisions are being made. Moeran's discussion in this volume of the importance of sake-drinking sessions for political manoeuvring is a good illustration of this point.

One is to some extent concerned here with a problem familiar to anthropologists, but by no means exclusive to them, of distinguishing between ideals and practice. In this case the distinction operates on two levels. At the level of the complex, 'modern' industrialized society, Japan has ideals and institutions not unlike those found in other industrialized nations. In practice, these operate at the grassroots level in quite different ways, as Goodman's chapter illustrates with regard to ideas of adoption and fostering. Kumon cited as an example 'the attitude most Japanese have *vis-à-vis* the present Constitution. They simply do not care much about its applicability to reality. The actual behaviour of the Japanese is not really determined according to laws like this' (1982: 15). At the grassroots level too, ideals are shared which may not represent actual behaviour – Moeran gives as an example the popular idea that statements made under the influence of drink are afterwards forgotten – but it is with an understanding of this distinction in mind that people are able to interact with each other.

Another feature of small-scale societies is that people come to know one another very well. There is a lot of role-play, since the same people wear different hats in the same arenas and with the same companions, so that there are various ritual mechanisms for distinguishing these roles from the individuals who play them. In a complex society, one may well play one's different roles on different stages, with quite distinct groups of people who rarely overlap. The description of the Japanese as 'contextual' would seem to provide an explanation of how they deal with the problem of combining qualities of both types of society. Linhart's chapter provides an illustration of the variety of behaviour possible among the same group of people.

In the context of a face-to-face group, much interaction takes place along lines understood only by members of that group (cf., Hendry 1993), or perhaps by other members of the same society who have been socialized to understand the type of symbolic communication which characterizes interaction between members of such a group. The training of a social anthropologist to interpret the symbolism of exchange, for example, or of ritual behaviour in general, would, I suggest, prepare him or her to examine group relations at a level which may be quite outside the experience of an observer from an individualistic society which places little emphasis on group identity. Indeed, it sometimes seems that Western writers feel they have 'explained' Japan when they describe the so-called 'group model', which has become so notorious these days. For an anthropologist, to identify the existence of face-to-face groups in a complex society should be just a beginning, a welcome aid to establishing a 'whole' to which they can apply well-established techniques of analysis.

NOTES

1 The work of Emiko Ohnuki-Tierney would seem to be an exception to this, although she is well aware of the problems. She returned, after many years in the United States, to the very area of her upbringing to carry out fieldwork for her *Illness and Healing in Contemporary Japan* (1984).
2 Parkin (1982: 5), referring also to Crick (1976).
3 Dore, as long ago as 1973 (1973: 10–13 and chapter 13), for example, addressed this problem and argued for at least a modified version of convergence theory, including some influence from the Japanese side.
4 An example of some of the possible implications of the contextualist argument has been published in English (Hamaguchi 1985).
5 Befu has for some time been seeking alternatives to this group model as the exclusive explanation of Japanese society and has organized a number of conferences in pursuit of this aim. The issue of *Social Analysis* referred to here appeared as a collection of papers presented at one such conference.
6 Interestingly, the chapters in this book which are most concerned with ready-made 'wholes', the studies of Beillevaire and Yoshida in islands of the Ryūkyū chain, are also particularly concerned with variations between them and structural features which appear to be common.
7 I have described elsewhere (1986) how this notion is fostered in small children.

REFERENCES

Ashkenazy, Michael and John Clammer (forthcoming) *Consumption and Material Culture in Contemporary Japan*, New York: Kegan Paul International.
Asquith, Pamela and Arne Kalland (eds) (1997) *Japanese Images of Nature: Cultural Perspectives*, Richmond: Curzon Press.
Befu, Harumi (1980) 'A Critique of the Group Model of Japanese Society', *Social Analysis*, nos 5/6, pp. 29–43.

—— (1984) 'Civilization and Culture: Japan in Search of Identity', in Umesao Tadao *et al.* (eds) *Japanese Civilization in the Modern World*, Osaka: National Museum of Ethnology (Senri Ethnological Studies, no. 16), pp. 59–75.

—— and Josef Kreiner (eds) (1992) *Otherness of Japan: Historical and Cultural Influences on Japanese Studies in Ten Countries*, Munich: Iudicum Verlag (Philipp-Franz-von-Siebold-Stiftung Deutsches Institut für Japan Studien, Monographien 1).

Ben-Ari, Eyal, Brian Moeran and James Valentine (eds) (1990) *Unwrapping Japan*, Manchester: Manchester University Press.

Benedict, Ruth (1946) *The Chrysanthemum and the Sword*, Boston: Houghton Mifflin.

Berque, Augustin (1997) *Nature, Artifice and Japanese Culture*, Northampton: Pilkington.

van Bremen, Jan and D.P. Martinez (1995) *Ceremony and Ritual in Japan: Religious Practices in an Industrialized Society*, London: Routledge.

Collick, Martin (1981) 'A Different Society', in Howard Smith (ed.) *Inside Japan*, London: British Broadcasting Corporation, pp. 9–58.

Crick, Malcolm (1976) *Explorations in Language and Meaning*, London, Melbourne and Toronto: Malaby Press.

Dore, Ronald (1973) *British Factory – Japanese Factory*, Berkeley and Los Angeles: University of California Press.

Evans-Pritchard, E.E. (1937) *Witchcraft, Oracles and Magic among the Azande*, Oxford: Clarendon Press.

Goodman, Roger and Kirsten Refsing (1992) *Ideology and Practice*, London: Routledge.

Hamaguchi, Eshun (1985) 'A Contextual Model of the Japanese: Toward a Methodological Innovation in Japan Studies', *Journal of Japanese Studies*, vol. XI, no. 2, pp. 289–321.

Hata, Hiromi and Wendy A. Smith (1983) 'Nakane's *Japanese Society* as Utopian Thought', *Journal of Contemporary Asia*, vol. XIII, no. 3, pp. 361–88.

Hendry, Joy (1986) *Becoming Japanese: The Pre-school Period*, Manchester: Manchester University Press.

—— (1993) *Wrapping Culture: Politeness, Presentation and Power in Japan and Other Societies*, Oxford: Clarendon Press.

Kumon, Shumpei (1982) 'Some Principles Governing the Thought and Behavior of Japanists (Contextualists)', *Journal of Japanese Studies*, vol. VIII, no. 1, pp. 5–28.

Lévi-Strauss, Claude (1966) *The Savage Mind*, London: Weidenfeld & Nicolson.

Nakane, Chie (1967) *Kinship and Economic Organisation in Rural Japan*, London: University of London, The Athlone Press.

—— (1973) *Japanese Society*, Harmondsworth: Penguin.

Nish, Ian (1987) *Contemporary European Writing on Japan: Scholarly Views from Eastern and Western Europe*, Tenterden: Paul Norbury Publications.

Ohnuki-Tierney, Emiko (1984) *Illness and Healing in Contemporary Japan*, Cambridge: Cambridge University Press.

Parkin, David (1982) 'Preface', in David Parkin (ed.) *Semantic Anthropology*, London: Academic Press (ASA Monograph 22), pp. v–vii.

Sugimoto, Yoshio and Ross E. Mouer (1981) *Japanese Society: Stereotypes and Realities* Melbourne: Monash University (Papers of the Japanese Studies Centre, no. 1).

Yoshida, Teigo (1987) 'Is Japan a Secular Society? A Report on the Third Japan Anthropology Workshop Conference', *Japan Foundation Newsletter*, vol. XV, no. 1, pp. 21–3.

Part I

Time, space and models of action

1 Time in the Japanese ritual year

Laurence Caillet

INTRODUCTION

Annual festivals are perhaps the most popular topic in Japanese ethnography. Most studies consist of monographs describing some annual festival in one village or throughout the country but we must also note historical analyses that attempt to recover the original, ancient form of a rite, and other kinds of essays that explain the structure of the festive year. The latter type of study is, of course, particularly conducive to the understanding of conceptions of time.

Yet such research, which attempts to expound the structure of a ritual year, involves nearly insurmountable difficulties in a country like Japan, which never elaborated its own astronomical calendar and contented itself with the importation of foreign ones. Through the course of history, this has resulted in the superimposition of three different calendar systems: the primitive agrarian calendar, the old lunar–solar Chinese calendar and the modern Gregorian solar calendar.[1] As a matter of fact, the Japanese have continuously shown a marked lack of interest in the computation of time and, generally speaking, in astronomy: they seem preoccupied only by the astrological use of calendars.[2] Consequently, the calendars themselves (two of which – the Chinese and the Gregorian – have been elaborated abroad) cannot provide us with any information about the Japanese rhythm of annual time. Therefore, I shall be discussing in this chapter only the ritual calendar – and not the ordinary, astronomical calendars – in an attempt to identify the differences between these two sorts of calendars. These differences will play a revealing role in the understanding of Japanese conceptions of time; I shall try not only to discover '*le rythme de l'activité collective*', which is the basis of calendars (Durkheim 1968: 15), but also to describe the characteristics of the calendar considered as a collective representation of time.

In fact, the superimposition of these different calendars gave rise to a complex ritual year. Its intrinsic complexity has indeed inevitably led to difficulties in interpretation, a situation which goes some way to explaining the sometimes strained efforts of Japanese scholars to elucidate simple principles. Roughly speaking, their attempts can be classified into two major tendencies, functional and structural. For Yanagita Kunio, a much-needed simplification is brought out by the distinction between calendar rites and agrarian rites;[3] for Origuchi Shinobu

(1973: 54), the apparent complexity of the calendar disappears when one considers the extreme monotony of the practices which, put in reductionist terms, seem to consist of nothing more than the multiple repetition of very few ritual elements. For Miyamoto Jōichi (1972: 128–34) as well, the rites are fundamentally repetitive, and the only difference which can be found between them concerns not the carrying out of the rites, but rather the nature of the spirits that are being worshipped – ancestors, or gods of nature. A similar hypothesis is developed, even more radically, by Ōshima Takehiko (1959: 82–98), who considers the establishment of two ritual categories: rituals dedicated to ancestors and rituals dedicated to unsatisfied spirits of the dead that cannot gain access to the status of ancestors.

Notwithstanding these rather functional points of view, which implicitly avoid the problem of the ritual calendar itself, the same authors apply themselves to the definition of an annual structure. They point out three essential structural principles: (1) the year is composed of two symmetrical segments; (2) its rhythm is sustained by the comings and goings of a ricefield god from mountain to fields, and from fields to mountain, where he takes the name of 'Mountain God'; (3) the interchange of temporal segments is metaphorically assimilated with the succession of human generations (see the discussion on the structure of the ritual year, p. 22).

All these theories are based upon a sort of historical analysis aimed at reconstructing an original simplicity which is supposed to be 'Japanese', and which contrasts with the degraded form of the rites at the present time. These theories are much too complicated to treat in detail here, but I shall try to consider their principal features in the light of contemporary ethnographic reality. As a matter of fact, the functional theories seem too empirical to make this reality intelligible, and the structural ones are, equally, too idealistic to make sense of it. In this chapter I shall consider successively the problem of the choice of ritual days, the structure of ritual periods and, finally, the structure of the ritual year as a whole.

RITUAL DAYS

Choice of ritual days

In present times, ritual days are fixed according to the numerical figure of the date of the month. Traditionally, however, there were three modes of determining ritual days: choosing the day according to the ordinal number corresponding to the figure of the month, called *jūnichi*, or 'double day' (such as the fifth day of the fifth month); fixing a day according to the Chinese signs of the zodiac; or determining a day by the phases of the moon.

Jūnichi

The festivals celebrated on 'double days' have their origin in China. Most of them were adopted by the Japanese court and, subsequently, by the urban population, before spreading to rural areas, where they were grafted onto pre-existing agrarian rites. Those celebrating 'double days' are usually aware of the foreign origin of the practices (concerning the zodiac, see Frank 1958: appendices).

Zodiac signs

Like the zodiac itself, many of the festivals celebrated according to the signs of the zodiac have been imported from China. Nevertheless, some purely Japanese rites are performed on days selected in accordance with the zodiac. One famous example is the ritual of *hatsu-uma*, the 'First Day of the Sign of the Horse'. Folk tradition relates that this day was chosen to commemorate the arrival of Inari, the Rice God, in Japan (this deity is supposed to have come to Japan on the first day of the sign of the horse in the fourth year of the Wado era, in AD 711). According to Yanagita (1972a: 246; 1951: 474) and Hashiura (1949: 169–70), the horse day was chosen to celebrate the Rice God because an old agrarian rite which had no link with the zodiac was performed on that day. This ancient rite is celebrated by a household head leading a horse with a magnificent harness to the mountain, so that the Mountain God (who goes to the plain at the beginning of spring to become the Ricefield God) can mount the horse and ride back with him. This particular role of the horse in spring may explain why the day of the sign of the horse was chosen to worship Inari.

The phases of the moon

Each month, most ceremonies fall on three dates: the fifteenth of the month, i.e. the day of the full moon in the old lunar–solar calendar; the seventh or the eighth, i.e. the day of the first quarter; and the twenty-third or the twenty-fourth, i.e. the day of the last quarter. This supposedly ancient mode of determining ritual days should permit the identification of rites of Japanese origin (Wakamori 1966: 8), though it should be noted that the date of the full moon was also very important in China and India. Examples that can be cited include the souls' festival, celebrated about the first full moon of autumn (*bon*), and the viewing of the full moon in the middle of autumn (*jūgo-ya*).

In fact, for a date to have been chosen according to the Chinese or primitive (and thus supposedly Japanese) calendar does not in itself inform us about the origin of the rite. All that can be said for certain is that the important dates of each month have exerted an attraction upon each other. Ceremonies of different origin tend to be grouped around one important day, while elements of a single rite are usually dispersed among various important and proximate dates. This has resulted in a great fluctuation in the dates of the ritual days, which, added to the previously mentioned superimposition of three different calendar systems, makes it extremely difficult to restore a coherent ritual calendar, even after an archaeological analysis of rites and practices has been made.

Definition of ritual days

In contemporary Japan, annual rites are usually referred to as the *nenchū* (or *nenjū*) *gyōji*, which literally means 'rites performed during the year'. However, this expression, which originated at the Heian court, did not at first signify the annual rites as such but designated a sort of table of rites (ibid.: 1). In fact, there was no generic term for annual rite; there existed only specific terms designating 'the day of the rite', such as *setsu-bi* (節日), 'joint day', an expression which makes an analogy between a day of ritual and a bamboo joint.

At present, many words meaning 'annual rites' still convey the idea of 'joint' or 'bamboo joint': the precise meaning of *sekku* (節句) in standard speech is 'the making of an offering [for the day of] joint'; and the dialect terms *shichi* or *sutsu* (Yanagita 1939: 1; Beillevaire 1982: 220), found in the southern islands, are none other than the local pronunciation of the word *setsu*.

Dialects provide us, in fact, with a great variety of terms which designate rites – thus, for example, *monbi* (in Ehime prefecture – see Yanagita 1946: 1608), a contraction of *mono-imi no hi*, the 'seclusion day'; *hata-bi* (in Kyushu – see Sakurada 1959: 1), the 'day for raising banners'; *shiba-bi* (in Kyushu – see Yanagita 1970a: 199), the 'day [for settling a sacred area] with faggots'; *kami-goto* (in Akita prefecture – see Yanagita 1946: 403), 'the god rite'; *orime* (in Kagoshima prefecture – see ibid.: 306), 'folding'; *toki-ori* (in Nara prefecture – see Yanagita 1939: 2; 1946: 1030), 'time folding'; and, lastly, *toki* (in Yamaguchi and Kagoshima prefectures – see ibid.), which according to ancient usage means 'moment' or 'opportunity'. Putting the matter succinctly, it can be said that there are two main ways of designating ritual days. The first refers to cult instruments, while the second characterizes the ritual day as a specific moment, a 'joint' or 'folding' in the everyday course of time. This form of conception of sacred times appears very clearly in Nara prefecture, where ritual days are called *toki-ori* or *toki-yori*, 'time folding', while ordinary days are known as *aida*, 'intervals' (ibid.). It should be noted here that nearly all these expressions do not literally designate the rites themselves, but rather the ritual days. They seem to signify that the ritual moment is more important than the ritual content. A rite seems to be a temporal link rather than a festival dedicated to a particular deity.

The multiplicity of meanings conferred on a single rite

A ritual day does not seem to have a finite, limited meaning in itself. It is just a moment where human and divine worlds come into contact, a moment the significance of which is not clearly stated. We shall consider here only one instance: the equinox festival known under the name of *higan*, the 'other shore', an expression which designates two weeks, one centred on the day of the spring equinox, the other on the autumn equinox.

The *higan* is considered everywhere in Japan as a Buddhist festival celebrating the arrival of the spirits of the dead on the other shore, i.e. in paradise. The choice of the equinox to celebrate this is founded on the fact that the equinox is the moment of the year when the sun sets the furthest to the west, in the direction of the very popular Amida paradise.[4] However, in many places the *higan* is, on the contrary, a festival welcoming ancestors returning to the village, exactly like the *bon* festival. For instance, in the Akita district of Akita prefecture people choose a day of the *higan* period to climb a hill. On the top of the hill, they make a great fire, the light of which guides the ancestors on their way back to this world. The rite is exactly the same as the one performed in other villages on the day of the famous *tanabata* (七夕) festival, on the seventh day of the seventh month, just a week before the souls' festival of the full moon, when the spirits of the dead begin to arrive in the village.

This walk in the mountain may also, at the same time, be the opportunity for solar rites. At sunrise people go to the east to make offerings to the rising sun; at noon they go to the south; and in the evening they go to the west. This rite, called *hi no tomo*, 'companion of the sun', may also be performed on the day of the village 'sanctuary festival' or *shanichi*.[5] This day is fixed, following Chinese custom, on those days of the signs of the elder-of-the-earth and of the rat that are closest to the equinox. Furthermore, most of the celebrations of *shanichi* may be performed for *higan*, especially the welcoming of the Ricefield God mentioned above (Berthier-Caillet 1981: 179, 339).

It is very difficult today to decide whether the solar rites are older than the festival for the spirits of the dead or older than the rites dedicated to the Ricefield God, because the *higan* is now a conglomerate of all these ritual elements.

Further examples will not be added here, but it must be mentioned that the description of most of the annual rites reveals how nearly all the ceremonies – like the *higan* – possess multiple meanings. It seems that a ritual has no finite meaning, but is fundamentally a moment in the course of the time which is considered sacred and on which is conferred a wide spectrum of possible meanings.

The local character of a ritual calendar

According to an investigation made in Shōwa 21st year (1946), 43.6 per cent of Japanese families celebrated the New Year at the beginning of the solar Gregorian year, 41.3 per cent did so at the beginning of the lunar–solar year (though to simplify matters people often prefer the same day of the following month) while 14 per cent mixed both calendars (Nishitsunoi 1958: 260). Today, because of the legal holidays, all families celebrate the solar new year. But the souls' festival, or *bon*, in the middle of the seventh month, is still often celebrated in the middle of August. The reticence felt over the celebration of rites that conform to the new calendar can easily be explained by the seasonal shift introduced when the Gregorian calendar was adopted. In the traditional calendar, the beginning of the year corresponds to the beginning of spring, and the *bon* festival must be celebrated at the beginning of autumn. The old year began in February (see Frank

1971), January and July coming too early to be considered as the beginning of spring and autumn.

In fact, the calendar unification, decreed by the Meiji government in order to reinforce political centralization, paradoxically added to the complexity of the calendar and gave support to its tendency to local variation, a tendency which, since the Middle Ages, has always been reasserted by the regular publication of provincial calendars.[6] Today, nearly every village possesses its proper ritual calendar, in which elements of different calendars are combined in conformity with local convenience.

In concluding the first part of this chapter, it can be stated that the coexistence of different ways of fixing ritual dates, the multiplicity of meanings attributed to a single rite and the local character of festive calendars all tend to prove that annual time is not perceived as a universal, but that it is considered as eminently contextual. Time does not seem to be conceived as an abstract category but rather as a concrete thing, which may be articulated and manipulated according to local ecological, agricultural or social necessities.

THE REPETITIVENESS OF RITES

In correlation with the multiplicity of meanings attributed to a single rite, and because of the reiteration of the same date according to different calendars, the ritual year as a whole seems to be composed of a small number of rites repeated many times with little variation (Origuchi 1973: 54ff.). The celebration of New Year, for instance, clearly shows this tendency towards reiteration. The main rites are centred on the 'Great New Year', celebrated according to the lunar–solar calendar on the first day of the first month, and on the 'Agrarian New Year', fixed to conform with the primitive natural calendar on the day of the full moon. Similar rites are also performed on the seventh day of the first month, the day which Chinese people used to call the 'Day of Man', and again on the eve of spring, the day called *setsubun*. Specialists usually try to characterize each of these four celebrations of the New Year. They consider the 'Great New Year' as the time of the restoration of the village community, and the 'Little' or 'Agrarian New Year' as the time of the restoration of agricultural fertility. The New Year celebration of the seventh day is characterized by numerous propitious rites, and the *setsubun* by exorcisms. This sort of differentiation is statistically possible, yet local analysis of New Year celebrations casts doubt on such conclusions (Hashiura 1949: 21; Kurata 1969: 5–42).

Consider, for instance, the ceremony of driving out the devils (*tsuina*), which originated in China. The ancient Chinese believed that demons could provoke particular trouble at each change of season (Wakamori 1966: 72; Bodde 1975: 75); this belief was introduced to Japan during the Muromachi period. Nobles and warriors used to expel evil forces at the beginning of spring; later on, the rite spread in Buddhist circles, and demon expulsions were added to Buddhist 'Meetings of the First Month'. Finally, the common people also adopted the belief – by scattering parched beans to drive out evil spirits for the *setsubun*. However, all these exorcism rites were mixed with welcoming rites dedicated to traditional Japanese demons, monstrous beings that regularly come from the other world to bring prosperity, and whose arrival to the village is celebrated at 'Great New Year', at 'Little New Year', or at 'Seventh-day New Year'. The interpenetration of these rites has been so intensive in the course of history that it is impossible to fix a single date for the accomplishment of a rite, or a single meaning for it.

This phenomenon is of sufficient significance that it seems difficult to consider it as simply contingent upon history, as have most Japanese ethnographers. On the contrary, it seems better to propose that this reiteration of the same rite is evidence of the Japanese cultural elaboration of the ritual cycle. To prove this, I shall now consider the example of autumn rituals.

One of the most famous Chinese festivals is celebrated on the ninth day of the ninth month (a 'double day') to ensure longevity. It was adopted at the Heian court, where people celebrated the 'double ninth' by drinking sake with chrysanthemums; and it later spread to rural regions, notably in the north-east, where it fused with harvest festivals. Moreover, in these remote north-east regions, people usually celebrate not only the ninth day of the month, but the 'Three Ninth Days' – i.e., the ninth, the nineteenth and the twenty-ninth days of the ninth month, 三九日 (*san-ku-nichi* in Tōhoku, or *mi-ku-nichi* in Chūbu) (Hashiura 1949: 253; Nishitsunoi 1958: 786; Wakamori 1966: 171).

The rites of the *inoko*, or 'young wild boar', celebrated in the south-west for the harvest, underwent a similar evolution. In China, the propitious rites of *inoko* were performed on the first day of the sign of the wild boar of the wild-boar month (the tenth month). They were celebrated on the same date when adopted by the Heian court, but the warriors who began to celebrate *inoko* during the Middle Ages chose the second day of the wild boar of the tenth month. Later, as a result of the reimportation of the warriors' rite to the court, nobles came to celebrate *inoko* three times a month. It is this triple celebration of *inoko* that peasants, in turn, finally adopted. They commemorate successively the first *inoko*, or '*inoko* for nobles and warriors', the second *inoko*, or '*inoko* for peasants', and the third *inoko*, or '*inoko* for merchants' – according to a process reflecting the social classes of the Edo period. It should be noticed, by the way, that the repetition of harvest rites implies the repetition of Ricefield God departures, as well as the indigenous creation of a corresponding welcoming rite for the deity in spring (Hashiura 1949: 261; Yanagita 1972b: 113). Thus the *inoko* festival, which is celebrated only once in China, is celebrated four times by Japanese peasants: once in spring, and three times in autumn.

The 'day of the sign of the bull', *ushi no hi matsuri*, which is commemorated in Kyushu at harvest time, attests to the same principle of repetition: one celebration in spring and three in autumn (Nishitsunoi 1958: 78; Yanagita 1972c: 417).

Ethnographers usually consider these repetitions to be the expression of the three great stages of the harvest process: the first-fruits offering, the harvest itself and the thanksgiving ritual (Inokuchi 1959: 151–60). Yet in most cases, the first-fruits offerings and the thanksgiving ritual are celebrated separately from the triple celebration of the ninth day, *inoko*, or the day of the sign of the bull.

Furthermore, peasants insist on the auspicious character of these repetitions and on the pernicious influence of 'unique' celebrations, which are often said to be *kata*, or 'one-sided' (Yanagita 1939: 5, 129). In Shimoina district in Nagano prefecture, celebrating 'Great New Year' and not 'Seventh-day New Year' is thought to be dangerous. In the Mino district of Gifu prefecture, people say the same thing about 'Great New Year' and *setsubun*, while in the district of Hiraka in Akita prefecture, celebrating the 'Great New Year' without celebrating the 'Little New Year' leads to the death of a mother or father.

The numerous moon-viewing rites of autumn are submitted to the same belief. Chinese custom calls for the contemplation of the full moon of mid-autumn, but Japanese rural rites prescribe viewing the moon not only on the fifteenth day of the eighth month for the yam-lifting (Yanagita 1946: 121–2, 589; Nishitsunoi 1958: 58, 443, 774), but also on the thirteenth day of the ninth month for the wheat harvest and chestnut gathering, and on the tenth day of the tenth month for the rice harvest and the lifting of giant radishes. The indissoluble links between these moon contemplations are made explicit by their denominations. The fifteenth day of the eighth month is called *otoko meigetsu*, 'men's full moon', and that of the thirteenth of the ninth month is called *onna meigetsu*, 'women's full moon'. *Kata* ('one-sided') celebrations are often strictly forbidden, and it is said that if clouds hide the moon on the fifteenth of the eighth month, it is better not to look at the thirteenth-day moon of the ninth month, as an unbalanced celebration of the rite may bring bad luck (ibid.: 197).

It may be thought that these repetitions are the expression of an obsessional temperament, but their objective consequence is that rites do not constitute definite points on the abstract course of time, but rather that they compose temporal segments. There is not one specific day celebrating the arrival of the Ricefield God, but rather a long period which may be called the period of his arrival. Rites are privileged moments, the meaning of which determines the meaning of ordinary days considered as *aida*. Berque (1982: 63) proposes to treat *aida* (or *ma*) as a spatial concept, such that the nature of its limits or boundaries constitutes part of its character or definition; similarly, the character of the *aida* (the ordinary days between rites) is in part defined by the character of the rites (*toki*) that they separate. Moreover, the intensive repetition of rites provokes a sense of some kind of real, concrete time which can be grasped only through the meanings given to it (auspicious, dangerous, etc.), and not through any mathematical model. The sort of time to which the annual rites give birth is not an empty medium, but rather an uninterrupted succession of various temporal segments. It is a qualitative time more than a quantitative one.

THE STRUCTURE OF THE RITUAL YEAR

It should now be clear that such complexity has led scholars to propose simple structures to the course of the annual ritual cycle. Three main structures have been pointed out.

The bipartition of the year

According to a Chinese commentary of the fifth century,[7] the Japanese did not know the four seasons and defined a year as the succession of spring and autumn, the season of ploughing and the season of harvest. This commentary informs us of two things: the agrarian character of the definition of the primitive year and the bipartition of this year. The former is confirmed by the etymology of the word *toshi*, which nowadays means 'year', but the original meaning is 'rice fruit' or 'rice crop', which developed in 'the duration between two rice crops', namely, 'year' (see, for instance, Ōno *et al.* 1974: 911).[8]

The problem of bipartition requires further discussion. Hirayama (1957: 93–4) pointed out that the *Shoku Gunsho Ruijū* (an important nineteenth-century compilation of classical texts) gives a list of the official rites for a half-year. For the first six months of the year, the rites are described in detail in one column, and for the last six months, at the same day of the month, there is written only 'idem.', with an indication of variants as appropriate. Furthermore, many ethnographers, following Yanagita (1970b: 37ff.), have attempted to prove the dual character of the ritual year, which they thought was symmetrically organized around an axis connecting its two most important ritual periods, the New Year and the *bon* festival. In fact, despite the influence of the Chinese ritual calendar on the New Year celebrations, and the Buddhist influence on the souls' festival, these two sacred moments still seem to resemble one another. They are very similar both in their calendrical structure and in the ritual practices performed.

When 'Little New Year' is counted as the climax of the New Year period (Yanagita 1972b: 32), the New Year and *bon* periods may both be seen to centre on the first full moon of the agricultural seasons.

It is true that today, the *bon* festival seems to be a Buddhist festival dedicated to prayers for the spirits of the dead, whereas New Year seems to be the celebration of a calendrical deity called *toshi-gami* or *toshitoku-gami*, 'Year God'. However, a detailed investigation shows that the *bon* festival is also an auspicious period, and that New Year celebrations are also dedicated to dead spirits (Yanagita 1970b: 59; 1972b: 92). In some places, for instance, the offerings to the Year God and to the ancestors coming for the *bon* festival are presented on the same domestic altar, which is renewed every year (Hayakawa, quoted in Ōshima 1959: 78).

That the *bon* festival and the New Year were originally similar festivals is very probable, and one may say that in olden times they effectively divided the year into two halves, separated from one another by the sacred periods of the ancestors' return. The real problem is to discover whether this symmetrical principle should or should not be regularly extended to the whole year, as many ethnographers have suggested. Certainly, the ritual year marks other instances of symmetry.

The most obvious of these is the symmetry of the first day of the sixth month with the first day of the twelfth month – both of them are under the sign of water and are dedicated to exorcisms of aquatic dangers. It is said that snakes slough on the first day of the sixth month, and that one must avoid going under mulberry trees, since this is where they do so. Everyone makes offerings to water deities (these deities are often represented by snakes) in order to avoid drowning. On the first day of the twelfth month, one must not go near rivers or the sea so as to avoid similar perils. As Wakamori Tarō (1966: 142) points out, the cause of the symmetry of these two ritual events is the ancient performance of purification rites before the beginning of the New Year and *bon* festival periods.

In fact, it can be suggested that the annual rites which are repeated every six months are all linked to the New Year and *bon* celebrations, and to the rites for the equinox. This corresponds to the four annual returns of the ancestors to this world. The reality of this symmetry raises no doubt, but its primitiveness must be questioned, since it is dictated by the astronomical calendar, which is of Chinese origin. It should also be noted that this 'original' symmetry can be discovered only through the difficult archaeology of ritual dates defended by Yanagita and his disciples. The very existence of this difficulty in itself tends to prove that the Japanese did not hold much store by such astronomical symmetry, which has since completely disappeared, owing to the historical evolution of ritual calendars.

Moreover, there seems to be another symmetry principle that gives structure to the ritual year, namely, the belief in the comings and goings of the Ricefield God/Mountain God.

The comings and goings of the Ricefield God

As Origuchi Shinobu (1973: 55) justly remarked, all Japanese folk rituals are repeatedly marked by the welcoming of a god on his arrival and the escorting of him back on his departure. This welcoming and escorting of gods provides the opportunity for elaborate processions, which may constitute the core of the ceremonies. The structural value of this principle (of the comings and goings of gods) is emphasized so much by folk beliefs that it dominates not merely the organization of most of the rites and festivals but also the development of the whole year. The beliefs differ slightly from province to province; it is generally said that the Mountain God comes down to the plain at the beginning of spring under the name of Ricefield God, in order to protect rice-growing. When the harvest is completed in the autumn, he leaves the plain and goes back to the mountain, where he becomes Mountain God once again. But in other places, the Ricefield God is said to live in human dwellings in the cold season. Some people also believe that the Ricefield God and the Mountain God are distinct deities, and each year they celebrate, at the end of autumn, the marriage of the Ricefield God with the Mountain Goddess. Lastly, in the south-west region of the country, the aquatic genii, or *kappa*, are substituted for the Ricefield/Mountain God, and their comings and goings in the seas, rivers and mountains determine the rhythm of the festive year (Kōda 1959: 233).

Roughly speaking, the visit of the Ricefield God (or the presence of the *kappa*) determines an agrarian year of approximately ten months (from the second month till the tenth or eleventh month), consequently leaving a sort of blank period, lasting two or three months, around the New Year. Thus, the partition of the year that is determined by the travellings of the Ricefield God does not coincide with the previously mentioned bipartition of annual time. In fact, the comings and goings of the god may rather constitute a reflection of the ecological complementarity of spring and autumn, and of the symbolic complementarity of the human and divine worlds – a religious context, in other words, which describes the other world not as the prolongation of this world, but as the immediate complement of it.

The anthropomorphic course of time

Some Japanese scholars interpret such contacts between this world's time and the other world's time as a sort of alternation of two different times that succeed each other in the same fashion as human generations. This third hypothesis elaborates the sexual metaphors originating in the assimilation of an agricultural process with the human life-cycle in a constitutive principle of the development of time.[9]

It should be noted that many agricultural tasks are evidently associated with sexual representations, like the immersion of rice seeds (for germination), which is compared to a resting after parturition, or the transplanting of rice, which is compared to sexual relations (Berthier 1980: 31). One should also note that the end of autumn and the beginning of winter, the time of germination and gestation for seeds, corresponds to the celebration of the gods' marriages, and quite often of human marriages also. But these agrarian representations are too scattered for one to be able to compose a coherent system covering the whole year.

In fact, the three hypotheses presented above must each be considered as partly correct. The bipartition of the ritual calendar reflects the symmetry of the astronomical year; the travellings of the Ricefield God attest the ecological complementarity of spring and autumn; and the anthropomorphic metaphors related to particular moments of the year confirm the essentially agrarian character of the Japanese symbolic universe. Yet these three hypotheses offer only a partial explanation, because they do not take into account the obvious complexity of the ritual calendar. As mentioned above, they require a historical analysis aimed at reconstructing an original simplicity, and they implicitly assert that 'Japaneseness' is 'original' and ahistorical. Paradoxically, this historical analysis results in a fundamental negation of historical processes. The problem of the structure of the ritual year must be reconsidered by taking into account the actual complexity of the rites. This complexity is, of course, the result of the historical process of the superimposition of calendars, but I think that the fact of the simultaneous use of different calendars in Japan, more or less skilfully juxtaposed, cannot be considered merely as contingent upon history.

Interrelations of temporal segments

Let us go back to the case of the symmetry of the first of the sixth and the twelfth months. It will be recalled that the discovery of their symmetry is founded upon the existence, on both sides, of rites whose purpose is the exorcism of aquatic dangers. But if we decide to take into account the multiple interpretations of the rites, it appears that the first day of the sixth month is linked not only with the first day of the twelfth month but also with the first day of the first month. Notice that the first day of the sixth month is often called *rokugatsu tsuitachi*, which means the 'New Year of the Sixth Month'. It is said that beliefs concerning the sloughing of snakes are the reflection of the renewal of the year, which takes place at about the time of the summer solstice. At this time of the year, people eat the last rice-paste cakes prepared for the 'Great New Year', and preserved until then, or else they prepare food similar to that of the New Year festival. People who are in dangerous years celebrate their personal birthday once more, on the first day of the sixth month, in order to add one more year at once and so to escape the perils bound up with their age (Wakamori 1966: 119).[10]

The complete examination of the correspondences between annual rites results, in fact, not in a symmetrical structure, but in the establishment of an intricate network. The New Year refers to the *bon* festival, which in turn refers to the equinox festivals, which in their turn refer to the complex of the welcoming and farewell rites dedicated to the Ricefield God (who is also the Mountain God and shares a common nature with the ancestors). The New Year celebration refers to the first day of the sixth month, which itself refers to the first day of the twelfth month. There are no isolated rites, and yet on the other hand there is no perfect symmetry connecting them all together either. The annual course of time appears like a cobweb bringing together all the annual rites.

Thus, the multiplicity of associations existing between annual rites transforms the annual course of time into an inextricable network similar to a spider's web. The intricacy of this structure blurs the succession of time segments. The portions of time arising from the ritual calendar are not units with a mathematical structure, but moments to which rites give different meanings. This sort of calendar does not measure time – it describes it.

Moreover, the multiplicity of associations between rites performed at different moments of the year makes it impossible to isolate a given ritual period: one cannot think of a ritual period without several others coming immediately to mind, leading in turn to all the other periods of the year, thus following a chain reaction. The course of continuous time as on an oriented arrow, with each moment being the cause of the next one and the consequence of the previous one, is submerged by those privileged moments which are the times of rites themselves rising to the surface; and the meaning of these does not depend on their situation in the course of time – it is, on the contrary, these festive times which give meaning to time in-between. Rites propose time, transforming it into a surface where the mind circulates in all directions.[11]

CONCLUSION

Thus, reality seems to be quite different from the idealistic bipartition recognized by Japanese ethnographers or, at least, is not reducible to this simple structure. The symmetry principles I have pointed out are the reflection of natural, temporally given conditions. They reflect the astronomical and ecological data which determine the spectrum of different possibilities for calendrical elaboration, but they do not in themselves provide us with any information about the choices among these possibilities.

The anthropomorphic hypothesis (which may be elaborated under the influence of Christian conceptions of annual time) is more interesting. It reveals a social factor, i.e. the celebration of marriages after the harvest, when people have a lot of food and no more work.[12] This custom, together with the fact of the actual germination and gestation of seeds during the cold season, gave rise to the belief in the marriages of the gods.[13]

The Japanese conception of annual time, such as it is, is based upon these natural and social realities, the harmony of which the calendar expresses. Yet this harmony does not seem to be realized by a regular mathematical symmetry, but rather by the constant relations between human and divine worlds. The bipartition which characterizes the annual Japanese cycle may be the reflection of the spatial contacts between these two worlds, which are constantly being actualized by the comings and goings of the gods. It might also be the constant infusion of the divine world into human activities that originates the cobweb-like structure of annual time.

In fact, the main characteristic of the annual ritual calendar seems to be the multiplicity of associations between rites, and it is this multiplicity, as seen above, that prevents us from grasping annual time as a simple mathematical structure.

Of course, neither in Japan nor in the West is there a unitary conception of time. At the two ends of the world, the analysis of the understanding of time comes up against the insoluble inadequacy of the two series of concepts which constantly coexist inside time: a subjective series, which takes into account the past, the present and the future, and an objective series, which takes into account simultaneity, duration and succession. Ever since Aristotle defined time as μέτρον, while admitting that only the individual conscience could grasp its unity, classical Western thought has tried to make time an object, apprehending it as the milieu of all changes; but it could not escape the tyranny of language which identifies 'presence' and 'being'. So this thought, in spite of its assertions, favoured the subjective definition of time (Derrida 1979: 33ff.). The Japanese attitude, as it expresses itself through the annual conception of time, does not require that a central subject compose the unity of time; it is, on the contrary, quite satisfied with the extreme mobility of the subject on the surface of time. Note the fact that the only purely Japanese word for time is *toki*. This word is often used with the same meaning as the term *jikan*, which is originally Chinese and literally means 'intervals between *toki*'; but *toki* is above all a word close in meaning to the French *quand*. Would this not mean that, instead of the linguistic tyranny of the present which Derrida stigmatizes, the Japanese understanding of time proposes, as the only reality, the reality of simultaneity or concomitance, namely, the reality of time coming above all from the context such as is expressed by the word *toki*? Of course, this is a much larger problem than the one I have tried to tackle in this essay, though it probably has something to do with non-linear time which the analysis of the annual calendar of rites raises to the surface.

NOTES

1 On the history of calendars see, for instance, Wakamori (1973).
2 Whereas in China there were both an Astronomy Office and an Astrology Office, in Japan the two offices were fused in a single Astrology Bureau (see Nōda 1956: 140).
3 Notice, for instance, that some agrarian rites – such as the ceremonial rice trans-plantation of the new year, *ta-uchi shōgatsu*, or the harvest rites of the day of the sign of the young wild boar, *i no kami matsuri*, which are both performed at fixed dates – can be found in Yanagita's *Vocabulary of Usages Concerning Annual Ceremonies* (1939). Nevertheless, rites at the beginning of rice transplantation, *hatsu-ta-ue*, or first-fruits rites, *ho-kake matsuri*, cannot be found in this first *Vocabulary* but appear in a later one of 1947 (*Classified Vocabulary Concerning Rural Villages*, also edited by Yanagita), in the chapter entitled 'Agrarian Ceremonies', *nōko girei*.
4 Of the four paradises described by Buddhism, the Western Paradise, also called the Paradise of the Pure Land, is the only one which became popular. The diffusion of this belief was perhaps helped by old autochthonous beliefs assigning the world of the dead to the western side (Yoshino 1972: 219ff.).
5 In China, *shanichi* rites were at first dedicated to earth and community gods, but they later developed into festivals for the ancestors as well as for the Earth God. In Japan, the rites are dedicated to the Earth God and to ancestors, and to the Ricefield God as well.
6 The provincial calendars, publication of which began in the Middle Ages, survived the interdictions successively promulgated by the *Bakufu* and by Meiji governments (see Okada 1973).
7 By Fei-songzhi, as a footnote to the chapter '*Woren-zhuan*' ('Book of the People of Wo' – or *wa* in Japanese), to be found in the section '*Weizhi*' ('Chronicle of the Wei') of the classical text *Sanguozhi* (*History of the Three Kingdoms*). A modern edition of *Sanguozhi* was published in Peking (1964) by Zhouhua Shuju; see vol. 1, p. 856, for the commentary referred to.
8 It seems that this phenomenon is not peculiar to Japan, since there was the same evolution in China (Granet 1959: 42).
9 These sorts of theories are all founded upon the description of *ae no koto* (饗の祭) rites (see Matsudaira 1957: 31). These rites are very localized, and it is difficult to extend conclusions to the whole country, even considering their archaic character.
10 For a detailed discussion of these 'dangerous years', see the chapter by Lewis in this volume.
11 This may be the reason why Gilles Deleuze and Asada Akira, his 'neo-academic' emulator, have enjoyed so much popularity in Japan.
12 Granet notes a similar custom in China (1982: 177).
13 The somewhat enigmatic belief that the gods travel to the province of Izumo and conduct negotiations relating to human marriages could well be considered in the context of the beliefs discussed here.

REFERENCES

Beillevaire, Patrick (1982) 'Le Sutsu Upunaka de Tarama Jima: Description d'un rite saisonnier et analyse du symbolisme spatial sur une île des Ryûkyû', *Bulletin de l'Ecole Française d'Extrême-Orient*, vol. LXXI, pp. 217–61.

Berque, Augustin (1982) *Vivre l'espace au Japon*, Paris: Presses Universitaires de France.

Berthier, Laurence (1980) 'La Fête des petits garçons', *Cahiers d'études et de documents sur les religions du Japon* (Centre d'études des religions et traditions populaires du Japon, Paris), vol. II, pp. 9–88.

Berthier-Caillet, Laurence (1981) *Fêtes et rites des 4 saisons*, Paris: Publications Orientalistes de France.

Bodde, Derk (1975) *Festivals in Classical China*, Princeton, NJ: Princeton University Press.

Derrida, Jacques (1979 [1972]) *Marges de la philosophie*, Paris: Editions de Minuit.

Durkheim, Emile (1968 [1912]) *Les Formes élémentaires de la vie religieuse*, Paris: Presses Universitaires de France.

Frank, Bernard (1958) '*Kata-imi* et *kata-tagae*: Etude sur les interdits de direction à l'époque de Heian', *Bulletin de la Maison franco-japonaise* (Maison franco-japonaise, Tokyo), vol. V, nos 2–4.

—— (1971) 'A Propos de la "vieille année" et du printemps', in Lydia Brüll and Ulrich Kemper (eds) *Asien Tradition und Fortschritt: Festschrift für Horst Hammitzsch zu seinem 60. Geburtstag*, Wiesbaden: Otto Harrossowitz, pp. 103–16.

Granet, Marcel (1959) *La Religion des Chinois*, Paris: Presses Universitaires de France.

—— (1982) *Fêtes et chansons anciennes de la Chine*, Paris: Albin Michel.

Hashiura, Yasuo (1949) *Matsuri to gyōji* [*Festivals and Rituals*] (reprinted 1955 under the title *Tsukigotono matsuri* [*Festivals of Every Month*]), Tokyo: Iwanami Bijutsusha.

Hirayama, Binjirō (1957) 'Nenjū gyōji no nijū kōsei [The Dual Structure of Annual Rites]', *Nihon minzoku-gaku* [*Ethnology of Japan*], vol. 4, no. 2, pp. 89–95.

Inokuchi, Shōji (1959) 'Nōkō nenjū gyōji [Agrarian Annual Rites]', in Omachi Tokuzō *et al.* (eds) *Nihon minzokugaku taikei* [*Ethnology Systems of Japan*], vol. 7, Tokyo: Hibonsha, pp. 117–66.

Kōda, Yōbun (1959) 'Nenjū gyōji noshakasei to chiikisei [Localism and "Sociality" in Annual Rites]', in Omachi Tokuzō *et al.* (eds) *Nihon minzokugaku taikei* [*Ethnology Systems of Japan*], vol. 7, Tokyo: Heibonsha, pp. 167–238.

Kurata, Ichirō (1969) (reprinted 1972) *Nō to minzokugaku* [*Agriculture and Folklore*], Tokyo: Iwanami Bijutsusha.

Matsudaira, Narimitsu (1957) 'Le Rituel des prémices au Japon', *Bulletin de la Maison franco-japonaise* (Maison franco-japonaise, Tokyo), vol. IV, no. 2.

Miyamoto, Jōichi (1942) (reprinted 1972) 'Minkan goyomi [Folk Calendars]', in *Miyamoto Jōichi Chōsakushu* [*Selected Works of Miyamoto Jōichi*], Tokyo: Miraisha, pp. 73–264.

Nishitsunoi, Masayoshi (ed.) (1958) (reprinted 1973) *Nenjū gyōji jiten* [*Dictionary of Annual Rites*], Tokyo: Tōkyō dō.

Nōda, Chūryō (1956) *Rekigakushiron* [*A Historical Essay on the Science of Calendars*], Tokyo: Kadokawa.

Okada, Yoshirō (1973) 'Nihon kakuchi de tsukurareta koyomi no subete [All Calendars which have been Elaborated in every Province of Japan]', *Rekishi dokuhon* [*History Reader*], vol. 18, no. 14, Tokyo: Kokutetsu, pp. 54–63.

Ōno, Susumu, Satake Akihiro and Maeda Kingorō (1974) *Kogo jiten* [*Dictionary of the Archaic Japanese Language*], Tokyo: Iwanami.

Origuchi, Shinobu (1930–2) (reprinted 1973) 'Nenjū gyōji [Annual Rites]', in *Origuchi Shinobu Zenshū* [*Complete Works of Origuchi Shinobu*], vol. 15, Tokyo: Chūōkōron-sha, pp. 47–124.

Ōshima, Takehiko (1959) 'Shinkō to nenjū gyōji [Beliefs and Annual Rites]', *Nihon minzogaku taikei* [*Ethnology Systems of Japan*], vol. 7, Tokyo: Heibonsha, pp. 67–116.

Sakurada, Shōtoku (1959) 'Nenjū gyōji sōsetsu [Synthetical Essay on the Annual Rites]', *Nihon minzogaku taikei* [*Ethnology Systems of Japan*], vol. 7, Tokyo: Heibonsha, pp. 1–16.

Wakamori, Tarō (1966) (reprinted 1973) *Nenjū gyōji* [*Annual Rites*], Tokyo: Shibundō.

—— (1973) 'Koyomi Nihonshi [The Japanese History of the Calendar]', *Rekishi dokuhon* [*History Reader*], vol. 18, no. 4, pp. 29–39.

Yanagita, Kunio (ed.) (1939) (reprinted 1975) *Saiji shuzokugoi* [*Vocabulary of Usages Concerning Annual Ceremonies*], Tokyo: Kokusho Kankōkai.

—— (ed.) (1946) (reprinted 1970) *Sōgō Nihon minzoku* [*General Folk Vocabulary*], Tokyo: Heibonsha.

—— (ed.) (1947) (reprinted 1975) *Bunrui nōson goi* [*Classified Vocabulary Concerning Rural Villages*], Tokyo: Kokusho Kankōkai.

—— (ed.) (1951) (reprinted 1973) *Minzokugaku jiten* [*Dictionary of Japanese Folklore*], Tokyo: Tōkyō dō.

—— (1970a) [1942] 'Nihon no matsuri [Festivals of Japan]', in *Yanagita Kunio zenshū* [*Complete Works of Yanagita Kunio*], vol. 10, Tokyo: Chikumashobō, pp. 153–314.

—— (1970b) [1946] 'Senzo no hanashi [About the Ancestors]', in *Yanagita Kunio zenshū* [*Complete Works of Yanagita Kunio*], vol. 10, Tokyo: Chikumashobō, pp. 1–152.

—— (1972a) [1946] 'Saijitsukō [Views about the Days of the Festivals]', in *Yanagita Kunio zenshū* [*Complete Works of Yanagita Kunio*], vol. 11, Tokyo: Chikumashobō, pp. 181–291.

—— (1972b) [1949] 'Nenjū gyōji oboegaki [Notes on Annual Rites]', in *Yanagita Kunio zenshū* [*Complete Works of Yanagita Kunio*], vol. 13, Tokyo: Chikumashobō, pp. 1–177.

—— (1972c) [1961] 'Mitoshiroda ko [Views on Mitoshiroda]', *Yanagita Kunio zenshū* [*Complete Works of Yanagita Kunio*], vol. 13, Tokyo: Chikumashobō, pp. 411–30.

Yoshino, Hiroko (1972) *Matsuri no genri* [*Principles of the Festivals*], Tokyo: Keikyūsha.

2   Spatial characterization of human temporality in the Ryūkyūs

Patrick Beillevaire

INTRODUCTION

Scholars dealing with Japanese cosmological representations seldom omit reference to the prefecture of Okinawa (Ryūkyū Islands) – a region that formed a kingdom vassal to both China and Japan prior to the 1870s – whether on a comparative basis or in search of a past that would have been preserved in these remote islands. The degree of cultural kinship between Ancient Japan and the Ryūkyūs is in fact a moot point, with political undertones, that will not be addressed in this paper. Let it be said, however, that in the domain of cosmology, as emphasized by numerous authors (see, for instance, Ouwehand 1964: 85ff.), there are obvious links between the concepts found in both places of a 'far-away land' (land of the dead, *tokoyo*, or land of the primeval deities, *ne no kuni*, as known in mainland Japan, and *nirai-kanai*, as known in Okinawa), or between the various ritual traditions of 'visiting deities' (*marebito*) related to those concepts.[1]

Though traditional Ryūkyūan culture and society have been slowly vanishing for many decades, one is nevertheless left with a complex and diversified picture of ancient cosmologies. In this respect, it is worth noticing that rites appear to last longer than explicit beliefs and representations, so that, when memories fail, the observation of rites may still provide relevant information about bygone times. In connection with the bare fact of the geographical isolation of these islands, the weak influence of organized Buddhism surely accounts for the rather well-integrated aspect of village cosmologies in the Ryūkyūs, as recorded during the present century. However, discrepancies between nearby villages should never be underestimated and need to be closely examined. The comparative analysis of local variations can prove very stimulating for the understanding of the fabric of Ryūkyūan culture, as shown in particular by Mabuchi Tōichi (Mabuchi 1968; 1980).

However, the subject I will be dealing with departs slightly from the usual approach to the relationship between space (i.e., symbolic orientations) and time (i.e., annual rites) in cosmologies. Here, I wish to restrict myself to some aspects of the way in which human temporality is figured in space – or, rather, 'characterized', since one is not dealing simply with a material space but rather with space that is symbolically oriented also.[2] The general intention of this chapter can be summarized by indicating that it gives support, in my view, to the statement of Durkheim and Mauss found in 'Les Classifications primitives' (1969: 74) according to which *'La considération des temps est parallèle à celle des espaces'*.

I will mainly be making use of data collected on Tarama Island during a stay of sixteen months (from March 1978 to July 1979). This small, round island, which is only twenty square kilometres in area, is located midway between Miyako Island to the north-east and Ishigaki Island to the south-west. It has received influences from both regions. It is a one-village island, with clustered dwellings. Its population, which has been steadily decreasing since the war, had fallen below 2,000 at the time of this enquiry.

I will consider, successively, observances occurring on three levels of space: inside the domestic unit, in the neighbourhood, and in the village – or island – taken as a whole.

FROM BIRTH ONWARDS

Briefly, as can quite commonly be seen all over the Ryūkyūs, houses (*yā*, 屋) in Tarama have a quadrilateral shape with two main front rooms. Most frequently – according to folk orientations – they face south (or sometimes east), but in reality they face south-south-west. Outside, the yard of the house is surrounded by a stone wall which also opens towards the south. The kitchen stands on the west side of the house, sometimes as a separate building. Due to its nature and function, it is essentially a women's place, where the fire-deity (*fī nu kam*, 火の神) is honoured. Guests (usually male) are entertained in the first and most honorific room, on the east side of the house (most often the greatest dignity seems to be attached to the north-east corner, but in Tarama there is some ambiguity between the north-east and south-east corners). Further to the west, the second room is used for meals and daily activities. When a house has been inhabited for several generations, it has its own altar for ancestor worship, built in the back wall of the second room. Outside, located in the north-west corner of the yard, there is a pigsty and a privy, which formerly had a ritual significance with regard to purification and fecundity.

From a static viewpoint, the Ryūkyūan house is a sort of microcosm which reproduces in the course of everyday life the cosmic hierarchy between east and west: the east side is superior (*wāra*, in Tarama dialect) to the west side (*stādi*). Heat, sunlight and masculinity are the main attributes of the east side, and their opposites – humidity, darkness and femininity – are those of the west side. From a dynamic viewpoint – that is to say, taking into account the meaning of certain rituals – females and the fire deity connect the west side of the house compound to the east side of the cosmos, displaying an instance of hierarchical reversal. Under Taoist influence the fire deity is conceived of as a go-between, reporting, at least once a year, near the end of the last month, the deeds of humans to the 'deities of Heaven' (*tin nu kam*, 天の神), thus ensuring protection to the household. Moreover, the fire deity seems to be akin to the primeval deities belonging to the 'far-away land' on the east side (for details, see Beillevaire 1982).

Until recently, the bringing forth of a child took place at the rear of the kitchen. The placenta was buried behind the house, in the north-west corner. In Tarama, four days after the birth there occurred a ceremony (*fuzu urusu*, Japanese *kujibiki*) for the selection of a name for the new-born child (*yarabi nā*, 童名, or 'domestic name').

I cannot here go into all the details of this ceremony, but the process of selection was of a divinatory kind, where first the fire deity, then the ancestors, would be asked to express their preference. On the same day, the mother carried the baby in her arms through the house and out into the yard through the door on the east side. There, she introduced her baby to the sun deity (*uputeda ganasu*). One may think of this quick and early move from west to east as an epitome of a person's destiny from birth to ancestorhood or *kami*-hood. This blunt statement calls for an explanation. But first, a few words are needed about what Lebra (1966) termed the 'life-sustaining human spirit' (*mabui* in Okinawa). In Tarama village this kind of 'soul' or vital principle, akin to the Japanese *tama* or *tamashii*, is honoured, or taken care of, on a small altar with an incense-burner located in the first room (in traditional houses on Tarama there are very few *tokonoma*, the slightly raised 'sacred dais' commonly found in Japanese country houses). It is called *mabvul*, but also referred to in conversations as *mamorigami*, or 'protective *kami*'. The *mabvul* comes to inhabit the body for life, and leaves it at the moment of death. There seems to be a closer relationship between the head of the house and the *mabvul* than with other members of the domestic unit.

Two main eschatological opinions, loosely related, coexist among Tarama islanders. One is the belief in the reincarnation of a deceased person whose name has been given to a descendant of either sex in the male line (it is the *mabvul* that is supposed to be reincarnated). The other possibility is for an ancestor to merge eventually with the *kami* (deities) of the cosmos who abide in 'Heaven' (*tin*), or more precisely on the horizon towards the south-east, a place commonly called *nirai-kanai* on other islands.[3] In Tarama, however, the *nirai-kanai*, or *nilla* in local dialect, is seen as a dreadful place located deep beneath the surface of the island and inhabited by *kami* whose function makes them reminiscent of the Greek *moira*. According to the opinion of some villagers, the 'spirit' of people who have just died would remain there for a short while during the liminal stage of funerary rituals.

The 'career' of an ancestor starts from the day of the funeral. The corpse lies in front of the altar for ancestor worship, or *kamidana* (神棚, also called *butsudan*). On that day, the west side of the house is laden with pollution, and food for the participants has to be conveyed out of the house from the kitchen to re-enter the house via the first room. In Tarama it is customary to put under the pillow of the deceased a small bag containing ashes taken from the incense-burner of the *mabvul* altar. The coffin is carried outside into the yard through the inferior side of the entrance way (the opening in the surrounding wall, being barred by a recessed wall, *tsunpun*, is divided in two ways – east and west, superior and inferior).[4]

From that day on, the deceased is remembered by means of a tablet (*ipai*, 位牌)

on the *kamidana*, and by a long series of rites. The *mabvul* of the dead is sometimes deemed to reside in the tablet itself. Usually thirty-three years after the burial (though this may vary a great deal), a last rite (*upu ninki*, 大年忌) is held, implying the 'deification' of the ancestor – literally his elevation to the status of *kami*, or *ubudatti* (大立ち) (although in fact the word *kami* is used for younger ancestors too). The tablet is then destroyed, or the name of the ancestor simply removed. However, these now anonymous *kami*-ancestors are still revered on the *kamidana*, but on the right side (facing it) – that is, towards the east, in a special part with a separate incense-burner (for a similar observation, see Newell 1980). Elsewhere in the Ryūkyūs, the place for deified ancestors is ordinarily found in the first room. The existence of an *ubudatti* section of the ancestral altar bears witness to the fact that a house has reached the status of 'stem-house', or *yā mutu* (屋元; *mutu yā* on Okinawa, a term with sociological implications somewhat different from the Japanese *honke*).

Much older ancestors, termed *uzugam* (in Japanese, *ujigami*), are given particular attention in some houseyards. Their altar is situated in the eastern part, most often in the north-east corner. These ancestors are sometimes said to be the founders of a domestic line of so-called *shizoku*, or people of 'gentry' status (良い人, *yukāl pstu* in dialect). It is difficult to check this assertion, because former *shizoku* were surprisingly numerous in Tarama (over 50 per cent, probably illegitimate descendants of court officials sent on duty or exiled on the island). What remains beyond doubt is the seniority of these houses (大屋元, *upu yā mutu*). Whether or not a privilege of status – and as a consequence of deeper genealogical memory – these *uzugam* are granted power of protection against disease, sterility, and malevolent spirits.

In Miyako, according to the *Dictionary of Okinawan Cultural History* (Maeda, Misumi and Minamoto 1972: 393), protective *yashikigami*, or 'deities of the residential site', termed *tokulgan* or *tokulnushi*, are also honoured in the north-east corner of the houseyard (associated with the 'direction of the tiger', *tura nu pa* – Japanese *tora no hō* – as derived from the Chinese zodiac). Evidence of the transformation of ancestors into *yashikigami* can be found in several places in mainland Japan (for an example from Miyazaki prefecture see Yonemura 1976: 180). In Tarama the protective power of *uzugam* is clearly exemplified when a house is situated along the north-west corner of a crossroads. In this situation the south-east corner of the yard of the house becomes a weak point through which there can enter the sacred but also deleterious energy of the *yū nusu* (世主), originating from far away in the 'horse direction' (午の方, *uma nu pa*);[5] entry to this part of the yard thus has to be prohibited. However, if the house is entitled to have an *uzugam* altar, it is placed in the south-east corner, and its protective power removes the prohibition on the use of the area.

To summarize, in opposition to the cosmic life originating from the east (or also from the south-east, according to folk orientations in Tarama; see Beillevaire 1982), which is the home of the primeval deities, human life starts from the west, on a mundane level. However, during a person's lifetime, his or her vital principle belongs to the eastern part of the house. Death is followed by a movement back to the west, but gradually the ancestor, unless reborn, moves east again, and tends to merge with the cosmic *kami*.

THE SPATIAL EXPRESSION OF SUCCEEDING GENERATIONS

The hierarchical relationship between east and west, and to a lesser degree between north and south, also appears in the spatial ordering of houses. Everywhere in the Ryūkyūs the inheritance of houses obeys strictly the rule of male primogeniture. As a consequence, younger children have to leave the house, at their wedding at the latest. Formerly, there was a tendency among Ryūkyūan villagers to cluster together not far from an older 'stem-house' (*upu yā mutu*) of their domestic line. But in doing so they had to comply with one rule: descendants' houses (the houses of younger sons) had to be built on the west or south side of the 'stem-house' – otherwise, all sorts of evil would have been brought about. I noticed several such cases of extended house-arrangement in Tarama, chiefly in the more densely populated Yoshikawa ward. The spatial subordination of the sites of younger sons' houses is often reflected in these house names (屋の名, *yā nu nā*, Japanese *yagō*); in that case, it is common to retain the stem-house name and to add a prefix such as *pai* or *il*, which mean south and west respectively. Nakamatsu (1972) has shown the existence of a similar ordering of houses on Miyako Island (especially in Karimata village), and in older villages on Okinawa Island.[6] Muratake (1975) also drew the conclusion that, because of the superiority and sacredness of the north side, ancient Ryūkyūan villages tended to expand southwards (as, for example, Nagusuku and Maezato villages on Okinawa Island). This also seems to be the case in Tarama, but contrary to Muratake's own opinion concerning Tarama, the north is not superior to the south in every ritual context, as will be explained later. Moreover, in Tarama the dangerous region of the tombs, where malevolent spirits are supposed to wander, is located north of the village.

The genealogical development of a family and village expansion are both open-ended processes in human experience. Nevertheless, the house-arrangement they display shows that they are also conceived as framed, at least partly, into the symbolic orientations of space.

Before taking the discussion further, it may be appropriate here to mention the spatial usage of the twelve animal signs of the Chinese calendar or zodiac, a subject that relates simultaneously to the various levels of the houseyard, the village section and indeed the whole island. Their usage is directly modelled upon the Chinese practice. Each animal sign corresponds in a fixed way with an orientation and, combined with other cycles, determines the fortune of units of time. At the houseyard level, each of the twelve orientations hosts a *kami*, but these are almost always collectively honoured as houseyard *kami*. The four signs – rat (north), tiger (east), horse (south), and cock (west) – refer to orientations significantly involved in important domestic or communal rites. In a more profane manner, they are also used within the village to designate each of the four wards.

MYTH, RITE AND HISTORY

Let us now look at some major events that take place at village level. Tarama village is clearly divided, following a north–south axis, into two sections which are nowadays administrative sub-units or *aza*. This division runs right across the island territory, north and south. Each *aza* consists of four *buraku* or wards. It should also be added that there are six main shrines (*utaki*, Japanese *otake*) for the whole community. Although in the course of ordinary life the symbolic meaning of this bipartite division is not so overt as in other villages of the southern Ryūkyūs (Sakishima), it nevertheless reveals itself in certain ritual settings, such as the Sutsu Upunaka and the Hachigatsu Odori festivals, at which times the west side of the village stands as primary and feminine, the east side as secondary and masculine.

The festival of the Sutsu (or Shitsu) Upunaka is the climax of the annual ritual cycle, and marks the renewal of the agricultural year. It is held around the end of May, on the 'water-days' of the Chinese calendar – formerly when the millet harvest was completed.[7] The word *sutsu* (節), cognate with *setsu* in modern Japanese, conveys the meaning of a transition or hinge between two seasons (and of a bamboo knot also). *Upunaka* (大中) means 'big' or literally 'great middle', also referring to the turning of the year. The word *shitsu* is not uncommonly used in the Ishigaki area as a term for festivals with a similar general signification, but with very different ritual proceedings.

On the second and most important day of this festival, the priestesses of the community (司, *tsukasa*) proceed from west to east, on the southern outskirts of the village. On sites revered by tradition are settled four ceremonial camps, each belonging to a pair of wards (*buraku*). The first site, Nagashigawa, from where the procession of the priestesses starts, obviously possesses more prestige than the other three sites. In fact, the first site is related to the two westernmost wards of the oldest part of the village. While they walk from one camp to the next, the priestesses ask the fertilizing power (*yū nusu*) to come down and bless the earth. In the four camps, all the ceremonial arrangements face east or south, save for the last ceremony on the third day, when the participants turn to the west. At that time, the secular order is reinstated and malevolent spirits warded off. During the ceremonies that are held at each camp on the second day, as well as on the route between these camps, the leading priestess is always the one in charge of the village shrine, called Ungusuku Utaki, where the tutelary hero of the whole community is worshipped. This half-legendary, half-historical character is worthy of some further remarks, but an enlargement of the context is needed first.

The myth of origin of the Tarama islanders relates the story of a brother and a sister who, very long ago, luckily escaped a tidal wave that drowned all the other villagers. The brother and the sister innocently became husband and wife, and after some initial failures begat the forebears of the present-day villagers. This story is but one version of a mythic theme widely found in the Austronesian area. Records of the same myth have been made elsewhere in the Ryūkyūs, especially on the island of Hateruma where, in a manner more conspicuous than in Tarama, the myth frames the local symbolic landscape (and particularly the bipartite division; for a detailed analysis see Suzuki 1977: 26–8). In Tarama, this myth is called the Bunaze myth, from the word *bunal*, meaning 'sister'.[8] The safe retreat that prevented the Bunaze couple from being drowned is a low hill located to the west of the village. Within a short distance from there, just on the boundary of the dwelling area, can now be seen a small sanctuary dedicated to the couple; it is deemed propitious against sterility.

After this rapid encounter with mythical beings, let us pass on to the second act of local history – associated with the famous (and better-attested) character called Ntabaru Shungen. The villagers say Ntabaru came from Amagawa (Ama well), the oldest part of the village, but in fact he might have been the son of an official dispatched from Miyako Island. Around the year 1500 Ntabaru, still in his teens, killed seven hooligans of the village. Then, by means of trickery and strength, he carried out the political unification of Tarama Island (prior to that time there had been three separate clusters of habitations). But the greatest feat in Ntabaru's eventful career took place when he sided with Nakasone from Miyako and helped suppress the rebellion fomented on Yonaguni Island under the aegis of a local chief, Untura. The victory substantially contributed to ensuring the hegemony of the Kingdom of Chūzan over the southern Ryūkyū Islands, and Ntabaru received the title of Tuyume as a reward for his services. (The Ryūkyū kingdom that developed on Okinawa Island retained its former name Chūzan, 'Middle Mountain', after it had superceded the two rival micro-states, located north and south of it, at the beginning of the fifteenth century.)

This brief historical outline will be sufficient to further an understanding of the symbolic setting. As mentioned above, Ntabaru was living near Amagawa, in the western and dominant part of the inhabited area. Ntabaru's presumed descendants share in their first name the character *shun* (春), and thereby form the Shun Uzu (the Shun 'clan'), the largest *uzu* in Tarama.[9] Nowadays, they still maintain special links with the western half of the village, and form a significantly higher proportion of the villagers who reside there. To that side also belong the two main shrines (*utaki*) dedicated to Ntabaru. The first and oldest shrine, Ungusuku, has been previously mentioned in connection with the Sutsu Upunaka festival. The second, called Tarama Jinja, was built at the beginning of this century, under the pressure of the growing nationalist ideology that favoured the unification of Shinto shrines. It is used both as an ordinary *utaki* for parishioners living in the western wards and, on official occasions, as a shrine representative of all the villagers. For this purpose, the memory of Ntabaru was reactivated by electing housewives from the domestic line of his most direct descendants (as claimed by the villagers) to be the priestesses in charge of this shrine. But yet another small sanctuary, located to the west, bears Ntabaru's name. It is in the surroundings of this sanctuary, called Ntabaru Ugan, that each year, in autumn, there commences the other great festival, gathering together the whole village. This festival, the Hachigatsu Odori, is a dramatic and colourful performance relating the surrender of the local chiefs in the southern Ryūkyūs. In olden times, the festival was held when the task of collecting taxes had been completed.

The festival lasts three days. On the first day, it takes place in Ntabaru Ugan.[10] On the second day, it is continued in the eastern part of the village, in a place where the house of Ntabaru's concubine is said to have been located. On the final day, the festival is performed simultaneously in both places. Despite its more profane appearance, the general signification of the Hachigatsu Odori, like the Sutsu Upunaka, is to call for abundance and prosperity. In this context too, the fact that the festival is started on the first day by villagers from the west side is definitely considered a token of its historical and ritual pre-eminence. People think of this side as the *mutu* (元) side – the root- or stem-side – of Tarama village. It should also be observed that the *shishi* (獅子, 'lion'), displayed at the start and close of each day's performance, is said to be female on the west and male on the east.

What can be concluded from this cursory presentation of ritual organization on Tarama Island? First – although this can hardly pass for a discovery in the Ryūkyūan context – the east–west axis is of the utmost importance for the annual renewal of fertility. On Tarama, it manifests itself during the Sutsu Upunaka as a procession, leading village representatives from west to east, and involving the participation of every ward and shrine. The complementary division between east and west also finds expression in the other great annual event, the Hachigatsu Odori. In both cases, the west side draws prestige from initiating the festival. A comparable procession, welcoming the *yū* (世迎い, *yūngai*) and moving from west to east, can also be observed on Taketomi islet, near Ishigaki (Ishigaki 1976: 81ff.). But in many other villages the east–west duality operates by means of a fixed contest between representatives of each side of the village (a boat-race or a tug-of-war). Most frequently, the west side has to be the winning side. By this symbolic victory, the west side acts on behalf of all the villagers as a receiver or purveyor of the fertility and prosperity annually bestowed by the deities from the outer world (usually the 'far-away land' to the east). Though this is without any doubt the dominant spatial perspective in Ryūkyūan culture, I am well aware that data from other places are not always perfectly consistent with this schema, in particular because of the adaptation to local topography (see Mabuchi 1968).[11] Nevertheless, my purpose here is restricted to the linking of Tarama's specific customs with the broad outline of Ryūkyūan concepts of space.

Second, the data from Tarama indicate that the Ntabaru legend and history take root in, or coalesce with, a pre-established symbolic pattern of space. This is not the only instance of such a tendency. Related to the aforementioned rites of bisection in villages of the main island of Okinawa (the tug-of-war), it is also the case that crests of the former royal house of Shuri, the capital of the kingdom, are borne by representatives of the west section (Muratake 1975: 307). Note that here, however, the west side occupies a dual role: it stands for the feminine and worldly (whence the presence of the royal crests), but its worldly status makes the west side the actual intermediary – like women – between this world and the outer world represented by the east side of the villages. More similar to the case of Tarama, at least two other places give evidence of the intermingling of history with spatial symbolism. In Hateruma, where the east–west polarity is quite pronounced, the children of a personage similar to Ntabaru who happened to die while fighting for the king of Shuri, were granted the charge of three shrines as a reward for their father's deed: following their rank of birth, the eldest brother and sister received the west shrine, the brother and sister coming next obtained the shrine situated in the middle, and the youngest pair the east shrine (Suzuki 1977: 33–4). Moreover, in Komi, on Iriomote Island, *shizoku* (people with 'gentry' status) inhabited the south section of the village (Miyara 1973: 168). Here, the village is divided between north and south. During the festival of the red and black masks (*akamata–kuromata*) incarnating visiting deities, the black mask of the begetter deity is an attribute of the south section, and consequently was previously worn by *shizoku* villagers. Another interesting case is the ancient court ritual called Agari-ūmai, or 'Pilgrimage to the east', which consisted in a yearly visit by the king and the high-priestess, originally the king's sister, accompanied by their respective attendants, to the sacred places that are scattered along the shore south-east of Shuri. The most important places are connected with some of the origin myths of Okinawan agriculture and consequently with the renewal of fertility. Origuchi Shinobu and other scholars after him brought to our attention the links between the ritual traditions of the small island of Izena, located to the north-west of Okinawa, from where the second Shō dynasty which created the ritual in the early sixteenth century originated, and the Agari-ūmai, as well as on a possible need felt by the latter to compensate symbolically for its western origin by laying stress on the east with solemnity.

CONCLUSION

Two notions of time are commonly held as primary and opposites (see Leach 1961): the notion of a repetitive or 'cyclic' time, based on periodic events such as seasons and the growth of plants, and the notion of a time that slips away, or 'linear' time, referring to the uniqueness of each human existence, the succession of generations from a founding ancestor or the irreversible course of history. From this analytical standpoint, birth and death fit either with the first or the second notion, depending on whether one chooses a subjective or a collective approach. Contrary to this dualistic presentation I have tried to show how, in Ryūkyūan society, these diverse sorts of events, whether recurrent or not, individual or collective, all tend to be concretely expressed within a symbolically oriented and encompassing space. No original concept of time is involved here. The perception of time displayed in Ryūkyūan folk culture might rather remind us of Aristotle's concept of a substantial time linked to physical movements or changes. This 'human temporality' consists precisely of such physical changes intervening in human life or in the natural environment, but also of invisible changes in culturally significant areas such as the incorporeal existence of the ancestors. In Ryūkyūan society (though presumably other specific examples could be found elsewhere) these changes are symbolically materialized as movements within space. History too, which is related to the development of a centralized kingdom, seems to some extent to be grafted onto the traditional spatial and cosmological pattern. In short, this oriented space can be described as a kind of mnemonic device embracing in lasting form different aspects of human temporality.

NOTES

1 For a parallel with the tradition of visiting deities on mainland Japan see Laurence Caillet's discussion of the Ricefield God (in the present volume).

2 In spite of conventional anthropological usage, the word 'time' should be dropped and replaced by the word 'temporality', which simply means 'being in time', since in practice one rarely grapples with the problem of what time actually is or consists of.

3 On this point see, for instance, Yoshida's description of the *hamaori* ritual on Tokunoshima (in the present volume).

4 This hierarchical scheme opposing east and west exerts a wide influence on the behaviour of villagers. For instance, three days after the funeral, women and children related to the house go to the north beach and clean the soiled clothes belonging to the deceased; on their outward journey they have to take a western (*stādi*) path (that is, western in relation to the village), whereas they come back home on an eastern (*wāra*) path.

5 Literally translated, *yū nusu* means 'master of the *yū*'. According to Origuchi Shinobu, the early meaning of *yū* (Japanese *yo*, as in *tokoyo*) was 'grain harvest', 'grain' (see Ouwehand 1964: 88). Each year, during the Sutsu Upunaka festival, the *yū nusu* visits the realm of humans, bringing renewed fertility and prosperity.

6 The *agere* house of priestesses mentioned by Yoshida Teigo in his paper on Tokunoshima (in the present volume) shows another instance of the symbolic superiority of the east side in the ordering of houses.

7 It is worth noting that the rite of 'rejuvenating water', clearly connected with the renewal of the year, still occurs in Tarama during the Sutsu Upunaka, while it takes place at the lunar New Year in the main island of Okinawa.

8 In the Ryūkyūs, sisters are supposed to be endowed with a protective spiritual power over their brothers' destiny, a power which is termed *onarigami* (*onari* and *bunal* are the same word). However, in Miyako and Tarama this attribute nowadays seems to be lacking, and the interpretation of past data is a matter of discussion. Anyway, in Tarama as indeed throughout the Ryūkyūs, women play the foremost part in religious activities. This notable feature of Ryūkyūsan culture first pervaded court life as well as peasant life, but from the seventeenth century it receded at court under the pressure of Confucian ideals.

9 Actually there is a genealogy showing how certain domestic lines branched off from some remote scion of Ntabaru in the sixteenth or seventeenth centuries.

10 In the morning, before the performance starts, villagers from the west side pay a visit to the Bunaze sanctuary.

11 But, whatever its topographical expression, one should bear in mind the pervasive existence in the Ryūkyūs of the complementary opposition between male and female elements, and between village divisions.

REFERENCES

Beillevaire, P. (1982) 'Le Sutsu Upunaka de Tarama Jima: Description d'un rite saisonnier et analyse du symbolisme spatial sur une île des Ryûkyû', *Bulletin de l'Ecole française d'Extrême-Orient*, vol. LXXI, pp. 217–61.

Durkheim, E. and M. Mauss (1969 [1903]) 'Les Classifications primitives', reprinted in M. Mauss *Œuvres II*, Paris: Editions de Minuit, pp. 13–89.

Ishigaki, H. (1976) 'Taketomi no yūnkai (yū makai) [The *Yūnkai* Ritual of Taketomi Island]', in *Yaeyama bunka ronshū* [*Essays on Yaeyama Culture*], Naha: Yaeyama Bunka Kenkyūkai, pp. 79–104.

Leach, E. R. (1961) 'Two Essays Concerning the Symbolic Representation of Time', in E. R. Leach *Rethinking Anthropology*, London: Athlone Press, pp. 124–36.

Lebra, W. P. (1966) *Okinawan Religion*, Honolulu: University of Hawaii Press.

Mabuchi, T. (1968) 'Toward the Reconstruction of Ryukyuan Cosmology', in N. Matsumoto and T. Mabuchi (eds) *Folk Religion and the Worldview in the Southwestern Pacific*, Tokyo: Keio University, pp. 119–40.

—— (1980) 'Space and Time in Ryūkyūan Cosmology', *Asian Folklore Studies*, vol. XXXIX, no. 1, pp. 1–19.

Maeda, G., H. Misumi and T. Minamoto (eds) (1972) *Okinawa bunka shi jiten* [*Dictionary of Okinawan Cultural History*], Tokyo: Tokyo dō.

Miyara, T. (1973) *Yaeyama no shakai to bunka* [*Yaeyama Culture and Society*], Tokyo: Mokujisha.

Muratake, S. (1975) '"Shakaiteki shōchōteki chitsujo" chōsa nōto [Field Notes on the "Symbolic and Social Order"]', in *Kami, kyōdōtai hōjō* [*Kami, Community, Abundant Harvest*], Tokyo: Miraisha, pp. 303–21.

Nakamatsu, Y. (1972) 'Hontō – Saishiteki sekai no hanei toshite no shūraku kōsei [Main Island Okinawa: Influence of the Ritual Sphere on Village Formation]', in *Okinawa no minzokugakuteki kenkyū* [*Ethnological Research on Okinawa*], Tokyo: Nihon Minzoku Gakkai Hen, pp. 1–63.

Newell, William H. (1980) 'Some Features of the Domestic Cult Organization in the Southern Ryukyus and Taiwan', *Asian Folklore Studies*, vol. XXXIX, no. 2, pp. 22–40.

Ouwehand, C. (1964) *Namazu-e and their Themes*, Leiden: E. J. Brill.

Suzuki, M. (1977) 'Hateruma jima no shinwa to girei [Myth and Ritual on Hateruma Island]', *Minzokugaku kenkyū* [*Japanese Journal of Ethnology*], vol. 42, no. 1, pp. 24–58.

Yonemura, S. (1976) '*Dōzoku* and Ancestor Worship in Japan', in W. H. Newell (ed.) *Ancestors*, The Hague: Mouton, pp. 177–203.

3 The Pythagorean view of time and space in Japan

Thomas Crump

The original version of this chapter, which was written on the basis of fieldwork carried out in 1983, was intended as a discussion of the way in which the Japanese conceptualization of time and space reflects certain ideas of number and cosmos traditionally ascribed to Pythagoras.[1] Since then the background to this subject has changed in three significant ways. First, I have myself returned to Japan seven times since 1983: in 1987, in particular, a long period spent in Kyoto and Osaka as a Japan Foundation Fellow enabled me to broaden my research into Japan's numerical culture to the point that I was able to write a whole book (Crump 1992) about it. Second, largely as a result of the continuing computer revolution, the place of numbers in Japanese popular culture has changed significantly since the early 1980s. Third, there have been significant developments, not so much in this field of research but in the attitudes deemed appropriate to any study of Far Eastern cultures. The present revised version of this chapter takes all these factors into account, largely by adding to and revising the notes. Even so, I believe that the fundamental principles that I set out to establish fifteen years ago still hold good (which largely explains the way I have accepted the invitation to revise this chapter).

Although Pythagoras is certainly known in Japan, it is not suggested that any Japanese concepts of time or space must be attributed, directly or indirectly, to Pythagoras or his school. Indeed, the origin of these concepts, so far as Japan is concerned, is undoubtedly Chinese (Nakayama 1969: 226); one would hardly expect otherwise.[2] On the other hand, in the present context their attribution to Pythagoras is not entirely adventitious, for to Pythagoras is ascribed a way of looking at the world which is still characteristic of the Orient, and which, in the Western world, only modern science – adopting the deductive methods first established by Plato[3] – has suppressed.[4] At popular level in Japan, just as elsewhere, Pythagoras is known largely for his theorem, although this attribution may have been unknown in premodern Japan.[5]

The Pythagoreans saw the universe in terms of number. According to Aristotle, 'they devoted themselves so intensively to mathematics and became so closely identified with it that they saw nothing in the whole world but numbers' (Burkert 1972: 413). The bias of Pythagorean mathematics was, however, to establish a numerical cosmology on the basis of the non-mathematical associations of numbers. The appreciation of mathematics was aesthetic,[6] not logical,[7] and although a number of fundamental theorems in arithmetic – such as the proof of the irrationality of the square root of 2 – are ascribed to Pythagoras, there was no attempt to use them as the basis of any logically based deductive system. Indeed, the fact that $\sqrt{2}$ is irrational meant that it was of no interest whatever, since Pythagorean arithmetic was based exclusively on whole numbers. The aesthetic bias of Pythagorean mathematics meant that numbers were important for their connotations, which had to be established extrinsically. The essential generality of any logical theory about the basis of arithmetic precludes any possibility of intrinsic connotations.[8] Pythagoras reputedly went so far as to say that all things are numbers (Russell 1946: 53), but what he meant, rather, was that all numbers were things. That is, any number which 'occurs', or any notable combination of numbers which 'occurs', such as that of 3, 4 and 5 in a right-angled triangle, must be significant.[9] As Burkert points out (1972: 473),

> One learns to count and calculate in childhood, and from the beginning the numbers are apprehended as things, with certain characteristics; they preserve this peculiarity even, at an unconscious level, in the mind of the adult.

The Pythagoreans systematically related the whole series of integers to different concepts, so that, for instance,

> One is νοῦς and οὐσία; two is δόξα; three is the number of the whole – beginning, middle, and end; four is justice – equal times equal – but it is also, in the form of the tetractys, the 'whole nature of numbers'; five is marriage, as the first combination of odd and even, male and female; seven is opportunity (καιρός) and also Athena, as the 'virginal' prime number; ten is the perfect number, which comprehends the whole nature of number and determines the structure of the cosmos, and with it ends the symbolic interpretation of numbers.
>
> (ibid.: 467–8)

This procedure[10] is suited both to number mysticism and the playing of games.[11] Inherent in the whole process is a tendency to secrecy,[12] for knowledge of the meaning of numbers is inevitably esoteric, and a source of power to those who have it. Plutarch, referring to the secrecy of the Pythagoreans and their prohibition of putting their doctrines down in writing (ibid.: 457),[13] noted that

> when their treatment of the abstruse and mysterious processes of geometry had been divulged to a certain unworthy person, they said the gods threatened to punish such lawlessness and impiety with some signal and widespread calamity.

Now what has all this to do with modern Japanese views of time and space? The use of writing, and particularly the use of *kanji*, provides a good starting-point for analysis. For where language 'breaks up the natural unity of the perceptual world – or at least imposes another structure on it . . . writing draws out, crystallizes and extends this discontinuity by insisting on a visual, spatial location which then becomes subject to possible rearrangement'.[14] In traditional Pythagorean mathematics, such rearrangement is to be found in the way in which 'numbers are represented by figures made with counters or pebbles, φῆφοι',[15] so that 'what at first seems merely a game leads to arithmetical combinations which are by no means trivial[16] (Burkert 1972: 427; Crump 1990: 119). If this has its parallel in the way in which modern Japanese fortune-telling makes use of the five basic elements (Yoshino 1983: 28ff.),[17] it is the Chinese characters themselves which form the basis of much popular mysticism.

The process can be illustrated by the familiar *kanji* connotations of the numbers 61, 77 and 88 associated with the so-called *juga*, or long-life celebrations. The number 61 is a somewhat special case, since it represents the first year of a new sixty-year cycle based upon the combination of the ten *kan* and the twelve *shi*, in which every one of the sixty years has its own distinctive meaning.[18] The special significance of the 61st birthday is to be found in some parts of the country in the custom of *kumi ni goshūgi o dasu*[19] which, together with comparable occasions on the 42nd and 77th birthdays, are familiar to any student of Japan. The cases of 77 and 88 are to be distinguished, in the Pythagorean sense, in that the connotations of the two ages can be derived directly from their *kanji* forms. Thus, the elements in the *kanji* 77, 七十七, can be recombined to give the cursive form of *ki*, 'rejoice', in the compound *kiju*, 喜寿, meaning the 77th birthday. This form of combination is somewhat more transparent in the form 米 , 'rice' in the compound *beiju*, 米寿, meaning the 88th birthday. A somewhat different and more arithmetical process gives 99 in the form 白, 'white' in *hakuju* (白寿), since this is obtained by subtracting *ichi* (一) from 100, or *hyaku* (百).[20] If the connotation 'white' is derived from 99 by a combined lexical and arithmetical process, the significance of the number 33 – which is important, in years, in the ritual relating to death, and in days, in that relating to birth (Tsuboi 1970: 18 ff.) – is purely arithmetical. This is but one case of what Gerschel (1962: 696) calls '*le nombre marginal*', which he defines as '*un nombre qui n'existe pas, puisqu'il surpasse d'une unité le dernier nombre réel, mais qui, en vertu des lois de la fiction, gagne en extension ce qu'il perd en compréhension*'. Such numbers occur as much at a trivial as at a cosmic level. They are, however, particularly significant when they exceed by 1 a power of 2, perfectly formed by the process of binary multiplication. This analysis makes the number 32 particularly significant for Gerschel (1962: 706), for with this number the limit attainable with four equal blocks of 8 is reached, so that 33 becomes '*un nombre marginal*'.

The significance of the number 33 in Buddhism manifests itself in a number of ways. A particularly striking example is given by Shorto (1963: 573–4) in his examination of the 32 *myos* of the medieval Mon kingdom of lower Burma:

> we may note first the widespread tradition that Thaton, the early Mon kingdom which was overrun by Anawrahta in 1057, had 32 *myos* like the later provinces, each the seat of a subordinate prince, and united by a *cetiya* cult. This tradition was current at least as early as the reign of Dhammacetî. In inscriptions at the Hpaya-ywa, Hsudaungbyè and Mokhainggyi pagodas which

he repaired near Pegu – the first named dated BE 848 or AD 1486 – Dhammacetî recorded how on the death of the Buddha the arahat Gavampati brought one of His teeth to Sirimâsoka, king of Thaton. In fulfilment of a promise made by the Master when He visited Thaton 37 years earlier, the tooth multiplied into 33, which the king enshrined in as many small stone *cetiyas*.

(ibid.)

This is but a particular case of the mandala, or 'geometrical and topographic "formulas" . . . usually fused with cosmological principles, which provided the design for the constitution of [a wide range] of communities [in Southeast Asia]' (Tambiah 1976: 102), and as Tambiah goes on to point out,

> It is possible to see Indian and Chinese precedents, Hindu and Buddhist sources, for these ideas, but one thing is clear: they could have taken root in Southeast Asia only because indigenous conditions and social practices favored their incorporation or because they represented a 'literate' culture's formalization of images already experienced and emergent in local conditions, a convergence that makes the quick and ready borrowing of classical Hindu–Buddhist charters readily understandable.

(ibid.)

In the Japanese Buddhist tradition the *mandara* also connotes a representation of the Buddha,[21] with the Buddha comprising the core, *manda*, and the *ra*, the surroundings, such as the holy Mount Sumeru:[22] as such it still plays a role in modern sects like Risshō Kōseikai (Takaki 1960: 128ff.). The most prominent manifestation of the number 33 is almost certainly in the well-known temple of Sanjusangendō in Kyoto, where 'thirty-three' is actually incorporated into the name, exemplifying the Pythagorean equation between names and numbers.[23] The correspondence with the case of the Buddha's tooth, described in the passage cited from Shorto, is very striking. The question is whether, not only in this case but in others also, these ideas 'could have taken root . . . only because . . . local conditions' were favourable according to the principle established by Tambiah (1976: 103).

What, then, in Japan, were the 'indigenous conditions and social practices [which] favored [the] incorporation' of a 'Pythagorean' number mysticism? The question is almost impossible to answer: the written record begins only with the adoption of the Chinese method of writing, which was but one part of the Chinese culture incorporated into the autochthonous tradition. Since the adoption of Buddhism – in which number mysticism has always been central – was part of the same process, there is hardly any need to establish that Japan, ecologically speaking, was particularly 'receptive'. In so far as 'indigenous conditions and social practices' were favourable, were they significantly different from those prevailing in China or Korea? If, however, the question is cast in a somewhat different form, so that it relates to the indigenous conditions and social practices as they developed under the influence of the culture imported from the mainland, then in terms of both time and space Japan does present particularly favourable conditions for a Pythagorean cognitive system to prevail – even if these conditions were largely the result of Chinese influence. In the first place the organization of space is based upon a permanent division into a number of discrete units, of which the ricefield (*ta*) may be taken as the prime example of the institution of *bun*, or 'part'. Wet-rice cultivation imposes a human geography composed of such fixed bounded elements, which in social terms are related to the *ie* as a corporate group (Bachnik 1983: 162). The world comprised of such elements may be comprehended in terms of the concept *uchi*, connoting 'inside', in contrast to that of *soto*, connoting 'outside'.[24] *Uchi* as cosmos, and *soto* as chaos combine to provide an image of Japan familiar to any visitor.[25]

The interdependence of the bounded elements comprising the spatial universe is determined and regulated by the time factor.[26] Once again, wet-rice cultivation provides the ideal type. The fact that the whole cycle of cultivation must be coordinated, in terms of time, over any integrated system of terraces, is decisive for the form of social organization.[27] It also puts a premium upon the organization of time in cosmic terms, which puts the ordering of the cycle beyond the caprice of any individual involved in it. This explains the Japanese preoccupation with calendars[28] and with all forms of mystical practice directed towards determining what times and periods are auspicious, or towards avoiding the consequences of the three 'calamities', or *sansai*, of fire, flood and storm.[29] In this respect the Pythagorean cosmos accords well with the Japanese life cycle, following the rule stated by Reader (1991: chapters 3 and 4) – 'Born Shinto . . . Die Buddhist' – and illustrated schematically by Crump (1992: 105).

The point could certainly be laboured further, but what has been said is sufficient, in the present context, for the first part of Tambiah's precept. As for the second part, the question is to what extent, in the case of Japan, a Pythagorean world-view represents a 'literate' culture's formalization of images already experienced and emergent in local conditions. The 'literate' culture, in the present case, can only be that of China, and in the case of China itself there can be no doubt that the extraordinary durability of its 'literate' culture must be related to its continuous capacity to 'formalize images already experienced and emergent in local conditions'. Everything said above in the context of the human ecology of Japan confirms that the position there is no different.

Although the significance of the use of *kanji* has already been discussed, there is one particular point still to be made. This is that only the Chinese 'have succeeded in devising numerals that represent their verbal numbers' (Menninger 1969: 53) – or, to put it another way, only in Chinese is there a perfect one-to-one correspondence between the written and spoken form of numbers. The significance of this point is that it is no more than one instance of the way in which anything in spoken Chinese is represented in writing. The case of the numerals may indeed have been decisive for the survival of the logographic form of written Chinese,[30] for were it not for the extreme simplicity of the algorithm for generating the spoken numbers, the written forms would have been too opaque to allow for the necessary 'rearrangements' mentioned by Goody (see above, at note

14), which are requisite for any sort of arithmetical operations, however elementary.[31] At the same time, the requirement of Chinese syntax that numbers should also be combined with one of a limited number of 'classifiers', equivalent to the Japanese *josūshi* (Crump 1992: 20), must be regarded as a factor tending to obscure their logical nature and enhance their mystical connotations.

If the conclusion is that the Pythagorean potential of Chinese numbers has a linguistic basis, this is even more pronounced in the case of Japanese. For although for ordinary counting purposes, and in the expression of numbers larger than ten, Chinese numerals supplanted the autochthonous Japanese numbers, the latter still survive as 'names' in the Pythagorean sense. According to Shiratori (n.d.: 27), the basis for this practice was established before the introduction of Chinese culture.[32] The present-day survivals are to be found in such words as *yaoya*, for 'greengrocer', whose written form, 八百屋, makes clear its literal meaning of the '800-shop'.[33] The cases are in fact so numerous that it needs a whole dictionary (Mori 1980) to list them, and if proper names are included the length of the list is much increased. This is indeed no surprise to anyone with a command of Japanese.

The distinctive form of *kanji*, combined with a fixed order for writing the strokes comprising any character, also provides the basis for the popular science of *seimeigaku* (姓名学), or 'full-name science'. The principle that names must be auspicious is to be found in the furthest reaches of Japanese history, as witness the constant changes in the name of an era in the course of the reign of a single emperor, generally as a desperate reaction to some natural disaster. In the present day the bestowal of a new name after death, for which the family must resort to the priests of the local Buddhist temple, is an example of the same tradition.

Since the original publication of this paper in 1984, the death of the Shōwa emperor in January 1989 has provided a textbook example of the application of Pythagorean principles to the choice of names. The modern practice was established with the Meiji restoration of 1868. The emperor himself, during his reign, is simply and unambiguously referred to as 'Tennō', but at the beginning of his reign he chooses a name, *nengō*, for it, which will then become the name by which he himself will be known after his death. Thus, on 7 January 1989, the Shōwa era came to an end, and its emperor took his place in history as Shōwa Tennō.

At the same time the new emperor had to find a *nengō* for his own reign. The choice was limited by rules long established by tradition. The name had to be represented by two *kanji* chosen out of a list of seventy-two derived from a group of sacred texts known as *shūkyō*. A name already used could not be repeated, and the Tennō's advisers came up with three possibilities.[34] Of these, two were ruled out because in *rōmaji* they would begin with s, as had Shōwa, leading to confusion in computer records.[35] This left Heisei as the only possible choice, so the present year (1998) is known officially as Heisei 10 – but, officially, Heisei Tennō, does not, indeed cannot, exist.

For ordinary Japanese *seimeigaku* provides a means of evaluating the fortunes to be associated with a given name according to the number of strokes in the different characters comprising it. The most common form of a Japanese name, consisting of four *kanji* – two for the family name and two for the given name – provides, therefore, four numbers which, in combination, and in relation to each other, determine in what respects the name is auspicious or inauspicious.[36] The complete method is explained in countless cheap paperbacks sold in supermarkets and station bookstalls.[37] In the early days of the Buddhist sect Risshō Kōseikai, it also played a role in attracting adherents (Takaki 1960: 127) who, by obtaining a new name according to the principles of the science, would enter into a new and more promising life (McFarland 1967: 187). This form of onomancy was an early preoccupation of Niwano, one of the two co-founders of the sect: his mastery of the relevant mysteries was an early source of his power. If now, the appeal of the sect is becoming more sophisticated and less reliance is placed on the practice of onomancy, this only means that it flourishes elsewhere.

This authentic 'Pythagorean' mystery, combined with the I Ching and the mystical use of the five elements, provides for four pages of entries under the heading *eki* ('divination')[38] in the Kyoto classified telephone directory, and the position is certainly little different in other Japanese cities. But what is its relevance to the themes of time and space in the cognitive universe of contemporary Japan? This question is most usefully examined in terms of Bachnik's (1983) discussion of recruitment strategies for household succession. The key is to be found in the relation of the household, or *ie*, seen as a continuing corporate group, to its position, or *tachiba*, in time and space (ibid.: 162ff.). A solution to the problem of succession, as the occasion arises and as it relates to individual members of the *ie*, is essential to its continued existence. If the problem, which is always critical, can be reduced to a choice between names, then its solution is moved out of the realm of domestic politics into that of supernatural forces governing the destiny of the *ie*. Here one sees, once again, the significance of the new names conferred by the Buddhist priests at the death of a member of the *ie*, who will be assured a permanent position as an ancestor commemorated in the tablets preserved on the shelves of the domestic altar.[39] But when it comes to the recruitment of new living members of the *ie*, the decision cannot be left to the priests – which explains the presence of the diviners listed in the Kyoto yellow pages and the popular manuals of *seimeigaku* on the supermarket shelves.

The fascination with numbers is even more widespread. Auspicious licence numbers for cars are advertised in the press, and games with a high potential for numerical legerdemain are particularly popular. Whiting (1977: 6) gives an idea of the Japanese obsession for baseball statistics, which would be confirmed by anyone who has looked at televised baseball during the summer season. Golf, the supreme status symbol among the elite, lends itself equally readily to this sort of analysis, with 18 holes to the course of varying lengths, determining whether they are bogey 3, 4 or 5, ranked in a predetermined order so as to decide each player's own handicap. Golf is the Pythagorean game *par excellence*: for not only is the 416-metre 7th hole (bogey four) at the Ichimatsu Country Club a statistical entity, it also has its own identity, and even its own folklore. And if golf and baseball are exogenous, they provide, as much as *go* and *shōgi* the means for ranking the players, reaffirming the Japanese obsession with hierarchy.[40] The analysis, if it goes too far beyond the themes of time and space, threatens to become trivial, but the phenomena observed are none the less dominant in popular culture.

How, then, does all this fit into the way in which the individual Japanese experiences life? One must start with a vision of life as a journey, mapped out in advance, with frequent if sometimes ambiguous signposts. It is a game with only one strategy indicated for the individual player, and that is laid down by the 'group' to which he belongs. There is always safety in numbers, so that individual choice is daunting. At the domestic level, questions of marriage and succession none the less require that such choice be made. The conflict can best be resolved by an appeal to the occult: the apparent merits of a potential daughter-in-law can be confirmed by the science of *seimeigaku*. The I Ching oracle can be consulted when it comes to questions of business strategy, such as opening a new branch. Calendric ritual, with all its means for predicting natural disaster, can ensure that 'forewarned is forearmed'.[41] If the signposts encountered on the journey through life lead in the wrong direction, the map can always be redrawn, so that the integrity of the structure is preserved. The accumulated store of mystical connotations provides the scope for endless reinterpretation, so that being 'wise after the event' can be transformed into being 'wise before the event'. The system, once established, can always be brought up to date – in the best Shinto tradition.[42] It can also provide the means of temporary escape from the strait-jacket of destiny, in the form of *pachinko* parlours, driving ranges,[43] *manga* (comics) or Suntory whisky from street-corner vending-machines – all institutions providing solace to be enjoyed in solitude.[44]

The picture is not meant to be bleak. It represents, rather, a continuing and successful adaptation to the exigencies of Japanese life, making use of traditional symbols of very long standing. The key to the symbolic system is to be found in the concept of 'guidance', best expressed by the Japanese *annai*. This represents the security of the beaten path,[45] and is in the authentic Pythagorean tradition. If, occasionally, the need to escape from 'guidance' cannot be denied, so that the transition is made from *uchi* to *soto*, that is no more than an instance of a process of reversal all too familiar to anthropologists.

Finally I must acknowledge that this paper is written from a *soto* perspective (a point so obvious that it did not strike me as particularly significant when working on the first version in the early 1980s). In the meantime, the publication of Said (1996) has led us to examine our consciences for the sin of orientalism,[46] while Fabian (1983) has made anthropologists aware of the dangers of conducting fieldwork from the perspective of visitors from another planet. Where Said (1996: 322) argues 'that "the Orient" is itself a constituted entity, and that the notion that there are geographical spaces with indigenous, radically "different" inhabitants who can be defined on the basis of some religion, culture or racial essence proper to that geographical space, is . . . a highly debatable idea', Fabian is nodding agreement. Almost any Westerner who has visited Japan knows only too well that this is precisely how many Japanese think of themselves.[47]

I am only half impressed: too much soul-searching makes for bad science, and the change in attitude asked for, at least implicitly, by Said and Fabian (and many others) can easily lead to a cure which is worse than the disease. Indeed, one reason for the crisis in contemporary anthropology (which tends to be a self-fulfilling prophecy) is that this process is already well under way.

The full significance of this fact in the Japanese context is far beyond the scope of this paper. None the less, the interaction between East and West is deeply embedded in contemporary Japanese culture, in a process that works both ways. Japanese popular culture is as prone to 'occidentalism' as much as any Western one is to orientalism (Crump 1994). In Japan, however, this interaction gets a new twist when traditional divination (*uranai*) is made available to the public in a manual (*Uranai no Kan 96*) which is sold with a CD-ROM for Windows 95. In the jargon of the computer age, this demonstrates that the basis of Pythagoreanism is essentially digital: in any context, Japanese or otherwise, this can only mean that it is completely demystified – at least when viewed from any scientific perspective. This is not, however, the perspective of Japanese who seek their fortune on a CD-ROM: for them, it is no more than a question of modern technology bringing an old mystery up to date.

NOTES

1 Heidel is extremely sceptical about the role of Pythagoras in Greek mathematics. The Pythagorean tradition, as described by Burkert (1972), is much more important than the individual achievements of Pythagoras himself, whatever they may have been.

2 Burkert (1972: 472) cites authority both for and against the possibility of direct connections between the Pythagoreans and the Chinese, but in any case finds the basic, underlying idea or attitude much more important, for 'speculation about numerical relationships in the cosmos is world wide, firmly established in ritual, and capable of being elaborated into a rich and ingeniously structured system without either presupposing or giving rise to mathematics in the proper sense of the word'.

   At all events, whatever China gained from Greek mathematics must have come via India, so the question, in any given case, turns on the relevant dates in the history of Indian mathematics. Greek mathematics came to India towards the end of the first millennium AD, so that the earliest records contain material that could not have come from Greece. This does not, however, solve the problem completely, since dating these records is itself extremely problematical, as has been demonstrated by the foremost expert in this field, Hayashi Takao, who is himself Japanese (Hayashi 1995: 149).

3 The key principle is to be found in Plato's injunction, μηδεὶς ἀγεωμέτρητος εἰσίτω, which, by establishing geometry as the basis of mathematics as a branch of deductive logic, provided the whole starting-point for the Western scientific tradition.

4 This came to be true only after the Renaissance. The position in medieval Europe is well described by Lewis (1964: 10ff.). Even in the West a Pythagorean view still prevails at the popular level.

5 The five-volume history of Japanese mathematics, *Meiji mae Nihon Sūgakushi* published by Iwanami Shōten for the Nihon Gakushi-in consistently refers to the hypoteneuse theorem (*kōkogen no teiri*), noting (I 17, 21, 73, 128, 222, 306, 405, II 194, 283, 570. V 154, 167, 466), however, the attribution to Pythagoras without ever disclosing when this was first recorded in Japan. The whole exhaustive study does not mention Pythagoras in any other context: indeed, the whole subject-matter of this chapter has no place in it at all. The same is true of short popular studies such as

Okura (1964) and Shimodaira (1986), although the latter, significantly, opens with a short section comparing the calculating skills of Japanese and Westerners (much to the disadvantage of the latter).

6 The recent debate on the proposition 'Aesthetics is a cross-cultural category' (Ingold 1996: 151–93) puts one on one's guard when taking for granted that the concept of aesthetics in premodern Japan existed in a form which makes it legitimate to refer to it in a twentieth-century journal article. I would insist, however, that no one familiar with the material culture of premodern Japan could possibly deny the pronounced aesthetic sense of those who created it. Aesthetics, whatever its precise meaning, is *par excellence* a characteristic of Japanese culture, during any historical period. I have no difficulty whatever about extending its domain to include the distinctive numerical culture described in this paper.

7 Compare the extreme position taken by the Cambridge mathematician, G. H. Hardy (1940: 70): 'pure mathematics [is] a rock on which all idealism founders: 317 is a prime, not because we think it so, or because our minds are shaped in one way or another, but because it is so, because mathematics is built that way'. Pythagoras would turn in his grave. For a modern approach see Restivo (1983, chapter 12 'Numbers and Cultures'). Even so, the austere Hardy must have derived some aesthetic pleasure from a life devoted to pure mathematics, although, as C.P. Snow has noted, the tenor of his book is profoundly pessimistic. This is not the way the Japanese approach mathematics.

8 This possibility is completely excluded by Russell's definition (1920: 18): 'The number of a class is the class of all those classes that are similar to it.' Russell himself acknowledged (ibid.: 3) that such views were the product of a high stage of civilization.

9 The Pythagorean explanation given by Burkert (1972: 473) is that 'where 3 is male, 4 is female, and 5, which mysteriously unites them, in the Pythagorean triangle, is "marriage" '.

10 A similar approach, in our own time, in the West, is taken by Grant (1982).

11 The calling numbers used in bingo are a perfect Pythagorean system, with numerous Japanese parallels.

12 According to Nakayama (1969: 159), 'the [Japanese] mathematicians' lack of contact with other fields of learning made their outlook narrow. Isolated from society as a whole and alienated from its intellectual tradition, they tended to form small groups in which a strong pupil-teacher relationship and an esoteric means of initiation were maintained.' The formation of such groups is still characteristic of Japan. In the modern Western world, 'secrecy' in mathematics has been used in inventing codes based upon the product of two very large prime numbers to form a composite number which cannot be factorised even with the help of the largest computers. Unfortunately for the military and the other users of the codes, advances in prime number theory – also computer based – have provided the means for cracking the codes, demonstrating that there is no ultimate secrecy in mathematics, and confirming Hardy's view (1940: 63) that 'mathematical reality lies outside us'.

13 Goody (1977: 61) notes how in the seventeenth century *Culpeper's Complete Herbal*, by publishing the secret knowledge of the medical profession, earned the author the enmity of the doctors, although he was compensated by the enormous sales of his book.

14 Here Goody (1977: 61) accepts Bruner's view (1966: 40-1) that 'symbolic representation in contrast to representation by perceptual similarity that occurs with iconic representation (images) [is] . . . specific to human language'. The implications with regard to written Chinese are quite far reaching. As for Japanese, they are dealt with by Crump (1988).

15 Hence the science of psephology, which the *Concise Oxford Dictionary* defines as the 'study of elections and voting'. The allusion is to the use of pebbles to cast votes in

the Athenian public assembly. For the use of pebbles in making up triangular numbers, see Crump (1982: 281).

16 One application of *janken*, the most elementary of all Japanese games, played by even the youngest children, led me into the mathematical theory of Markov chains (Crump 1990: 174,179).

17 According to Nakayama (1969: 63), 'The Chinese yin-yang and five-elements principles were expounded in Japan only among specialists at the court. The Japanese general public probably found this natural philosophy difficult to comprehend. Thus, purely Japanese aspects of the practice of fate calculation were developed in the form of a popular yin-yang art, *on'yōdō*. It had neither a simple core of principles nor a consistent system, but was a set of superstitious beliefs derived from various origins. Different writings of the court nobles show that both their public and private lives were strictly conditioned by the taboos of *on'yōdō*. The application of fate calculation attracted the people, not the theory itself.' The present position is described in detail in Crump (1992: chapter 6 'Fortune-telling'). Arithmetically, the rules are elementary (if surprisingly difficult to discover from the published manuals or *nyūmon*) and as such are well adapted to computer programming. Professional fortune-tellers are not ashamed to take advantage of this, and I have witnessed a number of cases of fortunes being revealed in the form of a computer print-out. Such a development should not surprise anyone who knows modern Japan.

18 The year 1966, the 43rd in the 60-year cycle, was marked by a very low birth rate because of a superstition, arising in the Edo era, that girls born in such a year would kill and eat their husbands. This was taken to be the result of the combination of *kan* '*hinoe*' and *shi* '*uma*' (Anon. 1983), representing a fatal juxtaposition of fire and the horse. The '*uma*' is one of the twelve animal signs of the Chinese calendar referred to by Beillevaire (in the present volume).

19 This special case (based upon Marshall 1983) should be distinguished from the general case of *kanreki iwai*, which means rather more than simply celebrating one's 61st birthday, in that the *kanji* components of *kanreki* import 'returning to the calendar'. When, in 1986, the 60-year cycle began for the second time in the Shōwa era, this was an event without precedent in Japanese history.

20 Is there a phonetic parallel here in that *hyaku* (100) less *i* (1) becomes *haku* ('white')? It should be noted here that *shiroi*, the normal word for white is based on the *kun* reading.

21 See, for example, in the National Museum in Tokyo, the Ryōkai Mandara tapestry from the Kojima Temple, dating from the Heian period.

22 For a more detailed analysis see Crump (1992: 37,120). For the Mandala outside Japan see Crump (1990: 71).

23 The Kannon Buddha, otherwise known as the 'Regarder of the Cries of the World', is a perfected bodhisattva characterized by boundless compassion and mercy. Chapter 25 of the *Lotus Sutra* (known in Japanese as the *Fumombon* chapter), after describing a number of catastrophes in which the Kannon Buddha will come to the rescue, goes on to list 33 bodies in which the living will be saved. This is the mystical basis of the number 33 in the Temple of Sanjūsangendō. In Japanese Buddhism the number 33 is almost always connected with the Kannon Buddha. Another example is provided by the *sanjūsansho* (literally, '33 places'), which refers to 33 temples in and around Kyoto (starting with Nyoiriu-ji on the Kii peninsular). It was believed in medieval Japan that anyone who had visited all of these temples would be preserved from hell. The number is ultimately derived from the 33 heavens situated at the top of the mystic Mount Sumeru, which is ruled by Indra, whose own heaven is located on the central peak, with the 32 other heavens being divided equally between the four cardinal points, after the pattern of the mandala (*The Threefold Lotus Sutra* 1975: 147). It is not surprising, therefore, that the number 33 connotes 'boundless'. It is also a '*nombre marginal*', relating directly to the 32 signs distinguishing the body of the

Buddha (ibid.: 7ff.), for by adding to the number 32, with its earthly connotations, the number 1, one enters into the realm of heaven, or unbounded perfection.

There are altogether 1001 statues of the Kannon Buddha in Sanjūsangendō, and this is another *nombre marginal*. (Compare 1001 with 10001, the binary representation of 33). There is one large central statue, with 500 identical but smaller statues on either side. The number 1000 (of the smaller statues) is equal to 25 x 40, the number 25 representing the 25 sorts of life and death of man. The derivation of the number 40 is more involved. Each statue should in principle have 1000 hands, but in fact each hand is taken to represent 25 hands: in practice each statue has 42 hands, but this number is reduced to 40, since one pair of hands is clasped in prayer, while another pair holds a small bowl.

The significance of the number 33 in Sanjūsangendō is also to be found in the 33 different figures into which the Kannon Buddha can be transformed, so that the 1001 separate statues in fact represent 33033 manifestations of the Kannon Buddha. It is also worth noting that the Buddha with 1000 hands (depicted in the same way) is to be found in seventeen of the the the temples comprising the *sanjūsansho*.

24 Note, for instance, the *shimenawa*, the ceremonial rope marking off a patch of holy ground.

25 Note also the *on* compounds of 外, such as *gaijin* (外人), 'a foreigner'.

26 Compare the use of spatial symbolism in Ryūkyūan folk culture described by Beillevaire (in the present volume). For a general discussion of time in Japanese culture, see Crump (1992, chapter 7).

27 For the Japanese context, this is described and explained in Beardsley *et al.* (1959: 114ff). The exchange of labour (*kattari*) is described in Embree (1946: 99ff).

28 This is apparent not only in the variety of calendars stocked in stationery shops and bookshops, but also in shops specializing in wedding gifts.

29 Described in detail in Yoshino (1983: 132ff).

30 If Kindaichi (1967: 18) is correct, 'the Japanese first imitated Chinese in counting numbers'. On a similar point in relation to the Spanish presence in the Maya area of Mexico, see Crump (1978).

31 This point is discussed in greater detail in Crump (1981: 3ff).

32 But Shiratori goes on to note that the Japanese, 'once in contact with the Chinese [were led by] their wonder at the excellence of Chinese customs and institutions . . . to a thoroughgoing imitation of everything Chinese. This tendency even affected the Japanese numerical conception until the odd numbers came to be valued and the even numbers to be slighted.'

33 Note also Shiratori (n.d.: 33): 'As to the frequent occurrence of eight in the mythologies, a question was raised by Japanese scholars of the Tokugawa period. Motoori Norinaga, in answering this question, says that this number eight simply means many, and should not necessarily be taken as the numeral eight.' There follows a long discussion of the mystical significance of the number eight in relation to the original Japanese pantheon.

34 The number of permutations of 2 out of 72 is 5112, and so far only 238 have been used for *nengō*, so it is at first sight odd that only three choices were available to the new emperor in 1989. Other limiting factors applied, however, to restrict the choice.

35 My plastic patient's registration card for the Kyoto University Hospital records the year of my birth, 1929, as S 4.

36 The point made by Hughes (1967: 86) in relation to the Chinese, that they 'concentrate more on categories of relationship than on categories of substance', applies also to the Japanese.

37 One of the many examples in a book entitled *Seimei handan nyūmon*, bought in a Toyama supermarket in the summer of 1983. It is significant that there is little variation in the explanations given in such books, suggesting a definite common origin. Quite how the necessary lore was first established is never made clear. Since

this whole process is well suited to computers, modern handbooks may well include appropriate software: an e-mail message received from my friend and colleague, Professor Takao Hayashi lists eight such publications, and this must be no more than the tip of the iceberg.

38 See note 1.

39 In the summer of 1983, three Buddhist priests of Higashi Honganji in Kyoto insisted that number mysticism, in whatever form, played no part in choosing the names to be given to the recently deceased.

40 For the subtleties of ranking in *go* see Kawabata (1972). It is interesting to note how hierarchy as a spatial concept corresponds to succession as a temporal concept.

41 This explains the enormous attention paid throughout Japan's premodern history to the predicting of eclipses. The tendency was always to over-predict, so that the astrologers could claim the credit for averting the catastrophes which an eclipse which had failed to occur would have brought with it.

42 McFarland, in his choice of 'The Rush-hour of the Gods', as the title of his book (1967), evokes the chaotic religious situation in modern Japan. For a more recent, and more analytical, study see Reader (1991).

43 This point is made very forcibly in Barthes' analysis of *pachinko* (1970: 43).

44 Such expressions as *jibun de* or *hitori de* suggest that the Japanese concept of solitude emphasizes doing something by oneself, no matter how many other people may actually be present.

45 This recalls, in the Christian tradition, the line of a well-known hymn: 'Be thou my guardian and my guide'. The longing for certainty can be very deep-seated in humankind.

46 Although Said is mainly concerned with the Islamic world of the Middle East, he does mention Japan in noting (1996: 285) that 'a wide variety of hybrid representations of the Orient now roam the culture'.

47 Just consider the case of Tsunoda (1978) – a popular best-seller – which argues that the functions of the left and right hemispheres of the brain are reversed among the Japanese.

REFERENCES

Ākurakuto (1996) *The Mansion of Divination 96*, Tokyo, Shōeisha (on-line software collection).

Anon. (1983) *Toshi no seikatsu kankaku to onyōdō* [*Yin and Yang in the Life of the City: A Folklore Calendar of the City*], *Rekishi Kōron* 9, 7, 54–9.

Bachnik, J. M. (1983) 'Recruitment Strategies for Household Succession: Rethinking Japanese Household Organisation', *Man*, n.s., vol. XVIII, no. 1, pp. 160–82.

Barthes, R. (1970) *L'Empire des signes*, Geneva: Albert Skira.

Beardsley, R. K., J. W. Hall and R. E. Ward (1959) *Village Japan*, Chicago: University of Chicago Press.

Bruner, J. S. (ed.) (1966) *Studies in Cognitive Growth*, New York: Wiley.

Burkert, W. (1972) *Lore and Science in Ancient Pythagoreanism*, Cambridge, MA: Harvard University Press.

Crump, S. T. (1978) 'Money and Number: The Trojan Horse of Language', *Man*, n.s., vol. XIII, pp. 503–18.

—— (1981) 'Le Problème linguistique du nombre', *Linguistique, ethnologie, ethno-linguistique (La pratique de l'anthropologie aujourd'hui) Actes de l'Atelier 'Linguistique et ethnologie' du Colloque International du CNRS organisé par l'Association Française des Anthropologues (Sèvres, 19–21 novembre 1981)*.

—— (1982) 'The Alternative Meanings of Number and Counting', in D. Parkin (ed.) *Semantic Anthropology*, London: Academic Press, (ASA Monograph 22), pp. 279–92.

—— (1988) 'Alternative Meanings of Literacy in Japan and the West', *Human Organization*, vol. 47, pp. 138–45.

—— (1989) *The Death of an Emperor: Japan at the Crossroads*, London: Constable.

—— (1990) *The Anthropology of Numbers*, Cambridge: Cambridge University Press.

—— (1992) *The Japanese Numbers Game: The Use and Understanding of Numbers in Modern Japan*, London and New York: Routledge.

—— (1994) 'Gendai Nihon ni okeru seiyō bunka no juyō to hen'yō [The Reception and Transformation of Western Culture in Contemporary Japan]', in T. Inoue, S. Motoda and K. Fukui (eds) *Bunka no chiheisen: jinruigaku kara no chōsen [The Horizons of Culture: The Challenge from Anthropology]* (essays presented to Professor Yoneyama Toshinao on the occasion of his retirement), Kyoto: Sekai Shisōsha.

Embree, J. F. (1946) *A Japanese Village: Suye Mura*, London: Kegan, Paul, Trench, Trubner & Co.

Fabian, J. (1983) *Time and the Other*, New York: Columbia University Press.

Gerschel, L. (1962) 'La Conquête du nombre: Des modalités du compte aux structures de la pensée', *Annales*, vol. XVII, no. 4, pp. 691–714.

Goody, J. (1977) *The Domestication of the Savage Mind*, Cambridge: Cambridge University Press.

Grant, J. (1982) *A Book of Numbers*, Bath: Ashgrove Press.

Hardy, G. H. (1940) *A Mathematician's Apology*, Cambridge: Cambridge University Press.

Hayashi, T. (1995) *The Bakshālī Manuscript: An Ancient Indian Mathematical Treatise*, Groningen: Egbert Forsten.

Heidel, W. A. (1940) 'The Pythagoreans and Greek Mathematics', *American Journal of Philology*, vol. LXI, pp. 1–33.

Hughes, E. R. (1967) 'Epistemological Methods in Chinese Philosophy', in C.A. Moore (ed.) *Chinese Mind*, Honolulu: East–West Center Press.

Ingold, T. (ed.) (1996) *Key Debates in Anthropology*. London and New York: Routledge.

Kawabata, Y. (1972) *The Master of Go*, Tokyo: Charles E. Tuttle.

Kindaichi, H. (1967) *Language and Culture of Japan*, Tokyo: Nihon Kokusai Kyōiku Kyōkai.

Lewis, C. S. (1964) *The Discarded Image*, Cambridge: Cambridge University Press.

McFarland, H. N. (1967) *The Rush-hour of the Gods*, New York: Macmillan.

Marshall, R. C. (1983) 'Giving a Gift to the Hamlet: Rank, Solidarity and Productive Exchange in Rural Japan', unpublished manuscript.

Menninger, K. (1969) *Number Words and Number Symbols*, Boston: M.I.T. Press.

Mori, M. (1980) *Meisū Sūshi Jiten [A Dictionary of Number Compounds]*, Tokyo: Iwanami Shoten.

Nakayama, S. (1969) *A History of Japanese Astronomy*, Cambridge, MA: Harvard University Press.

Nihon Gakushi, in. (1954) *Meiji mae Nihon Sūgakushi [A History of pre-Meiji Japanese Mathematics]*, 5 vols, Tokyo: Iwanami Shōten.

Okura, K. (1964) *Nihon no Sūgaku [Japanese Mathematics]*, Tokyo: Iwanami Shinsho.

Reader, I. (1991) *Religion in Contemporary Japan*, London: Macmillan.

Restivo, S. (1983) *The Social Relations of Physics, Mysticism and Mathematics*, Dordrecht: D. Reidel.

Russell, B. (1920) *An Introduction to Mathematical Philosophy*, London: Allen & Unwin.

—— (1946) *A History of Western Philosophy*, London: Allen & Unwin.

Said, E. (1996) *Orientalism*, London: Penguin.

Shimodaira, K. (1986) *The Japanese Feeling for Mathematics*, Tokyo: PHP Kenkyūjo.

Shiratori, K. (n.d.) 'The Japanese Numerals', *Memoirs of the Research Department of the Tōyō Bunko* (The Oriental Library, Tokyo), vol. IX, pp. 1–78.

Shorto, H. L. (1963) 'The 32 Myos in the Medieval Mon Kingdom', *Bulletin of the School of Oriental and African Studies*, vol. XXVI, pp. 572–91.

Takaki, H. (1960) *Nihon no Shinkō Shūkyō* [*Japan's Newly Established Religions*], Toyko: Iwanami.

Tambiah, S. J. (1976) *World Conqueror and World Renouncer*, Cambridge: Cambridge University Press.

The Threefold Lotus Sutra (1975) New York and Tokyo: Weatherhill and Kosei.

Tsuboi, H. (1970) 'Nihon no Seishikan [The Japanese Way of Life and Death]', in *Minzokugaku kara mita Nihon* [*Japan in the Light of Folklore*], Tokyo: Kawade Shobōsha, pp. 18–34.

Tsunoda, T. (1978) *Nihonjin no Nō* [*The Brain of the Japanese*], Tokyo: Taishūkan Shōten.

Whiting, R. (1977) *The Chrysanthemum and the Bat*, Tokyo: Permanent Press.

Yoshino, H. (1983) *Inyō Gogyō to Nihon no Minzoku* [*Yin–Yang, the Five Elements and Japanese Folk Customs*], Tokyo: Jimmon Shoin.

4 The question of space

From Heidegger to Watsuji

Augustin Berque

SPACE, SOCIETY, MEDIANCE

In his essay *Fūdo* (*The Human Milieu*, 1935), Watsuji Tetsurō[1] initiates a hermeneutic phenomenology of the relationship of societies with their environment, which refers explicitly to Martin Heidegger's *Sein und Zeit* (*Being and Time*, 1927), while radically diverging from it on two grounds. First, Watsuji criticizes Heidegger for not having given enough importance to space. Second, correlatively, he criticizes Heidegger on account of his conception of *Dasein*, which, according to Watsuji, acknowledges only the individual dimension of the 'being-human' (or human existence, *ningen sonzai*), not its social dimension.

Watsuji stresses that the structure of human existence is no less spatial than temporal, and no less social than individual; consequently, one cannot subordinate spatiality to temporality, as Heidegger does, and one must always take into account the social–individual duality of the human (*ningen*). This leads Watsuji to pose a triple parity: to temporality responds spatiality, to history, milieu (*fūdo* – we shall understand here the relationship of a society with its environment), and to historicity mediance (*fūdosei* – we shall understand here the meaning, sense and orientation (the French *sens*, or the Japanese *omomuki*) of the above relationship[2]).

It is thus the stress which Watsuji puts on space and socialness (*aidagara*) which leads him to conceptualize mediance. For him, structurally, mediance is the necessary counterpoint of historicity – or more exactly, as we shall see, of historiality (*Geschichtlichkeit*) according to Heidegger. Watsuji even establishes mediance, in the first line of his book, as the 'structural moment of the being-human' (*ningen sonzai no kōzō keiki*); that is, more simply, an essential motivation of our existence.

I shall here attempt to delineate the logic of Watsuji's move, regarding Heidegger on the one hand, and regarding on the other hand philosophers like Emmanuel Levinas or Didier Franck, in whose works the accent is put on spatiality while leading to perspectives quite other than that of mediance. This examination will necessitate an anthropological approach, as the social, here, evidently appears to interfere with the ontological. Why, indeed, is it a Japanese philosopher, Watsuji, who first thought of, and named mediance?

SPATIALITY IN HEIDEGGER

The question of space is not absent at all in Heidegger's works (see Dewitte 1992: 201–19). However, it has only a secondary importance before the 1950s, during which decade, on the other hand, it becomes central. *Bauen, Wohnen, Denken* [*Building, Inhabiting, Thinking*] (1951) and *Die Kunst und der Raum* [*Art and Space*] (1969) illustrate this period, in which Heidegger's problematic focuses notably on the notion of place or site (*Ort*). His leading idea is that the place does not precede the work but, on the contrary, proceeds from it; in other words, a site is such only as a function of a human building or project.

This idea, as is well known, distinguishes radically Heidegger's approach from the presuppositions of the modern movement in architecture and urbanism, according to which space supposedly contains the work and therefore precedes it. Space, here, is considered as universal. For Heidegger, on the contrary, there is an opening, by dint of the work itself, of a certain space, which is relative to it; this is what he calls *räumen*, that is, 'spacing' or 'making place', or even 'giving rise'. By giving rise to a space, the human work 'spaces'.

This problematic does not appear yet in *Sein und Zeit*, the reference in regard to which Watsuji posed himself when he wrote *Fūdo* (that is, in the form of successive articles, the most important of which, for our purposes here – this in the book corresponds to chapter I, which is entirely theoretical – dates back to 1929, with minor additions and changes written in 1931 and 1935). One must of course bear this chronology in mind in order to appreciate Watsuji's judgement. Nevertheless, this judgement concerns some positions which have not varied in Heidegger's works, and which were already firmly established by *Sein und Zeit*. It is therefore in this book that we shall examine Heidegger's conception of spatiality. This reveals two principal traits.

In the first place, Heidegger introduces, in sections 22 to 24, an essential distinction between the spatiality of the world (*Welt*) – or, more particularly, of the ambient world (*Umwelt*) – and 'space' (*der Raum*). Correlatively, he distinguishes place as an attributive position (*Platz*) from place as an accidental location (*Stelle*). The world is made out of things which all have their attributive place, whereas 'space' contains a virtual infinity of accidental places, which interchangeable objects can indifferently occupy. An attributive place cannot be dissociated from a certain thing, nor from the relationship that one entertains with that thing. The hammer – a famous example – is either in its place, where I expect to find it without even having to be conscious of this place as such; or it is not, in which case only I become conscious of this place as such. On the contrary, an accidental place can perfectly be dissociated from the object which occupies it. This is because the space which it presupposes is an abstract one.

Heidegger shows that, contrary to the modern postulate, what is first is not 'space' but the world. From the latter to the former leads an evolution at the end of which, notably, attributive places become accidental places, 'de-stance' (*Entfernung*) becomes a measurable distance (i.e., the presence of things in mind is replaced by their objective remoteness), and the ambient world itself disappears, giving way to an objective environment. This evolution, which Heidegger calls 'deworlding' (*Entweltlichung*), is none other than the movement of modernity.

The second trait of Heidegger's conception of space consists in subordinating spatiality to temporality. The *Dasein* is spatial indeed, but it is first temporal, as is firmly established in section 70. The spatiality which de-stance induces, for instance, presupposes an anticipation by dint of which the *Dasein*, so to say, projects itself close to the thing it is awaiting. This projection is an 'ek-stasis', i.e., a being-out-of-self, which causes the *Dasein* to be always 'ahead' of itself. It is a purely temporal movement, a presenting (*Gegenwärtigen*) which makes present the thing waited for, although it still is objectively away. De-stance presupposes this 'ekstatic' temporality. Therefore, Heidegger writes (1993: 369) that the spatiality of the *Dasein* is possible only as founded in temporality. It is only secondarily that the *Dasein* is spatial.

FROM SPACE TO MEDIANCE

Watsuji agrees with Heidegger on several fundamental points. Although he does not explicitly adopt the latter's problematic concerning the distinction between world (a phenomenologic–hermeneutic notion) and space (a geometric and physical notion), what he deals with – mediance – belongs evidently to the world, not to 'space'. We shall examine later the reasons why he neglects, by so doing, a distinction which in Heidegger is a primordial one; anyhow, *Fūdo* accumulates examples which are perfectly in tune with *Sein und Zeit*: in the ambient world which is that of the human milieu, 'cold wind is a *yamaoroshi* or a *karakaze*. A spring wind is that wind which disperses the petals of cherry flowers, or that wind which caresses the waves. The damp heat of summer is that heat which makes full-blown greenery wither up, or which makes children play on the beach' (1962: 11).

In a word, Watsuji's 'phenomena of milieu' (*fūdo no genshō*) undeniably possess the 'aroundhood' (*Umhafte*) and the 'horizontalness' (i.e., the fact of being limited by a horizon of sense) specific to Heidegger's *Weltlichkeit* (world-liness). They do not belong to a universal and abstract 'space', but to the 'togetherness' or 'going-along-with' (*Bewandtnis*) of things in the historiality or epochality of the Heideggerian world. To add just one French example: in the aroundhood and horizontalness of the Parisian milieu, sunset glow goes along with Notre Dame's big rosace, whereas the chirping of birds at dawn goes along with its apse. This accord – a mediance – supposes both nature and culture, indissociably attuned to each other.

Let us remark, in addition, that if Watsuji does not distinguish historicity (the objective relation of the past) from historiality (the reality of an epoch for those who are living it) in the same way that he does not distinguish 'space' from the world, what he says refers evidently to the latter. As well as the peculiar sense of the different milieux on Earth, the matter at stake is indeed the discontinuous and heterogeneous temporality of successive worlds and epochs, not the continuum which historical science considers, with its universal time marks. Quite logically,

Watsuji associates mediance with a given epoch, not with universal time. As in Heidegger, there is indeed in his mind a historiality or epochality of the human milieu, even though he does not use that vocabulary: milieu is 'straight off a historical milieu . . . If one separates them, both history and milieu are no more than abstract things, without a concrete basis. The milieu which we are questioning here, it is the originary milieu, before that abstraction' (pp. 16 and 17).

What Watsuji calls here 'abstraction' is no other than what we have seen above under the name of 'deworlding' in Heidegger's case: that movement by dint of which the world becomes an object for scientific knowledge, composed in its turn of separate objects, metrically disposed in a pure space. Watsuji, for certain, does not speak of such a space but the distinction which he immediately establishes, in his introduction, between milieu (*fūdo*) and the natural environment (*shizen kankyō*), exactly points at the terms of that same movement: environment is an object, analysable as such, whereas the milieu consists in phenomena which, as such, presuppose the existence of the human subject, who lives, perceives and interprets them.

On such bases, why does Watsuji's conception of spatiality oppose that of Heidegger? Correlatively, why does Watsuji, although so sensible to the question of space that he accuses Heidegger of not taking it into account sufficiently, present his theory of milieu without developing – as Heidegger, in contrast, does – a problematic of space?

Regarding the primordial status which Watsuji accords to spatiality (by refusing to subordinate it to temporality), one should first remember that this Japanese philosopher thinks and writes in Japanese. Now, the two Chinese characters used in that language for expressing 'Being' or 'existence', *sonzai*, originally incorporate spatiality: *zai*, which comprises the radical 'earth', means 'being in a place', or 'the place of Being'. Similarly, the second element of *ningen* (human being) is quite directly spatial: read for example *ken*, it is the length of a tatami; read *ma*, it is (among other things) a room in a house, and read *aida*, it is an interval or relationship between two things, events or persons. These figures are not hidden in etymology; they are made immediately sensible by the sinograms of *sonzai* and *ningen*. In a word, in Japanese, one cannot figure the properly human Being (the being-human, *ningen sonzai*) if not spatially.

We shall see below that Watsujian spatiality does not base itself ontologically solely on Chinese writing. Let us first ask ourselves how it can be that, instead of a problematic of space and worldliness (as in Heidegger), Watsuji immediately derives from his assumptions a theory of mediance. Second, why such a theory, and not, say, a theory of corporeity as in Emmanuel Levinas, who also refused to give temporality a primary status? On the contrary, indeed, as Didier Franck comments, *De l'existence à l'existant* poses that there is not only 'irreducibility of the spatiality of the existing to ekstatic temporality', but also 'priority of the position of the body over time' (1992: 88). Similarly, Franck considers that 'the spatiality of the *Dasein* . . . presupposes a manual space irreducible to temporality since the hand, flesh and life are not constituted by time' (1986: iv).

In answering these two questions I shall undertake an anthropological analysis. First, however, in order to remain at the level of the properly philosophical foundations of Watsuji's argument against Heidegger, one must remark that the former – once more – does not take up a distinction which is essential for the latter: that between *existential* and *existenziell*. As is known, for Heidegger, the existential is ontological, i.e., engages the very humanity of every human being; the *existenziell*, on the other hand, is ontical, i.e., it concerns the character of such and such a person. In such a view, mediance (which Heidegger does not conceive of) could only belong to the *existenziell*, since it is a differentiation which is not essential to humanity. Indeed, a human being can pertain to one or other milieu and be no more nor less human (in this sense, one should remember that the differentiation of terrestrial space into diverse milieux has nothing to do with the degree of humanness of their inhabitants). Now, this is what Watsuji dismisses from the first line of *Fūdo* – where he defines mediance as the 'structural moment of the being-human'.

In other words, for Watsuji, one cannot be (ontologically) human except (ontically) in the guise of belonging to a certain milieu. Therefore, indeed, distinguishing here the existential from the *existenziell* becomes meaningless, and one should not be surprised that Watsuji did not attempt to do so (if he had, he would certainly have considered mediance as an existential!). On the contrary, he poses explicitly the interpretation of mediance as 'ontologic-ontic', adding that 'inasmuch as one questions the types of milieux, it can only be so' (1962: 23).

Whether 'it can only be so', or otherwise, philosophy alone cannot ever decide; accordingly, we shall pursue our argument on different grounds: the problem of the collective identity of the Japanese, the examination of which will also suggest why Watsuji attached himself to mediance and not, like Levinas or Franck, to corporeity. Before that, though, we must examine Watsuji's second criticism against Heidegger: namely, his reducing of the human to the individual. In fact, the whole matter depends on the relation of the individual to the collective.

MEDIANCE AND SOCIALNESS

It is in the first pages of *Fūdo* that Watsuji, after proposing that having under-estimated spatiality constitutes 'the limit of Heidegger's work' (1962: 1), since 'a temporality which is not founded in spatiality is not yet true temporality', attributes this limitation to the fact that 'if Heidegger confined himself to that, it is because his *Dasein* is after all no more than an individual. He apprehends the being-human [*ningen sonzai*] only as the Being of man [*hito no sonzai*]' (1962: 2).

The distinction between *hito* and *ningen* is essential in Watsuji's works. These two terms are, usually, indifferently translated as 'man' or 'human being' in English. Yet, for Watsuji, *hito* – like its European equivalents *anthrōpos*, *homo*, *homme*, *man*, *Mensch* – renders only the individual dimension of the human (*ningen*). As can be seen in the two characters of this last term – the first one is read in Japanese *hito, jin, nin* and the second one *gen, kan, ma* and *aida* – the human is that which is inbetween (*aida*) men (*hito*). In other words, socialness or social linkage (*aidagara*) is inherent to humanity. The human is, at the same time, individual as *hito* and social as *aida*.

European readers will probably react immediately and quote a passage in *Sein und Zeit* showing that the 'being-with' (*Mitsein*) is given as an existential, and thus conclude that the *aidagara* is only its Japanese version; which would of course annihilate Watsuji's argument. Does not Heidegger say that being-in-the-world is being-with-others (*miteinandersein*)?

We must here question cautiously the presuppositions of our own culture. This point will be dealt with later. But first I shall stress that Watsuji's remark is acccompanied by a consequence which is unthinkable in Heidegger's perspective. The latter poses that 'death as end of the *Dasein* is the *Dasein*'s most proper, not relative, certain and as such undetermined, unsurpassable possibility' (1993: 258–9), which leads him to establishing being-toward-death (*Sein zum Tode*) as an existential. Watsuji writes the following: 'man dies, the linkage between men changes, but while dying and changing, men live and the betweenness [*aida*] of men continues. It is in the fact of ending ceaselessly that this linkage continues ceaselessly. That which, from the point of view of the individual, is being-toward-death [*shi e no sonzai*], is being-toward-life [*sei e no sonzai*] from the point of view of society' (1962: 16).

In other words, in the human, the social being transcends the finitude of the individual being; or, more abstractly put, the relational field transcends the finitude of the substance. We must now question the implications of this transcendence.

MEDIANCE AND IDENTITY

As Watsuji himself writes, it is his reading of *Sein und Zeit* which made him conceive of mediance; not so much because his general perspective, that of hermeneutic phenomenology, is that of Heidegger too (at least in principle), but mainly, as we already saw, by making him react toward what he perceived as a lack and a bias in the German philosopher's work.

This bias, in other words the determination of Heidegger's ontology by a factor which the German philosopher was not conscious of, is precisely attributed to mediance by Watsuji, who also writes that he himself became conscious of it by dint of his own feeling of being out of place during his long sea voyage, from Japan to China, India, Arabia, the Mediterranean, and on to his destination Germany:

> It may be that this sort of question appeared to me precisely because my heart was full of impressions from very varied milieux, as I was absorbed in [Heidegger's] minute analysis of temporality. Yet it is also precisely because these questions appeared to me that I started ruminating over my impressions of milieux, or paying attention to them. Thus I can say that what made me conscious of the question of milieu is the question of temporality and historicity. Without this mediation, my impressions of milieux would have

remained mere impressions of milieux. That this mediation worked indicates precisely that mediance and historicity correspond to each other.

(1962: 2)

A physical shift (travel), and correlatively the transfer of a point of view, a re-semantization, a new concept: we can see here at work in an exemplary way, a *trajection* – this process which brings forth mediance by dialectically combining the physical and the phenomenal, the ecological and the symbolical in human milieux and in the totality of human milieux, i.e., the *ecumene* (which is thus to be distinguished from the biosphere, just as Watsuji distinguished the milieu fom the environment). Yet, if Watsuji lucidly analyses the process which led him to conceive of mediance, in his turn he does not consciously figure the determination which he undergoes by dint of the mediance he himself is soaking in.

To make up for that, with the double distanciation which time and cultural otherness can give us, some of the characters of that mediance – and, by contrast, some of the characters of the European mediance (in which Heidegger was soaking) – can nowadays be clearly seen in *Fūdo*.

Most revealing in this respect is the way Watsuji and Heidegger respectively deal with socialness. In the latter, the being-with of the common world (*Mitwelt*) brings forth a 'one' (*Man*) which deprives the *Dasein* from its proper Being. According to Heidegger, this deprivation is a downfall (*Verfallenheit*). Such an expression well enough indicates that the German philosopher perceived individual identity positively and collective identity negatively. On the contrary, in Watsuji, the *aida* is, as we have seen, what in the human is the basis of being-toward-life. One could not express more vividly that, here, relation is perceived positively, whereas substance – that of *hito* in its individuality – founding being-toward-death, is of course perceived negatively.

This difference is crucial, both ethically – because it is the status of the person which is here at stake – and ontologically. So relational and contrary to the substance of the Cartesian subject as the *Dasein* may be, that which Heidegger has on his mind, most fundamentally, is the constancy or the interruption of an individual being in its identity; whereas Watsuji, for his part, considers the impermanence and insubstantiality of the individual being as that which connects it to and subsumes it in the more stable collective identity of the we (*wareware*).

It stands to reason that both philosophers express here an atavistic drive: that to substantialism in European thought on the one hand and, on the other, to relativism, or rather relationalism, in 'oriental' thought (especially as Mahayana Buddhism expressed it, from its Indian sources to Japan).

Without insisting on the metaphysical reach of this heredity, let us yet again pay attention to the problem of the determination which mediance exerts upon individual thinking. Watsuji's outlook reveals what, at first glance, might be called a culturalistic option: in his eyes, Heidegger merely expresses the individualism which is proper to European culture. Nevertheless, the Watsujian theory of mediance fundamentally pertains to environmental determinism; because, in the last analysis, the dependent variable there is culture, and the independent one is nature. Without delving here into the details of Watsuji's reasoning (which belong to classical deterministic analogies between climate and temperament), this can be read from the outset in the choice of his chapter titles, e.g. the third one: 'The Peculiarity of Monsoonic Milieux' (*Monsūnteki fūdo no tokushu keitai*). This indeed is a perspective, the firmest landmark of which can only be physical geography, phenomenological though the stance of the first chapter may be.

Heidegger, for his part, speaks on the contrary of a 'space of play' when dealing with the spatiality of the *Dasein*. This is quite another outlook – one founded on an initial human choice: 'The *Dasein* [. . .] has each time already set for itself a space of play [*einen Spielraum eingeräumt*]'. 'It determines each time its own place [*Es bestimmt je seinen eigenen Ort*]' (1993: 368).

Both perspectives are relational, for certain, but their focus is not the same. In Watsuji, the focus of the relation is no other than Mighty Nature; in Heidegger, as well as in European phenomenology in general, for instance in Merleau-Ponty, the focus is the body of the individual subject. Symptomatically indeed, Heidegger's vocabulary refers fundamentally to the hand of the acting subject, e.g., the *Vorhandene* (being-before-the-hand) and the *Zuhandene* (being-at-hand), which in their relation to the *Dasein* constitute the reality of the world; whereas Watsuji's refers to nature (as shows the very word *fūdo*, i.e., wind-earth).

Watsuji, for sure, from the start and without any ambiguity, discards environmental determinism. He also explicitly speaks of the liberty of the human subject *vis-à-vis* the natural environment; but he immediately adds that this liberty, in its very expression, necessarily expresses a mediance.

Thus it appears clearly that, in Watsuji, not only is the identity of the individual being subsumed under that of a collective being, but the latter is rooted in nature by dint of mediance.

We are touching here one of the most curious aspects of *Fūdo*; namely, the fact that, while defining clearly the phenomenological mechanisms by dint of which mediance determines the ways of being of the human subject, and while showing how this phenomenality makes it escape from the determinations of the natural environment as such, Watsuji himself, in the non-theoretical part of his book, in fact illustrates exemplarily the approach of environmental determinism; that is, in a word, explaining cultural characters by natural factors. Here I shall not discuss this reading in detail, but rather try to uncover what it implies.

We have already seen that Watsuji does not consider Heidegger's distinction between world and space, although he stresses spatiality. From that point, he immediately passes to mediance. Let us assume that, by so doing, Watsuji partakes of that tendency, proper to Japanese thought, which according to Nakamura Hajime (1960) is prone to consider the phenomenal world as sole absolute. In particular, this way of thinking attaches itself to the sensible manifestations of nature, rather than referring them to some abstract principle. This is what Bashō's adage illustrates: *Matsu no koto wa matsu ni narae* (what a pine is, learn it from the pine).

Yet if this tendency was elaborated, particularly in Buddhism, into a genuine philosophical tradition, it is already present in the Japanese language itself. The sentence which I have just quoted indeed does not distinguish whether the matter is about one pine in particular or pines in general. This amounts to saying that here, Being and being (*Sein* and *Seiendes*, *sonzai* and *sonzaisha*) are one and the same entity. Similarly, when Watsuji poses mediance as 'structural moment of the being-human', it can be understood either as '*the* structural moment' or '*a* structural moment'. Japanese, here, does not distinguish the definite from the indefinite.

The consequences are immense. From an ontological point of view, it means that it does not matter whether the determination of mediance exerts itself on Being or on a being; i.e., that Heidegger's fundamental distinction between existential and *existenziell*, ontologic and ontic, is not relevant. Indeed, as we have seen, Watsuji considers milieu as 'ontologic-ontic'. It is for the same reason that, instead of developing a problematic of space, he attaches himself from the outset to the phenomena of milieu. As a matter of fact, when Being is not distinguished from being, there is neither 'time' nor 'space' but only sensible phenomena.

The consequences of this indistinction are just as significant on anthropological, social and political planes; because it entails that mediance indifferently soaks through the general (society) or the particular (the individual). In other words, individual identity and collective identity form one and the same whole.

As a matter of fact, this indistinction is clearly illustrated by Watsuji's own reasoning in *Fūdo*. He begins indeed by stating that milieu supposes human subjectivity; i.e., that medial phenomena exist in as much as they are perceived by human subjects. But what kind of subjects? When reading the first chapter, which presents Watsuji's theory of mediance, one cannot but understand the sense as the human subject in general, whether individual or collective, and one infers, consequently, that the study of mediance requires an objective analysis of the concerned subjects' subjectiveness.

Now, it appears in the following chapters that, in fact, Watsuji uses his own travel impressions for defining the mediance of the milieux he deals with. Certainly, he previously has proposed, quite explicitly at the end of the first chapter, that intuition is the key to understanding mediance; but the fact remains that he never questions the relevance of *his* intuition as such, making thus no difference between his subjectiveness and that of the people he writes about.

By doing so, Watsuji completely inverts the hermeneutical approach, though he invokes it expressly. Instead of an effort to understand objectively the otherness of the other's proper subjectiveness, his approach is in fact a sort of introspection of his own feelings. In other words, Watsuji's own subjectivity (*shukansei*) absorbs and suppresses the respective subjectivity or sovereignty (*shutaisei*) of the other subjects, thus falling into a complete contradiction with the premises of *Fūdo* (which, as we have seen, state that what is at stake in mediance is human subjectivity).

In a homologous way, roughly at the same time, in a phantasmal inflation of its own collective subjectiveness, Japan pretended to embody the destiny of the nations of East and South-east Asia, in defiance of the proper sovereignty of these nations.

Such homology was no accident at all, since it originates in the same lack of definition of the subject in Japanese culture; particularly in what Nishida Kitarō, at about the same time, called 'the engulfment' (*botsunyū*) of 'the plane of the subject' (*shugo-men*) into 'the plane of the predicate' (*jutsugo-men*) (1966: 208–89). I interpret this logic as an identification of the subject with the milieu which subsumes it. This identification works in two ways: by suppressing the other's alterity and by subordinating the individual to the whole (e.g. the ultra-nationalistic motto *botsuga kiitsu*, 'suppress the self, return to the One').

Inverting the hermeneutic approach is but one of the transformations performed by Watsuji in his interpretation of Heidegger's thought. It is only an unconscious homologue to the shift which he performed consciously when he substituted the point of view of mediance to that of *Dasein*. Certainly, both endeavours – Heidegger's and Watsuji's – are rejections of the modern classical subject, i.e., Descartes' self-instituted and substantial *cogito*. Yet, from the former to the latter, one passes from a perspective focusing on human existence to a perspective focusing on the natural determination of this existence, which in its turn is collective rather than individual.

To borrow Nishida's image of an engulfment of the subject, one might say that if the *Dasein* swallows up the consciousness (and conscience . . .) of the modern classical subject, the *Dasein* in its turn is swallowed up by the milieu. In other words, Being is engulfed into the place (*basho*) of its being. Nishida's 'logic of place' (*basho no ronri*) is indeed relevant to these phenomena, the actuality of which cannot be denied if one pays attention to what history and the social sciences have shown in our own century (including Heidegger's, Nishida's and Watsuji's compromises with totalitarian ideologies).

Yet, I would like to stress, as a conclusion, that this engulfment is only one aspect of human reality; the other one being, dialectically or rather trajectively, the ontological emergence of the individual subject's consciousness and conscience out of the milieu and out of the community (which indeed are the places of its being). Engulfment (belonging) and emergence (liberty) are the two sides of human reality, each of which alone is both necessary and insufficient. If we are to overcome the dualism of the modern classical paradigm, this can in no way be accomplished by merely reducing this complex relation to an engulfment of the modern classical subject into *Dasein* and mediance, from which, in fact, it had historically emerged. It is through the objective recognition that we *are* also our milieu (which entails that humanity is also the *ecumene*), that we can reach a new stage in the continuous development of Being (see Berque 1996).

NOTES

1 Japanese philosopher (1889–1960). I refer to vol. VIII in the complete collection of his works: *Watsuji Tetsurō zenshū*, Tokyo: Iwanami, 1962. For Heidegger, I refer to the 1993 edition of *Sein und Zeit*, Tübingen: Niemeyer.

2 These are my own definitions, those in *Fūdo* being either obscure (for mediance, as will be seen) or loose (for milieu). See A. Berque (1997) and (1996).

REFERENCES

Berque, A. (1996) *Etre humains sur la Terre: principes d'éthique de l'écoumène*, Paris: Gallimard (also published in Japanese as *Chikyū to sonzai no tetsugaku: kankyō rinri wo koete*, Tokyo: Chikuma, 1996).

—— (1997) *Nature, Artifice and Japanese Culture*, Northampton, NY: Pilkington.

Dewitte, Jacques (1992) 'Monde et espace: la question de la spatialité chez Heidegger', in *Le temps et l'espace* (Brussels: Ousia, 1992).

Franck, Didier (1986) *Heidegger et le problème de l'espace*, Paris: Minuit, 1986.

—— (1992) 'Le corps de la différence', *Philosophie*, vol. 34.

Heidegger, Martin (1993) *Sein und Zeit*, Tübingen: Niemeyer.

Nakamura, Hajime (1960) *Ways of Thinking of Eastern People*, Tokyo: Ministry of Education.

Nishida, Kitarō (1966) *Nishida Kitarō zenshū* [*Complete Works of Nishida Kitarō*], vol. IV, Tokyo: Iwanami.

Watsuji Tetsurō (1962) *Watsuji Tetsuro Zenshū* [*Complete Works of Watsuji Tetsuro*], Tokyo: Iwanami.

5 Contested identities and models of action in Japanese discourses of place-making

An interpretive study

Eyal Ben-Ari

INTRODUCTION

Towards the end of my first period of fieldwork in Japan, I interviewed an 80-year-old villager about the history of the area in which I was working. At the end of our conversation he asked where I lived. I answered that I lived in, and was studying, Hieidaira, the new suburban housing estate neighbouring his village. He thought for a while and then declared:

> Hieidaira is actually a little Tokyo. It's like Tokyo in that you have people from all over the country. They're all so occupied with their jobs or businesses that there is almost nobody willing to invest his time in the neighbourhood association. Well, what do you want? They're all first generation in the estate; There's no feeling of *furusato* [hometown or homeplace], and little contact between people.

At that time I sensed that calling a residential area, located hundreds of kilometers away from the capital, 'Little Tokyo', evoked a rich variety of connotations and associations, but, like many insights garnered during fieldwork, I put the incident aside. It was only years later, when I began to think about the manner in which people talk about – that is, describe, analyse, and evaluate – their residential community, that I began to discern the metaphor's meaning.

At first I thought that the image simply exemplified the 'reputational content' (Suttles 1984) of the housing estate: the series of typifications and images that capture the character and 'spirit' of a place. But then I realized that the strength of the 'Tokyo' metaphor used by the elderly villager lay in the 'missions' (Fernandez 1986: chapter 2) it seemed to be carrying out. First, it illuminated many of the qualities commonly associated with 'modern' Japanese communities: urban impersonality and heterogeneity, self-interest bordering on selfishness, and a lack of communal commitment and involvement. Second, this image under-scored an attitude towards such localities. The villager's declaration seemed to have an appeal as much for its critique of contemporary Japanese society as for its expressing a quest for the warmth and intimacy of the 'traditional' community. And third, the metaphor predicated a 'folk' model (Quinn and Holland 1987) of community dynamics: that is, a set of assumptions and interpretive schemes that lie at the base of mundane or common-sense knowledge about communities. These models are of great importance because they are the basic points of reference for 'what we are' and 'what we are trying to do' through which people's reality is constructed. Here the man I interviewed seemed to be assuming – much like many older sociological theories of community – that a particular locality could be taken as a microcosm of wider social processes. More specifically, this man proposed that the case of Hieidaira exemplified a causal chain linking the effects of industrialization and urbanization to involvement in, and a sense of belonging to, a community.

But how is this image – or, more correctly, the properties, viewpoints, and causal chains it predicates – related to wider discussions about present-day residential localities and their place in contemporary Japanese society? In what follows I will attempt to show how a set of analytical tools from symbolic anthropology can aid us in answering this question. The last decade has seen the publication of a number of excellent studies centred on the ways in which 'old' places – whether real or imagined – are discussed as part of a nostalgic search for identity in the post-war era. Martinez (1990), for instance, shows how people have begun to look for the good in Japan, and to spend their holidays in places that represent the real but lost Japan. Bestor (1989) illuminates how the old urban label of *shitamachi* is now being reapplied to make sense of, and legitimize, contemporary community life and lifestyles in Tokyo. Finally, Robertson's (1992) work, which focuses on a newly urbanized suburb of Japan's capital, emphasizes the (problematical) traditionalizing practices of 'place-making' in today's Japan.

Such studies have done much to further our understanding of what is entailed by 'talk' about a locality. These studies show how 'traditional' communities – whether real or imagined – are represented in contemporary public culture as idealized versions of the 'good' Japan, and how the purported qualities of such places are part of the nostalgic quest for identity in the post-war period. Furthermore, they illuminate a peculiar combination of notions of space and time. These investigations reveal how, through addressing specific places and their attendant qualities, people constantly promote or denigrate another level of imagery: certain visions of what Japan was, is or should be like. In this article, however, my aim is not to add yet another explication of spatial concepts such as 'urban' or 'rural' or temporal notions like 'tradition' or 'old' as they are used in contemporary Japan. Rather, I will demonstrate how the use of a set of theoretical tools based in anthropology may illuminate issues involved in current Japanese discourse about local communities.

Recent studies in anthropology and related disciplines have well underlined the contested – essentially labile and political – nature of community identity (Cohen 1986; McDonogh 1991; Bendix 1992). According to this set of approaches, local identity is no longer conceptualized as a given but rather as an assortment of typifications and images that are constantly negotiated and struggled over. But maintaining that such typifications and images are contested is not enough. We need to theorize the cultural contours within which these contestations take place: to delineate the underlying grounds of, and the limits on, such public debates. This paper seeks to address these issues through examining what Mullins (1987) has identified as a primary task of urban anthropology: namely, the links between discourses about local communities and the larger society. In this article I extend these understandings to the study of Japan in two directions.

My first point involves the type of community I have chosen to examine. The overwhelming majority of previous studies of Japanese localities have been examinations of 'traditional' or 'historic' communities or neighbourhoods (Ben-Ari 1992). Against the background of these works, the lack of systematic treatments of how *newly* built residential communities figure in public discourse about the plight of contemporary Japan is readily evident. I propose that the importance of studying such localities lies not only in their quantitative significance: by some estimates more than a third of Japan's population now resides in such recently established suburbs (Allinson 1979: 5). It is also important because these communities are among the primary means through which the ideology – the central symbols and goals – of Japan's new middle class is discussed and debated. In other words, new residential areas often provide concrete instances through which different groups debate the lifeways shaped by this ideology. As Kelly (1990: 69; 1986) puts it, both 'official policy and public opinion have idealized career employment in large organizations, meritocratic educational credentialing, and a nuclear division of labour between working husband who takes care and domestic mother who gives care'. While these idealizations may contradict the reality of many Japanese, this middle-class ideology nevertheless defines 'standards of achievement, images of the desirable, and limits of the feasible' (ibid.). Along these lines, an examination of the discourse about localities said to be populated by representatives of the new middle class may prove fruitful in furthering our understanding of both their 'reputational content' and their use in broader debates about contemporary Japanese society.

My second point stands in direct contradiction to much of the stress found in recent analyses. To take two examples, while Martinez (1990) shows how people now look for the 'good' in the lost Japan, Bestor (1992) illuminates how the old urban label of *shitamachi* is now being reapplied to legitimate contemporary community life in Tokyo (see also Dore 1978 and Smith 1988). In such works the accent is on a specific version of the past: the benevolent, harmonious and cooperative 'historical' community. These works charge that in contemporary representations the 'negative' or adverse features of past communities have been glossed over. According to these studies, this favourable version of rural and urban localities has essentially replaced or supplanted older views. But what of other images – of anti-democratic practices, of conservative attitudes towards authority, and of social control – which have also guided post-war understandings of various localities. I will argue that these images still figure in the contemporary discourse about localities, and that the newer images have been grafted on, rather than having replaced, older ones. Accordingly, in my examination I uncover both the complexity and contestation that mark the discourse about such places.

THE COMMUNITY

Hieidaira, the housing estate I studied (Ben-Ari 1991a), offers a useful entry into a consideration of these issues. I begin with a short description of this estate and then turn to the imagery and talk attendant upon it. Hieidaira, which means 'plain of Hiei', was developed in the late 1960s. It is set against the rather picturesque Hieizan Mountain chain to the east of Kyoto's northern suburbs. Together with a small neighbouring village, Hieidaira is part of an independent administrative district within the city of Ōtsu in Shiga prefecture. Initially developed as an area for second (summer) homes, the estate's location made it economical for standard residential development as the urban centres of Kyoto and Osaka expanded in the 1970s. Hieidaira now resembles many other newly constructed housing estates in the country. Its three wards are divided into neat, rectangular blocks of detached dwellings giving the area an appearance of being thrust upon the mountains. As in many Japanese residential areas (Smith 1979: 95), residences tend to be owner-built and thus appear less monotonous than their European or American counterparts.

The estate has a population of nearly 3,000 people, of which *sarariiman* (salaried employees) are the largest minority. While we shall return to this point shortly, suffice it to note here that other sizeable occupational groups include merchants, teachers and artisans. Again, in ways similar to other Japanese suburbs, the tempo of daily living revolves around the flow of people from the community in the morning and their return at night. Only on weekends, or occasional holidays, are there many men around during the daytime. Hieidaira partakes of a dualism that characterizes many suburban communities: while it is linked politically and administratively to the city of Ōtsu (population 0.25 million), it is to the neighbouring giant of Kyoto (population 1.5 million) that most of the local residents are oriented. It is to Ōtsu that they turn for public services (schools, libraries, welfare aid) and major utilities, but it is predominantly to Kyoto that they turn for jobs, higher education, and the provision of daily needs such as medical care, shopping, and entertainment.

THE PHYSICAL SETTING: A DISTANT 'COUNTRY'

Let me begin with the physical imagery of the estate, not only because it is the most tangible but because it is also one of the most remarked upon aspects of the place. Among the hundred or so comments I have recorded about the place in my fieldnotes, two types were most common: remarks about the locality's distance from urban centres and statements about its spaciousness. For example, local residents reported that when told about the estate, outsiders' reactions were often sympathetic comments such as, 'it must be very difficult to live in Hieidaira because it is such a distant place'. Interestingly, the impression of distance appears to be related to a perception of Hieidaira as an 'other' place, remote in an historical sense or removed spatially from the confines of Japan's national borders. Thus, outsiders often associated the estate with the Buddhist temples located in Mount Hiei to the north of the estate. In this view, Hieidaira is isolated just like this religious complex (belonging to the Tendai sect) which has figured as a pilgrimage site for hundreds of years. One day a local resident, a professor of Chinese studies at a private university in Kyoto, explained:

> Historically speaking this area has an image of being far away. I think it has to do with the image of Mount Hiei which is a deep and faraway place; that's why the image of the neighbourhood is fused with this religious image. The name Hieidaira is written with the same Chinese ideogram [as Mount Hiei] and that's why people tend to think of this as being in the middle of the mountains and being a place 'far away'. People are really surprised to learn that it takes me only twenty minutes to reach my university.

Similar explanations that I received for the image of distant place associated the estate with Kyoto's northern neighbourhoods. In the past these areas have been perceived by people living in the ancient capital as being far away from the city's centre.

The image of Hieidaira as an 'other place' is also related to its spatial surroundings. Reactions to the mountains and greenery surrounding the neighbourhood are epitomized by those of a doctor who runs a small clinic in the estate who told me that 'Hieidaira is a little like America'. Other people talked of Hieidaira being like 'Europe', 'France', 'Germany', and, in a Japanese twist to 'other' places, like 'Hokkaido'. Hokkaido is Japan's northern and most spacious major island and in the popular mind is often associated with the ambience of foreign countries. Stating the resemblance between the estate and foreign places served at one and the same time to play up the 'natural' advantages of the area – the good air, expansiveness and greenery purportedly found outside of Japan or in the northern island – and to contrast them to the usual plight of urban life in Japan.

It is around this contrast that people's comments tended to conflate the 'physical' side of the area with its social ambience. Much of this imagery has to do with the countrified atmosphere of the locality. My fieldnotes are replete with testaments about the 'calm' or 'leisurely' feelings elicited by the area. Frequently, such qualities were compared with the characteristics of people's previous places of residence. One woman, in a rather humorous tone, told me of growing up in the centre of Kyoto and of having to get used to the 'country' (*inaka*) with all of its creepy crawly insects when she came to the neighbourhood. Another man used the label 'country' when telling fellow workers in Kyoto that he 'commutes from the country, a place of good air'.

A GOVERNING IDENTITY: URBAN AMBIENCE AND EDUCATION

Yet despite its location in the mountains, surrounded by forests and streams, the neighbourhood has – as I was told time and again by people both within and outside the area – a distinctly urban mark. One prime expression of its urban character is the constant mention of the *variety* of its residents. Such commentary about local diversity obviously served to differentiate the estate from older, purportedly more homogeneous villages. But on another level – that of 'folk' understandings of cities – these comments underscored what Fischer (1976: 37) has so aptly illuminated as *the* social mark of cities: the existence of a variety of separate social worlds. The following excerpt, from a conversation I had with the head teacher of the local school, expresses this point graphically:

> Listen, it's as though they took a multi-storey apartment building and turned it over: people just sort of 'spilled out'. The people here live in private, detached houses but the contact between them is like that in an apartment building. They are not really conscious of the area as a community, and you sometimes get the feeling that they think only of themselves, a sort of selfishness.

Another man, a real estate agent, commented that Hieidaira was very 'Tokyo-like' (*Tōkyōteki*): living in the area are people from a variety of places, with a distinct feeling among them that they can do what they feel like doing without others' intervention.

But more is said to mark the neighbourhood than urban heterogeneity and self-centredness. The educational achievements of Hieidaira's residents repeatedly came up in interviews and conversations. This point may be clarified through the lists residents and outsiders provided when I asked about the kind of people living in the estate. While lists varied somewhat between individuals, all included the following core of vocations: *sarariiman*, doctors, merchants, lawyers (I never encountered any) and school teachers. In addition, a number of other, rather special, categories of people were said to inhabit the neighbourhood: musicians ('enough to set up a whole orchestra', one man exaggerated), artisans (using traditional forms found in Kyoto), artists and, above all, university lecturers. Thus Hieidaira has a rather strong 'governing identity' (Suttles 1972: 248–50): it is said to be marked by people with high educational achievement. Typically, a teacher at the local school (she lives outside the area) told me that this was 'a *hai reberu* (high-level) area, one of university teachers', and a number of people told me the residents 'have a high level of knowledge' (*chishiki ga takai*). In its most overstated form, the assertion – put to me by numerous people – was that the estate is inhabited by many Kyoto University teachers. Kyoto University is the second-ranked institution of higher education in Japan, and certainly the first-ranked in this area of the country.

This governing identity is encapsulated by the most common label used for people living in the estate: *interi*. The dictionary translation of *interi* is intellectuals or the intelligentsia, but in more common parlance it means people with high educational attainments, or simply highly educated people. As one astute local put it, the academic background of a graduate of an elite university is often perceived as a measure of that person's success, hard work and intelligence. More generally in Japan, such people are usually accorded respect, prestige and above average salaries. The image of *interi*, however, includes not only an emphasis on educational achievement, but also elements of political progressivism.

The labelling of the neighbourhood as *interi* has roots in the 1970s when the locals (led by a number of university lecturers) organized a series of campaigns to force local government and the private developer of the estate to provide such local amenities as a new sewerage system, school and playgrounds (Ben-Ari 1991a: 113–14). So successful were the residents that one head of the neighbourhood association was labelled by a former employee of the developing company as 'an expert in human engineering, a specialist in putting demands to local government officials and getting their cooperation'. What is of significance from the point of view of the present analysis, however, is that the label *interi*, originally attached only to the local leadership, was generalized into a designation for the whole area. Two points merit mention in this regard. First, the estate's identity was not solely the result of processes by which only highly educated people moved into the area, for in reality in-migration was very diverse. Rather, it crystallized out of the management of the community's 'external relations': out of the success of the original leaders in forging a sense of local identity, and the labelling of the neighbourhood by outsiders such as officials at the city office. Second, the general label of *interi* was the outcome of amplifying small differences between the Hieidaira and other essentially similar neighbourhoods. Hieidaira's minority of university teachers began to be taken as representative of the whole area. Small differences were amplified into what were then taken to be fully fledged representations of the community's governing identity.

Closely related to the image of educational achievement is a conception of relatively high economic standing. The same teacher who used the image of an apartment house which had spilled out, said, 'the level of people here is higher than the average in the country. Both in their income and in their awareness of education they are the elite [*jōryu*].' Referring to the Hieidaira-ites, a city official told me that 'their prosperity is very conspicuous', while a young school-teacher said that some houses looked as though they came out of home fashion magazines.

Such labels, however, are not merely abstract designations of the neighbourhood's main qualities, but also figure in the way people reason about its social dynamics. Talk about the tone set by the *interi* of the area revolves around two issues: a highly competitive 'passion' for education, and an assertive politics. A member of the city's Board of Education stressed that Hieidaira was similar to many of the newly built areas of the city populated by people who put a heavy emphasis on education. In a corresponding manner, the principal of the middle school to which the children of Hieidaira commute, observed that, like residents of other such areas, Hieidaira's parents are very enthusiastic about education and participated avidly in school-related activities. The children, he added, usually got high grades. Such comments simultaneously asserted the typicality of Hieidaira as an area populated by a new generation of people educated after the Second World War and its distinctiveness as the embodiment of interest in education.

IMAGES OF POLITICAL ACTION

Teachers at all levels – kindergartens, and elementary and middle schools – often placed the enthusiasm for education in a causal scheme related to politics. In their thinking, the label '*interi*' provided a bridge between education and politics by linking the stress on education to the articulation of local demands. Accordingly, I was often told that parents in the area had an interest in education and therefore came forward with many demands; or, that the heavy stress on achievement at home led to constant claims put to educational authorities. Almost all of the educators thus underscored what they perceived to be a widespread sentiment – again, Hieidaira being both a typical and an extreme example of such expectations – that educational authorities be responsive to the demands of parents. In a similar vein, the image of Hieidaira's aggressive progressivism came up time and again in conversations with people who have had dealings in city-level politics: leaders and activists in neighbourhood organizations, politicians and city bureaucrats, and schoolteachers and principals. A local resident (a kindergarten teacher working outside the neighbourhood) linked collective participation and relations with authority to education:

> Because you have many people who have a high educational level here, they tend to be independent; and they go directly to heads of departments in the city government, to the mayor or to people in charge. There is much less fear of going to managers among them than among other people living in Ōtsu.

This attribution was echoed (in a disapproving tone we shall return to presently) by a self-employed man in his fifties:

> I see this as part of what has been happening in Japan in the last twenty or thirty years. Hieidaira is Japan in miniature. It reflects general things that are going on outside: the strengthening of people's power or citizens' power. If something does not work out, or if they don't like the answer the city government gives them then they go running off to the newspapers.

Another woman related the stance towards authority to income, occupation, and exposure to America, and through these elements to the future image of Japan:

> People in Hieidaira have an independent income and independent work, and in this respect they are different from other people. This is a general problem in Japan and not only in Ōtsu: the relation between people and the administration. It should be like, well, the grassroots movement in America, or the movement against the Vietnam war. One has, as an individual . . . independently to decide about one's environment and whether there is a need to go against the political or administrative authorities.

Again, the ex-principal of the school contrasted Hieidaira with older neighbourhoods where the dominant force was usually a local oligarchy. 'Hieidaira,' he said, 'is exceptionally open and democratic.'

It is important to understand the wider context within which this kind of talk takes place. Since at least the end of the 1960s public struggles in Japan have been influenced by a variety of groups: citizens' and environmental movements, consumer cooperatives, students' groups, and some labour unions and political parties. These movements have succeeded in placing new issues on the country's political agenda and have been instrumental in crystallizing the idea that Japan's citizens have something called 'rights' which the system owes them (McKean 1981: 267–8; Pharr 1990: 11). In this sense, the Hieidaira-ites are taken to be representative of these new kinds of groups and attitudes.

MATERIALISM, INDIVIDUALISM AND EVALUATION

Yet for all of this, the qualities associated with Hieidaira are rarely described in purely positive or affirmative tones because they belong to a contested terrain in Japan's public culture. The debate about these qualities centres on the value of (Western) individualism and democracy, the excesses of competition and the loss of a quintessential Japanese identity.

Materialism

If awareness of consumer issues is the positive side of people's tangible wealth, materialism is its negative side. One element often cited in critical terms was the 'showiness' of the neighbourhood's residents. For instance, a number of people mentioned the ostentatiousness of some of the houses and furnishings. Another indicator was a Japanese version of 'keeping up with the Tanakas'. One anthropologist living in the area characterized what was happening among a coterie of friends as a sort of 'potlatch':

> We started it off by inviting a few friends around here to a party. Soon we began a round of going to each other's houses, drinking beer, sake and whisky, singing *karaoke*, and sometimes dancing. Pretty soon some of the original friends began to invite more people to the parties and the group grew from about sixteen to about thirty-two. It was too much, it became a kind of potlatch: people began to notice and comment about each other's furniture, and what they had bought for the kitchen. It's crazy!

A closely related theme pervading comments about the materialism found in the neighbourhood was self-centredness. An elderly man talked of the estate's young mothers as *tonde-iru okāsan*: 'flowery' mothers who are basically interested only in going out and having a good time. One of the local newspaper agents said that there were more educated people here who read a variety of newspapers and journals, but that they were also marked by a sort of individualism. He linked education to snobbery and to a lack of concern for others. A 60-year-old resident specializing in the property market, contended that

> there are a lot of people here who have a feeling of 'only my (own) house'. They don't care what others think, they have their own way and want to live it without interference. It's such a Western style of living: people who went to America, France, or Europe, saw life there and decided to live like that here. That university professor was in Virginia for his sabbatical and he told me that Hieidaira reminded him of America. This man in the art gallery was in France

and wants to live like a French painter . . . Hieidaira is so European, not very Japanese-like.

In a few chosen words this man not only posits a causal chain linking international influence to self-centredness, but drives his point home by stressing the alien quality of such an individualistic orientation. The reasoning here also seems to answer certain expectations about what it means to be Japanese. Japanese travel brochures often use such phrases as 'my pace' or 'my plan' to make tourists realize that they can do as they want once they have escaped the confines of Japanese society (Moeran 1983: 105). According to the logic of this man's assertion, it is the same kind of escape from 'Japanese' norms of behaviour which is risky within neighbourhoods such as Hieidaira, because it can lead to a stress on individualism. To reiterate a point made earlier, the comparison with America or with Europe is not limited to the physical side of the estate, but perhaps more significantly it is a means of attributing certain social characteristics to the area.

The excesses of education

It is in the debate about educational achievement that local matters are even more explicitly linked to a discourse about the ills of contemporary Japan. A resident of the estate, a carpenter who was born in and still works in Ōtsu, stated:

> I feel that the competitive spirit here is very strong. This is probably related to the high education of the parents, doctors, many university teachers: their children are really smart and many of them go to *juku* [private supplementary schools] from a very early age and they are taught this sense of competitiveness. I wouldn't like my daughter to go to a *juku*. I want her to be much freer; to come home and do all sorts of things.

On the one hand, this passage underscores the effects of Japan's 'examination hell': the gruelling preparations for entrance examinations into Japan's top universities. The carpenter's comments well underline the prospects of his daughter's having to enter such an educational 'rat-race'. On the other hand, this passage underscores how this competition is localized, in an area of *interi*. The very act of living in such an area, this man feels, forces his daughter to compete. A 40-year-old mother of two school-age children, talked in similar terms about the local primary school:

> Because people here tend to be more educated, there is strong pressure for education, an enthusiasm for education. This may lead to sides which are not so good for the children, not so healthy. There are strong demands put on the kids, sometimes too strong. Moreover, mothers with higher education tend to be very proud and to branch off into various factions around the type of education system they would like.

Many polemics about the educational system focused on these mothers, labelled *kyōiku* mama. This term means 'education mama', but as one local wit translated it for me, its connotation is more akin to 'education-crazy mother'. While not entirely a negative designation, it does indicate a radical stress on achievement. One teacher, again invoking the imagery of Hieidaira as social microcosm, said that the neighbourhood was characteristic of all of Japan in terms of the anxieties suffered by families dominated by such women, but hastened to add in a much more positive light that it was definitely easier to teach the children of such mothers because they tend to be more inquisitive and open to learning.

Along with competitive education and materialism said to characterize the neighbourhood, other anxieties – questioning key assumptions about life in Japan – emerge. The woman who ran an afternoon facility catering for children until the time their parents came home noted:

> Parents here have a feeling that they have come to a place that is free, to a place where they can live a life that is relatively freer than in the city; and they give their children this kind of feeling. There are a number of outcomes to this situation. For instance, the children are unskilled in group activities, especially when I compare them to the previous place where I worked [in Kyoto]. You have to struggle with them until you achieve anything, and this is a reflection of their parents' difficulties in group activities. Another aspect is that there is a leisurely feeling here and very little stress is put on physical effort. That's why they lack sturdiness and are poor in sports. This is all part of a general feeling here of selfishness, that anyone can do what they feel like.

The kindergarten's head teacher linked selfishness to materialism. She mentioned that, while it was nice to have large houses and wide gardens, there was always a feeling here that the children will not feel a need to go out to the street to play. The emphasis in the estate, she concluded, is too much on the house and on the individual, and leads to children who lack group activities in their lives. Such comments encapsulate a major criticism of the 'educated folks' of Hieidaira – as they do of many representatives of Japan's new middle class: one of their greatest weaknesses is in their apparently poor ability to inculcate a sense of 'groupishness'. The ability to 'group' is seen as so central as to define what being Japanese itself is. Thus by purportedly 'doing their own thing', the Hieidaira-ites are questioning the very foundations of 'traditional' values.

Politics and commitment

Many administrators and politicians I interviewed complained that in place of 'warm' relations between governors and governed the residents of Hieidaira have begun to place demands on them on the basis of rights. A rather outspoken city bureaucrat said, 'We've invested a lot of the city's money in Hieidaira, but today the residents have forgotten this. They've forgotten the basic cooperation with the city government. All they do is to come to us with their demands.' Another senior official formulated an explanation of the changing attitudes in historical terms:

> There is a big difference between the attitudes of citizens to the City Office before the war and after it. In the past the municipality was called the

Oyakusho. The [honorific] *o* showed the deference that was shown to us. People used to make a fuss if a city official came around to their neighbourhood. Today they just say *shiyakusho*, that is, just plain City Office. They see themselves as being on an equal footing with the people who work in the municipality. Many feel that public services are 'owed' to them.

The new attitudes signal a significant change from the pre-war conception of a hierarchy leading from the Home Ministry down to the community (and to the household): 'the purpose of this pyramidical structure was . . . the transmission of the *will* of those above to those below, and the *feelings* of those below to those above' (Dore 1959: 104; emphasis in original). That the Hieidaira-ites are questioning this cultural conception was clarified in the words of a member of the municipality's social welfare department. He explained that many newly built areas like Hieidaira were populated by young couples with no restraint (*enryō*) in demanding things of government authorities. Here again, the use of the word *enryō* resounds not only with a questioning of authority, but also with a threat to some deep-seated Japanese views of appropriate behaviour and communication between status levels (Kondo 1990: 150).

Similar critiques were directed towards the political organization in the locality. The head of the neighbourhood association (an executive in a Kyoto department store) talked about the locality's occupational make-up:

A lot of university teachers, self-employed, artists, and so on live here. On the one hand this makes for people who are willing to be mobilized for the gains of the whole neighbourhood. On the other hand this makes things disjointed: it's very difficult to get some kind of uniformity of opinion before putting demands to the administration.

This view of the difficulties in reaching a consensus is shared by city officials. In the words of an official liaising with the neighbourhood association: 'In Hieidaira you have people with all sorts of opinions, from all sorts of places, and with all sorts of ways of thinking. Under these circumstances there is very little local solidarity. Maybe this will come about in the next generation, but now it's difficult to get them to work together.' As other government officials put it, the residents' individualism hindered local communication and led to an inability to reach decisions.

Similarly, some persons linked the occupational make-up and the educational level of the Hieidaira-ites to lack of involvement in communal affairs. The head of the local neighbourhood association talked of the snobbery of many university teachers and doctors, who thought they were somehow 'superior' and thus unwilling to participate in community functions (such as sports days) or in community action (such as signing petitions). Interestingly, this view is shared by many of the politically progressive residents of Hieidaira. One woman (a participant in the students' movements of the late 1960s) observed:

There is a bad side to middle-classness. People with education and money have a lot of pride. Sometimes they become indifferent; they think only of their lives and their business. This is the negative side of individualism. That why it's sometimes difficult to set up a citizens' movement in such a place [as Hieidaira].

The stress on the negative consequences of Hieidaira's social characteristics is related, in turn, to a set of 'solutions' which are aimed at rectifying such social ills and which have been at the heart of much public debate in the past few decades.

ORGANIZED SOLUTIONS: THE INTENTIONAL CREATION OF *FURUSATO*

When I mentioned the rather weak participation of Hieidaira-ites in the voluntary fire brigade, an official from the city's fire fighting unit said:

> In Hieidaira you have a hodgepodge of people from all sorts of places like Osaka and Kyoto and they have little awareness and commitment to the area. That's why it's difficult to get volunteers for fire fighting . . . Hieidaira's the same as areas where there are mostly apartments, big apartments, where most people live in an area only for a short time and have no attachment and little solidarity. Any cooperation between such people and the [local] area is difficult.

This short passage includes more than a portrayal of the qualities attendant on urban residences. It posits two elements which many people see as a 'resolution' to the social maladies of newly built areas like Hieidaira. The first is a causal model linking length of residence in the area to the emergence of solidarity and attachment. The second is a postulate that local solidarity and attachment are preconditions for the emergence of communal involvement action. Implicit in these contentions is a solution based on the creation of a *furusato*, a 'home-place' or 'home-town' in Hieidaira. At base this solution involves the establishment – within new residential communities – of the sentiments of belonging and involvement which are said to have characterized 'old' villages. A nostalgia for and a desire to be associated with the past are universal to all rapidly changing societies. But the contents, the meanings and the means by which this quest is undertaken shift with the context. Thus the question becomes one of delineating the peculiarly Japanese version of the past which is involved here (Ben-Ari 1991b).

It is useful to follow the lines of Robertson's (1992) argument as she has done much to clarify the notion of *furusato-zukuri* (the making of a home-place). The dominant representation of *furusato* is infused with nostalgia, a dissatisfaction with the present on the grounds of a remembered or imagined past plenitude (ibid.: 14). As Allinson (1978: 458) notes, Japanese scholars, critics, novelists and poets have all engaged in a orgy of public display over the loss of community, the sense of anonymity and the widespread isolation that are said to afflict urban Japan. Since the early 1970s, however, academics and intellectuals, government officials and party activists, as well as ordinary citizens, have begun to call for a resolution to these circumstances. They have discussed such concepts as *komyuniti* (community) (Ben-Ari 1991a), *mai taun* (my town) (Tokyo Metropolitan Government 1982), *machi-zukuri* (creating a hometown) (Nussbaum 1985; Bestor 1992), or *chihō no jidai* (the age of the local) (Smith 1988: 381). But as Robertson (1987) astutely observes, all of these terms revolve around the notion of 'native-place building'. The notion of *furusato-zukuri* is a practical project. Essentially, it involves remaking the past as the condition for bringing about a social transformation in the present: the idealized characteristics and practices of the 'village of the past' are used as prescriptions for creating a similar set of traits and conventions in contemporary residential communities (Robertson 1992: 9). The modes of sociability of the 'good old days' which were based on harmony and camaraderie, while long since abandoned or dismantled are taken to be capable of revivification and reconstruction.

Yet the creation of a 'native-place' in such communities as Hieidaira reveals the complexity of recreating 'past things' in the framework of large-scale urban or suburban localities. A number of suggestions raised at a meeting between the mayor and Hieidaira's community leaders were enlightening in this respect. Such meetings were held in all of Ōtsu's neighbourhoods throughout the early and mid-1980s. During the meeting various details of the neighbourhood's infrastructure and services were discussed. But about midway through the assembly other issues began to be raised when the mayor suggested that as part of creating a sentiment of community in Hieidaira the locals should cultivate traditional Japanese dances (*odori*). Along with municipal officials he proposed setting up a variety of 'citizens festivals' such as arts meetings, exhibitions or a city citizens' sports day. Such community-related activities, he reasoned, may inculcate the spirit of the traditional locality with its emphasis on self-help, self-reliance, and solidarity. Indeed, Robertson (1987: 124) has shown how citizens' festivals are staged in cities throughout Japan as a conscious effort on the part of municipal governments to reclaim from inexorable urbanization, and more recently 'internationalization', the indigenous village within the city.

But these kinds of suggestions should not be understood as rather simplistic manipulations of residents by institutional interests. The promulgation of such evocative catchwords as *fursato-zukuri* is, to be sure, related to the attempt by various levels of government to do such things as implement social change (Kelly 1986), promote tourism (Ivy 1988), strengthen neighbourhood associations (Takayose 1979), and create political platforms (Nagashima 1981). But to over-stress the political and economic interests linked to the promulgation of such terms is to lose sight of their power and depth for modern Japanese. It is to lose sight of the place of locality in the search for personal and collective meaning in today's world.

These dimensions were brought home to me rather poignantly in the meeting with the mayor during which an elderly pensioner asked the municipality for help in finding a place for a cemetery in the area. He continued that until the age of 60 he hadn't thought about these things, but after he dies he would like his children to be able to visit his grave in the area. Taking up this point, the head of the estate's over-60s club explained that a cemetery was necessary 'as it is the foundation of a *furusato*. It is the way in which everyone can take root in the area.' Similarly, in Hieidaira it is the older and middle-aged individuals, raised in pre-war villages or neighbourhoods, who call for the construction of a local Shinto shrine. Pointing to the existence of such a sanctuary in a neighbouring village, these people justify their claims in terms of the importance of shrines in ensuring the estate's intergenerational continuity. A retired civil servant from Hieidaira talked about the advantages of joining the adjacent village in an administrative union of neighbourhood associations:

> There are a lot of good things about the union. It's important that the village join in *furusato-zukuri*. The village has a long history; they have a Shinto shrine and three [Buddhist] temples. Here in Hieidaira we have many *interi*, some of whom don't want a shrine, and some of whom do want a shrine. . . . Personally, I think it's important to have a shrine, even to join the village's shrine; even if it costs money. Alternatively we could join the big shrine in Ōtsu; Hieidaira will improve if we will be able to hold various services like the memorial service for the dead.

Another segment of the local populace, overwhelmingly parents of children at school, not only take an active part in organizing, but are continually defending the Buddhist children's festival which is held during the summer. Their explanation – directed at some critics citing the need to leave religious affairs to individual choice – is that without such religious practices the children will find it difficult to develop a notion of spiritual matters and an attachment to the area. Similarly, it is a small group of intellectuals – authors, social commentators and journalists – who talk of the need to arrange for a chronicle of the estate. As in other Japanese communities (Brown 1979), writing a local history is seen as a way to create a sense of place. While I was doing fieldwork the book to be based on my doctoral thesis was envisaged as one such document.

The importance local residents attach to festivals is not limited to religious or 'spiritual' events. Such occasions as bazaars, shows, hikes, trips, summer camps or singing competitions organized by neighbourhood groups are also considered valuable. But what is evident in regard to these latter kinds of activities is the extent to which Hieidaira's residents recognize that these must be consciously and intentionally organized. This is no mean point, for it underscores how, in the contexts of complex urban societies, it is only organizations that can make arrangements for large-scale localities. In Hieidaira – as in Japan in general – it is through the activities of a host of committees, clubs, associations and other organized groups that the creation of a sense of locality can be actualized. The need for organized action as a remedy for the lack of local solidarity was explained by the president of the PTA:

> Its hard to strike up contacts here. The kids may get to know those who live on their street, but a little farther away it becomes difficult. That's why school is important for creating friendships. It takes time, and that's why we need

activities like dance parties, bazaars, lecture meetings and rice-ball-making parties.

The example of the annual sports day discussed in the first edition of this book (Ben-Ari 1986) further illuminates the importance of organized action for local residents. A member of Hieidaira's sports committee related the significance of the day to the process of community-building: 'One of the most important ways in which neighbourhoods are formed is the process by which people become familiar with each other. The importance of the sports day lies in the possibilities it provides for such things.' Time and again, the head of the sports committee stressed that such occasions were especially important in areas like Hieidaira where there are hardly any communal festivals and functions and relatively little contact between people. But the observations of the head of the neighbourhood association about the sports day underlined a different set of attitudes towards the locality:

> The sports day is the festival [*matsuri*] of the whole area. There are plenty of people who want to take part in the whole affair with its lively and enjoyable atmosphere. But other people none the less feel that taking part in such events poses a restriction on their free time . . . Sunday.

Thus, alongside a harking back to the past 'village' is also a stress on the importance of the right 'not to neighbour'. At one and the same time, the same people may argue for setting up a local shrine engendering local solidarity and also argue for building a community where minding one's own business is a prime value. These sentiments can be found not only among younger members of the community, as I found out when I asked an elderly professor of Buddhist studies about his ideas of an ideal neighbour. Before replying, he got up and fetched a book of Chinese proverbs. He painstakingly translated a proverb by Confucius into English: 'The communication of gentlemen is like water.' Giving a little chuckle, he continued in Japanese, 'It isn't like milk or juice, you see. This kind of communication is brief and frank. It involves little interference in each other's affairs and no real commitment.' Thus for all of the stress on *furusato-zukuri*, many people said that it was also important to preserve the atmosphere of non-interference and minimal contact with neighbours. They may hark back to an idealized version of the old village, but the freedom 'not to participate' is just as important: they want the freedom to choose whether to take part in the 'village of the past' or to withhold their participation.

These ambivalences are related to doubts about the artificiality of attempting to 'traditionalize' modern settings. Following the sports day in which members of the estate's neighbouring village had participated, I interviewed an elderly member of the neighbourhood association. The women's association of the village had performed a traditional Japanese dance during the interval between the sports day's two parts. He began rather condescendingly and then spoke of the incongruity of the setting:

They [the villagers] are provincial [*hōkenteki*]. This has good sides to it like in their excellent participation in sports events and other community activities. But it also has funny sides, like when they got up at the intermission and dressed up in traditional clothes and danced that traditional dance. It gave me a funny feeling. It didn't fit in; a traditional dance in the sports day.

This passage well underscores the discomfort many people feel with the synthetic creation of traditional practices in inappropriate contexts. He seemed to be saying that there are appropriate places for the expression of the village's traditionality.

CONCLUSION

In this article I have examined 'talk' about newly built residential areas populated by representatives of Japan's new middle class. I began by situating my argument in relation to a number of recent studies which have examined idealized representations of a combination of space and time: 'local communities of the past'. These works have furthered our understanding of what is entailed by talk about such localities. As they show, such discourse is related both to the 'reputational content' of a locality and to the way the locality is used as a medium for discussing wider issues. Yet I would propose that my study bears wider import for the study of Japanese communities.

First, I have contended that understanding discourse about local communities involves juxtaposing two levels of analysis: the local and the national. I use the word juxtapose, because it is not only a matter of how localities are represented according to the logics of national debates about a 'vanishing' tradition or a new kind of neighbourhood. It is also a matter of how wider understandings are mobilized by locals in their dialogue with a variety of significant others about local identity. The national discourse is actualized in – and fixes the contours of – local dialogue. In this respect, Hieidaira is marked by a plurality of images. While it is countrified in one sense, it is definitely not the country of the 'old' Japan in another sense. Being both urban and a residential area for the highly educated it is taken to be representative of a new type of community which is characteristic of post-war Japan. In this manner talk about Hieidaira is talk about the new middle class and what it represents. More generally, talk of such localities is part of wider Japanese discourse about modernity, nostalgia, the politics of civic involvement and (interestingly) about Japan's internationalization.

The second point is related to the causal assumptions underlying the discourse on contemporary localities. This point is clearest in regard to the terms 'past' and 'tradition'. The superiority of the 'past' is not simply an abstract idea, but one based on invoking – sometimes implicitly and other times explicitly – a causal scheme. 'Tradition' is seen to grant a local community strength in communal participation and action by providing the locality with a sense of solidarity and unity. In other words, in the Japanese 'folk' theory of 'traditionality', community-wide activities are both indicators and products of the power of the community which is (in turn) based on its 'past' legacy. Yet for all of the stress on the edifying nature of tradition, there is an accompanying discourse about the detriments of the 'village of the past'. This discourse focuses – just like the nostalgia-driven discourse – in part on real and in part on imagined places. But what is evident is that the previous images of 'traditional' communities as locations of 'old ways of thinking' and feudal attitudes which lead to strong social control have not been completely supplanted. In contemporary Japan assertions about 'old' places as repositories of traditional values compete with claims about such places as exemplars of pre-war values.

This idea brings me to the third and final point which bears import for the anthropology of Japan. Anthropological discussions of this society have long been dominated by analyses placed at the level of villages and neighbourhoods, of communities and subcultures or of 'minority' groups. Only more recently have anthropological enquiries focused on a grander scale to ask questions about the wider processes that keep parts of this society together or separate them. But as I have shown here, the move to a more macro focus should be undertaken cautiously. The current stress on openness and the pluralism of perspectives now in fashion in anthropology (Cooke 1990; Gupta and Ferguson 1992) should not blind us to the 'topography', that is, to the broad contours or configurations, of possibilities within which the experiences of place in such societies take place. By focusing on the specific folk models or schemas that are used to make sense of the world, my study tries to map out some of the *limits* of the pluralism entailed by newer approaches. For example, the reality of the residents of Hieidaira comprises a limited field of issues such as leisure and collective commitment, individualism and groupishness, or democratic rights and traditional authority relations. While these issues, of course, change at the same time that the self-definitions of the Japanese change, they nevertheless encompass the broad possibilities within which localism and 'Japaneseness' are defined. We must be wary of an all too neat emphasis on the 'invention' of Japanese traditions. To reiterate, a stress on contestation, mutability, and change does not imply that 'anything goes'. We may miss continuities and limits on invention without a recognition of the elements of more enduring coordinates in the way Japanese conceptualize their communities and through these localities the way they think of themselves, their history and their tradition.

REFERENCES

Allinson, G.D. (1978) 'Japanese Cities in the Industrial Era', *Journal of Urban History*, vol. IV, no. 4 pp. 443–76.
—— (1979) *Suburban Tokyo: A Comparative Study in Politics and Social Change*, Berkeley: University of California Press.
Ben-Ari, E. (1986) 'A Sports Day in Suburban Japan: Leisure, Artificial Communities and the Creation of Local Sentiments', in J. Hendry and J. Webber (eds) *Interpreting Japanese Society: Anthropological Approaches*, Oxford: JASO Occasional Papers, no. 5, pp. 211–25.
—— (1991a) *Changing Japanese Suburbia: A Study of Two Present-Day Localities*, London: Kegan Paul International.

—— (1991b) 'Posing, Posturing and Photographic Presences: A Rite of Passage in a Japanese Commuter Village', *Man*, vol. XXVI, pp. 87–104.

—— (1992) 'Uniqueness, Typicality and Appraisal: A "Village of the Past" in Contemporary Japan', *Ethnos*, vol. LXVII, nos 3–4, pp. 201–18.

Bendix, R. (1992) 'National Sentiment in the Enactment and Discourse of Swiss Political Ritual', *American Ethnologist*, vol. XIX, no. 4, pp. 768–90.

Bestor, T.C. (1989) *Neighborhood Tokyo*, Stanford: Stanford University Press.

—— (1992) 'Conflict, Legitimacy, and Tradition in a Tokyo Neighborhood', in T.S. Lebra (ed.) *Japanese Social Organization*, Honolulu: University of Hawaii Press, pp. 23–47.

Brown, K. (1979) 'Introduction', in Keith Brown (trans) *Shinjo: The Chronicle of a Japanese Village*, Pittsburgh: University Center for International Studies, University of Pittsburgh (Ethnology Monographs Number 2), pp. 1–45.

Cohen, A. (ed.) (1986) *Symbolizing Boundaries*, Manchester: Manchester University Press.

Cooke, P. (1990) 'Locality, Structure and Agency', *Cultural Antropology*, vol. V, no. 1, pp. 3–15.

Dore, R. (1959) *Land Reform in Japan*, London: Oxford University Press.

—— (1978) *Shinohata: A Portrait of a Japanese Village*, London: Unwin.

Fernandez, J. (1986) *Persuasions and Performances: The Play of Tropes in Culture*, Indiana: Indiana University Press.

Fischer, C.S. (1976) *The Urban Experience*, New York: Harcourt Brace.

Gupta, A. and J. Ferguson (1992) 'Beyond "Culture": Space, Identity, and the Politics of Difference', *Cultural Anthropology*, vol. VII, no. 1, pp. 6–23.

Ivy, M.J. (1988) 'Discourses of the Vanishing in Contemporary Japan', PhD thesis, Cornell University.

Kelly, W. (1986) 'Rationalization and Nostalgia: Cultural Dynamics of New Middle-Class Japan', *American Ethnologist*, vol. XIII, pp. 603–14.

—— (1990) 'Japanese No-Noh: The Crosstalk of Public Culture in a Rural Festivity', *Public Culture*, vol. II, no. 2, pp. 65–81.

Kondo, D. (1990) *Crafting Selves: Power, Gender and Discourses of Identity in a Japanese Workplace*, Chicago: University of Chicago Press.

McDonogh, G. (1991) 'Discourse of the City: Policy and Response in Post-transitional Barcelona', *City and Society*, vol. V, no. 1, pp. 40–63.

McKean, M. (1981) *Environmental Protest and Citizen Politics in Japan*, Berkeley: University of California Press.

Martinez, D.L. (1990) 'Tourism and the *Ama*: The Search for a Real Japan', in E. Ben-Ari, B. Moeran and J. Valentine (eds) *Unwrapping Japan*, Manchester: Manchester University Press, pp. 97–116.

Moeran, B. (1983) 'The Language of Japanese Tourism', *Annals of Tourism Research*, vol. X, pp. 93–108.

Mullins, L. (1987) 'Introduction: Urban Anthropology and U.S. Cities', in L. Mullins (ed.) *Cities of the United States: Studies in Urban Anthropology*, New York: Columbia University Press, pp. 1–15.

Nagashima, C. (1981) 'The Tokaido Megalopolis', *Ekistics*, no. 289, pp. 280–301.

Nussbaum, S.P. (1985) *The Residential Community in Modern Japan: An Analysis of a Tokyo Suburban Development*, PhD thesis, Cornell University.

Pharr, S.J. (1990) *Losing Face: Status Politics in Japan*, Berkeley: University of California Press.

Quinn, N. and D. Holland (1987) 'Culture and Cognition', in D. Holland and N. Quinn (eds) *Cultural Models in Language and Thought*, Cambridge: Cambridge University Press, pp. 3–40.

Robertson, J. (1987) 'A Dialectic of Native and Newcomer: The Kodaira Citizens' Festival in Suburban Tokyo', *Anthropological Quarterly*, vol. LX, no. 3, pp. 124–36.

—— (1992) *Native and Newcomer: Making and Remaking a Japanese City*, Berkeley: University of California Press.

Smith, H.D. II (1979) 'Tokyo and London: Comparative Conceptions of the City', in A. Craig (ed.) *Japan: A Comparative Perspective*, Princeton, NJ: Princeton University Press, pp. 49–99.

Smith, R.J. (1988) 'Postscript to Ella L. Wiswell: Suye Mura Fifty Years Later', *American Ethnologist*, vol. XV, pp. 380–4.

Suttles, G. (1972) *The Social Construction of Communities*, Chicago: University of Chicago Press.

—— (1984) 'The Cumulative Texture of Local Urban Culture', *American Journal of Sociology*, vol. LXXXVI, pp. 283–304.

Takayose, S. (1979) *Komyuniti to Jūmin Soshiki* [*Community and Residents' Movements*], Tokyo: Keiso Shobo.

Tokyo Metropolitan Government (1982) *Tokyo Tomorrow, My Town Concept Consultative Council*, Tokyo: Tokyo Metropolitan Government Library Publication no. 17.

Part II

Kinship and social relations: perceptions and practice

6 Time, space and person in Japanese relationships*

Jane M. Bachnik

INTRODUCTION

The Japanese are often characterized by great sensitivity to relationships. As Lebra writes, 'The overwhelming impression from the literature, as well as from my personal observations, is that the Japanese are extremely sensitive to and concerned about social interaction and relationships' (1976: 2). 'For the Japanese *ningensei* ('humanity', or 'human-beingness') takes precedence over everything else' (ibid.: 6).

Such sensitivity is not directed primarily towards marital or family relationships, but towards 'other relationships, *even at the expense of the former*' (ibid.; emphasis added). This means that relationships are primarily identified with the broad spectrum of social life *outside* the primary group or family. It has been well documented that ties are central to many arenas of Japanese social life, including enterprise productivity, which is increasingly related to a 'fundamental humaneness about the mode of organizing people' (Cole 1979: 252). In addition, government ministries, Diet representatives, political parties and large-enterprise families are linked in extensive networks (Yanaga 1968; Hamabata 1983); and large-scale enterprises have extensive sub-contracting ties. Both religion and morality are also based on human ties: ethics on '*the relationship between man and man*' (Watsuji, cited in Lebra 1976: 12), and Confucianism, as Smith (1983: 103) puts it, on 'the centerpiece of the Cosmos [which] is human society and its manifold relationships'.

Yet major difficulties remain in the conceptualization of relationships. For example, there is considerable agreement among scholars of Japan that relationships are constituted by practice (meaning performance) and exist in space and time (Kumon 1982; Lebra 1976; Maraini 1975; Nakamura 1968; Nakane 1970). Words for 'relationship', such as *tsukiai*, or *tsukiai kankei*, have strong connotations of doing. Furthermore, human beings are consistently described as 'always . . . existing in a network of human relationships' (Smith 1983: 192), 'invariably identified as acting in some kind of human relationship, never autonomously' (ibid.: 49). Even the word for human being conveys this sense. *Ningen* (人間) is made up of two terms: *nin* (人) meaning 'person' or 'people' (also read *hito*), and *gen* (間) meaning 'space', 'space between', 'space of time', 'an interval' (also read *kan, ma* or *aida*). *Ningen* is often used with the word *kankei* (relation), which implies both 'connectedness' and 'participation'.

The strong implications from these translations are that Japanese relations are constituted by practice and exist *in* space and time. The analytical difficulty stemming from such characterizations is that of objectification and the relation of objectified models to performance in space and time. In his extensive (and excellent) discussion of this question, Bourdieu (1977) has pointed out that objectification omits time, and that time is essential to the practice of social life. For example, in gift-giving reversible patterns of reciprocity are experienced by the participants as *irreversible*, because of the interval between gift and counter-gift (ibid.: 6–7). The abstracted patterns do illuminate one aspect of social life (reciprocity), but they omit the equally crucial aspect of how reciprocity works in time.[1]

Like gift-giving, relationships are experienced in time, and time constitutes them as a dialogue with the 'other' which is constructed as it goes along. As Lebra puts this (1976: 7),

> The Japanese Ego acts upon or toward Alter with the awareness or anticipation of Alter's response, and Alter in turn . . . influences Ego's further action . . . . Activation of the chain cannot be attributed to either Ego or Alter exclusively but to both or to the relationship between the two.

Smith also notes that both self and other can be expressed only in relational terms. 'There are no fixed points, either [for] "self" or "other"' (1983: 77). The implication is that the self is constituted in interaction with others, and both Plath (1976, 1980) and Smith (1983) have called for an interactionist approach to the Japanese self.

Nakane has also noted this aspect of relationship in a set of figures which she presents on 'self' and 'other'. In Figure 6.1 self and other are separate entities, who must create a connection between them (a Western view). In Figure 6.2 self and other are interconnected by a tie (a Japanese view). Nakane comments that

SELF   OTHER

Figure 6.1 Self/other relationship (polar)
Source: Nakane (1972: 138)

SELF   AND   OTHER

Figure 6.2 Self *and* other relationship
Source: Nakane (1972: 138)

the focus in Figure 6.1 is on the '*poles*' of self/other, in Figure 6.2 on the '*and*' between the two (1972: 138).

Nakane's figures capture in a nutshell virtually all of the problems involved with the idea of 'relationship'. Relationship as a connective 'and' between self and other cannot be extracted from the context in which it exists (between self and other). Relationship is not substantive, but dynamic. It has to do with the creation of self and other.

Because of this, Nakane's diagram is paradoxical. The very point Nakane is trying to communicate (that relationships are *in* time and practice) is negated by the way in which the relationships have been removed from time and practice in this representation. Only in time and space can *ningen* be defined in a field of ties (*ma*), or a social nexus (*aidagara*). Nakane is not the only one caught in this paradox. Lebra's definition of a 'Japanese ethos', whose chief characteristics of social interaction and relationships are depicted in the term 'social relativism', is also paradoxical – since the interactional context which is necessary to give 'social relativism' its meaning has had to be abstracted to arrive at the label.

Because the contradictions involved in 'relationship' seem basic to Japanese society, I think it is imperative to acknowledge the existence of these paradoxes, rather than to gloss over them. But what is really at issue here? The issue of self and other which Nakane attempts to represent in such diagrams is not simply the relationship of a particular self and other, as Nakane indicates. It is also related to a more general set of issues regarding self and other, that of the relation of the individual to a more general other – that of society. In this sense we can read the figures on two levels: as representing two perspectives toward self and other, and also as representing two perspectives for approaching the self and society.

This opens up the perspective of 'relationships' to include much more complex issues. Instead of viewing relationships as objective data on the social horizon, the issue of approach itself must be consciously examined, as the relation of the researcher to that social horizon. This relation, in turn, must be included in the ultimate depiction of the social order. Objectification is of critical interest here because it permeates social science approaches so thoroughly that it goes largely unrecognized. By objectification I mean not only the objective stance of the observer, but a stance toward *social life* itself as observed and objectified so that 'in taking up a point of view on the action, withdrawing from it in order to observe it from above and from a distance, [the anthropologist] . . . . constitutes practical activity as an *object of observation and analysis, a representation*' (Bourdieu 1977: 2). This is illustrated by both of the polar dichotomies of self/other in Figure 6.1.

I am proposing that objectifying relationships has obscured important issues in Japanese social life. As 'things' (data) which are perceived on the social horizon, relationships are problematic, as I hope to demonstrate. But even more problematic is that as 'things', they are passive rather than active, and the productive part they play in the construction of social life is obscured. In this sense I believe relationships to be crucial in understanding Japanese social organization since, by viewing relationships as constructed in practice, we can also view social life as constructed in practice. This changes the perspective of the enquiry – from an investigation of what relationships are, to an investigation of how they work; from how relationships are organized to how they organize.

Relationships will be approached here, not as the lowest-level 'building blocks' of society, which must be integrated into higher levels, but as organizing factors themselves. The very term 'relationship' means a linkage, a connecting, and it is perfectly reasonable that relationship is a connective in a higher-level sense – relating self not only to other but to the social order (in the sense of what are usually considered as rules, structures and patterns. See Note *).

APPROACHES TO SELF AND OTHER IN JAPANESE SOCIETY

In order to demonstrate that issues of approach such as those raised above have practical consequences, I will now explore a set of problems currently being raised about the portrayal of self and other in Japanese society.

There are two issues that have been focal points regarding the definition of self and other in Japan, and both of these revolve around the organization of 'person'. The first is the problem of variation in defining 'person', both in the Japanese language and in the psychology of the self. The second is the excessively holistic and unified representation of Japanese society via the group, or 'group model' (commented on by Sugimoto and Mouer [1980] and Befu [1980]); it virtually leaves the 'individual' out of the account.

Let me first briefly elaborate on both these matters. The problem of variation in Japanese person terms is well known and commonly cited in cross-cultural descriptions on Japan (for example, Befu and Norbeck 1958; Fischer 1964; Neustupný 1978; Suzuki 1973, 1976, 1978b; Wolff 1980). To illustrate the point: Fischer (1964) reports ten terms used for reference and address in one three-member family; Smith (1983) notes a minimum of fourteen terms used by boys and girls for reference and address. The terms also vary from family to family and person to person. Thus, where 'I' and 'you' would be used in English, multiple terms are required in Japanese, and these include names, age-status terms, kin terms, place-names and zero terms. In addition, the self is defined as 'open-ended' (Suzuki 1976, 1978a, 1978b), 'relational' or 'variable' (Araki 1973).

However, the perspectives on person and self which define the self as variable are those of the *pole* of self (Figure 6.1), rather than the relationship between the poles; this difficulty has been noted by Plath (1980) and Smith (1983).[2] It is the focus on the pole of self (and the expectation of consistency at the pole) that defines either self or person in interaction as variable.

On the other hand, the pole of the other as abstract collective has most often been approached in terms of the human collective, or group, which has thus been considered as *the* unit of Japanese social organization. The second set of criticisms has focused on the group as a model, which depicts the human group as too rigidly organized, too uniform and too devoid of personal self. The complete submergence of the self in the group, and the characterization of the group by consensus, harmony, paternalism, loyalty, dependency, hierarchy and holism have also been brought into question.[3]

These criticisms are both astute and relevant. Yet I notice an inverse relationship in the way these two problems of self and other are defined. They are like two sides of the same coin. While the self is characterized by enormous variation, the group and its members are depicted by virtual uniformity. The extreme situational flexibility of the self can also be contrasted with rigid obedience to the minutely defined rules of the group.

Moreover, the change of logical type from 'group' to 'group model' is important, since the latter is a meta-level statement. The unacknowledged slippage from 'group' to 'group model' leaves an important question unresolved: is the *model* or is the *human group* too rigidly organized, uniform and devoid of personal self? Do holism, consensus, harmony, etc. reflect characteristics of the model (as the social-order pole of Figure 6.1), or characteristics of the human *group*? Confusion over the logical level of these characteristics leads to constant slippage from human practice (which may be varying and inconsistent in social context) to analytical constructs which cannot be human, in this sense. The connection between analysis and practice is re-established by making the characteristics *prescriptive*, applicable to *all* group interaction. The construction of the model then eliminates conflicts, dissent and tension from Japanese groups. It is precisely this situation which has led to severe criticisms of the inability of the group model to deal with conflicts, dissent and tension (by Befu [1980] and Sugimoto and Mouer [1980]).[4] Befu rightly points to the relationship between group harmony and *tatemae* (the presentation of group life to outsiders) as representing only one aspect of group social life – its public version, or *kireigoto* (1980: 36, 39). *Tatemae* is simply one facet of the group's portrayal of itself, rather than a blueprint for its organization. But here again it should be stressed that *tatemae* (as self-defined ideology) and the group model (defined from the researcher's perspective) reflect different logical levels of analysis.

I think it is significant that not only the self but also the group has been repeatedly described both by Japanese and others as located in experience, time and space. Kumon translates group as *sō* (1982: 23–4) – 'our' company, 'this' household, 'us' – which specifies the group as 'placed', or located in experience. A number of basic concepts for Japanese society all relate to the experiential context of the group: for example, *bun*, *mibun* (position, place) (Lebra 1976); *shozoku* (belonging) (ibid.); 'identity' (Kumon 1982); *ba*, or group 'frame' (defining 'this' group) – in contrast to 'attribute', which transcends the group (Nakane 1970). Kumon also relates the group to *ma* (field of ties) and *aidagara* (social nexus), both of which are connected with *ningen* as 'human relationship' (1982: 12).

These difficulties with self and other again bring us back to the paradox of Figure 6.2. The problems of consistency in the self and of lack of variation in the group can be related directly to the polar perspectives of the self/other dichotomy. I am proposing that these are not empirical problems, but rather problems of definition. But the question at issue, rather than the definition of a more consistent self or a less uniform group, can now be posed as a problem on a different level: as the relation of self and social order; the relation of consistency and variation; and of multiplicity and unity in Japanese social life.

It is now useful to examine Figures 6.1 and 6.2 more carefully, to ascertain better the relationships of self and social order which they express. Here, Figure 6.1 represents the dominant approaches to social thought in the history of the West as being located at the poles of the individual and the social order. The two poles represent two perspectives which are prominent in philosophical and social-science terminology. Thus, the pole of the individual is also concrete, empirical and 'real'; while the pole of the social order is abstract and ideal (and viewed as form, pattern, structure, rule or norm). The pole of the social order is also at a different level of abstraction from the pole of the individual, for it is generalized, while the latter represents the particular, the case.[5]

The larger issues which each of the pair of polar perspectives addresses is the relation of multiplicity (or multiple different individuals) to unity (or one social order). Each of the polar perspectives is valid, as Stark points out (1962), because each addresses a facet of the relation of self to society. The difficulty stems from the multiplicity of perspectives on social life which must co-exist: the visible manifestation of society is the individual, yet individuals share traditions which they do not originate (including those which produced and defined the individual as individual). The shared traditions, patterns and institutions (which make up the social order) are not empirically visible, but must be abstracted from the instances of individual situations.

In addition to the poles of the individual and the social order, a third perspective is possible, as Stark points out: that of the relation of self to the social order, of multiplicity to unity. Although this perspective is relatively rare in the history of Western social theory, I would argue that it dominates the Japanese approach to self and social order. The perspective is present in the Japanese interpretation of Confucianism, as well as Shinto. But this should not confuse the issue that the perspective of self *and* social order is expressed primarily in practice – i.e., in terms of everyday interaction in Japan – in contrast to the academic discourse of philosophers and social scientists in the West:

> Western pragmatism appears historically on the scene of thought as a reaction to idealism . . . . [It is] academic, it originally took birth, as a theory, in the heads of philosophers . . . . Japanese pragmatism has its roots in the life, work, beliefs of the people, it is something born in the thought processes of farmers, fishermen, potters, carpenters, and their like.

> (Maraini 1975: 70)

Thus the problem of defining 'relationship' in Japanese society emerges as a set of complex and important issues. These include the relation of self to other in time and space, versus relations-as-objectified; the relation of self to the social order, versus polar views of self *or* social order; the relation of concrete to abstract, multiplicity to unity, versus the dichotomies of concrete *or* abstract, multiplicity *or* unity. The ethnographic issue of Japanese relationships emerges as a double discourse, in the broad sense of this term – both at the level of ongoing social life and at the meta-level of significant issues in Western philosophy and the social sciences. The subject thus has the potential to be illuminating on both of these levels.

TIME, SPACE AND PERSON IN JAPANESE DISCOURSE

I will now turn to the question of time, space and person in Japanese society, toward developing a perspective which approaches self *and* other in time and space. There are three parts to this perspective. First, I will discuss an approach to relationship which is more compatible with the Japanese perspective. I will then relate this approach to a specific ethnographic context, that of the *ie* (translated as 'household'). Finally, I will discuss more broadly the implications of this perspective *vis-à-vis* Japanese society.

In developing a perspective for relationship which can move between the polar dichotomies I have delineated, I will proceed by discussing language, and specifically differentiate between referential versus indexical perspectives toward meaning. I will focus on indexing, and indexical meaning, as relevant for approaching Japanese social life. My focus is not only on language, however, but on social life, and I wish to show how these perspectives on language are also perspectives on social life.

The very problem with defining person in Japanese may be a by-product of the expectation of a consistent set of terms for self and other (Bachnik 1982). Most linguists agree that no class of pronouns exists in Japanese, and that names, age-status terms, kin terms, place-names, and zero terms are all used where pronouns would be used in Indo-European languages. Thus, not only do person terms vary, but also the circle of terms is considerably expanded in Japanese. Yet 'person' (and pronouns) in other Asian languages – such as Vietnamese (Luong 1984), Kawi (Becker and Oka 1974), Indonesian (Geertz 1960, 1973), Korean, Burmese, Cambodian, Thai (Head 1978) – are also characterized by wide variation in terms used, and this is increasingly linked to a definition of person in discourse situations. Here it is extremely significant that person terms in Japanese are usually omitted in discourse, meaning that person is defined in discourse situations without reference to terminology.

Thus one says '*Ikimasu*', to mean 'I am going'. *Ikimasu* literally specifies 'going' (from the verb stem *iku*, 'to go'), as well as formality (from the formal suffix *masu*). But person (here 'I') is unspecified and must be understood from the context. Furthermore, one can also say 'I am going' in a variety of other ways – for example, '*Iku*' (using the verb stem without the *masu* suffix), which communicates informality, as well as 'going'.

Although Japanese often communicate without using person terms, it is impossible to speak without using register. *Keigo*, or 'register' (also known as honorifics, speech levels or polite language) is unavoidable in Japanese. As Jorden notes, 'Almost without exception even single utterances are marked for politeness and formality, and certainly anything longer than a two-item exchange will be so marked' (1978: 144). Register communicates a message about the relation of the speaker to the addressee (and/or the referent), and this message communicates varying degrees of social distance as well as deference or respect in Japanese (as well as in other Asian languages, such as Burmese, Cambodian, Korean and Javanese; see Head 1978: 187).

Thus, a close relationship exists between register usage and the definition of person. In addition to reference, or naming (and often in lieu of it), the Japanese speaker is defining a continuum between self and other which is signified by the use of register. Nor is this distance continuum peculiar to person in Japanese, or in other Asian languages. Linguists acknowledge that reference is not the only function, even for Indo-European pronouns. 'I' is defined *in relation to 'you'* (see Forchheimer 1953). Becker and Oka refer to this relation between 'I' and 'you' as a distance cline which is central,

> perhaps *the* central thread in the semantic structure of all languages . . . Between the subjective, pointed specific pronominal 'I' and the objective, generic common noun, between these poles *the words of all languages* are ordered and categorized according to their distance – spatial, temporal, biological, and metaphorical – from the first person, the speaker.
>
> (Becker and Oka 1974: 229; emphasis added)

Edmund Leach has also discussed a self/other distance cline (1964) and argued that distance to or from the speaker defines the choice of animal terms used in verbal abuse. (We say 'You pig', 'dog', 'goat', 'swine' or 'ass', but not 'you ant-eater', 'son of a hippopotamus', or 'koala bear'.) Leach also spells out other clines – kinship and locational space – and relates closeness on one cline with closeness on others. (We neither eat our pets nor marry our sisters and brothers.)

The perspectives on language of both Leach and Becker are worth attention here. They both regard language not only as classifying 'things' in the environment, but also as defining the location of things-in-the-world in relation to us. To take this one step further, the 'world' of 'things' is not simply that of nature, which we learn by naming. *It is our relationship to the world which allows us to name things in the first place.*

This is an important point. At issue are two different approaches to language (and the world outside ourselves): through reference (naming), and through the distance cline the speaker signals between self and other. The second approach relates more closely to Charles Franklin Peirce's system of signs than it does to that of Ferdinand de Saussure. Peirce's approach to signs is defined in terms of relationships, and breaks down into tripartite sets of relationships between symbol, icon and index. The index, considered by Peirce to be the most important of the three kinds of signs, communicates a relationship between the entity signalled and the signalling entity (smoke is an index of fire; a rap on the door is an index of someone seeking entry; see Hartshorne and Weiss 1931; Buchler 1940).

More pertinent to this discourse, a pointing finger is also an index, which 'is based upon the idea of identification, or drawing attention to, by pointing' (Lyons

1977: 637). For example, 'this' and 'that', 'here' and 'there', 'now' and 'then' – all these are pointers, and each is defined in relation to a set of coordinates, gauged from the speaker's perspective. The speaker, as 'I', *anchors* the discourse as the zero-point from which spatio-temporal distance is gauged; the relationship between speaker and addressee (and/or referent), which indexing communicates, is also spatio-temporal. My use here of the term 'index' corresponds to the meaning of the term 'deixis'.[6]

Indexes are thus performative, rather than purely referential. 'I' does more than simply 'name' the speaker – 'I' is also in space and time, the very 'I' who is uttering this statement *here* and *now* (ibid.: 645). To put this even more strongly, 'I' is what allows 'here' and 'now' to be understood in the first place. Seen in this way, pronouns are pointers; and one of the major functions which 'I' performs is that of 'locating', 'anchoring' the discourse (ibid.; Benveniste 1971: 226).

These two perspectives on language – reference and indexing – can be related to the two perspectives on self and other, as objectified and in practice, which have already been discussed above. Thus, the objectified poles of self/other can be related to reference – and a focus on *what* the participants say. The continuum between self and other can be related to index – and a focus on *how* the participants anchor and index the 'world' both of reference and of social ties (the other) in relation to themselves. Yet in approaching language, as well as social life, we in the West have focused predominantly on the poles rather than the continuum; on reference rather than index; and on *what* rather than *how*.[7]

One of the unfortunate consequences of this focus has been the lack of application of indexing and deixis to the investigation of social life (Silverstein 1976). Yet indexicality, with its close connection to performative discourse, as well as to time and space, is unavoidably social, just as discourse is social. Moreover, it is also ontological, for the speaker who anchors time and space is *in* time and space. The implications of this are extremely important: the indexical perspective, to make an unavoidable inference, is one of being *in* the world. This means it can be linked both to practice and to phenomenological perspectives, such as those of Ortega (1957), Heidegger (1962), Merleau-Ponty (1962) and Erwin Straus (1967).

For all of these, the basic starting-point for social life is that of being in the world. 'It is not the case that man "is" and then has, by way of an extra, a relationship-of-Being towards the "world" – a world which he provides himself occasionally' (Heidegger 1962). Rather, being in the world is crucial for our orientation both to self and the world: 'We don't live in a homogeneous, isometric, isotropic space – or a geometric space – *but a space in which we orient ourselves*' (Straus 1967: 117; emphasis added).

This orientation is accomplished by a set of spatio-temporal coordinates for the cardinal directions, defined by Straus (ibid.: 118) as above and below, in front and behind, left and right. All of these coordinates require the existence of a zero-point (my body), in relation to which they must be defined (also Merleau-Ponty 1962). Ortega puts the point clearly:

[This orientation] does not allow me to be ubiquitous. At every moment it fixes me to one spot like a nail and exiles me from everything else . . . . I can change my place, but whatever place it may be, it will be my 'here'. Apparently, here and I, I and here, are inseparable for life. And since the world, with all the things in it, must be for me from 'here', it automatically becomes a perspective – that is, its things are near to or far from *here*, to right or left of *here*, above or below *here*. And this perspective is a perspective *in time* as well – the *here* is a *now*.

(Ortega 1957: 74)

Thus the indexical relationship between 'here' and 'there', 'now' and 'then', 'I' and 'you', of time and space in discourse, can also be related to the directional coordinates of vertical and horizontal, front and back, left and right, which orient the self toward the 'world', both physical and social. We locate ourselves constantly in time and space by a set of coordinates which tell us 'where things are'. We also locate ourselves socially (for example by introductions and genealogies), and by our perception of our relationships *vis-à-vis* others (which we then objectify as 'status' and 'role'). The process is similar to reading the spatial coordinates of a map, using the little red dot which says 'You are here'. Without this dot one is unable to read a map; while without locating or 'reading' the social distance between self and other, one is unable to perform adequately in social life.

Yet our spatio-temporal orientation through the use of these coordinates is more than simply a means by which we locate *our* relation to the world. The world is located by orienting it *in relation to ourselves*, just as a camera requires constant adjustment of the lens in focusing the picture. While we have generally assumed the *world* to be 'given', and such spatio-temporal orientation to be riding on the 'given-ness' of the world, the evidence suggests that it is rather the other way round – that spatio-temporal orientations are crucial in organizing our perceptive frame of reference which emerges as 'the world'.

In order to illustrate the point that indexing is essential to our comprehension of the 'objective' world of reference, it is necessary to consider examples of situations where reference fails because indexing fails. I will use two sets of cases: the first, documented by a surgeon, Marius von Senden, who in 1932 investigated the spatial conceptions of congenitally blind patients after successful cataract surgery. The second case refers to the record of two neurosurgeons concerning the aphasic victim of a car accident (Yamadori and Albert 1973).

Von Senden documented the differences between tactile and visual senses of space:

Before the operation a doctor would give a patient a cube and a sphere; the patient would tongue it or feel it with hands and name it correctly. After the operation the doctor would show the patients the same objects without letting them touch them; now they had no clue as to what they were seeing.

(Dillard 1974: 27)

The lack of spatio-temporal orientation, normally derived from sight, drastically affected these patients' orientation to the world. When asked how large his mother was, one patient put his thumb and index finger about an inch apart to show the size (von Senden 1960: 52). 'A house that is a mile away is thought of as nearby, but requiring the taking of a lot of steps' (ibid.: 41). One patient took off one of his boots, threw it some way off in front of him, attempted to gauge the distance, took another few steps and tried to grasp it, then moved on again and groped for the boot until he finally got hold of it (Dillard 1974: 28). When asked what he could see when he first opened his eyes, the patient

> saw an extensive field of light, in which everything appeared dull, confused, and in motion. He could not distinguish objects . . . . Soon after his operation a patient generally bumps into one of these colour-patches and observes them to be substantial. . . . In walking about it also strikes him . . . that he is continually passing in between the colours he sees, that he can go past a visual object, that a part of it . . . disappears from view . . . . Thus he gradually comes to realize that there is also a space behind him, which he does not see.
>
> (ibid.: 27–8)

Von Senden's cases document what cognitive psychologists have already told us – that the world is not passively 'seen' but actively constructed. 'Seeing' is learned through experience, and understood from spatio-temporal coordinates in relation to the self. This is such a basic skill that we are largely unaware that we are doing it. Yet it was so difficult for an adult to learn that many of the patients investigated by von Senden preferred to close their eyes and affect blindness.

The second case, documented by the two neurosurgeons Yamadori and Albert (1973), concerns a 54-year-old man who suffered a skull fracture, and severe motor and speech disturbances, as the result of a car accident. He recovered completely, except for certain difficulties, including an inability to name the basic categories of his body and ordinary objects in his room:

> When asked to point to a chair the patient stood up, looked around the room, then sat down, spelling to himself C-H-A-I-R; C-H-A-I-R . . . . He finally said, 'I have to double check that word later. I don't know.'
>
> (ibid.: 114)

The patient kept a notebook in which he made word-lists and diagrams. In it he drew a picture of the relation of ceiling, wall and floor. On this he had marked: 'Wall – from bottom to top; used from floor to ceiling . . . . Floor – walk on this area.' Another diagram portrayed the relation of his thigh, knee, leg, foot and toes. He drew in arrows to point out 'foot': 'below leg then knee and last thigh'. He demonstrated remarkable difficulty in naming the first day of the month and year, drawing maps, and drawing clock settings (ibid.: 116–19).

In this case, what the patient lacked in being unable to name his own parts of the body, or a chair, wall or floor, was not the names themselves, but a zero-point by which he could relate himself to his surroundings. His problem was thus most acute (because most visible) in his inability to identify those aspects of his surroundings (including his own body) which were closest to him. This case demonstrates that even objects in the environment – chairs, walls, tables, floors, etc. – are not wholly objectified, but rather are understood by us in relation to a zero-point (ourselves).

I have developed these issues at some length because they bear directly on problems in approaching Japanese social life. Two basic perspectives exist for viewing self and other: the polar views of self (individual) and other (social order), and the relationship between these poles. These can be seen in a figure/ ground relationship, such that if either the self/other poles or the continuum between the poles is regarded as 'figure', the other perspective becomes 'ground'. Although both the polar perspectives and the continuum cannot be brought into simultaneous focus, it is significant that both perspectives do exist in all cultures, and both are necessary for understanding social life. Yet Japan and the West have each tended to focus on the opposite perspective as 'figure' for viewing social life. The West has tended to view the poles (and this has resulted in the development of concepts of 'structure' and the 'individual', as well as objectification and referential meaning). The Japanese have developed to a fine art the relationships *between* the poles, *between* self and social order. This has resulted in a focus on social life in practice, and on being in time and space.

Because each of the two self/other perspectives involves an approach to social life, they are incompatible, in the sense that each must define the other. The issue is whether to start with 'names', the world of reference, and use this to define time, space and distance (in the path of Newton) – or whether to start with a zero-point (for example, the 'I' of Indo-European discourse), a distance cline *between* self and other, and thus to work from the other direction, using distance to define reference.

I believe that the zero-point and distance cline are much more appropriate than referential meaning as a starting-point for approaching Japanese social life. This means that index (rather than symbol), distance *between* (rather than figure or name), and pointing – 'this'/'that', 'here'/'there' – (rather than reference) should be used as starting-points in the study of Japanese social life.

The spatio-temporal (deictic) coordinates between self and other are acknowledged as organizational parameters for discourse. Deixis is also acknowledged to be universal (Lyons 1977: 646). As organizing parameters, index (or deixis) is in no way unique to Japan. What I am proposing, however, is that the Japanese have utilized the deictic parameters which organize discourse for social organization as well – hence the emphasis on 'place' or 'field' (*ba, tachiba* [Nakane 1970: 1]), 'share', 'fraction' (*bun, mibun* [Lebra 1976: 67]), 'position' (Embree 1939; Norbeck 1954; Cornell 1956; Beardsley *et al.* 1959; Plath 1964; Nakane 1967; Kitaoji 1971; Bachnik 1983), and the extensive use of distance and directional coordinates in linguistic register. These coordinates are spatio-temporal – but they are not abstract. They are located in the here and now by human beings interacting in space and time; they are used to relate self to other, and self to the environmental universe.

It should be obvious that the study of Japanese social life in this way will require a reorientation of approach. For example, it will require a situation (and an anchor-point). It must depict the process of social life (such as dialogue); and it must be in time. The researcher must also be *in* the situation and *in* time. These reorientations relate to many of the issues being raised about ethnography at present – such as social life as dialogue (Marcus 1980; Bakhtin 1981; Gumperz 1982; Marcus and Cushman 1982; Clifford 1983), the relation of time to social life (Bourdieu 1977), and the relation of the researcher to the ethnographic text.[8] Note that it is inappropriate to raise 'objectivity' as a problem of method in this case, since objectification is the very issue which I bring into question (and therefore is the *subject* of the enquiry).

TIME AND SPACE: TWO SCENES

It is impossible to carry out the entire programme defined above in the space which is available here.[9] Instead, I will briefly sketch a context of two small scenes, which are not meant as any kind of empirical 'proof' for the theoretical position I am outlining.[10] The scenes are necessary to deal with the paradox I have pointed out in the portrayal of Japanese social life – that being anchored in time and space is omitted in objectified social-science models. This makes portrayal of a social context necessary. I am aware that this cannot be the actual context, but only a report of it.

The scenes took place in an *ie* (household), which I shall call the Katō house, where I lived and undertook research during a series of visits totalling five years over a sixteen-year period, from 1967 to 1984; the scenes I shall be describing took place when I had known the members of the Katō household for about five years (the word *ie* is variously translated as 'family' or 'household' since it has components both of kinship and enterprise; neither translation is fully adequate). The Katōs are a farm household in Nagano prefecture.

Scene 1

The setting: a large farmhouse fronting onto a garden which is blooming profusely on a mild September day. The house is opened up all along the front (south) side, and four guests are making their way along the stepping-stones through the garden. Beckoned onward by those inside the house, they walk up a stone stairway, remove their shoes, step up to the *tatami* mats and kneel, bowing so their heads touch the floor, as they meet those in the house. They present gifts to those in the house, who bow just as low in return. The guests return the bow of the hosts, and then rise, as they are invited over to sit at a low table on *zabuton* (cushions).

The guests are the bride-to-be, who will soon marry the eldest son (and successor of the household), her father, mother, and father's sister. The hosts are the wife (*okāsan*) and her husband's sister (*obasan*). I am also there, greeting the guests. The *okāsan* and *obasan* bring tea for the guests, and we all sit, quietly sipping the tea, and enjoying the view of the garden. The hosts leave, and I am left to talk with the guests. The room is open to the garden on two sides, and this openness makes it seem as if we are almost in the garden. Flies buzz in and out, and the sun shines into the room. At the far end of the room from the garden is an alcove which has a flower arrangement – made from flowers in the garden – and several scrolls, mounted on silk, hanging on the walls.

Eventually, the two women return with the first course of an elaborate meal which is tastefully arranged on hand-painted porcelain and lacquerware dishes. Although it is now nearly three o'clock, the guests are reserved as they approach the food. They sample a few pieces from each dish, eating delicately, remarking on the freshness of the farm vegetables, but they do not finish all the food.

Conversation in the meal is punctuated by quiet pauses. We finish with tea, which seems to accentuate the quiet calm of the afternoon, and the laziness of the feeling of sunshine coming in from the garden. There is a feeling of calm, making us feel removed from the hustle and bustle of daily life.

Scene 2

The setting: several hours before Scene 1, in a different room of the same farmhouse. Three women are sitting at the *kotatsu* (a table with a hole cut into the floor beneath it, used as a place to sit at and for warming oneself in winter). This room also fronts onto the garden, but does not have a good view. The room is cluttered and looks lived in; holes have been poked in the paper-covered doors (*shōji*), and magazines and children's schoolbooks are lying about. A TV is in the corner. The *tatami* mats are old and worn, and there are cracks in the fittings of the doors and windows.

The three women at the *kotatsu* are the *okāsan*, the *obasan*, who has come on a visit for the day, and myself. The two women are talking about goings-on in their households (the husband's sister has married into another house), gossiping and drinking tea. Conversational register is very informal and the talk is punctuated by howls of laughter and slaps on the back, performed with great gusto by the *okāsan*. Suddenly the telephone rings in the next room, and the *okāsan* goes to answer it. We hear a loud shriek through the walls – then a pause.

The *okāsan* comes back into the room and begins talking in an even more animated fashion than before. '*Ah komaru. TaiHEN komaru!*' I gather from what she is saying that the eldest son, who is about to be married, has just arrived at the railway station in the next town with the bride-to-be and her relatives – seven hours early. Nothing is ready; the preparations have not even been started – and yet they will be here within half an hour.

The *okāsan* is still recounting the conversation, and moaning about what she can do, when the *obasan* gets up and begins climbing out of the *kotatsu*, unwrapping a bundle which she has beside her: 'Don't worry about a thing! I've brought my work clothes [*mompei*], and I'm all set to help. We'll have things ready in no time.'

The *okāsan* protests – rather weakly – that the *obasan* is a guest and certainly cannot be expected to help. The *obasan* responds by pulling on her *mompei*, saying as she does so, 'Can't work in a kimono. Slows you down something terrible.'

The *okāsan* protests – even more weakly – while they move off in the direction of the kitchen, and then, quickly, they get down to business, and I am delegated to go to the shop. The two women work furiously and manage to have a complete meal ready within a couple of hours, while I am again delegated to occupy the guests after they arrive.

As empirical manifestations of social life, both scenes are different – in almost every way. At the same time each is connected to the other, for each produced the other (the kitchen scene was produced by the telephone call, and the kitchen scene in turn produced the meal which was central to Scene 1).

Each of these scenes is characterized by communication in a number of different modes: for example, the greetings, bowing, the giving and receiving of gifts and food, spatial communication, speech register, kind of dress worn, and communication content. There are two kinds of messages (following Bateson 1972): 1) information messages ('They're seven hours early!'), communicating *what* people say (content); and 2) relational meta-messages (like that of distance in register usage), communicating *how* far away people define themselves *vis-à-vis* each other (form).

The expression of self and other which took place in Scene 1 in Parlour 4 (see Figure 6.3) was characterized by formality of dress and speech register, by the giving of expensive and aesthetically pleasing gifts (by the guests), and by the giving of a specially prepared and artfully arranged meal (by the Katōs). In this scene relatively few informational (content) messages and a great number of relational (form) messages were communicated.

The messages 'say' that the two groups of people (the Katōs and the house of the bride-to-be) are *distant*, and the message is similar in each mode. Distance is communicated in both cases by formality, which can also be viewed as *difference* from everyday life. Aesthetics is important in communicating this difference, so that the sparse furnishings, indeed 'emptiness' of Parlour 4, the arrangement of the garden *vis-à-vis* the room, the art objects in the room, the tasteful arrangement of the food presented by the Katōs, and the gifts and dress of the guests – all these give much attention to aesthetic form, and at the same time communicate little *content*.[11]

The communication of self and other which took place in Scene 2, in contrast, was characterized by informality of dress and use of speech register, by the giving of much more ordinary gifts (cakes for the house ancestors), and by the receiving of tea and crackers (*senbei*) by the guest. The relational messages in Scene 2 were both informal and close; this scene was striking in the lack of aesthetics exhibited. For example, the number of household artefacts in the room, its degree of clutter, the lack of a good view of the garden, the cracks in the doors and windows, the informal dress, the informal speech register and the howls of laughter and slaps on the back, and the informal gifts and mode of tea-drinking – all these contrast with the formality in Scene 1.

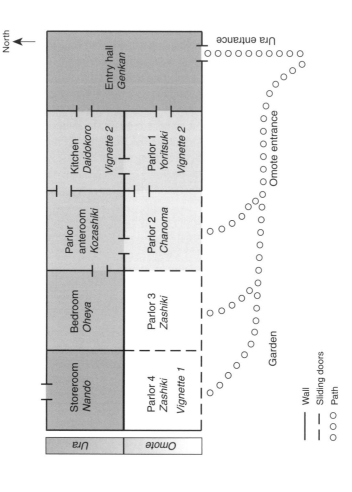

Figure 6.3 House plan of the Katō household

Thus in the first scene all the modes of communication expressed formality, emptiness of content, and difference from ordinary everyday life – in other words, what people did and said expressed their relationship as 'far' (or as 'outside-ness'). Communication in the second scene expressed informality, everydayness, and a high degree of *content* – what people did and said expressed their relationship as 'close' (or as 'inside-ness').

Two concepts which express these clusters of relationships are *ura* ('inside-ness', content, informality, everydayness) and *omote* ('outside-ness', form, formality, difference from everydayness); both are major concepts in Japan. The communication in Scene 1 is obviously characterized by *omote*, and this word is also used to describe the section of the Katō house which makes up the four parlours. The communication in Scene 2 is characterized by *ura*, the word used to describe the section of the house which consists of the four back rooms. *Omote* and *ura* are much used in everyday discourse, in expressions such as *omote no hanashii* (literally, 'appearance talk', viz. 'what they do in order to impress others whose presence puts them on guard') and *ura no hanashii* (literally, 'inside' or 'inner talk', viz. 'their secrets which they will disclose only to those who are closest to them') (Doi 1973a: 259).

None of these glosses is adequate as a definition, for my point here is that *omote* and *ura* are indexes, rather than referential terms – that they define a distance cline, *between* self and other, rather than naming or describing any characteristic of either. Index thus hinges on context, on the perceived relationships between the Katō household and the two different sets of guests. The basis of defining the bride-to-be and her relatives as distant is that the marriage has not yet taken place; and this is the initial meeting of the people in Scene 1. The basis of defining the *okāsan*'s husband's sister as close is that she is the only sibling of the household head.

Most important of all, *omote/ura* (and these two scenes) do not represent dichotomies. Rather than specifying some 'thing', *omote* and *ura* index *degrees of distance* between self and other. Moreover, distance in turn also functions as an index – pointing out *degrees of difference* between self and other. Rather than formality versus informality, or 'ordinariness' versus 'non-ordinariness', *omote* and *ura* indicate the *degree of formality* (from formal to informal, along a continuum).

Yet, this is not all. I have already defined two levels of communication – that of the message (information), and that of the meta-message (relationship message). If we think of the information message as *content* and the relational message as *form*, then *omote/ura* have a double-level relationship as well, since *ura* has to do with content (as well as *lack of form*), while *omote* has to do with form (as well as *lack of content*). Scene 2 was also characterized by much more content, which was most obvious at the point of the telephone message when the *okāsan* let the *obasan* in on the crisis which had just arisen for the Katō house. This conversation produced a change in distance communication between the two women so that the guest (the *obasan*) left the *kotatsu*, changed into work clothes, and changed rooms (moving to the kitchen) in order to help the *okāsan* deal with the crisis created by the imminent arrival of the other guests. All of these changes virtually erased the little remaining distance between the *okāsan* and *obasan*, and the latter became (temporarily) like a household member herself.

Thus *omote* and *ura* are related to one another in a manner similar to that in which the sand in one side of an hour-glass is related to the emptiness (or lack of sand) in the other. This is an inverted continuum – in the sense that the degree of existence of one term means the lack of existence of its counterpart, to the same degree. To give an example, the greater the formality that is expressed, the less the informality that can be expressed in the same situation, and vice versa. Thus, the frantic scene taking place in the kitchen (and the crisis brought about by the telephone call) are not communicated to the guests in Parlour 1. Nor are the aesthetics of Parlour 4 communicated in Scene 2, which takes place in a setting which is both ordinary and unaesthetic. Yet both parts of the continuum are necessary for social life, and the Japanese are well aware of this. Guests in Parlour 4 know that the *ura* is being modified, just as guests in Parlour 1 know that the *omote* is not present. The *omote* is necessary for dealing with outsiders, and the *ura* is essential in creating the *omote* – so the scene in the kitchen is clearly necessary for the scene in Parlour 4 to take place at all.

A number of other sets of terms also express the relationship of an inverted distance continuum. For example, *tatemae* – 'the surface reality' (Hamabata 1983: 7), 'a . . . formal principle . . . palatable to everybody concerned so that the harmony of a group is maintained' (Doi 1973a: 259) – and *honne*, 'the world of inner feelings' (Hamabata 1983: 8). Doi and Hamabata (as well as Barthes [1982] and numerous other writers) make it clear that *honne* (as inner reality) is no more 'real' than *tatemae* (as surface or appearance) for the Japanese. Both *tatemae* and *honne* are considered equally 'real', as are all expressions of *omote* and *ura*. In addition, *giri* (social obligation) and *ninjō*, 'the world of personal feelings' (Hamabata 1983: 22), are also an interrelated set of terms; as Doi puts it, 'it is possible to consider *giri* as the vessel . . . and *ninjō* as the content' (1973b: 34). Other sets of terms are *yoso* or *soto* (outside), and *uchi* or *naka* (inside); *hare* (sacred, extraordinary, formal) and *ke* (profane, ordinary, informal); *oyake-goto* (public) and *watakushi-goto* (private). The meanings of many of these sets of terms overlap (Doi 1973a: 259). This makes sense if the terms are indexical, and if they all index a continuum which is similar as between self and other, or self and the social order.

IMPLICATIONS

The differences in these scenes are familiar enough to members of a Western society, for we too use different degrees of formality in language use, in dress and in gift-giving. There are occasions when we act formally, and occasions when we act informally. We also are able to shift from scene to scene, and we can understand distance clines.

The difference between ourselves and the Japanese lies in our perspective, which is oriented toward reference, not index; toward objectifying the world, not relating it on a continuum *vis-à-vis* ourselves; and toward perceiving both self and other as dichotomous. The difference in perspective has important consequences in the way social life is approached and defined in Japan. In other words, both the distance cline and the poles exist in both societies, for ordinary people in everyday life; but the Japanese focus on the distance cline (or indexing) and arrive at the poles (reference) through indexing. We, on the other hand, start with the poles and move in the opposite direction. The result is a difference in focus: on self (the individual), and on society as structure, norms, or patterns. For the Japanese, however, the focus is on the relation of self to society, both of which are closely connected to time and space.

This means that relationship in Japanese social life is not an issue of empirical data, nor are relationships adequately viewed as 'objects' or 'things' on the social horizon. Instead, relationship is a way of *defining* that social horizon, and is therefore crucial for an understanding of the process of Japanese social life.

Relationships can be seen as both ontological (in time and space) and indexical (relating time and space to self and other). They are like gauges according to which people define degrees of difference between self and other and index their communication (both in content and form) according to the *degree of distance defined*. Social life should therefore be approached as continuing discourse, consisting of both words and action.

A major difference in perspective follows from the focus of social life on index (and distance) as distinguished from perspectives focused at either of the poles of individual or social order. This is evident from the way in which Doi defines social maturity in Japan as 'the ease with which one shifts from *omote* to *ura* and back again without much strain' (ibid.). Rather than mastering either the performance or rules of a particular situation, the goal of maturity here is that of being able to define the difference between situations, in ways which are culturally agreed upon. Doi further elaborates (ibid.) that a person's integrity is not damaged by taking 'recourse to *omote* or *ura* depending upon the particular situation he finds himself in. Rather his integrity rests upon the complete mastery of *omote* and *ura*.' 'Integrity' here is not defined by recourse to the 'inner' self (as *ura*), but as the ability to shift appropriately between *omote* and *ura*. The focus on shifting means that mastery (or knowledge) of *omote/ura* is not encompassed in any particular expression of *omote/ura*, because the differentiation necessary for shifting appropriately between scenes requires knowledge of the whole range of possibilities.

In the same way, what people say or do (for example, in gift-giving or greetings) has different implications depending on whether this is defined referentially or indexically by the observer (or on whether reference defines index or index reference). If reference is primary the message is important (i.e., the *gift*). If indexing is primary, however, the referential message is nested in the relational context (which includes the relation between giver and receiver, and the expression of the gift as a particular point on the continuum of self/other or *giri/ninjō*). Thus each scene carries an indexical message – of who communicated the scene and their relationships with each other; and moreover it is these relationships that literally *produce* the scene. The two scenes used above illustrate this, by the degree to which the expression of content and form in the scenes was indexed by the relationships perceived between the participants.

I am proposing that a continuum is the paradigm for this type of study of Japanese social life – but this is a specific kind of continuum. It is defined by indexing, performed in the communication of self and other in a number of simultaneous modes of social expression. It is neither real nor ideal; it does not exist in time and space. It is potential – consisting of possibilities which can be expressed in time and space.

These possibilities are ranged along the entire continuum which is defined by degrees of closeness to or distance from the self, including everything in-between. Each of the perspectives indexes a different expression of social discourse (through the whole range of possibilities of content and form relationships), although only one of these possibilities can be expressed in a given social situation. Another way of putting this is that rather than there being a single social reality, a number of possible perspectives of both self and social life are acknowledged. Interaction in Japanese society then focuses on the definition of the appropriate choice, out of all of the various possibilities. This means that what one says and does will be different in different situations, depending on how one defines one's particular perspective versus the social other.

In a society where social life is defined via interaction along a distance continuum, priority would be placed, not on defining 'the' world or 'the' self, but on understanding the relationship between the different possible perspectives which can define both self and the world. The meta-level nature of indexicality is important here. Rather than a focus on congruency in the communication of messages (such as gift-giving or the treatment of guests), the focus is on the relationship between different messages, at different times and in different situations. The perspective is in fact on *difference*, and on all the possible degrees of difference between the ways of expressing a message, in all combinations of content/form ranging from extreme *omote* to extreme *ura*.

It is now possible to see that indexing is a means for relating social life *between* scenes but this is done by difference, rather than similarity. Thus the degrees of difference between points on a distance cline index the interactions *within* Scenes 1 and 2. But they also relate the different interactions *between* the two scenes. This means that if slices of scenes are extracted and compared without taking indexing between scenes into account, the result will be unexplained variation, just as a comparison between Scenes 1 and 2 of gift-giving, greeting interactions, behaviour toward guests, eating or tea-drinking would produce variation in each kind of behaviour. The indexing between scenes is defined, of course, by the different relationships of the participants – which are omitted from objectified accounts of social life.

The relationships of the Katōs may be located along the entire range of the distance continuum, and the house plan indicates the entire range as well. The relationship between difference is expressed in the sliding scale of formality of each of the four 'guest' rooms, which locate points along that continuum. In this sense, Benedict's characterization of the Japanese as 'the most fantastic series of "but also's" ever used on earth' (1946: 1) should not be explained away. The question which Benedict has raised is not of collapsing the 'but also's', but of explaining the relationships between them.

Indexing also provides a means for dealing with the problems of rigidity and inflexibility in definitions of norm and rule. To return to the problem of minutely defined rules, in Scenes 1 and 2 the indexing of distance (in the use of register, definition of space and placement of seating at tables) defined the giving of gifts and food, the choice of room and seating at the table, the speech register used and the amount of content (or lack of it) which was communicated. The question here is whether minutely defined should refer to the redundancy of communication in *indexing* or to rule-governed behaviour. I think that these scenes *can* be characterized by minutely defined rules and rigidity, but only if they are viewed retrospectively, like a strip of film run backwards, so that virtually all of the behaviour is seen as rule-governed. Since the interaction is generated by the parameters of the scenes themselves, the argument is circular. The fluidity of choices, the ambiguity of more than one correct possibility for indexing distance and the flexibility of response in interaction (which is evident in the reaction of the *obasan* to the crisis) are all omitted from this perspective. The entire significance of the communication of self and other and the mutual generation of the scene between them are missed, if situations are viewed as virtually prescribed.

The question of whether such rules are really indexical commentaries on *interactions* is important because, if approached objectively, indexes (like 'here', 'there', 'now' and 'it') are empty. Many of the rule statements about Japanese society focus on interaction and/or relationships, and there is a high degree of emptiness in their definitions (also noted by Sugimoto and Mouer 1980: 11). For example, terms such as 'situational ethic', 'social relativism' and 'interactional relativism' are very commonly used to describe Japanese society. These terms specify merely that situations are crucial in defining interaction, ethics and social organization. But since they require the very situation which they are supposed to explain, in order to explain it, they are not only empty but also circular.

A large number of statements about structure and rules in Japanese society also concern interaction, and the question is whether these statements refer to indexing of distance or principles of rule. For example, 'horizontal' and 'vertical' are both commonly used to define relationships. But do they refer to abstract principles of 'horizontalness' or verticality? Or to interaction and the distance cline between self and other?

These questions may be asked as well of virtually all of the terms used to define the group model: dependency, harmony, paternalism, consensus, loyalty and hierarchy. The translation of virtually all of these terms is problematic, as Doi (1973b), Rohlen (1974) and Smith (1983), among others, have pointed out. Thus *wa* (harmony) is not, according to Rohlen, a metaphor, nor is it merely an element in a system of abstract distinctions. Rather, it is relational, referring to 'the cooperation, trust, sharing, warmth, morale and hard work of efficient, pleasant, and purposeful fellowship' (1974: 47). 'Hierarchy' is also an important term because it has been so often used to describe Japanese society. As Smith points out, 'most scholars who deal with Japanese society place at the center of their scheme of Japanese values something usually called a sense of hierarchy. Less thoroughly analyzed is this sense of *hierarchy in action*' (1983: 48; emphasis added). Each of the group-model terms refers to a complex way of interaction between self and other, which the translation does not adequately convey; and all of them raise questions about whether they should be indexically defined.

Thus 'relationship' is not an empirical issue (i.e., the investigation of relationships), but instead involves the relationship *between* self and social order, part and whole, one and many – issues which are as complex (and at least as important theoretically) as any issues stemming from the polar dichotomies themselves. To those who say that Japan has not contributed in an important way to the theoretical development of the social sciences, I would respond that if this is so, it must be due to the basic level of the issues which confront the Western researcher in Japan, rather than to any real lack of potential contribution. The researcher must confront such basic matters as the relation of self to society, of space and time to social practice, of self to the empirical world, of the empirical to the abstract, particular to general, and subject to object. The basic nature of these issues also means that one ignores them at the risk of prejudicing one's research, or, to put this another way, that consciousness of one's approach to research in Japan is a necessary part of attention to the 'data', because each defines the other. I do not mean to imply that this is not also true elsewhere, but simply that all of these relationships are central to the everyday working of Japanese culture. Therefore the relationship between theoretical and practical becomes central, as well.

In conclusion, it should be greatly significant to us that the Japanese perspective on social life focuses on the relationship *between* what we in the West have most often perceived as dichotomies. But this significance will be lost if we try to perceive the Japanese through dichotomous lenses. Instead, the importance of Japanese society for us should lie in the possibility of reaching new perspectives on issues which have long perplexed us, including the relation between the individual and the social order; variation and rule; flexibility and constraint; time and continuity; and particularity and general unity.

NOTES

*   I believe my main argument in this paper still stands, and so have chosen not to rewrite it. But I would like to clarify certain points which may make the argument more accessible for the present-day reader. The paper sketches out a thorough theoretical refocus on Japanese society. That refocus has now been more thoroughly presented in Bachnik and Quinn (1994) and Bachnik, in press.

Viewed from the vantagepoint of 1998, the paper seems to juxtapose two perspectives on language and meaning: 'reference' and 'indexing', a juxtaposition that seems itself to partake of the very kinds of dualisms it is supposedly arguing against. Recent research on indexical meaning, especially that of William Hanks, makes clear that what I am regarding as 'index' should instead be considered as 'indexical reference'. 'Indexical reference' more clearly specifies a theoretical perspective that is focused on the vantagepoints *between* self and other (and between self and social order). In this sense, Hanks points out that 'indexical reference' is strongly linked to Bourdieu's outlines of the theory and logic of social practice.

In this sense it is not an either/or question of reference or index, but rather which is the more appropriate starting point for viewing ongoing relationships between them. We can pose a parallel question about self and social order. The major question posed by this paper then, is: Do we adopt the starting point of viewing self and society through indexing (or indexical reference), which then points us toward the theoretical organization of practice (as eloquently elaborated by Bourdieu)? Or do we view practice (and a social order constituted by practice) as objectified (through a referential focus) from the very practice that gives it its organizational basis? The paper suggests that 'relationships' in Japanese society raise organizational issues about self and social order, and their relationship to the organization of practice that still has much more to inform us.

This is a revised version of a paper first presented at a Conference on The Social Anthropology of Japan, held at the Nissan Institute of Japanese Studies, Oxford University, in March 1984. The material presented is based on five years of field research in Nagano prefecture, Japan, conducted in 1967–8, 1970, 1972–5 and 1984. The research was supported in part by a grant from Fulbright-Hayes (Institute of International Education), by two NDEA Title VI grants, and through a Harvard Comparative International Program Ford Foundation Grant. I am grateful to T.M.S. Evens for extensive comments on this and earlier versions of this paper.

1 '[E]ven if reversibility is the objective truth of the discrete acts which . . . are called gift exchanges, it is not the whole truth of a practice which could not exist if it were consciously perceived in accordance with the model' (Bourdieu 1977: 6).

2 Smith puts this strongly (1983: 74): 'It is not mere idle speculation to suggest that our understanding of these matters would be very different today if over the past thirty-five years research had been conducted in the framework of the interactionist social psychology of figures like George Herbert Mead and Henry Stack Sullivan . . . . Had the intellectual influences been different, we should long since have had an eminently plausible picture of the Japanese conception of the self.' Plath's *Long Engagements* (1980) is an intriguing experiment toward an interactional portrayal of the life-cycle.

3 These criticisms are extensive, and include three conferences on alternative models: at Shaker Town, Kentucky, in August 1978 (organized by Harumi Befu); in Yamanashi prefecture, Japan, in July 1979 (organized by Befu and Nakano Takashi); and in Canberra, Australia, in May 1980 (organized by Sugimoto and Mouer). The latter produced a special issue of *Social Analysis* (December 1980), as well as a newsletter (*Dialogue*) and a series of research projects aimed at focusing on the individual, instead of the group.

4 For further discussion on logical types see Bateson (1955; reprinted in 1972: 177–93). Confusion over logical levels in 'group model' and 'group' results (in Bateson's words) in a mistake of the order of eating the menu instead of the food.

5 I do not wish to imply that the polar representations are consistent; Evens (1977) discusses the contradictions, paradoxes and confusions surrounding these terms. Stark (1962) uses them as the basis for a history of social thought.

6 On indexicality and deixis see, for example, Jakobson (1957), Benveniste (1971), Fillmore (1975), Silverstein (1976), Lyons (1977), Levinson (1983).

7 As Silverstein puts this (1976: 15), 'All of our analytic techniques and formal descriptive machinery have been designed for referential signs, which contribute to referential utterances in referential speech events.' Index has been approached through reference, as 'riding on' reference, and for this reason has been largely the province of linguists (as well as philosophers).

8 The literature on this subject (including ethnographies) is too extensive to cite. Excellent discussions include Marcus (1980), Marcus and Cushman (1982) and Clifford (1983).

9 See Bachnik and Quinn (1994) and Bachnik (in press).
10 Such a 'proof' is incompatible with the focus of this paper, which assumes (and investigates) the relationship between subject and object, between 'data' and their construction by the researcher, and between the poles of empirical and abstract reality, discussed above.
11 'Emptiness' in Japanese aesthetics may even be related to the emptiness in content of formal (*omote*) communication in such contexts.

REFERENCES

Araki, Hiroyuki (1973) *Nihon no kōdō yōshiki* [*Japanese Behavioural Styles*], Tokyo: Kodansha.
Bachnik, Jane (1982) 'Deixis and Self/Other Reference in Japanese Discourse', *Working Papers in Sociolinguistics*, vol. XCIX, pp. 1–36.
—— (1983) 'Recruitment Strategies for Household Succession: Rethinking Japanese Household Organisation', *Man*, n.s., vol. XVIII, no. 1, pp. 160–82.
—— (in press) *Family, Self and Society in Contemporary Japan*, Berkeley: University of California Press.
—— and Charles J. Quinn (eds) (1994) *Situated Meaning: Inside and Outside in Japanese Self, Society and Language*, Princeton: Princeton University Press.
Bakhtin, Mikhail Mikhailovich (1981) 'Discourse in the Novel', in M. Bakhtin *The Dialogic Imagination: Four Essays* (trans. Caryl Emerson and Michael Holquist), Austin: University of Texas Press, pp. 259–422.
Barthes, Roland (1982) *Empire of Signs*, New York: Hill & Wang.
Bateson, Gregory (1955 [1972]) 'A Theory of Play and Fantasy' (originally published in *A.P.A. Psychiatric Research Reports*, vol. II, 1955), reprinted in G. Bateson *Steps to an Ecology of Mind*, New York: Chandler, pp. 177–93.
Beardsley, Richard K., John W. Hall and Robert E. Ward (1959) *Village Japan*, Chicago: University of Chicago Press.
Becker, A. L. and I. Gusti Ngurah Oka (1974) 'Person in Kawi: Exploration of an Elementary Semantic Dimension', *Oceanic Linguistics*, vol. XIII, nos 1/2, pp. 229–55.
Befu, Harumi (1971) *Japan: An Anthropological Introduction*, San Francisco: Chandler.
—— (1980) 'A Critique of the Group Model of Japanese Society', *Social Analysis*, nos 5/6, pp. 29–43.
Befu, Harumi and Edward Norbeck (1958) 'Japanese Usages of Terms of Relationship', *Southwestern Journal of Anthropology*, vol. XIV, pp. 66–86.
Benedict, Ruth (1946) *The Chrysanthemum and the Sword*, New York: Houghton Mifflin.
Benveniste, Emile (1971) *Problems in General Linguistics*, Coral Gables: University of Miami Press (Miami Linguistic Series, no. 8).
Bourdieu, Pierre (1977) *Outline of a Theory of Practice* (trans. Richard Nice), Cambridge: Cambridge University Press.
Buchler, Justus (ed.) (1940) *The Philosophy of Peirce: Selected Writings*, London: Routledge & Kegan Paul.
Clifford, James (1983) 'On Ethnographic Authority', *Representations*, vol. I, no. 2, pp. 118–46.
Cole, Robert E. (1979) *Work, Mobility and Participation: A Comparative Study of American and Japanese Industry*, Berkeley and Los Angeles: University of California Press.
Cornell, John (1956) 'Matsunagi', in R.J. Smith and J.B. Cornell *Two Japanese Villages*, Ann Arbor: University of Michigan Press (Center for Japanese Studies, Occasional Papers, no. 5), pp. 113–232.
Dillard, Annie (1974) *Pilgrim at Tinker Creek*, New York: Bantam Books.
Doi, L. Takeo (1973a) '*Omote* and *Ura*: Concepts Derived from the Japanese Two-fold

Structure of Consciousness', *Journal of Nervous and Mental Disease*, vol. CLV, no. 4, pp. 258–61.

—— (1973b) *The Anatomy of Dependence* (trans. John Bester), Tokyo: Kodansha.

Embree, John F. (1939) *Suye Mura: A Japanese Village*, Chicago: University of Chicago Press.

Evens, T.M.S. (1977) 'The Predication of the Individual in Anthropological Interactionism', *American Anthropologist*, vol. LXXIX, no. 3, pp. 579–97.

Fillmore, Charles J. (1975) *Santa Cruz Lectures of Deixis 1971*, Bloomington: Indiana University Linguistics Club.

Fischer, J.L. (1964) 'Words for Self and Other in Some Japanese Families', *American Anthropologist*, vol. LXVI, no. 6 (part 2, special publication), pp. 115–26.

Forchheimer, Paul (1953) *The Category of Person in Language*, Berlin: Walter de Gruyter.

Geertz, Clifford (1960) *The Religion of Java*, Glencoe, IL: The Free Press.

—— (1973) 'Person, Time, and Conduct in Bali' (first published New Haven: Yale University Southeast Asia Studies 1965), reprinted in C. Geertz *The Interpretation of Cultures*, New York: Basic Books, pp. 360–411.

Gumperz, John J. (1982) *Discourse Strategies*, Cambridge: Cambridge University Press.

Hamabata, Matthews M. (1983) 'Women in Love and Power: Social Networks and Business Families in Modern Japanese Society', PhD dissertation, Harvard University.

Hartshorne, Charles and Paul Weiss (eds) (1931) *Collected Papers of Charles S. Peirce*, Cambridge, MA: Harvard University Press, vol. 3.

Head, Brian (1978) 'Respect Degrees in Reference', in Joseph Greenberg (ed.) *Universals of Human Language*, Stanford: Stanford University Press, vol. 3, pp. 151–211.

Heidegger, Martin (1962) *Being and Time* (trans. John Macquarrie and Edward Robinson), New York: Harper & Row.

Jakobson, Roman (1957) *Shifters, Verbal Categories and the Russian Verb*, Cambridge, MA: Harvard University Press.

Jorden, Eleanor (1978) 'Linguistic Fraternization: A Guide for the *Gaijin*', in *Proceedings of the Symposium on Japanese Sociolinguistics, 1978*, San Antonio, Texas: Trinity University, pp. 103–23.

Kitaoji, Hiranobu (1971) 'The Structure of the Japanese Family', *American Anthropologist*, vol. LXXIII, pp. 1036–57.

Kumon, Shumpei (1982) 'Some Principles Governing the Thought and Behavior of Japanologists (Contextualists)', *The Journal of Japanese Studies*, vol. VIII, no. 1, pp. 5–28.

Leach, Edmund (1964) 'Anthropological Aspects of Language: Animal Categories and Verbal Abuse', in Eric H. Lenneberg (ed.) *New Directions in the Study of Language*, Cambridge, MA: M.I.T. Press, pp. 23–63.

Lebra, Takie (1976) *Japanese Patterns of Behavior*, Honolulu: University of Hawaii Press.

Levinson, Stephen C. (1983) *Pragmatics*, Cambridge: Cambridge University Press.

Luong, Hy Van (1984) '"Brother" and "Uncle": An Analysis of Rules, Structural Contradictions, and Meaning in Vietnamese Kinship', *American Anthropologist*, vol. LXXXVI, no. 2, pp. 290–315.

Lyons, John (1977) *Semantics*, Cambridge: Cambridge University Press, vol. 2.

Maraini, Fosco (1975) 'Japan and the Future: Some Suggestions from *Nihonjin-ron* Literature', in Gianni Fodella (ed.) *Social Structures and Economic Dynamics in Japan up to 1980*, Milan: Institute of Economic and Social Studies for East Asia, Luigi Bocconi University, (Series on East Asian Economy and Society, no. 1), pp. 15–77.

Marcus, George E. (1980) 'Rhetoric and the Ethnographic Genre in Anthropological Research', *Current Anthropology*, vol. XXI, no. 4, pp. 507–10.

Marcus, George E. and Dick Cushman (1982) 'Ethnographies as Texts', *Annual Review of Anthropology*, vol. XI, pp. 25–69.

Merleau-Ponty, Maurice (1962) *Phenomenology of Perception* (trans. Colin Smith), London: Routledge & Kegan Paul.

Nakamura, Hajime (1968) 'Consciousness of the Individual and the Universal among the Japanese', in Charles A. Moore (ed.) *The Status of the Individual in East and West*, Honolulu: University of Hawaii Press, pp. 141–60.

Nakane, Chie (1967) *Kinship and Economic Organization in Rural Japan*, London: Athlone Press.

—— (1970) *Japanese Society*, Berkeley and Los Angeles: University of California Press.

—— (1972) *Tekio no jōken* [*Situational Adaptation*], Tokyo: Kodansha.

Neustupný, J. V. (1978) 'The Variability of Japanese Honorifics' in *Proceedings of the Symposium on Japanese Sociolinguistics 1978*, San Antonio, Texas: Trinity University, pp. 125–46.

Norbeck, Edward (1954) *Takashima*, Salt Lake City: University of Utah Press.

Ortega y Gasset, José (1957) *Man and People* (trans. Willard R. Trask), New York: W. W. Norton & Co.

Plath, David W. (1964) 'Where the Family of God is the Family', *American Anthropologist*, vol. LXVI, pp. 300–17.

—— (1976) 'Cycles, Circles, Selves: Consociation in the Japanese City', paper presented at Workshop on the Japanese City, Mount Kisco, New York, 23–7 April.

—— (1980) *Long Engagements: Maturity in Modern Japan*, Stanford: Stanford University Press.

Proceedings of the Symposium on Japanese Sociolinguistics 1978, (The Summer Institute of the Linguistic Society of America at the University of Hawaii, 1977), San Antonio, Texas: Trinity University.

Rohlen, Thomas P. (1974) *For Harmony and Strength: Japanese White-collar Organization in Anthropological Perspective*, Berkeley and Los Angeles: University of California Press.

von Senden, Marius (1960 [1932]) *Space and Sight* (trans. Peter Heath), Glencoe, IL: The Free Press.

Silverstein, Michael (1976) 'Shifters, Linguistic Categories, and Cultural Description' in Keith Basso and Henry Selby (eds) *Meaning in Anthropology*, Albuquerque: University of New Mexico Press, pp. 11–54.

Smith, Robert J. (1983) *Japanese Society: Tradition, Self and the Social Order*, Cambridge: Cambridge University Press.

Stark, Werner (1962) *The Fundamental Forms of Social Thought*, London: Routledge & Kegan Paul.

Straus, Erwin (1967) 'On Anosognosia', in E.W. Straus and R.M. Griffith (eds) *The Phenomenology of Will and Action*, Duquesne: Duquesne University Press, pp. 103–26.

Sugimoto, Yoshio and Ross Mouer (1980) 'Reappraising Images of Japanese Society', *Social Analysis*, nos 5/6, pp. 5–19.

Suzuki, Takao (1973) *Kotoba to bunka* [*Language and Culture*], Tokyo: Iwanami Shoten.

—— (1976) 'Language and Behavior in Japan: The Conceptualization of Interpersonal Relationships', *Japan Quarterly*, vol. XXIII, pp. 255–66.

—— (1978a) '*Hito* as a Self-Specifier and *Otaku, Kare* and *Kanojo* as Other-Specifiers', in *Proceedings of the Symposium on Japanese Sociolinguistics 1978*, San Antonio, Texas: Trinity University, pp. 195–204.

—— (1978b) *Japanese and the Japanese: Words in Culture* (trans. Miura Akira), Tokyo: Kodansha International.

Wolff, Jonathan Hart (1980) 'Linguistic Socialization, Self and Personal Referents in Japanese', MA thesis, Cornell University.

Yamadori, Atsushi and Martin L. Albert (1973) 'Word Category Aphasia', *Cortex*, vol. IX, no. 1, pp. 112–25.

Yanaga, Chitoshi (1968) *Big Business in Japanese Politics*, New Haven: Yale University Press.

7 Is the *ie* disappearing in rural Japan?

The impact of tourism on a traditional Japanese village

Okpyo Moon

The *ie*, or the traditional family system in Japan which used to be characterized by strong patriarchal control and inequality among its members, was formally abolished in 1947 with the introduction of the New Constitution. The New Constitution prescribed instead a more 'democratic' family system based on the equal rights of husbands and wives (Ōtake 1995). The continuous trend of the so-called 'nuclearization' of household composition witnessed since the early 1950s has also led many sociologists to believe that the *ie* no longer functions as a real sociological entity even in rural Japan.[1] Hasumi writes, for instance:

> The postwar Japanese capitalist economy, founded on highly advanced technology and state monopoly, has a reproductive structure that is quite different from that of the prewar period. Contrary to the prewar Japanese system (which is rooted in the functioning of the *ie* and the *mura*, or 'village' organisation), postwar Japanese capitalism has in fact developed by undermining the foundations of rural familes. What has become critically at issue nowadays is not the *ie* or the *mura* organisations themselves but the 'undermined' family life, the various kinds of responses to the dissolution of traditional *ie*, and the new organizations that have emerged in this process.
>
> (1973: 6)

The importance of the *ie* in understanding contemporary Japanese society has been denied even by some anthropologists who are more interested in emphasizing the changing aspects of Japanese village life rather than in delineating the constant cultural features: 'Much of what has been written concerning the household (*ie*), extended household (*dōzoku*) and hamlet (*buraku*) expresses an ideal that may have been true in the past, but is no longer strictly adhered to in practice' (Moeran 1981: 42).

Notwithstanding such denials, my own experience in the field makes me more inclined to agree with the following remarks made by a rather 'culturalogically' oriented Japanese rural sociologist.

> Once one enters into a Japanese village, one cannot avoid admitting, sometimes with pain, that the reality of what has been talked about, for want of a noble term, as "family life" comes to one much more vividly if one describes

it as the *ie* life. . . . Even the modern volunteer organisations such as environmental movement groups work on the basis of the *ie* and the *mura*. . . . Undoubtedly there are many aspects that distinguish the postwar *ie* and *mura* from the prewar *ie* and *mura* and in those respects we may say that they are different. However, the substance still seems to be what can only be expressed as *ie* and *mura* and nothing else.

(Torikoe 1996: iii)

Among the specifically cultural features that 'can only be expressed as *ie* . . . and nothing else', we may include an emphasis upon continuity, succession practices and some of the socio-religious functions that still occupy an important place in contemporary rural family life in Japan. On the basis of an analysis of detailed ethnographic materials drawn from one particular village in central Japan, this paper aims at depicting the actual process of the transformation of the *ie* in the face of drastic economic changes in the country. The paper is based mainly upon data collected during my original fieldwork in the village in 1981–82 (see Moon 1989), but I visited the village again in 1991, 1992 and 1993 for further research, and some of the results of these latter visits have also been incorporated.

THE VILLAGE

The village, Hanasaku, is located about 800 metres above sea level at the north-eastern end of Gunma prefecture. Before the Second World War, the economy of the village was based mainly on a half-yearly farming of staple food crops such as barley and soybeans, with sericulture as a major supplementary source of cash income. Charcoal-burning and timbering were also pursued during the agriculturally slack seasons. As in many other Japanese villages, agriculture in Hanasaku has undergone several significant changes since the Second World War. The most notable of these is the drastic reduction of the farm population.[2] The village economy was further shattered by the post-war decline in the demand for charcoal as a fuel, as well as for nationally produced timber and dry-field crops.[3] As a consequence, many villages under similar circumstances, especially in the north-eastern part of the country, have lost a substantial portion of their population to the urban industrial sector through migration; and by the mid-1960s, the problems of rural under-population (*kasomondai*) had already become one of the major issues of rural sociology in Japan.[4]

Events in Hanasaku have followed a somewhat different path, however. During the early 1960s, a ski resort was opened on the village territory, and this resort, together with the subsequently developed shops and country inns (*minshuku*), have provided the people with alternative winter-time occupations. In 1981, after some twenty years, these developments finally began to curb the constant outflow of the village population. Table 7.1 shows how the population of the village had decreased from 1,160 to 881 between 1960 and 1975. It has begun to increase since then, however, and had reached 1,013 in 1993. On the other hand, we may note that the number of households has increased from 205 to 214, even during

Table 7.1 Population of Hanasaku village, 1960–93

Year	No. of households	Male	Female	Total
1960	205	569	591	1,160
1965	207	554	550	1,104
1970	202	493	492	985
1975	207	441	440	881
1980	214	440	448	888
1993	256	—	—	1,013

the period of constant population decline between 1960 and 1975. By 1993 there were 256 households in the village.[5] These statistics closely reflect the ways by which the traditional household organization, the *ie*, adapts itself to the changing economic situation in Hanasaku. To examine this process is the focus of this study.

THE CORPORATE FUNCTIONS OF THE *IE*: PAST AND PRESENT

In the past, most households in the village used to function as corporate productive units. Farming of the family estate used to be carried out jointly by household members under the supervision of the household head. The average holding of farmland per household is about three to four acres in this village. The intensive cultivation of this area and the two-yearly croppings of silk worms used to require the labour of the whole household. The pattern was similar for another household enterprise, charcoal-burning, which was pursued by most families in Hanasaku until some time after the Second World War. For the construction of the family kiln, for instance, all the members of the household, including women and children, used to work together, and although the charcoal itself was produced by the male members alone, the women cooperated by making the sacks.

The way in which people distributed the trees for charcoal-making also indicates the indivisible character of the household as an economic unit. As in many other parts of Japan, the residents of this village used jointly to purchase a part of the state-owned mountain forest each year for charcoal-making. Once trees were purchased in the name of the village, however, their division was always done on the basis of the number of households in the village and never by the number of individuals who were able to pursue the occupation. Depending on the developmental stage of each household, therefore, some may have had no male members to do the job, while others may have had two or three. In such cases, the former usually resold their own share to the latter at a higher price.

The post-war decline of the charcoal industry has already been mentioned. Agriculture has suffered a similar decline. The spread of new technology, including farm machinery, chemical fertilizers, insecticides, herbicides and so forth, has been such that the agricultural population has been greatly reduced. Nowadays, most households in Hanasaku have only one or two members working on the land, and most of these are women. For certain tasks such as rice-transplanting or harvesting, the husbands, most of whom now work in one of the wage-earning occupations, sometimes cooperate with their wives, but younger members of the household rarely participate in farm work. These changes in the pattern of the household economy have had some consequences for succession practices.

HOUSEHOLD SUCCESSION AS AFFECTED BY ECONOMIC CHANGE: A COMPARISON BETWEEN AGRICULTURAL AND *MINSHUKU* HOUSEHOLDS

As has been amply documented by ethnographers on Japan, the *ie* is based on a one-child inheritance system, and the commonest form of household composition in Hanasaku is what one may term a 'stem-family', namely, a family containing two or more married couples in successive generations with one married couple in each generation. Succession to the household mainly consists of succession to the office of the household head, who assumes the role of manager of the household property and its enterprise, and has responsibility for the ancestor ritual as well as for the aged parents. Although it became necessary in Meiji law to register the property as legally belonging to the household head as an individual (Isono 1964: 40–1; Dore 1958: 101), in practice the property is still conceived of as belonging to the household as a whole, and the household succession also involves the transmission of a large part of its property as well.

Although there are regional variations, in general two sets of preferences are observed in the selection of the successor within the household: male rather than female, and older rather than younger. In short, the eldest son is the preferred choice.[6] As Bachnik has pointed out (1983: 164), however, in the selection of the successor, the emphasis is always placed on the continuity of the household as a corporate group rather than the continuity of any particular individual within the group.

This raises difficulties for the labelling of succession practices in Japanese households by means of conventional anthropological terminology, such as 'patrilineal', 'matrilineal' or 'bilateral', all of which refer to individual continuity rather than corporate continuity. The generally preferred strategy based on male/female and older/younger hierarchies can always be reversed for the greater benefit of the household group. If the eldest son is physically or mentally incompetent, or if he is considered incompatible with the group for various reasons, a younger son may be chosen as the successor, even when the eldest son wants to remain in the household. Similarly, a daughter or, in theory, a completely unrelated person may also be chosen as the successor. In fact, only about half the present heads of households in Hanasaku are the eldest sons of the previous heads; the rest are either branch households or households succeeded by a junior son, a daughter or an adopted child.[7]

The succession practices in Japanese households thus allow a good deal of scope for flexibility to accommodate a changing situation. Since, theoretically, any of the children may succeed to the household, migration of the young to cities may take place with relatively less disruptive effects on the continuity of their households in the village (cf. also Tauber 1951; Vogel 1967). On the other hand, it may also be stated that the recent increase in economic opportunities other than agriculture has reduced the number of potential successors.

In the past, when land was the major means of production, succession to the existing household also meant access to a livelihood. In that situation, therefore, one may assume that the parents were in a better position in choosing a successor than nowadays, when few young people are interested in farming as an occupation. Moreover, even when a child is secured as the successor to the household, the second problem is to recruit his or her spouse to reproduce the household. As already indicated, the recent pattern requires women to work on the land while their husbands may be employed elsewhere. Many of the farm households are therefore having considerable difficulties in finding a daughter-in-law for their successors. One of the consequences is that successors to farm households tend to marry late.

To find a man willing to be adopted into the household as husband of the succeeding daughter is similarly difficult. As a married-in member the status of the adopted husband within the household is relatively low. Even in the past, therefore, it was not considered a desirable course for a man. Hence the proverb, 'If you have three measures of rice bran, don't go as an adopted husband' (*Kome nuka sango areba, yōshi ni wa ikunazo*). When other economic opportunities were limited, however, many of the second or third sons had to marry into another household for their livelihood. Moreover, although some young people in Hanasaku work as wage labourers in the ski grounds, the construction fields or one of the few local shops and factories, none of these jobs has been stable or prestigious enough to attract young people. As a result, young people who do not want to work on the farm and are not interested in the other occupations available tend to leave the village. Many villages in similar circumstances have either become commuter villages, if they are close to urban centres, or in remoter areas have become underpopulated.

THE IMPACT OF THE DEVELOPMENT OF THE TOURIST INDUSTRY

After the advent of tourism in Hanasaku one of the ways adopted by people in the village to keep the young at home and thus to ensure the continuity of the household has been to start a *minshuku*. *Minshuku* is a blanket term for all the kinds of inn and small hotel developed in the countryside for the lodging and entertainment of tourists. The word apparently came into common usage in the early 1960s with the growth of what is known as *rējabūmu*, the Japanese transcription of 'leisure boom'. The literal meaning of *minshuku*, 'staying with the people', seems to have attracted many city-dwellers, especially young people, with its rather romantic idea of learning about country life and mixing with the local people.

As the volume of tourism within the country rapidly increased with the general improvement of the country's economic conditions in the early 1960s,[8] many *minshuku* villages appeared in the Japanese countryside. Usually, *minshuku* villages appear in an area where there are already some natural tourist attractions such as well-known mountains, lakes, hot-springs, and so forth. Some more recent ones, however, seem to start *minshuku* first as a means of earning supplementary cash income, and to develop tourist attractions later. The bulletin of the national association for country inn operators includes some rather bizarre but ingenious inventions such as hot milk baths, perfume baths or herb saunas. Others concentrate more on local specialities such as special mushroom cooking, mountain vegetable dishes or seafood dishes, etc. Another way of attracting the attention of city people is to build sports facilities. Spiritual as well as physical discipline is often strongly emphasized in Japan, and sports seem to provide an effective means toward this end. During the summer, therefore, many young people are encouraged to stay together and to have training for one kind of sport or another. Such an activity is commonly known as *gasshuku*, literally meaning 'staying together', and *gasshuku* teams of young people in large numbers have been one of the major attractions for *minshuku* villages.

Minshuku in Hanasaku began to appear immediately after the opening of the Olympia ski resort, so called to signify that it was opened in 1964, the year of the Tokyo Olympics. As the tourists gradually outnumbered the lodging capacity of the Olympia hotel attached to the resort, the company owning the hotel and the local branch of the association for commerce and industry encouraged local people to open *minshuku*, and the number gradually increased. In 1993 there were eighty-eight *minshuku* altogether in the village, while the number was only about sixty in 1981, when I did my first fieldwork. As business developed, the inn operators began to build other sports facilities to attract tourists even during the non-skiing seasons, especially during the summer when the weather remains comparatively cool in this area. There are now in the village two gymnasia, one owned by the Olympia company and the other by the village, sports grounds equipped with electric lights for night games, and numerous tennis courts. Many *minshuku* in the village now own individual tennis courts for their own guests. In addition to the Olympia, there were in 1981 two more ski resorts near the village on the state-owned mountain slopes, and many people from Hanasaku also worked there during the winter. In 1993, when I revisited the village, four more ski slopes had been opened nearby, three of them owned and managed by the local government itself, which is eager to develop tourism in the area.

Unlike farm households, *minshuku* households have largely maintained the character of the traditional household as an economic unit, due to the nature of their business. Most *minshuku* households in Hanasaku carry on farming as a supplementary occupation to varying degrees. Within the household, therefore, there is a certain degree of division of labour in carrying out the two 'combined-household' enterprises. In a three-generation household, for instance, the older couple tends to concentrate on farming while the younger couple is mainly in charge of the inn business. The division of labour, however, is not always clear-cut, since there are always tasks to which any member of the household can contribute when required. Such tasks as cleaning up the guest rooms, preparing the beds, washing up in the kitchen, setting the table, cooking, receiving or fetching guests in a car can be done by any of the members. The inn business, therefore, provides far more occasions for the cooperation of household members than does farming. Even children of school age who almost never participate in farm work usually contribute labour to *minshuku* work. Unlike kin employed from outside the household, the members of the household are not paid separate wages, since, as the people put it, they are carrying out 'the work of the house' (*uchi no shigoto*), which is for the household as a whole and not for any particular member of the group.

By contrast, we may note a different tendency in farm households. I have already mentioned that there had been a general decline in agriculture after the Second World War. To compensate for the income deficiency, many Japanese farmers adopted a strategy of diversification of the household economy, that is, a strategy of combining agriculture with other work for the survival of the household as a whole. The result was a rapid increase in the so-called 'part-time farm households' (*kengyōnōka*). Even at the time of my original research in 1981, there were very few households relying solely on farming for their livelihood. When I visited the village in the early 1990s, some ten years later, I found that the agricultural population had further decreased as the aged parents retired from farmwork, while few of the younger generation took up the job.

In the case of the households which combine farming and other relatively unstable wage-earning jobs, therefore, the continuity is clearly threatened. On the other hand, by providing their successors not only with land and a house but also with an occupation more attractive than farming, the *minshuku* households are in a much better position to secure a successor than the farm households. Similarly, it can be stated that the ideology of household continuity has played a significant role in determining the pattern of the changing village economy, especially that of the emergence of numerous small-scale country inns as household enterprises.

CHANGES IN THE INTERNAL STATUS STRUCTURE OF THE HOUSEHOLD

A certain change in the status structure of the traditional household is, however, noticeable. In the past, when all the members of the household were engaged in the same economic activities, whether farming, silk-worm raising or charcoal-burning, skills and knowledge largely obtained through experience had always been transmitted from parents to children, from the previous head of the household to the successor. Nowadays, most of the young people have had city experience of varying periods and so accumulated a different kind of knowledge from that of their parents, most of whom have never left the village. Some of the inheriting children of *minshuku* households have had training as professional chefs, while others may have had brief experience working in a hotel in the city. Even without such specific qualifications, the simple fact of youth and urban experience makes the young better suited to the newly developed tourist industry.

Most young people have high-school education nowadays and they usually speak standard Japanese. Hanasaku has a fairly strong dialect whose vocabulary differs substantially from standard Japanese. People of the village, therefore, find it difficult to deal with tourists from Tokyo and surrounding urban areas. Most tourists are young, and the young hotel workers understand them better.

Within the household, therefore, there has been a diffusion of authority. In many of the *minshuku* in Hanasaku the actual head of the household is not always the boss (or *oyakata*) of the work of the *minshuku*. Even when the parents are still mainly in charge of the business with regard to its major financial transactions, the actual dealings with the guests are often delegated to the younger members of the household. In general, it seems that the opinions of the young are much more respected than before in the running of the household enterprise.

Changes in status structure are even more striking in farming households in the village. Since most men are not fully engaged in farming they are no longer the chief decision-makers within the household either. In many farm households it is the wives, the actual farmers, who decide which crops to cultivate, what area is to be given to each crop and so forth. It is also these wives who most frequently represent the households in hamlet meetings concerning agricultural matters. Moreover, it is mostly the women who order and purchase fertilizers, seeds, and silk-worm eggs, as well as household goods through the agricultural cooperative. During the harvest all the farm households in each hamlet take turns in recording each day's delivery of crops, another task mostly carried out by women.

Most of all, however, it is knowledge of the new agricultural machinery that enhances women's status within the household in general. To drive the powered cultivator, for instance, one needs a licence, which must be obtained by taking a written and practical examination in a nearby town and which has to be renewed every two years. Most farm household women in the village now have this licence. In addition, most of them are able to manipulate the powered huller, the thresher or the rice mill. Such skills are unknown to the previous generation. In the traditional Japanese household the male head is often referred to as the 'principal pillar' or *daikoku bashira* of the house. Commenting on the increased responsibilities of women and their recent importance in the household, therefore, old people often remark that the *yome*, the daughter-in-law of the house, is nowadays as much a *daikoku bashira* as the household head.

The diversification of farm household economy has also affected the traditional authority of the household head over his successor. In the past the household head was the manager of the household property, the supervisor of the household work-group and the keeper of the family purse. When land was the only meaningful source of livelihood, the authority of the household head was often economically reinforced, especially in his relationship with the potential successor, since the former could always resort to the threat of disinheritance whenever disagreements occurred between the two. As more people have become involved in wage-earning or salaried occupations, however, the economic basis of this authority has also inevitably been undermined. It is in the light of these changes that starting an inn becomes a significant advantage for the parents in consolidating the household unit. Unlike farm households, where successors now inherit merely the household headship, duties for parents and ancestors, and community obligations, successors to *minshuku* households also inherit the business. Although the latter sometimes involves a certain amount of debt as well, it nevertheless seems to be more appealing to the young, both male and female.

CONTINUITY IN SOME OF THE SOCIO-RELIGIOUS FUNCTIONS OF THE HOUSEHOLD

I have so far argued that the new economic opportunities created by the advent of tourism in Hanasaku have been incorporated into village society in a way that helps perpetuate household organization in its traditional form, and that the ideology concerning the continuity of the household unit has played a significant role in shaping the newly developed tourist industry in the village. Certain aspects of the people's religious life also support this argument.

The traditional importance of the household or the *ie* in village life is reflected in the numerous rituals centring around the houses and household members. Each house in Hanasaku, for instance, has a tutelary deity of its own known as *yashiki-inari*, a small wooden or stone statue contained in a miniature house, usually found at one corner of the back garden. The deity belongs to the house itself and is believed to protect its contents and inmates. In addition to the *yashiki-inari* of the main building there are a number of minor deities for each of the smaller buildings usually found in a farmhouse compound (barn, godown, warehouse, etc.). Most of the farm households in Hanasaku also have their own gods of the fields and water sources somewhere in the mountains. Although no specific rites are performed in relation to any of these gods, except for the daily offering of rice to the *yashiki-inari*, all are recognized annually at the New Year by the offering of a pine branch decorated with some auspicious objects such as dried cuttlefish, sardines and mandarin oranges. The purpose of these ritual decorations is said to be to purify these places for the coming year, and the offering is often preceded by a general cleaning of the house.

Apart from the purificatory New Year decorations of pine branches, the month of January, the least busy month for agriculture, used to be the month devoted to numerous ritual activities centring around the household group. Many rituals such as the 'first fetching of water' rite or the New Year's ceremonial call around the hamlet by household heads, have now disappeared. Similarly, as a consequence of economic diversification and of the changes in the people's work-cycle, some of the rites which are specifically related to certain agricultural enterprises such as silk-worm raising or rice-transplanting are no longer observed either. What is significant in the present context, however, is the recent increase in the volume of rituals by which people can express the relative social status of their households within the community. These rites include the *yakudoshi* feasts and the ancestor memorial services.

The rite of *yakudoshi* is a rite performed for those who in that year reach the ages which are regarded as especially vulnerable and inauspicious. The custom is widespread in Japan,[9] but the actual years which are considered unlucky vary from area to area. In Hanasaku, these unlucky years or *yakudoshi* are the 19th and 33rd year for a woman and the 25th and 42nd year for a man. These years are considered 'dangerous' because they are the times when people undergo mental and physical changes. To exorcise or drive out possible attack by an evil spirit, therefore, a purification rite is performed by a communal burning of the New Year decorations. Around 13 January, for instance, people take down their decorations, remove the food items and leave them on their doorsteps. The branches are then collected by those who have advanced to unlucky ages in that year, and on 14 January, the members of their households make a bonfire with these branches. During the display, to which all the other hamlet members are invited, the mandarin oranges are distributed and the dried cuttlefish are grilled on the fire and shared among those present. The explanation given is that the burning of pine branches is to 'purify' (*yaku o harau*), and the sharing of food is to share the 'spiritual danger' (*yaku*) which has fallen on one member of the household.

Later in the evening, after the bonfire, the families of the *yakudoshi* people again hold a big feast at their own houses for relatives and neighbours. The idea of 'sharing the spiritual danger' is still prevalent. The occasion, however, also provides an opportunity for social recognition of the respective standing of each household within the community, especially when those who fall in the unlucky years are men, household heads or the would-be successors of the households. When, for instance, it is a daughter or a daughter-in-law who has reached one of the unlucky ages, those who are invited to the household feast include in most cases only the members of one's immediate neighbourhood group and relatives who live within the same hamlet. For succeeding sons and household heads, on the other hand, their guests include the members of all the associations to which the *yakudoshi* person belongs, those of his workplace, those of his age-group, as well as neighbours, relatives and members of the extended household.[10] Relatives living in other hamlets are also supposed to visit. The larger the number of visitors the better, since all the visitors are believed to share the spiritual danger of the person concerned. Since there are usually a number of *yakudoshi* people every year, villagers usually make a round of visits during the course of the night, or else different members of the household are sent to different households according to the sex and age of the *yakudoshi* person concerned.

As already indicated, the *yakudoshi* feasts have greatly increased in scale in recent years. Even in one of the six hamlets in Hanasaku, where the largest number of country inns has grown up, and where the purificatory bonfire ceremony was dropped a few years ago owing to poor attendance – January being the busiest skiing season – the *yakudoshi* feasts prosper more than ever before. Another example of a household ritual which has increased in recent years is the ancestor memorial service. In theory, memorial services for ancestors are supposed to be held on the first, third, seventh, thirteenth, seventeenth, twenty-third, twenty-seventh, thirty-third and finally the fiftieth calendar year after the death of a person. In former times, however, these services could be held only by the most well-to-do families in this village, and even then only for a limited number of years. They have become much more ubiquitous nowadays, and these household feasts are sometimes used for a political end. For instance, anyone who is interested in local political office often holds as many household feasts as possible to invite neighbours and relatives. While giving out money to the voters is illegal, these activities are considered acceptable. On the whole, with the general improvement in living standards, these household rituals seem to have provided many with a means by which they can translate their newly gained economic prosperity into social influence, and thus enhance their relative status within the community.

In this connection, one may note a similar tendency in new house buildings and new gravestones. In the past, people apparently erected a small gravestone for each of the dead members of the household. Nowadays they often erect a huge gravestone in the name of the household as a whole. At grave sites, therefore, one often finds nowadays huge gravestones with an engraving of the 'House of such-and-such', with a smaller flat stone standing beside it, on which the names of a number of the recently deceased household members are engraved. By its size and shape most people in the village can tell immediately approximately how much such a stone has cost. Like house buildings, therefore, these stones clearly express the relative prosperity of each household. Another relevant example may be the posthumous Buddhist names presented to the dead members of the household. The rank of posthumous names differs with the kind of Chinese characters used (e.g. *tokuingo*, *ingo*, *kengo*, etc.) as well as depending on the number of characters. The rank of one's posthumous name is supposedly determined by one's deeds and achievements during one's lifetime. In reality, however, it more often reflects the worldly success or failure of one's descendants, and for this reason, posthumous names have provided another opportunity by which people can express their relative status.

CONCLUSION

In their attempt to explain the relationship between economic development and social change, those advocating what is commonly known as 'the modernization approach' assume that one can describe the general features of 'traditional' and 'modern' societies and treat development as the transformation of the one type into the other (cf. W. Moore 1963: 89). The change from a traditional to a modern society is conceptualized as entailing the eventual modification or elimination of 'traditional' pattern variables (see also Hoselitz 1960; Eisenstadt 1966, 1970; Bennett 1967; Dalton 1971). The data analysed in this article seriously challenge this generalized view of the unilineal transformation of societies. As has been indicated, many aspects of post-war economic change in Hanasaku match the elements which are believed to affect social transformation: the mechanization of cultivation techniques, the introduction of cash crops, greater involvement in wage-earning activities and increased individual mobility. Not only has the wealth in the village greatly increased, but its economy has also considerably diversified over the past twenty-five years, as more people have become involved in small businesses, shops, construction work and the like, with the resultant increase in cash income and general prosperity in the village. These changes in the economic sphere, however, have not brought about concomitant changes in social organization, and particularly so as regards the household unit.

As we have seen, the development of a tourist industry in Hanasaku has provided those of its residents who are faced with a potential crisis in household continuity with a positive adaptive strategy with which they can manipulate the changing economic situation to their advantage. The household or the *ie* remains the basic unit of social, political and religious life in Hanasaku, and, as I have discussed elsewhere (Moon 1989), its relative stability accounts for many of the persistent features in the village.

NOTES

1 The percentage of the households with 'nuclear' composition has increased from 43.4 per cent in 1955 to 62.9 per cent in 1988 (Ōtake 1995: 14).
2 According to Fukutake (1981: 50), the population engaged full time in agriculture has dropped from 18 million in 1950 to about 13.9 million in 1960, and again to 5.3 million in 1980. In 1993, the number came to just over 4.5 million.
3 The proportion of national supply of grain crops decreased from 53 per cent in 1955 to only about one per cent in 1970 (Sugano 1976: 17).
4 See Kawamoto (1967); Nakayasu (1965); Nōrinshōnōseikyoku (1967); Kunimoto (1973); Fukutake (1981: 18–22). Although it has been more serious in some remoter areas, the phenomenon of rural–urban exodus has been noted for the country as a whole, and the ratio of rural to urban population has almost reversed between 1945 and 1990 from 72: 28 to 23: 77.
5 For a detailed analysis of population changes in Hanasaku, see Moon 1989: chapter 1.
6 It is generally agreed that this practice of male primogeniture became widely prevalent only after the promulgation of the Meiji civil code in which the rule of inheritance was supposedly modelled after the dominant custom among *samurai* families. Until the effects of that civil code became pervasive, however, other types of succession were also practised in certain parts of Japan, such as succession by the youngest child or by the first-born regardless of its gender (cf. Takeda 1951; Izumi and Nagashima 1963; Naito 1970; Suenari 1972; Maeda 1976).
7 According to Nakane (1980: 16), the authority of the household head was greater in wealthier families. Reports also indicate that a choice other than the eldest son was much more frequent for big merchant and warrior households during the Tokugawa period (Nakano 1964; Takeuchi 1954; R. Moore 1970).
8 For a statistical survey of the national and international tourism of the Japanese, see Tamao (1980).
9 For example, David Lewis (in the present volume) reports that *yakudoshi* observances are common among well-educated professionals and white-collar salaried employees in the particular urban area he studied.
10 For detailed description of this ritual, see Moon (1989: 108–10).

REFERENCES

Bachnik, Jane M. (1983) 'Recruitment Strategies for Household Succession: Rethinking Japanese Household Organisation', *Man*, n.s., vol. XVIII, no. 1, pp. 160–82.

Bennett, John W. (1967) 'Japanese Economic Growth: Background for Social Change', in R.P. Dore (ed.) *Aspects of Social Change in Modern Japan*, Princeton, NJ: Princeton University Press, pp. 411–53.

Dalton, George (ed.) (1971) *Economic Development and Social Change: The Modernization of Village Communities*, New York: The Natural History Press.

Dore, Ronald P. (1958) *City Life in Japan*, London: Routledge & Kegan Paul.

Eisenstadt, S. N. (1966) *Modernization: Protest and Change*, Englewood Cliffs, NJ: Prentice-Hall.

—— (1970) 'Social Change and Development', in S. N. Eisenstadt (ed.) *Readings in Social Evolution and Development*, Oxford and London: Pergamon Press, pp. 3–33.

Fukutake, Tadashi (1981) *Japanese Society Today*, Tokyo: University of Tokyo Press.

Hasumi, Otohiko (1973) Nōson Shakaigaku no Kodai to Kōsei [*Tasks and Structure of Rural Sociology*]: *Readings in Sociology 4*, Tokyo: Tokyo University Press.

Hendry, Joy (1995) *Understanding Japanese Society* (second edition), London and New York: Routledge.

Hoselitz, B. F. (1960) *Sociological Factors in Economic Development*, Chicago: Free Press.

Isono, Fujiko (1964) 'The Family and Women in Japan', *The Sociological Review*, vol. XII, no. 1, pp. 39–54.

Izumi, Seiichi and Nobuhiro Nagashima (1963) 'Katoku Sōzoku kara mita Nihon no Higashi to Nishi' [East and West Japan from the Viewpoint of the Succession System], Kokubungaku Kaishaku to Kanshō 28 (5): 121–6.

Kawamoto, Akira (1967) 'Kenkarison no Shakai Kōzō-shimane-ken Sanson no Jirei' [Household Migration and Village Structure: A Case Study of a Mountain Village in Shimane Prefecture], Nōgyō Keizai Kenkyū 38 (1).

Kitahara, Atsushi (1983) 'Mura no shakai' [Village Society], in Mitsusei Matsumoto (ed.) *Chiiki Seikatsu no Shakaigaku* [*Sociology of Country Life*], Tokyo: Sekai Shisosha.

Kunimoto, Yoshiro (1973) 'Deserted Mountain Villages of Western Japan', *Japan Quarterly*, vol. XX, no. 1, pp. 87–96.

Maeda, Takashi (1976) *Summary of* Ane Katoku [Elder Sister Inheritance], Osaka: Kansai University Press.

Moeran, Brian (1981) 'Japanese Social Organisation and the Mingei Movement', *Pacific Affairs*, vol. 54, no. 1, pp. 42–56.

Moon, Ok-pyo (1989) *From Paddy Field to Ski Slope: The Revitalisation of Tradition in Japanese Village Life*, Manchester: Manchester University Press.

Moore, Ray A. (1970) 'Adoption and Samurai Mobility in Tokugawa Japan', *Journal of Asian Studies*, vol. XXIX, no. 3, pp. 617–32.

Moore, W. E. (1963) *Social Change*, Englewood Cliffs, NJ: Prentice-Hall.

Naito, Kanji (1970) 'Inheritance Practices on a Catholic Island: Youngest Son Inheritance', *Social Compass*, vol. XVII, pp. 21–36.

Nakane, Chie (1967) *Kinship and Economic Organisation in Rural Japan*, London: Athlone Press.

—— (1980) Ie no Kōzō [Household Structure], in *Ie*, Tokyo Daigaku Kōkai Kōza 11: 3–27.

Nakano, Takashi (1964) *Shōka dōzokudan no kenkyū* [*A Study of Merchant Dōzokudan*], Tokyo: Miraisha.

Nakayasu, Sadako (1965) 'Kenkarison' [*Household Migration*], Nihon Nōgyō Neapo 14: Henbō suru Nōson, Tokyo: Ochanomizu Shōbo.

Nōrinshōnōseikyoku [Agricultural Department of (Tokyo) City Hall] (1967) *Kasochiiki jittai chōsa hōkoku* [*Reports on the Conditions of Underpopulated Areas*].

Ōtake, Hideo (1995) *Gendai no Kazoku* [*Modern Family*], Tokyo: Kobuntō.

Smith, Robert J. (1978) *Kurusu: The Price of Progress in a Japanese Village, 1951–1975*, Folkestone: Dawson.

Suenari, Michio (1972) 'First Child Inheritance in Japan', *Ethnology*, vol. XI, pp. 122–6.

Sugano, Shunsaku (1976) 'Sanson Keizai Shakai no Kaitei to Saihensei no Ruikei' [The Patterns of Integration and Disintegration of the Economy and Society of Mountain Villages], Sonraku Shakai Kenkyū 12: 1–66.

Takeda, A. (1951) 'Anekatoku to Yōshisei' [Elder Sister Inheritance and Adoption], Minkan Denshō 15 (3): 12–16.

Takeuchi, Toshimi (1976) *Shinshū no Sanraku Seikatsu* [*Village Life in Nagano Prefecture*], vol. I, II, III, Tokyo: Myocho Shuppan.

Tamao, Tokuhisa (1980) 'Tourism Within, From and To Japan', *International Social Science Journal*, vol. XXXII, pp. 128–50.

Tauber, Irene B. (1951) 'Family, Migration and Industrialization in Japan', *American Sociological Review*, vol. XVI, no. 2, pp. 149–57.

Torikoe, Hiroyuki (1996) *Ie to Mura no Shakaigaku* [*Sociology of Family and Village*], (third edition), Tokyo: Sekaishisōsha.

Tsukamoto, Tetsujin (1992) *Gendai Nōson ni Okeru 'Ie' to 'Mura'* [*Ie and Mura in Contemporary Rural Japan*], Tokyo: Miraisha .

Vogel, Ezra F. (1967) 'Kinship Structure, Migration to the City and Modernization', in R. P. Dore (ed.) *Aspects of Social Change in Modern Japan*, Princeton, NJ: Princeton University Press, pp. 91–111.

8 Death rites in Japan in the twentieth century*

Jan van Bremen

> Only through time time is conquered
> T.S. Eliot

DEATH RITES

This chapter takes up the themes and builds on some points made in the first JAWS volume. In her introduction to that collection, Joy Hendry touched on such highly emotive events as abortion, illness and death, and remarked that the anthropologist, as outsider, may be able to take a more dispassionate view (Hendry 1986: 5). In my chapter in that volume, Japanese anthropologists were left undiscussed. The present chapter brings these issues together. It is about rites related to death and abortion, and it is built on work mostly by Japanese anthropologists and folklorists. It may shed light on the seemingly endless but typically vehement discussion over insider versus outsider studies in anthropology. One should see the discipline as a whole.

Space and time are basic variables to any social order and constitute a theme worth taking further. Rites of passage negotiate the breaks in these realms, with birth, marriage and death first among them. Mortuary rites accomplish the disposal of the dead. They can include burial, reburial, cremation, exposure or burial in water. The different forms have the same purpose and function. The rites which involve such procedures are varied in their symbolic meaning. Such rites may, for example, involve the reincorporation of a spirit with its ancestral lineage or the rebirth of a spirit in another world. This is the case in Japan and other societies in Asia.[1]

The theory behind this general notion of mortuary rites was launched by Robert Hertz (1882–1915) in his 1907 work. It distinguishes between primary and secondary death rites, and single and double burial. The impermanent corpse is housed in a single or a double disposal ceremony. Some peoples have a series of secondary rites to help the dead soul on its journey into death. The primary and secondary rites, single and double disposal, beliefs held about the soul of the dead, and the rules of mourning are all sides of death that express the idea of transition. In Japan it is the reincorporation of a spirit with its ancestral lineage or the rebirth of a spirit in another world.

The core of Hertz's study was an analysis of death rites mostly among the Dayak peoples. In the 1970s the Berawan of Borneo (Kalimantan) had double burial and secondary death rites (Metcalf 1982) that structurally resemble rites and beliefs found in other places in Asia where double burials and secondary death rites are prominent such as China, Korea and Japan. It is not important whether a society is simple or complex, literate or illiterate when it comes to considering the purpose and function of mortuary rites.

The term 'complex society' came to be used to refer to peasant and industrialized societies with large populations, state organization, cities, social stratification and literacy, in contrast to small-scale societies which lack most or all of these qualities. It has also been used in a different way: not to contrast complex with simple but to term societies where a number of different civilizations have merged and mixed.[2]

The differences hardly seem to matter when one considers the purpose and function of death rites in Japan and other places in Asia. From the perspective of social organization, primary rites, and rites of double disposal and secondary death rites, occur at different places and times, done by overlapping and different sets of people. The intergenerational rites are performed in the framework of a sociotope by members of past, present and coming generations.[3] The primary death rites tend to be brief. They deal with the remains and should bring about a separation of the dead soul from this world. The secondary death rites take longer to complete and consist of daily, seasonal and special rites. The commencement, continuation, and completion of these rites are an intergenerational work for the members of Japanese families (*ie*) or corporate groups.

The Japanese family does not easily fit the framework of kinship or descent on account of two interrelated features of the *ie*. First, the *ie* is a structural unit consisting of certain roles or positions rather than a group of persons. Roles or positions are defined in the context of the *ie*, a corporate body with its own name, house and property, occupation, status and goal. The members are recognized as such by virtue of the functions they perform in contribution to the *ie*. The second important feature is the mandatory perpetuation of the *ie* through succession over generations. In this context, '*ie*' is best rendered as 'stem-family'. Stem-families consist of at least two generations of conjugal units. Rights and property are handed down from generation to generation and each inheritor becomes the focus for the family organization in that generation. A religious element extends *ie* membership to ancestors as well as to posterity.[4]

If the *ie* continues to exist as a sociotope in spite of its abolition as a legal person, fragmentation of the family, bilaterality, gender equality and individuation subvert the *ie*. Disintegration often surfaces on the death of a household head. Women play a key role in mortuary ritual. New customs such as the separation of mortuary tablets (*ihai wake*) at marriage, the bilateralization of tombs, the merging into a single tomb by two single-child families (*ryōke baka*), joint burial by unmarried or homosexual couples and the co-burial of friends appear. Temples offer 'eternal memorial tombs' (*eidai kuyō baka*) attending to dead souls. Some individuals have their ashes scattered in the sea or over the mountains, a practice reminiscent of traditional graves of disposal (*sute baka*).[5] New ideas have appeared such as the belief in a post-mortem life-cycle.

EXAMPLES OF MEMORIAL RITES IN THE TWENTIETH CENTURY

In the twentieth century in Japan, amid technological and industrial development, primary and secondary death rites have been held on a larger scale than in preceding times. This is due to population growth, the large numbers of dead in wars, natural disasters and accidents, and increased longevity of people. In the first half of the century millions died overseas, in colonies and in wars. Millions died in peacetime in the second half of the century in work accidents, traffic accidents, illnesses, suicides and natural disasters. This has left tens of millions of dead souls to take care of through secondary rites. Endowing not only people but also animals, plants, and things with souls, adds the very large number of dead souls of animals, fish and plants raised, killed, caught and harvested by industries, which have reached unprecedented numbers in the twentieth century.

Rites aimed at the reincorporation of a spirit with its lineage or the rebirth of a spirit in another world are a persistent feature in the religious landscape of the twentieth century in spite of the massive changes unprecedented in rapidity and scale, and in the face of stark contrasts such as war and peace, want and prosperity, death and longevity, safety and danger, perpetuity and change.

Memorial rites for the souls of the dead are widespread in Japan, held by state, civil and religious authorities, families, groups of friends, and individuals. The performing or neglect of these rites is believed to affect the well-being of the souls of the dead and the living members of a household or group. As the living serve the dead, so the dead serve the living, it is believed. If the service is neglected, or discontinued, both the living and the dead souls suffer and fare ill.

Three examples of memorial death rites are offered to illustrate these secondary rites. The main example to be discussed is ghost marriage, a new practice that arose in the 1940s and 1950s in north-east Japan, mainly an agrarian and primary producing area. It was confined to the region until the 1980s. The second example is to be found in memorial rites for the dead souls of founders and employees held by companies mainly in the industrial west of Japan beginning in the 1940s and booming in the 1970s. The third example are nationwide rites for the souls of dead fetuses, and for animals, fish, plants and personal tools and discarded articles.

GHOST MARRIAGE IN NORTH-EAST JAPAN

Before the Ryūkyū Archipelago was claimed by the Japanese government in 1872 and made into Okinawa prefecture in 1879 the practice of ghost marriage was not found in Japan. It was known as a Chinese custom, portrayed in popular literature and theatre. Ghost marriage in Okinawa adheres to the principle of patrilineal descent and succession and is influenced by Chinese culture. Folklorists and anthropologists studied ghost marriage at first hand in the Ryūkyū chain. Then the field widened as the Japanese empire came to embody Taiwan, Korea, Manchuria and parts of China. The period from the 1920s to the 1940s was the first heyday of ghost marriage studies by Japanese anthropologists.[6] They studied ghost marriage and kinship, and the history of marriage. After the war much of the field was recaptured. Studies resumed in Taiwan, Korea, China, and in new places such as Hong Kong and Singapore, and, for the first time, Africa (Wada 1988). Since the 1970s studies of ghost marriage are booming again. The research topics, as before, are ghost marriage and kinship, and the history of marriage. But new topics have been added. They include souls and the world of the dead, the role of shamans and shamanism, the role of women, oral traditions and new religions (Matsuzaki 1993a: 539–40).

Besides Okinawa, and in Chinese and Korean communities in Japan, ghost marriage was discovered in the north-east (Tōhoku) in the 1980s by anthropologists and folklorists doing research or being employed in the area. North-east Japan comprises the prefectures of Aomori, Yamagata, Miyagi, Iwate and Akita. Most prominent are research and publications by Sakurai Tokutarō (b. 1917), Takeda Akira (b. 1924), Takamatsu Keikichi (b. 1934), Matsuzaki Kenzō (b. 1947), Ikegami Yoshimasa (b. 1949) and Nakao Katsumi (b. 1956). More than half of these scholars add comparative studies of ghost marriage in Asia to the north-eastern field.

Ghost marriage in the north-east differs from ghost marriage in the south-west (*Seinan*) and the practice is not related. In the north-east they take a special form. The dead soul of a real person is married to a make-believe partner. A ghost marriage in Okinawa and elsewhere in Asia involves real partners, dead or alive.

The practice, which began in the 1940s and 1950s, was by parents who made a ghost marriage for the dead soul of a son who had died young and unmarried in the Pacific War or its aftermath. It may have been adapted from stories by natives of the region who lived in Manchuria and North China as settlers among Han people who practised ghost marriages.[7] The practice seemed to disappear in the 1960s. But as modernization theorists predicted its demise as a result of rapid economic development of the region, new forms became popular. Now ghost marriages are made for the dead souls of a son or daughter who died young and unmarried as the result of an accident, illness, natural disaster, suicide or abortion. This kind of ghost marriage grew and spread in the north-east in the 1970s but it remained confined to the north-east until 1982. Then a television broadcast, 'Wedding celebrations in the world of the dead: Tsugaru peninsula's 500 wedding dolls', made it known nationwide. Since then clients who live outside the north-east request ghost marriages for the souls of dead children.

The particular form of north-eastern ghost marriage is a memorial rite for a dead soul and a posthumous rite of passage, enabling the dead soul to reach adulthood and eventually ancestorhood. The idea is reflected in posthumous rites of passage for the dead souls of young children, such as the first day of entering a school.[8] Appeasing the dead soul is thought to protect the living. These ghost marriages are performed by folk practitioners (*minkan fusha*), priests of Buddhist and, more rarely, Shinto establishments, and last by new religions. The material evidence of the practice in the north-east appeared largely in chronological order as votive boards (*mukasari ema*), photo-collages and display cases containing a photograph and doll(s), which represent a ghost wedding.[9] This north-eastern ghost marriage is an example of a new mortuary rite, not dictated or forestalled by the state laws that have regulated and made more uniform public and religious cemeteries since they were first promulgated in 1884. It is an example of a local cult that off-sets the mortuary practices of the state, professionals, and commercial stakeholders in the domain of death.

New cults, urban and rural, arise in the midst of nationwide and worldwide shifts in mortuary rites this century in complex societies. In Japan, a main change is that self-help by family members, relatives and neighbours, or local mortuary associations (*sōshiki gumi*), makes way for the service of a local undertaker (*sōgi ya*). The change began early in the century, but in the second half the small entrepreneur in turn lost ground to funeral funds and companies operating funeral parlours. Another change in death rites in this century is the shift from interment (*dosō*) to cremation (*kasō*). It followed the construction of a public crematorium in every Japanese municipality in the 1910s and 1920s. The trend was reinforced by a second construction wave in the 1950s, and is nearly complete today. A century ago about a quarter of all bodies were cremated. At mid-century the figure stood at half. Now cremation is nearly total, at over 90 per cent for the nation and nearly 100 per cent in the cities.

The latest shift is a move from cemeteries to memorial parks as the site for the family stone. Local government, business and religious bodies construct these parks, large and small, in urban and suburban surroundings. A plot in a memorial park (*reien*) is sought because a place in a temple cemetery is not available or because it is preferred to one in a cemetery (*bochi*). Memorial parks have been laid out offering hundreds or thousands of plots in a park-like location within easy reach of large cities. The memorial parks are new and tidy. They resemble the new housing estates, where many of the owners of the plots live. Aoyama Cemetery in Tokyo may be seen as a prototype. Tama Cemetery near that city is one of the first new-style *reien*.[10]

Memorial parks large and small continue to be built. The Chiba Memorial Park of Perpetual Blessing (*Chiba Eifuku Reien*), operated by a temple, is new. The area covers 1,842 square metres and offers room for 300 plots of 3 square metres, beginning at 1,3000,000 yen with a yearly administration fee of 6,000 yen. Chiba Memorial Park East (*Chiba Higashi Reien*) is a commercial venture. It is also new and offers 3-square-metre plots costing 645,000 to 735,000 yen with an annual administration fee of 4,300 yen. The Japan Memorial Park Service Society (*Nihon Reien Saabisu Kyōkai*) with head office in Tokyo and branch offices in Chiba, Osaka, Yokohama, Funabashi, Shizuoka and Wakayama, offers a choice between a plot in a public memorial park (*kōei reien*), a temple cemetery (*ji-in bochi*) and a park cemetery (*kōen bochi*). The fee for a lot begins at 152,000 yen. One of the largest memorial parks in the country is the *Osaka Hokusetsu Reien* opened in 1973. The non-profit organization manages an expanse of nearly 100 hectares with room for about 24,000 plots. At present nearly 20,000 plots are taken. Clients can choose between a 1-square-metre plot in a general area (*ippan bosho*) costing between 316,000 and 397,000 yen; a plot on a terrace (*kaidan bosho*) for 207,000 to 246,000 yen; or a Western-style stone on a lawn (*shibafu bosho*) costing 264,000 yen. The management fee is 2,000 to 2,800 yen per year. Parks tend to offer a bus service, particularly frequent during All Souls' (*bon*) and the spring and autumnal equinoxes (*higan*).[11] The preference for memorial parks is reflected in the choice of the site for a memorial of the dead soul of a domestic pet. Memorial parks for pets are becoming popular (Matsuzaki 1993a).

In big cities one may rent an ancestor-locker in a storehouse to place the memorial tablets for the dead souls of people or pets. Lockers at eye-level are the most expensive, cheaper are those above and below that line. A robot-priest may be available to read a sutra. Clients are happy with the innovation. Are not prayer wheels spun by water or wind? The fee is fixed, and one need not deal with another person.

Throughout this century the altar has become an increasingly important part of funerals. It shows the status and the power of the deceased and those who hold the wake (Yamada 1996). This reflects an urban trend in rites of passage to display power and wealth. The rite of passage industry offers a range of services that diversify and standardize practices and it sets standards of conspicuous consumption in Japan, as in other places where people are prosperous.

In the first half of the century the military were responsible for most premature deaths. In the second half of the century, when birth control was encouraged, members of the medical profession increased the ranks of the souls of the dead by performing tens of millions of abortions. Accidents, illnesses, suicides and disasters added young dead souls. Industries have substantially added to the production of dead souls of fauna, flora and goods.

In the north-east, as far back as the nineteenth century at least, it has been customary to offer a statue of the Bodhisattva of Mercy (Jizō) to a child who died young. The statue is chiselled with features and its worldly name is written on it. It is offered in a Jizō temple where a priest is asked to put the spirit in the statue. A second statue may be added to suggest a pair and a ghost marriage. The Jōan temple in Fukaurachō, a harbour on the Japan Sea Coast on Tsugaru peninsula, is a centre of Jizō beliefs and cults. Villagers have put some 150 stone statues there over the years. The inhabitants of this part of Japan man large fishing fleets in waters around the world. Young unmarried men are away for long periods of time and their profession is accident-prone. Ghost marriage is also found here.

A place where ghost marriage began is the Jizō Hall in Kawakura in Kanagichō on the Tsugaru peninsula in Aomori prefecture. In the late 1960s the Jizō festival held annually on 23 July drew people from the vicinity who come to the temple and crowd together in the small Jizō Hall. Many of those who come have lost a child. In order to console such a child they place small Jizō statues near the Jizō, who is the main object of veneration. Many statues had white faces and red lips. In the war Jizō statues dressed in military uniform were venerated, but it is rare to see such a statue carved entirely in stone (see figure 8.1).

In the 1960s during the yearly festival for Jizō, local people gathered and

Figure 8.1 Eirei Jizō, guardian deity for the spirits of the war dead. In the court of the Batō Kanzeon Temple in Niikappu, Hokkaidō, is a rare specimen of a statue of the compassionate Ksitigarbha, Jizō in the Japanese form of the underworld bodhisattva, carved in the likeness of a soldier. Before the deity are offerings of flowers and candles in their ritual basins. A vessel to hold lit incense sticks is found in the middle; it is also used for putting in flowers. Two swords offered to the deity's left show the memorial's size. The name *Eirei Jizō* is chiselled in the base. (Photo with permission by Fujita Shōichi. Reproduced by courtesy of the *Oosters Genootschap in Nederland*.)

offered prayers, food, candles and incense, took part in Jizō dances and stayed throughout the night. Outside the hall *itako* (see below) plied their trade, particularly speaking with the dead (*kuchiyose*) (Miyamoto 1975).

Twenty years later the Jizō Hall in Kawakura is a place famous in the northeast for ghost marriage. In 1987 a photo dating from 1937 and another dating from 1946, were found. The oldest doll was from 1980; the next one from 1982. From the mid-1980s, the offerings of ghost marriage display cases began to rise from twenty to thirty a year. The cost of keeping a case and performing the memorial services was 5,000 yen for a period of five years. The term could be renewed and a case kept for ten years. Expired or abandoned dolls are ritually burned each year. Unfortunately, this continually destroys the material evidence.[12]

The bereaved who come to this temple live in the vicinity of the temple or come from Tsugaru peninsula. In 1987 thirty-five cases were received and 200 were being kept by the temple (Takamatsu 1993b: 24–7). For a while Jizō statues and ghost marriage cases shared the same space. With the steep increase in numbers, the temple erected a separate building in 1985 for the ghost marriage cases (Nakao 1995: 107). The practices meanwhile continue to exist side by side.

The Kōbō temple, popularly called '*Nishi no Kōya san*', in the city of Kizukuri on the Tsugaru peninsula, is another place where ghost marriage has appeared. The oldest photograph of a ghost marriage here also dates from 1937. In August 1987 the temple had 1,360 ghost marriage display cases in its keeping. Since old ones are ritually burned every year the precise number offered to the temple is not known. The temple records that were being kept in 1987 go back only ten years. Labelling began in 1971 for administrative purposes. The record lists the shelf number, place number, address and name of the donor, and the worldly and posthumous name of the bride or bridegroom and states the cause of death. The record is not always straightforward on that score. It is not uncommon, for example, to register a suicide as an accident.[13]

Seen by region of origin, of the 763 cases on record in the Kōbō temple, 728 came from Aomori prefecture: 349 from the cities of Aomori and Hirosaki, and 171 from South Tsugaru. The remaining 35 were from outside the prefecture, namely Akita, Hokkaido, Yokohama, Fukushima, Fukuii, Ibaraki and Tokyo. In 1987, the price of a display case with a doll of a bride, bought in a department store was about 10,000 yen; a bridegroom cost about 20,000 yen. Due to the high cost of a display case, votive boards (*mukasari ema*) are becoming popular again.

The first display cases with doll(s) were offered to the temple by a few families in 1955 for sons who died unmarried as soldiers. The number rose by ten to fifteen per year until it reached a peak in the late 1960s. The temple did not advertise but the news spread by word of mouth and on the advice of shamans (*itako*, *kamisama*). One explanation of the rise is the ageing of the population through increased longevity. Ageing parents entrust the memorial services for the dead souls of their child to a temple. In 1978 the number was rising again to a yearly forty to fifty dolls. The second peak began in 1982 after the nationwide broadcast of an NHK documentary about the temple and the practice. The number of ghost marriages and display cases increased to eighty or ninety per year. Most of the bereaved are from Hirosaki and Aomori city (Takamatsu 1993b: 12–23). These parents came to commemorate a child who died young and unmarried but also to give a ghost marriage to the dead soul of a child aborted two decades or so ago who would have reached the age to marry.

A ghost marriage may be conducted for various reasons. One is for the sake of propriety, for instance, the rule that an elder sibling should marry before a younger one. Here the weight is on memorialization. A ghost marriage may be made on the advice of a shaman who attributes ill to the emanations of a dead soul of a sibling who died young and unmarried. It nearly always involves a family member, but a case is on record of a family who had to make a ghost marriage to satisfy the dead soul of a princess who perished where they lived while awaiting marriage a few hundred years ago. More usual is a case recorded in 1987 of the young mistress of a household who suffered three miscarriages in a row. Consultation with a shaman eventually revealed that the misfortune was caused by the envy of the dead soul of her husband's elder brother, who died unmarried, a soldier in the war. A ghost marriage remedied the situation. It commemorated the dead soul and exorcized its unhappy influence. The soul consoled, proper order is restored, if only in the shadow world, and the problem ceased (ibid.: 33–6). About one-third of the ghost marriages in the north-east are made on the advice of a shaman.

North-eastern shamans may be divided into two large groups: *itako*, dwindling in number, and *kamisama* taking their place.[14] As shamans they call down the souls of gods or the dead, diagnose what causes a dead soul to interfere with the lives of the living, or empower the ghost marriage depicted on a votive board, a photo-collage or a display case of the dead soul and the virtual partner. Their background is different. *Itako* are organized in professional groups, centred on a teacher, her house and groups of students. A teacher has ties to lay Buddhist associations (*kō*) and temples. They are (with one exception on record) women, and blind or nearly so. Early in their youth they were trained in recitation and austerities for about two years in the house of a teacher. If they passed the initiation rite, the teacher gave them the licence to work as a professional shaman. Under the tight pre-war state control religious establishments and practitioners needed a state licence. In addition to their teacher's permit obtained on initiation, the *itako* needed a special permit which her teacher had to obtain from a temple. Possession was checked by the local police.

A visually handicapped girl was apprenticed to an *itako* as her siblings might be apprenticed to a master or mistress in another trade. It taught the girl a skill and gave her the chance to earn a living. Since schools for the blind opened after the war, however, not many parents or girls seek training as an *itako* any longer. The group has grown old and rarely takes in a new student. The places on the religious markets are being taken by *kamisama*. These are shamans who did not seek it as a profession at an early age, nor are they visually handicapped. They became shamans for better or worse, against or of their own volition, later in life. They have taken over and changed the roles *itako* play, including calling down the souls of the dead (*hotoke oroshi*). *Kamisama* are mostly women but there are men among them. They are unorganized, independent practitioners. When they gain followers or believers (*shinja*), they may found a new religious sect or break away from the school of a teacher. New religions in the north-east have begun to offer ghost marriage among their services. The *Taiwa Kyōdan* in the city of Sendai in Miyagi prefecture established by Hozumi Hisako (b. 1908) has a following of 55,000 believers (Fujita 1992; Inoue *et al.* 1990: 745–6; 929). It may be only a matter of time before new religious sects elsewhere take up the practice.

MEMORIAL CULTS IN COMPANIES AND FETUS CULTS IN FAMILIES

A ghost marriage in north-east Japan is a memorial rite and a rite of passage for a dead spirit that parent(s) or sibling(s) hold for the dead soul of a son or a daughter, sister or brother who died young and unmarried. Memorial rites have been held for an assortment of dead souls in Japan, in the twentieth century and earlier. They are held for the dead souls of people, animals, fish and plants, and for souls acquired by such personal articles as a pair of spectacles, or tools, for example a needle (Kretschmer 1996). These rites increase in times of prosperity. The scientific, industrial and private sectors began to order the memorial rites. Scientists are on record as among the earliest requesting these rites. In the Shōan temple in Tōyōnaka city near Osaka the practice of performing a ceremony for animals was begun in 1956 when scientists, veterinarians and other professionals who had to kill animals in their work first asked the temple to perform a ceremony. They were followed in subsequent decades by people who wished to erect a memorial marker for their dead pets or favourite animals. In 1982 there were 18,845 markers counted. The rate of increase was 700 to 800 per year (Asquith 1990: 183). Rites of gratitude and commemoration for the dead souls of all kinds of flora and fauna come from the sectors and people directly involved, those who procure the animals, fish or plants and put them to death. With industrialization, the scale of deliberate life-taking of animals, fish and plants has risen to unprecedented heights. The people who hold the rites are those who perpetrate the killing. They live and work in the scientific and industrial sectors, the heartland of technological civilization. Anatomists hold memorial rites for the dead souls of the human remains handled in an anatomical theatre for teaching or demonstration.

The primary life-takers, the whalers, hunters, fishermen, butchers and foresters perform rather than explain the rite. It is surmised that the rites are an expression of gratitude, a wish for replenishment and for a better rebirth for the souls of the plants or animals, and to protect the life-takers from retribution. The rites for the dead souls of animals, plants and objects are held by the specialists – technicians, managers and workers – who are personally involved.

These cults are local and are restricted to a social body such as a family or a company. Some cults for the souls of the dead that arose in the post-war decades remain local, such as north-eastern ghost marriage. Others have been disseminated widely, such as the rites to commemorate the dead souls of aborted children (*mizugo kuyō*) that can be performed at certain temples. This cult is linked to a shadow population of tens of millions of dead souls created through abortions in the post-war period. Doctors and medical assistants began these rites. Parent(s) too have begun to extend the rites for these dead souls. They may be put on a par with older dead souls and helped to reach liberation, even ancestorhood. That is a new element in the memorial rites carried out for the dead souls of miscarried, still-born or aborted fetuses, short-lived babies and victims of infanticide nationwide since the 1960s and 1970s.

A knot of government regulations and pharmaceutical and medical interests has helped maintain the situation whereby abortion is a common method of birth control in the second half of the twentieth century in Japan for most of the population. The memorial cult has been spread and exploited by the mass media, first via women's magazines, then photographers, specialists in occult matters, and religious establishments seeking new income since state support for religious institutions ended after the war (Morikuri 1994).

CONCLUSION

Typically, Shinto shrine rites are said to be for the living while Buddhist rites are said to be for the dead. In reality it is not so simple, as this example and the example of the *Yasukuni Jinja* in Tokyo, the first shrine where the dead souls of the soldiers who fell for the country in the past century are commemorated, make clear. Folklorists and anthropologists think that the Buddhist house altars are ancestor and spirit shelves rather than places of Buddhist worship. So popular practices force scholars to alter their perceptions and schemes.

NOTES

* I am indebted to Wada Shōhei, Ōmori Yasuhiro, Sugishima Takashi, Yoshimoto Shinobu and the National Museum of Ethnology in Osaka, Matsunaga Kazuto, Matsuzaki Kenzō, Nakao Katsumi, Itō Hiroshi, Pamela Asquith, Robert Smith, and Elmer Veldkamp for materials put at my disposal. I should like to thank Joy Hendry and Itō Keiko for editorial comments and help.

1 Adapted from the *Encyclopedia of Social and Cultural Anthropology* (Barnard and Spencer 1996: 614–15) and Evans-Pritchard (1981: 173, 175).

2 Adapted from U. Hannerz in the *Encyclopedia of Social and Cultural Anthropology* (Barnard and Spencer 1996: 122–4) and C. Ouwehand (1965: 137).

3 The neologism 'sociotope' is coined here after 'biotope' to convey the idea that the members of a social group live in environments and conditions vulnerable, interconnected, life-supporting, bearing and taking.

4 Adapted from Lebra (1993: 108–11), Itō (1982), and Sorensen (1993).

5 Based on the lecture 'Culture, Self and Death in Japan' delivered by Takie Sugiyama Lebra in the Centre for Japanese Studies in Leiden University on 14 May 1997.

6 The situation was different inside the country. Shamanism was a taboo word to apply to Japan until the end of the war (Sakurai 1988: 7).

7 Based on the lecture 'Tsugaru no shigo kekkon' delivered by Nakao Katsumi in the Centre for Japanese Studies in Leiden University on 2 February 1996.

8 The rite of school entrance (*nyūgaku shiki*) has been depicted on votive boards

showing the child accompanied by its father, mother and siblings, if any, all dressed in their finest. Illustration no. 97 in Sakurai (1988, p. 547) is an example.

9 '*Mukasari*' is a noun made of the contraction in the dialect around Sendai and Yamagata of the phrases: '*Mukō e saru*' or '*mukae saru*'. The meaning of the word is matrimony (Wada 1990: 2–3).

10 The difference felt between memorial parks and temple graveyards is articulated by a protagonist in a tale published by Mishima Yukio in 1952, *Death in Midsummer* [*Mannatsu no shi*]: 'Tomoko, who had never been to the Tama Cemetery before, was astonished at its brightness. So wide a space, then, was given to the dead? The green lawns, the wide tree-lined avenues, the blue sky above, clear far into the distance. The city of the dead was cleaner and better ordered than the city of the living' (Mishima 1966: 18; translation Edward G. Seidensticker).

11 Information gleaned from leaflets and advertisements.

12 The number of articles related to north-eastern ghost marriage in the collection of ethnographic museums is low.

13 Data gathered in Uba-dera in Ōhata-chō, Shimokita district in Aomori prefecture show that the make-believe partner typically bears a common name. If the dead man's name was Yoshio, his bride doll's chosen name may be Yoshiko. If the wordly name of a man was Norio, his bride doll's name may be Noriko. Names like Hanako or Tarō are common (Takamatsu 1993a: 30, 38).

14 The shamans go by different local names and the different types are not always distinguished by the public. Scholars classify shamans in a number of ways. Sakurai (1988: 12–30) for instance distinguishes three types: professional shamans, shrine shamans and local lay shamans. The clients are mostly local people. They talk about a shaman in terms of her kinship ties, place of residence, or Shinto or Buddhist guardian god. For example: 'Kimura *kamisama*' (family name); 'Ishikawa *no kamisama*' (place name); 'Yamada no Ryūjin *sama*' (place and god name). The term '*gomizo*' is widely used. It has a demeaning undertone. Children of '*gomizo*' are often bullied (*ijimeru*) (Ikegami 1992: 15, 16, 28).

REFERENCES

Asquith, Pamela (1990) 'The Japanese Idea of Soul in Animals and Objects as Evidenced by *kuyō* Services', in D. J. Daly and T. T. Sekine (eds) *Discovering Japan*, Toronto: Captus Press, pp. 181–8.

Barnard, Alan and Jonathan Spencer (eds) (1996) *Encyclopedia of Social and Cultural Anthropology*, London: Routledge.

Evans-Pritchard, E. E. (1981) *A History of Anthropological Thought*, London: Faber & Faber.

Fujita, Shōichi (1992) 'Misogi-sai. Taiwa kyōdan [Purification Rituals: A Discussion]', in Fujita Shōichi *Reinō no higi* [*Esoteric Rites of Spirit Control*], Tokyo: Fusōsha, pp. 127–46.

Hendry, Joy (1986) 'Introduction: The Contribution of Social Anthropology to Japanese Studies', in J. Hendry and J. Webber (eds) *Interpreting Japanese Society: Anthropological Approaches*, Oxford: JASO, pp. 3–13.

Hertz, Robert (1907) 'Contributions à une étude sur la représentation collective de la mort', *Année sociologique*, vol. 10, pp. 48–137.

Hori, Ichirō (1971) *Nihon no shamanizumu* [*Japanese Shamanism*], Tokyo: Kodansha.

Ikegami, Yoshimasa (1987) *Tsugaru no kamisama: Sukui no kōzō wo tazunete* [*The Gods of Tsugaru: Considering the Anatomy of Salvation*], Tokyo: Dōbutsusha.

—— (1992) *Minzoku shūkyō to sukui: Tsugaru, Okinawa no minkan fusha* [*Folk Religion and Salvation: Private Ritual Practitioners of Tsugaru, Okinawa*], Kyoto: Tankōsha.

Inoue Nobutaka, Kōmoto Mitsugi, Tsushima Michito, Nakamaki Hirochika and Nishiyama Shigeru (compilers) (1990) *Shinshūkyō jiten* [*Encyclopedia of New Religions*], Tokyo: Kōbundō.

Itō, Mikiharu (1982) *Kazoku kokka kan no jinruigaku* [*Anthropology of the Nation as a Family*], Tokyo: Minerva shobō.

Kimura, Hiroshi (1988) 'Dōshokubutsu kuyō no shūzoku [The Custom of Holding Memorials for Plants and Animals]', in *Bukkyō minzoku taikei* [*Outline of Buddhist Folklore*], vol. 4, of Fujii Masao (ed.) *Sosen saishi to sōbo* [*Ancestor Rituals, Funerals and Graves*], Tokyo: Meicho shuppan, pp. 375–90.

Kretschmer, Angelika (1996) *Harikuyō. A Case Study of Tradition and Change in Religious Behaviour*, Erlangen: Friedrich-Alexander-Universität Erlangen-Nürnberg (Diskussionsbeiträge Erlanger Japanstudien no. 2).

Kusunoki, Masahiro (1984) *Shomin shinkō no sekai. Osorezan shinkō to oshirasan shinkō* [*The World of Folk Religions: Mt Osore and Oshira Beliefs*], Tokyo: Miraisha.

Lebra, Takie Sugiyama (1993) *Above the Clouds: Status Culture of the Modern Japanese Nobility*, Berkeley: University of California Press.

Matsuzaki, Kenzō (1993a) 'Petto no kuyō – inu, nekko wo chūshin ni [Pet Memorial Services – Focusing on Dogs and Cats]', *Shinano*, vol. 45, no. 1, pp. 1–21.

—— (1993b) (ed.) *Higashi Ajia no shiryō kekkon* [*Ghost Marriage in East Asia*], Tokyo: Iwata shoin.

—— (1996a) 'Dōshokubutsu no kuyō oboegaki. Kuyōhi konryū shūzoku wo megutte [Notes on Memorial Services for Plants and Animals And the Custom to Erect Shrines for them]', in Matsuzaki Kenzō (ed.) *Minzokuteki sekai no tankyū: Kami, hotoke, mura. Kamata Hisako Sensei Koki Kinen Ronshū* [*Research into the World of Folklore: Gods, Buddha and Village. Essays Presented to Professor Kamata Hisako*], Tokyo: Keiyūsha, pp. 162–85.

—— (1996b) 'Yorikujira no shochi wo megutte. Dōshokubutsu no kuyō [Concerning the Disposal of Beached Whales: Memorial Services]', *Nihon Jōmin bunka kiyō* [*Journal of Japanese Folk Culture*], vol. 19, pp. 31–76.

—— (1996c) 'Kibutsu no kuyō kenkyū josetsu. Kutsu no kuyō wo chūshin ni [Memorial Services for Utensils: Concerning Memorial Services for Shoes]', *Mingu kenkyū* [*Folk Artefacts Research*], no. 112, pp. 23–32.

Metcalf, Peter (1982) *A Borneo Journey into Death: Berawan Eschatology from its Rituals*, Philadelphia: University of Pennsylvania Press.

Mishima, Yukio (1966) *Death in Midsummer* (trans. Edward G. Seidensticker), Tokyo: Tuttle.

Miyamoto, Tsune'ichi (1975) 'Kawakura jizō [Jizō of Kawakura]', in *Miyamoto Tsune'ichi Chosakushū* [*Miyamoto Tsune'ichi Complete Works*], vol. 18, Tokyo: Miraisha, pp. 189–91 (first published 1969).

Morikuri, Shigekazu (1993) 'Sai no kawara no gendai: shiryō kekkon, mizuko, kuchiyose, nagare tekiya [*Sai no kawara* in the Present Day: Ghost Marriage, Funerals for the Newborn, Spirit Channelling and Wandering Fortune Tellers]', *Kyōto Minzoku* [*Bulletin of the Folklore Society of Kyoto*], no. 11, pp. 59–65.

—— (1994) 'Mizuko kuyō no hassei to genjō [The Origins and Current Practice of Memorials for the Stillborn]', *Kokuritsu rekishi minzoku hakubutsukan kenkyū hōkoku* [*Bulletin of the National Museum of Japanese History*], vol. 57, pp. 95–127.

Nakamaki, Hirochika (1986) 'Continuity and Change: Funeral Customs in Modern Japan', *Japanese Journal of Religious Studies*, vol. 13, nos 2–3, pp. 177–92.

—— (1992) *Mukashi daimyō ima kaisha. Kigyō to shūkyō* [*Yesterday Warlords, Today Companies: Business and Religion*], Tokyo: Tankōsha.

—— (1995) [zōho (enlarged edition)] *Shūkyō ni nani ga okite iru ka* [*What is Happening in Religion*], Tokyo: Heibonsha.

Nakao, Katsumi (1995) 'Tsugaru no shigo kekkon [Posthumous Marriage in Tsugaru]', *Miyagi Gakuin Joshi Daigaku Kirisutokyō Bunka Kenkyūsho Kenkyū Nenpō* [*Miyagi Gakuin Women's University Annual Research Bulletin of the Department of Christian Studies*], no. 28, pp. 97–115.

Ōsaki, Tomoko (1995a) 'Ueno Kan'eiji Bentendō no shōhi wo megutte [Concerning the

Destruction of the Benten Hall in Ueno Temple]', *Jōmin Bunka* [*Folk Culture*], no. 18, pp. 59–80.

—— (1995b) 'Ueno Kan'eiji Kiyomizu Kannondō no ningyō kuyō', *Nihon Minzokugaku* [*Bulletin of the Folklore Society of Japan*], no. 201, pp. 109–19.

Ouwehand, C. (1965) 'De Japanse volkskultuur', in P. van Ernst (ed.) *Panorama der Volken*, vol. II, Roermond: Romen, pp. 137–66.

Sakurai, Tokutarō (1977) 'Meikon no shūzoku to shamanizumu. Tōhoku chihō minkan miko no yakuwari [Ghost Marriage Customs and Shamanism. Role of the Female Shaman in Folk Societies in Tōhoku]', in Sakurai Tokutarō (ed.) *Nihon no shamanizumu. Minkan fūzoku no kōzō to kinō. Gekkan* [*Japanese Shamanism: The Structure and Function of Folk Traditions*. Vol. II], Tokyo: Yoshikawa Kōbunkan, pp. 457–69.

—— (1988) *Nihon Shamanizumu no kenkyū. Denshō to seitai, Sakurai Tokutarō chosakushū* [*Study of Japanese Shamanism: Image and Reality: Collected Writings by Sakurai Tokutarō*], vol. 5, Tokyo: Yoshikawa Kōbunkan.

Satō, Noriaki (1981) 'The Initiation of the Religious Specialists *Kamisan*: A Few Observations', *Japanese Journal of Religious Studies*, vol. 8, nos 3–4, pp. 149–85.

Sorensen, Clark W. (1993) 'Asian Families: Domestic Group Formation: Ancestors and In-laws: Kinship Beyond the Family', in Grant Evans (ed.) *Asia's Cultural Mosaic: An Anthropological Introduction*, New York: Prentice-Hall, pp. 89–151.

Takamatsu, Keikichi (1993a) *Fūzoku to takaikan no minzokugakuteki kenkyū* [*Ethnological Research into Customs and Concepts of the Afterlife*], Tokyo: Hōsei-daigaku Shuppankyoku.

—— (1993b) 'Aomori-ken no meikon [Spirit Marriage in Aomori Prefecture]', in Matsuzaki Kenzō (ed.) *Higashi Ajia no shiryō kekkon* [*Ghost Marriage in East Asia*], Tokyo: Iwata shoin, pp. 11–42.

Takeda, Akira (1990) 'Shiryō kekkon no hikaku minzokugaku. Chūkoku, Nihon, Kankoku [Comparative Research on Ghost Marriages: China, Japan and Korea]', in Sakurai Tokutarō (ed.) *Sorei saishi to shiryō kekkon: Nikkan hikaku minzokugaku no kokoromi* [*Ancestor Ceremonies and Ghost Marriage: Attempting a Japan–Korea Comparative Ethnology*], Kyoto: Jinbun shoin, pp. 156–206.

—— (1993) 'Higashi Ajia ni okeru shiryō kekkon. Kankoku no shūzoku wo chūshin ni [Ghost Marriages in East Asia: Focusing on Korean Tradition]', in Matsuzaki Kenzō (ed.) *Higashi Ajia no shiryō kekkon* [*Ghost Marriage in East Asia*], Tokyo: Iwata shoin, pp. 211–60.

Wada, Shōhei (1988) 'Bōrei kekkon to wa nani ka [What is Ghost Marriage?]' in Sakurai Tokutarō (ed.) *Sei to kekkon no minzokugaku* [*The Ethnology of Sex and Marriage*], Kyoto: Dōhōsha shuppan, pp. 105–204.

—— (1990) 'Michinoku ema no tabi [Discovering Rural Shrine Portraits]', *Dōhō* [*Countrymen*], no. 151, pp. 2–4.

Yamada, Shinya (1996) 'Shi wo juyō saseru mono. Koshi kara saidan e [How We Come to Accept Death: From the Hearse to the Altar]', *Nihon Minzokugaku* [*Bulletin of the Folklore Society of Japan*], no. 207, pp. 29–57.

Ethno-cinema-photography

Nakamaki, Hirochika (1992) *Mukashi daimyō, ima kaisha. Kōyasan no kuyōtō ni saguru* [*Yesterday Warlords, Today Companies: The Memorial Pagodas of Mt Kōya*], 42 min. and 40 sec. Osaka: The National Museum of Ethnology.

Ōmori, Yasuhiro (1994a) *Tsugaru no kamisama* [*Shamanic Mediums of Tsugaru*], 1 hr, 33 min., 38 sec. Osaka: The National Museum of Ethnology.

—— (1994b) *Reijō Osorezan* [*The Holy Site of Mt Osore*], 1 hr, 23 min., 24 sec. Osaka: The National Museum of Ethnology.

9   A child in time*

Changing adoption and fostering in Japan

Roger Goodman

INTRODUCTION

The impetus for this chapter comes in part from challenges thrown down separately by anthropologists in the United States and Japan. At the level of general anthropology, John Terrell and Judith Modell (1994: 160) in their 'Anthropology and Adoption' accuse anthropologists of having been deficient in their attempts to explain the significance of practices such as adoption:

> A study of adoption becomes an inquiry into fundamental beliefs about the person and personal connections as these intertwine with political, economic, and historical developments. . . . We want to strengthen public awareness of the diverse ways that people in different parts of the world . . . build and value human relationships, family ties and obligations. In the process we should demonstrate that anthropology importantly is . . . a 'way of seeing' for those other than its practitioners.

In the specific case of anthropological work on Japan, Sekimoto Teruo (1988: 6) takes to task those who have worked on kinship:

> I feel that [the] interest in Japanese families and kinship has come to a dead end. . . . Students in that field were too interested in traditional aspects. Sometimes they created some idealised traditional form of the Japanese family, and their work was not about actual families and kinship. They could not deal with changing aspects of contemporary family life. Thus I believe that some radically new approach will definitely be necessary in order to re-develop this field. . . . [C]ontemporary, changing aspects have not been well studied.

In responding to these challenges, this chapter draws on nine months of fieldwork undertaken in 1991 while based in a children's home (*yōgoshisetsu*) in western Tokyo. There are some 530 *yōgoshisetsu* in Japan with around 30,000 resident children. Japanese institutional care for children whose parents cannot look after them differs from that in other OECD countries in a number of interesting and significant ways which need to be outlined as an introduction to the topic of this chapter.

- Children generally spend a very long time (on average nearly five years) in residential care homes. Placement is essentially a matter of chance and is decided by the workers at the local Jidōsōdanjō (Child Consultation Centre), who are generally unqualified (in terms of social work) local government bureaucrats ultimately responsible for the care and treatment of children in homes (see Goodman forthcoming).
- In Japan, there is very little family support social work. The workers in the Jidōsōdanjō each have 100 or so children on their books and hence there is little possibility of supporting individual children at home as opposed to seeking alternative care arrangements.
- For reasons which this chapter intends to explore, very few children are fostered as an alternative to residential care, and virtually none are adopted from children's homes. Table 9.1, widely disseminated by the Japanese Foster Parents' Association, stresses just how much Japan is out of line with other OECD countries.

Table 9.1 Proportion of children in welfare institutions and in foster home placements in various countries

Country	Foster placement (%)	Welfare institutions (%)
England	70	10
Holland	54	46
Sweden	85	15
Finland	67	33
New Zealand	60	40
America	79	14
Japan	9	90

Note: The figures in Table 9.1 for England appear very out of date, but are reproduced here in this form since these statistics are taken-as-given in the debate that is taking place in Japan.
Source: Sato Oya Kai (1990)

TRADITIONS OF ADOPTION AND FOSTERING IN JAPAN

The relative absence of fostering and adoption from children's homes seems somehow all the more surprising in the light of there being long traditions of both in Japanese society, albeit in different contexts. According to Bachnik (1988: 14): 'Adoption has been widely practised in Japan for at least 1300 years.' To some extent, indeed, adoption might be said to be *the* defining feature of the Japanese kinship system; patterns of adoption are certainly more widespread and flexible in Japan than in neighbouring countries such as China and Korea with which it shares so many other cultural practices.[1] Adoption was particularly prevalent among the upper classes, though also practised lower down the social hierarchy; samurai records suggest that by the nineteenth century up to 40 per cent of families adopted sons or daughters. The practice was so widespread that, in the Tokugawa period, one scholar picked it out as a major cause of social chaos describing it as both 'barbaric' and 'evil' (see Lebra 1993: 107ff.).

The type of adoption that was practised in premodern Japan, and which indeed remains the most prevalent type today, was essentially adoption for purposes of succession and can only be understood in relation to the basic form of Japanese kinship system – the *ie*. Figure 9.1 shows the *ie* in diagrammatic form. The *ie* had become fixed, in theory if not necessarily in practice, as the basic social unit by the Tokugawa period (1600–1868) and was disseminated as an ideal kinship model in the period of Meiji modernization. In the context of this chapter, a number of important features about the *ie* need to be kept in mind.

- Certain roles and positions – e.g. head, successor – are defined in the context of the *ie*; hence, it should be seen as distinct from 'family' where genealogy rather than position is paramount.
- It is a corporate body which has its own status, assets, career and goals.
- Its existence as an entity over and above its immediate membership means that the members are only temporarily looking after it and their main purpose is to pass it on, in the best possible condition and with the best possible leadership, to the next generation.

Ideal succession within the *ie* is male primogeniture, but if the eldest son is not considered competent, then a younger son may replace him. If there is no eligible successor within the family, then an 'outsider' should be recruited through adoption. Continuity is the key.

This type of adoption, unlike fostering, creates a fictive parent–child relationship by law; the adopted child – or adopted couple – have the same legal rights as a natural child or children. In some sense, it might be considered similar to traditional ideas of marriage in that it has primarily economic and political aims. In terms of economics, it is noticeable that the adoption of a competent heir was particularly stressed among merchant families. In terms of politics, it is significant that adoption is generally known in Japanese as *yōshi engumi* (sometimes shortened to '*yōshi*'). *Yōshi* means both adoption and the adopted person; *engumi* consists of two characters meaning 'relation' and 'matching', and hence can be translated as 'alliance'. Like marriage, too, the adoption ties of this type can be broken, a type of 'divorce' (*rien*).[2]

Japanese adoption, therefore, is distinguished by the following characteristics (see Bachnik, 1988: 14–15):

- primary focus is the 'house' (*ie*) not the adoptee;
- adoptees are not foundlings, but usually close relatives whose natal home is known;
- age of adoptee is relatively old (the vast majority are adults);
- no legal distinction is made between adoptive and 'real' child.

According to Jack Goody's (1969) seminal comparative study of adoption, this type of adoption – which maintains the line of the family or 'house' (in Lévi-

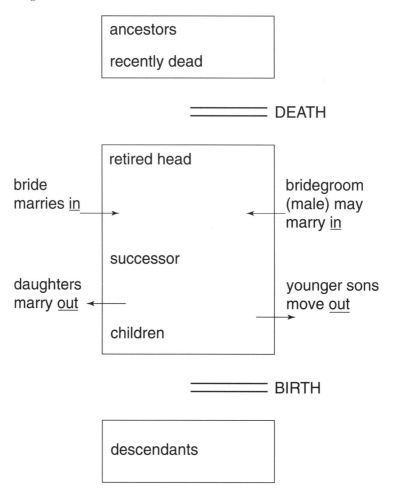

Figure 9.1 Ie – Japanese household
Source: Adapted from Hendry (1986a: 17)

Straussian terminology) – is common in many traditional East Asian societies, but also existed in ancient Greece and Rome, and then disappeared in Europe after the medieval period. Goody does not discuss, though, whether there ever existed in ancient Greece or Rome such a variety of forms as in Japan, where virtually any method of adoption is allowed in order to continue the family line: a sister's son or daughter's son is as good as a brother's son; a brother can be adopted as a son; a son-in-law can be adopted, as can a married couple. If the ranks or reputations of two houses involved in marriage are considered incompatible, then a daughter can gain suitability by being adopted by another house, although there is no need for her ever actually to live with her adoptive parents, as indeed was the case with the bride of Prince Chichibu, brother of the Shōwa emperor and uncle of the current emperor.[3]

In order to make a concubine respectable in pre-war Japan, a father could be chosen for her from the right sort of family ('father adoption'). In extreme cases, a man on the verge of bankruptcy would sell his entire property to a total stranger known as a *kaiyōshi* ('buyer-adoptive son'), who was willing to take over the family occupation and adopt and continue its name (Befu 1962: 38).

In the civil code the only limitations on adoption are, in the case of kin, the prohibition on adopting someone of a higher generation, such as an uncle or aunt and, in the case of non-kin, adopting someone who is older.[4] Otherwise, not only has any other pattern been possible in theory, it has also been found in practice. As Lebra (1993) in her work on the pre-war Japanese aristocracy sums up: 'Adoption functioned like a panacea to restore the appearance of normalcy in the case of all sorts of actual anomaly.' Rather than undermining the strict idea of patrilineal blood lines (*chisuji*) in Japan, the flexibility of the adoption system, combined with what she calls 'genealogical amnesia', actually served to maintain it.[5]

The concept of fostering also has a long history in Japan. The origins of the word '*satogo*' seem to lie in the idea that in the Middle Ages many children among the aristocracy were brought up by their mother's family *ie* [matrilateral cognates] (Nihon Shakai Minzokugaku Kyōkai 1954: 503–5).[6] Fostering was certainly widespread in pre-war Japan, especially among the elite. In describing how the status culture of the aristocracy was acquired and passed on, Lebra shows how not only fathers but also mothers were generally uninvolved in childrearing and children were largely brought up by servants (what she calls 'surrogate parenthood') or else, quite frequently, foster parents (*sato-oya*) – as happened for example with the late Emperor Shōwa and his brother.[7] Interviewees in her study recall the abuse they received at the hands of these caregivers; many children indeed were left permanently (*sato nagare*) with their working-class foster parents who needed them for labour by their natal families who wanted fewer mouths to feed.[8] Sometimes these peasant families would receive money (*satobuchi*) for caring for the children on the understanding that they would be returned if the designated successor died or proved unsuitable. Noguchi (1988: 26) suggests that some urban families in Tokugawa Japan thought that the experience of living in the countryside would enable the children to grow up strong and healthy; others, however, have argued that the practice related more to keeping children, particularly those born in 'unlucky' years, out of harm's way – both for their own good and the good of the family.

Prior to 1945 foster children lacked civil or social rights, especially in their relationships with their foster parents. There were advocates of a state fostering system such as Ishi'i Jūji, the famous founder of an orphanage in Okayama, but fostering was essentially undertaken in the private sector; foster parents received at best minimal state support; and the experience of fostered children differed enormously, from treatment as full-kin to an extra pair of hands (Komatsu 1992: 143–7). Though perhaps not to quite the same extent, there is then a good case for suggesting that fostering, as with adoption, was a system that very much suited the interests of the *families* concerned and paid little attention to the interests or rights of the *child*.

MODERN PATTERNS OF ADOPTION AND FOSTERING

How did these pre-war practices, which can be traced far back in Japanese history, translate into the modern period? In theory, the post-war civil code (1948) banned any adoption that was enacted purely in the interests of the *ie*. Emphasis was laid on the rights of the individual and it was expected that the Japanese system would become more similar to that of the United States where adoption was undertaken for the good of children whose natural parents were unable, for whatever reason, to look after them. In practice, as with much of the new civil code, it ran alongside rather than replaced the previous code. Adult adoption and child adoption for purposes of succession remained, when combined, by far the two most popular categories of adoption. In post-war village studies, Beardsley *et al.* (1959: 238) and Befu (1962: 37) suggested that around 25 per cent of all households were succeeded by adoption; Nakane (1967: 67) gave a figure of nearly one-third of the households in some villages. Among elite families, where the political and economic considerations of adoption were even more important, the figures may have been even higher; among post-war prime ministers, Yoshida Shigeru was adopted, and two other prime ministers, Kishi Nobusuke and Sato Eisaku, were actually brothers – the younger brother, Nobusuke, being adopted to succeed to his father's natal household (the Kishi family), his father having been adopted to his mother's natal household (the Sato family) (Hara 1995: 3).

A third category of adoption – step-child adoption and adoption of one's own illegitimate child or own grandchild – relate to the family register law (*koseki-hō*), a complex and somewhat controversial system of family registration which has existed in one form or another for 1400 years in Japan. It places every Japanese individual in one and only one family register (*koseki*) which provides legal proof of his or her identity. Each *koseki* can consist of a married couple or a married couple and their unmarried children (natural or adopted) of the same surname or an individual with unmarried children (natural or adopted) of the same surname, or just an individual over the age of 20. Many step-parents adopt their step-children in order to set up a new *koseki* that includes them as a way of ensuring legal guardianship.

A fourth category of adoption – the idea of adoption for the protection of the child; what Goody (1969) describes as the modern European understanding of the term – has only very recently been introduced into Japan (in part under the banner of 'internationalization') and it is the introduction of this system and its fate in a Japanese context that will be the focus of much of the rest of this paper.

In the case of fostering, in the immediate post-war period – a time of great social, political and economic upheaval in the country – there is evidence of a large number of private arrangements being made, often leading to private adoptions (Vogel 1963: 240–41). There was little state intervention or support for these arrangements (Komatsu 1992), nor was there any system to check on the well-being of the children involved (Kikuchi 1991). The first state fostering system was not set up until the 1947 Child Welfare Law was enacted – thirty years after western Europe adopted a similar procedure – though as Table 9.2 suggests,

Table 9.2 Number of registered foster families, families fostering children and children in foster care, 1953–91

Year	Registered foster families	Active foster families	Children being fostered
1953	13,288	7,271	8,041
1955	16,827	8,370	9,169
1960	19,022	7,751	8,737
1965	18,230	6,090	6,909
1970	13,621	4,075	4,729
1975	10,230	3,225	3,851
1980	8,933	2,646	3,188
1985	8,659	2,627	3,322
1991	8,163	2,183	2,671

Sources: Nihon Sōgō Aiku Kenkyūjo (1988: 236); Kōseitōkeikyōkai (1992: 116)

the system has never been fully utilized and the number of registered foster-parents and children fostered declined, consistently, over the next forty years.

MODERNIZING FOSTERING AND ADOPTION IN JAPAN

In 1988 a new adoption law was introduced in Japan. Known as *tokubetsu yōshi* (special adoption), this was the first attempt to introduce and regularize adoption for the good of the child rather than the *ie*, and it meant that there were, in effect, three different systems of adoption operating alongside each other as shown in Table 9.3.

In the case of adult adoption and the registration system of children (A1 and B) the adoptive parents know the background of the child or adult who is being adopted and the adoption does not need to go through the court. In the vast majority of these cases the two families are related. In the A2 category, many of the children would be known to the adopting family, and often would have been related to them; some, however, will have been adopted from children's homes or were fostered specifically for the sake of continuing the family line. In the

Table 9.3 Estimated numbers of different types of adoption in Japan per year in mid-1990s

A 'Traditional' (Futsu yōshi)	B To register children on Koseki	C 'New' Tokubetsu yōshi
A 61,100/year of which: A1 60,000 adult A2 1,100 children	B 26,5000/year	C 500/year

Sources: Figures for A1 and B are extrapolated from a survey by the Supreme Court which was part of the discussions leading up to the revision of the adoption law (Saikō Saibansho Jimu Sōkyoku 1988, 5–6) and a report by Yonekura (1984: 2). Figures for A2 and C are extrapolated from Iwasaki (1992: 56) and Ministry of Foreign Affairs, Japan (1996: 54)

Table 9.4 Estimated numbers of adoptions by age and gender in Japan, 1983

By age:

Age	Annual number	Average number per age year
0	874	874
1–5	8,588	1,718
6–11	12,768	2,128
12–14	2,850	950
15–19	3,268	654
20–29	33,364	3,336
30–39	14,706	1,471
40–49	4,978	498
50–59	3,116	312
60–69	760	76
70–79	114	11
TOTAL	**85,386**	

Adoption of Minors (under 20): 28,348 (33.2%)
Adoption of Adults (over 20): 57,038 (66.8%)

By gender (figures in percentages):

Age range	Male	Female
0–19	51.2	48.8
20–39	86.2	13.8
Over 40	50.8	49.2

Source: Yuzawa (1983: 24). Yuzawa has extrapolated these figures from a 1982 Justice Ministry Survey of some 2,247 cases

immediate post-war period there were many such adoptions – 43,849 in 1949 – but numbers have declined consistently and dramatically since. Such adoptions have since the war needed to be approved by the courts. While the absolute number of 'traditional' and 'registration' adoptions has dropped considerably over the past twenty years – from some 150,000 to about 90,000 today – there clearly remain many who think that adoption is necessary for continuing the family line. As Table 9.4 shows, though, the majority of all such adoptions are of adults – some quite elderly – of whom most are male.

While it is easy and still not uncommon to undertake adoption to continue the family line, the general perceptions of this practice are confused and, according to some informants and researchers (see Yonekura 1984: 6), rather negative or suspicious (*'kurai'* – dark – is the term often used). Ideas expressed include that there must be something wrong in the family that they need to adopt or even that there may be something suspicious (*inchiki-teki*) behind the adoption. Adoption can be used as a means to avoid inheritance tax (*sōzoku-zei*) – 80 year olds, therefore sometimes adopt 70 year olds; relatives sometimes adopt children so that they can live in the catchment area of a particularly good state school; employers, in the current period of shortages of blue-collar manual workers, adopt illegal overseas workers so as to keep them in the country (Kikuchi 1991). The most common response in discussions about adoption, however, is '*kawaisō*' (how sad) for all concerned, though perhaps particularly for a marrying-in man who, so the saying goes, should refuse to be adopted if he still has three cups of rice to his name. The idea that there is something philanthropic in adopting a child whose parents cannot look after it has very little history in Japan.

The impetus behind the introduction of the *tokubetsu yōshi* system in Japan can largely be traced back to a famous case in the 1970s. Kikuta Noboru was a doctor who specialized in both abortions and infertility – and could see certain inherent contradictions in his work. Abortion rates in Japan not only historically but also today are, by international standards, high, and it is still used as one of the main forms of 'contraception'. Kikuta believed that one reason for the high abortion rate was because anonymous adoptions were impossible.

The main obstacle to the adoption of unwanted children has been the *koseki* (family register) system that has been in force since 1872 and makes it compulsory to record that a woman has given birth – under any circumstances. Since the *koseki* has in the past been needed for such basic acts as obtaining a driving licence or a passport, applying to schools or companies, and may even still today be examined by prospective parents-in-law, the potential stigma involved in recording an illegitimate birth may cause major problems later in life not only for the mother but also her family.

Kikuta claimed that it was easy to find potential adoptive parents – from among those he assessed as infertile – if only he could persuade the mother to give up her child for adoption rather than have it aborted; he claimed to have relayed some 220 babies illegally to adoptive parents from the early 1970s and to have recorded them (illegally) as their natural children (*jisshi*) and ensured that there was no trace on the natural mother's family register.

Partly as a result of Kikuta's lobbying, a new adoption law was introduced in 1988 by which children could be registered by adoptive parents as their natural children. The law, moreover, contains a number of strict regulations which – for the first time in Japan – are meant to protect the welfare interests of the child:

- the adoption must be concluded by *katei saibansho* (family court);[9]
- it ends all legal relationship between the adopted child and biological parents;
- parents must be married and over 25, child must be under 6;
- adoption is possible only in cases where biological parents are really unsuitable and adoption is in interests of child;[10]
- it may not be nullified by the adoptive parents;
- there will be a six-month trial period during which adoptive parents remain under investigation by Jidōsōdanjō;
- normally parents will be encouraged to become foster parents first.

Under this system, adopted children are no longer expected to support their blood parents, only their adoptive parents in old age – an important issue in Japan, where social welfare for the elderly is still relatively underdeveloped; nor do the children have any right to inherit from their biological parents, a measure which is intended to reduce what has been an ongoing area of conflict between adopted children and their blood siblings. The fact that the *biological* mother has delivered and given up a baby for adoption, however, continues to be marked on *her koseki* – to prevent consanguineous marriages.

The new law, however, has not, in numerical terms, had the impact that Kikuta's early work appeared to suggest it might. While there were 1,814 adoptions in 1988 through the *tokubestu yōshi* system, numbers declined successively over the next three years to around 500 a year in the mid-1990s (Aoki 1994: 24). As Table 9.5 shows, indeed, the total number of child adoptions, through either the *futsu* or the *tokubetsu* system has declined dramatically since the *tokubetsu yōshi* system was introduced. We shall explore reasons for this decline later.

Table 9.5　Figures for *futsu* and *tokubetsu yōshi* adoptions of children, 1985–95

Year	Futsu yōshi * – under 20 ** – under 18	Tokubetsu yōshi all under 6	Total of child adoptions
1985	3,245*	–	3,245
1986	3,296*	–	3,296
1987	2,876*	–	2,876
1988	2,421*	1,814	4,235
1989	2,151*	1,933	4,084
1990	2,037*	1,178	3,213
1991	1,529**	619	2,148
1992	1,310**	509	1,819
1993	1,258**	520	1,778
1994	1,205**	491	1,696
1995	1,111**	521	1,632

Note: The *tokubetsu yōshi* system came into effect in 1988
Sources: Iwasaki (1992: 56); Ministry of Foreign Affairs (1996: 54)

Similarly, the first revision of the foster care law to be introduced since 1947 that came into effect in 1987 has had little effect on patterns of fostering. Administratively, the new law transferred authority in this area previously exercised by prefectural governors to local public bodies. More practically, it attempted to increase the number and improve the image of foster parents through reducing the amount of investigation potential foster parents had to go through before registration; by providing better training for foster carers; by utilizing non-government organizations to publicize[11] (and train) the activities of foster carers; and by simplifying the criteria expected of foster parents to simply having an understanding of childcare and offering a stable family life, not necessarily involving marriage. Nevertheless, in a population of 120 million, still only 3,000 children are being fostered and the figures have continued to decline (see Table

9.2). As we shall see, there are a number of interesting factors which may help explain why neither the new adoption law nor the new fostering systems have been as effective as hoped.

THE FAILURE OF THE ADOPTION AND FOSTERING REFORMS

It must be said that many doubt Kikuta's claims as to the ease with which he found adoptive parents who were prepared to take children without knowing their background.[12] Part of the problem is that there exists in Japan – and the *tokubestu yōshi* system has in some ways exacerbated this – a fundamental confusion between fostering and adoption. There remains strongly the idea that one fosters so as to adopt, and there is much evidence from the fostering agencies which try to place children from *yōgoshisetsu* that many of the registered foster parents are very fussy about which children they will foster because they are in fact searching for a child to adopt. Of total numbers fostered, 50 per cent are under 3 years of age; 80 per cent are under 6. Only 7 per cent of registered foster parents, according to surveys, are not fussy at all about the child they take (see Tokyo-to Yōiku Katei Centre 1991: 10): very few indeed are prepared to foster – let alone adopt – disabled children, who, if they find a family at all, tend to go overseas or to foreign couples in Japan through the services of organizations such as the Japan International Social Service (Nihon Kokusai Shakai Jigyōdan). Mixed-blood children have been almost impossible to place in Japan and a whole community for such young people born during the post-war American Occupation was set up in the 1960s in tropical Brazil (see Hemphill 1980: 140ff). This reluctance to adopt unknown children is normally summed up in the expression '*Doko no uma no hone ka wakaranai*' (You don't know from which horse the bone comes) – an expression which is also commonly used when choosing a spouse.

Alternatively, Ozawa (1991: 13) argues that the recent decline in fostering in Japan (and, perhaps by association, in adoption for the sake of the child) is related not so much to social attitudes towards unknown children but to economic factors: the increase in housing costs (which was particularly significant during the bubble economy of the 1980s) and the expanded participation rates of women in the labour force. The idea that fostering could itself be seen as an occupation for those properly qualified, so-minded and accredited has not been accepted in Japan. One of the main concerns of the 1947 Act was that there should not be abuse of child support expenses, and anyone who considers fostering with any financial motives is viewed very suspiciously by the social workers who approve foster families; this explains, in part, the reluctance of those without substantial means to volunteer to foster.

Jidōsōdanjō workers argue that it is the natural parents and guardians of the children – who in Japan have the weight of the law on their side to such an extent that it is difficult even for courts to override them – who, again confusing adoption and fostering, do not want their children fostered in case they lose control over them and cannot get them back. The Katei Saibansho (family court) does have the power to place children in children's homes, but it does not have the power to keep them there, and parents are able to take their children out whenever they want. Hence, it is that courts have no option but to place such children in infant and children's homes and that some children (about whom social workers have particular concerns) are literally hidden in, or moved around between, homes to avoid being removed from the system altogether.

Foster placements, when they have been made, have often proved unsuccessful, with a high rate of breakdown. Komatsu (1992: 146) explains this in terms of lack of state support for the foster carers who, he says, 'More than anywhere else . . . are squeezed between low practical support on the one hand and high expectations on the other.' The following case of a boy in the home where I did fieldwork is not atypical and was told to me by a psychologist who had been brought in to advise staff on how to alter their practice in working with 'problem' children.

> X was abandoned when he was less than one and placed in an infant's home [*nyūjiin*)] from where he graduated to a *yōgoshisetsu*. Unusually, a foster family was found for him but, at the age of 4, he was rejected and returned to the children's home. His foster mother said he was continually peeping at her while she was having a bath and that it was beyond her ability to deal with such unhealthy behaviour. [The therapist related this behaviour to the boy having been in a Catholic *nyūjiin* where nuns showed him no affection; he desperately wanted it from his foster mother but she thought his attentions were perverted and returned him to the home.][13] X was found another foster family with whom he stayed until 10 or 11 when he started stealing money from the family and again was returned to a home. Now [aged 17] he was having a lot of problems in the home; stealing from other children and staff. [The therapist explained that his motivation, in part at least, was that he wanted 'to be loved even if bad' since the one thing he had always been denied was unconditional love.[14]]

This sad tale supports Komatsu's (1992) account of the lack of support for foster (and other carers) by the Japanese state, which prefers to play the role of what he describes as 'peripheral non-responsibility'. In the case of fostering, this role is particularly problematic and may be exacerbated by the age of many of the foster parents – in 1990 almost 10 per cent of fathers and 6.5 per cent of mothers were over 60 years old; 40 per cent and 30 per cent respectively over 50; and only 0.4 per cent and 1.1 per cent under 30 (Sato Oya Kai 1990: 9) – and the majority are themselves childless and have little or no experience of childcare.

Despite a high rate of breakdowns, the average length of time in foster care for those so placed is in fact slightly higher than the average placement in homes (Takahashi 1987: 9), so perhaps of at least equal significance in explaining the failure of the new ('Western-style') adoption and fostering policies are the vested interests of the *yōgoshisetsu* which currently look after over 90 per cent of children in care. In a sense, some of the homes want to keep hold of the children in their care and it is interesting that in Tokyo just six, generally viewed as the more progressive, of the thirty-seven homes provide half of all the children who are fostered (Tokyo-to Yōiku Katei Centre 1991: 9).

Many children who come into care are first placed in a children's home which some see as a major weakness of the system since subsequent fostering is even more disruptive.[15] The subsequent chance of being fostered from residential care has actually been declining in recent years. Since 1955, the number of children in foster homes has dropped by over 65 per cent, while that in *yōgoshisetsu* has fallen by less than 15 per cent; less than 40 per cent of foster placements are taken up, 83 per cent of places in children's homes are occupied (see Table 9.6). The argument put forward by the homes as to why this is so is that they provide 'professional care' whereas foster parents supply amateur care particularly in the case of children with emotional problems (see Yamamoto 1988: 6; Zadankai 1991: 21).

There is another reason, however, that needs to be considered which relates to the institutionalization of the homes themselves: to a certain extent, the homes are run by, and for, the families who set them up and who have a vested interest in maintaining them as going concerns. This idea was clearly apparent at the annual conference for the Heads of all the Children's Homes held in Kyoto in November 1991, where the main item on the agenda was how they were going to respond to the '1.53 shock' – the fact that women were having only 1.53 children during their childbearing years and hence there would be a great decline in the number of children in the population and, by inference, in the homes in the near future.[16] Some homes might well need to be closed.

Table 9.6 Comparative proportion of children in foster home placements and in child protection institutions, 1955–89

Year	Foster care	Children's homes	Infant homes
1955	9,111 (56.2%)	32,944 (?)	2,755 (?)
	[100]	[100]	[100]
1965	6,909 (33.4%)	32,346 (88.0%)	3,188 (82.6%)
	[75.8]	[98.1]	[115.7]
1970	4,729 (29.9%)	30,933 (90.3%)	3,331 (81.5%)
	[51.9]	[93.9]	[120.9]
1975	3,851 (31.5%)	30,084 (86.6%)	3,292 (?)
	[42.2]	[91.3]	[119.4]
1980	3,188 (29.6%)	30,787 (88.2%)	2,945 (69%)
	[34.9]	[93.5]	[106.8]
1985	3,429 (30.2%)	30,717 (87.7%)	3,004 (73%)
	[37.6]	[93.2]	[113.0]
1989	3,069 (39.1%)	28,252 (83.1%)	2,661 (67%)
	[33.6]	[85.8]	[95.5]

Key:
( ) = % of available places being taken up
[ ] = relative percentage in different types of care compared to 1955

Source: *Shakai Fukushi Happyō* (1952–90)

The implications of the 1.53 shock for running a children's home appear very considerable. For example, because of the long history of the *yōgoshisetsu* and their links with other social welfare institutions, considerable political power and social status can accrue from being the head of a home, even more from being the head of the *rijikai* (board of governors) of several welfare institutions centred around a home that have formed a joint *shakai fukushi gakusha* (social welfare corporation). It would appear not uncommon for the head of a *yōgoshisetsu* to be on the local government *shakai fukushi kyōgikai* (social welfare council), and from there political elevation to higher local government positions is possible.

There are also potentially significant financial issues at stake. When one visits, or meets for the first time, the head of a private *yōgoshisetsu* there are two pieces of information which one quickly discovers: the age of the home and its capacity. When talking about numbers of children, heads of private homes always cite the home's capacity (*teiin*) rather than the actual number of children (about which they can at times be rather vague). The reason for this is that should a home's intake drop too far below its capacity (the figure is unspecified), it is in danger of having its capacity reduced or even of being removed from the *sochi seido* (government placement system) altogether and hence losing its public funding. Clearly, there is little political or economic incentive for the heads of homes to find adoption or fostering placements for the children in their care.

CONCLUSION

The attempts to introduce new forms of fostering and adoption into Japan and the debates surrounding them raise interesting questions about a whole range of issues: the perception of welfare in Japan; the relationship between the state and the individual; the concept of the child and children's rights; and indeed the type of society Japan is and should become.

On the one hand, there are increasingly vocal groups that are attempting to introduce 'Western' ideas of both adoption and fostering practices where the focus is on the interests of the child and not the adoptive family (who want to adopt to continue the family line or occupation) or the foster family (who want to foster with a view to adoption if all works out well). They insist that personal social services should be organized and provided to meet the needs of those who require them, rather than in the interests of those who provide or pay for them. Much of what they write and say is supported by examples from outside Japan – especially the United States, Canada, Scandinavia and the UK, where they aver that such systems exist – and is presented under the banner of 'internationalization', the current 'buzzword' rhetoric in Japanese society that some draw on to try and bring Japan in to line with Western, OECD counterparts.

Other groups in Japan, however, argue that such practices go against Japanese 'tradition'. Some of those who work in the children's homes argue strongly that it is more beneficial to the children for them to stay in such homes than be fostered or adopted out: they argue that the shared and cooperative life children lead in such institutions (with up to 200 other children) suits them as East Asians who 'naturally' enjoy living in large groups (see Nozawa 1991; Zadankai 1991) and contrast Japanese experience with the large number of foster-home breakdowns in some Western countries (see Berridge and Cleaver 1987).

Many of those who work in childcare institutions in Japan cite the absence of fostering and adoption as among those practices which characterize Japanese children's homes and which have developed naturally out of Japanese cultural practice. Underlying such practice is a different concept of the relationship between the individual and the state to that in the West: in Japan, the care system is still discussed in terms of *hogo* (protection) rather than any idea of service. The state provides for those members who cannot look after themselves, but this is on the basis that they are in absolute need of that help, not that they have rights as citizens to a minimum standard of living. The stigma attached to receiving welfare benefits grew during the 1980s, as the government has turned away from the seeming convergence course with Western European systems that it followed in the early 1970s, to an attempt to construct a 'Japanese-style welfare' system (*Nihongata fukushi seido*) with an emphasis on self-reliance, independence and the market mechanisms of the private-sector economy (see Tabata 1990). The lack of support for foster carers is a good example of the 'small state' in welfare matters. The state argues that it is culturally compatible (and financially healthy) to intervene as little as possible in everyday foster-carer-receiver relationships and it continues to treat foster parents as 'traditional national parents' and hence gives them minimum practical support (Komatsu 1992: 145).

Many similar debates took place over the ratification by Japan of the UN Convention on the Rights of the Child (see Goodman 1996). At their core is the idea of whether the child should be seen as a separate being to be respected as an individual or whether, as it has often been viewed in Japan, as something to be moulded (*kitaeru*) into a social being (*shakaijin*) (Hendry 1986b) to play a particular social role.

Underlying these debates, though, are differing ideas not just about the 'person' and the 'child' but also about 'time' and 'continuity'. It has been difficult to introduce UN conventions based on Anglo-Saxon concepts of the rights of the child, when they have had to compete with notions of the role that a child is supposed to play in Japanese society in the continuity of families. Very few families in Japan either adopt or foster children if they already have children of their own, since they have already fulfilled their commitment to their ancestors to continue the family household. While practices of adoption and fostering may appear to be 'natural' outcomes of indigenous kinship systems, they are in fact, like all cultural forms, constructs that demonstrate important economic, political, historical and social features. These are always open to change and challenge or, as Terrell and Modell (1994: 156) put it: 'what adoption means . . . is malleable, contingent, pragmatic', and as Esther Goody (1982) demonstrates in her work on adoption practices among West Africans in London, terms such as 'adoption' and 'fostering' are culturally and historically relative. There is no reason why the concepts of time and of the child cannot change in Japanese society. Nevertheless, the fact that, throughout their long histories, both fostering and adoption in Japan have generally been conducted primarily in the interests of the families concerned rather than of the individual children has made problematic the acceptance of new systems in which the interests of the child are given primacy. Indeed, as the evidence presented in this paper suggests, such attempts to introduce new concepts of fostering and adoption may actually have been counter-productive so that even the number of children who are adopted to continue the family line – and thereby find a family and an all-important network of connections – has been in decline. As we have seen, the current debate on adoption and fostering reflects important internal cultural debates over the concepts of children, rights and the state. There is little evidence yet, however, to suggest that children have been the beneficiaries of these discussions.

NOTES

* Any project based on fieldwork necessarily incurs enormous debts, not all of which can be acknowledged. I would like to thank here, however, the help I received while preparing this paper from Itō Yone, Nakagawa Yuri, Tsuzaki Tetsuo, Chikuchi Midori and Hino Katsumi. The fieldwork on which this paper is based was funded by a grant from the Japan Society for the Promotion of Science.

1 According to Bachnik (1988: 15), Japanese adoption is first mentioned in the Nara period (710–94) where it had already developed its own Japanese flavour and diverted from Chinese practice.

2 In the mid-1980s, there were almost 19,000 cases of adoptions being revoked a year, a ratio of around 20 per cent of all adoptions, a figure that was remarkably consistent over the previous ten years (see Saikō Saibansho Jimu Sōkyoku 1988: 5–6).

3 Hence, in this context it is important to note that adoption does not necessarily mean co-residence while fostering does.

4 While most adoptions are of adults, whose competence can already be judged, child adoptions allow for emotional ties to develop between adopters and adoptees. Since the future abilities of a boy who is adopted must be in doubt, in the case of childless couples, adoption is often of a girl, who can be brought up as a 'daughter', and for whom a capable man can be adopted later as a husband. It should be stressed that sexual relations between adopted children are not considered to be incestuous. Another method for childless couples is to adopt an already married couple, sometimes at the time of their wedding.

5 The classic example here, of course, is the Japanese imperial family where adoption has allowed it to claim unbroken continuity for 124 generations since the 'foundation' of Japan in 660 BC.

6 The expression '*sato no oya*' is still used in Japan to talk about the parents of one's wife or by wives to talk about their own parents. *Sato* means 'natal place'; *oya* means parent or parents.

7 There are interesting parallels between the case of the Shōwa Emperor and some Oceanic societies, such as Hawaii, where such fostering practices were also common (see Terrell and Modell 1994: 156–7).

8 One can compare this with African ideas of what Kopytoff and Miers (1977: 55ff.) call 'adoptive slavery' or 'acquired persons'.

9 The Court needs to be convinced by the applicant and the family court social worker that the potential adoptee is in need of the care being offered (*yōhogoyōken*). If it is not convinced of this, then the application for adoption will be rejected, thereby ensuring that the child's, and not the applicant's, rights and needs are placed first (see Ishizaka 1990: 34).

10 Technically under the new adoption law (Minpō, clause 815), a child after the age of 15 can sue to return to his or her biological parents if they can prove that they can look after him. Since adoption was initially approved only because it was 'proved' that their parents were not capable, this is very unlikely to occur.

11 Many in Japan still think, for example, that foster parents receive no payment for taking in children, when in fact they received in 1994 between Y75,000–115,000 a month, depending on individual circumstances and the prefecture in which they lived.

12 Different sources put the number of adoptions Kikuta arranged as variously between 100 and 220. His sudden death in August 1991, age 65, left many questions unanswered.

13 The desire for close physical contact (known in Japanese as 'skinship') is something that is often mentioned in the context of children in care by teachers, carers and foster parents, who say that children are often excessively demanding in their search for affection (*hitonatsukkoi*). The staff : child ratio in homes means that children are often deprived of 'skinship' which is considered an essential element of child socialization in Japan.

14 The classic work on the importance of unconditional love in Japanese childhood is Doi Takeo's *The Anatomy of Dependence* (1973).

15 Virtually all infants who come in to care are placed in *nyūjiin* rather than fostered since only those with 'special skills', such as nurses, are allowed to foster such young children.

16 The number of children under age 15 in Japan fell from 30.1 million in 1955 to 26.5 million in 1984 to 20.8 million in 1993 (Keizai Kōhō Center 1995: 8).

REFERENCES

Aoki, Susumu (1994) 'Tokubetsu yōshi engumi no Saibansho no Mondaiten [Issues in the Special Adoption Court Judgement System], *Hōritsu no Hiroba*, February, pp. 24–30.

Bachnik, Jane (1988) 'Adoption', *Kodansha Encyclopedia of Japan*, vol. 1, pp. 14–15.

Beardsley, R. K. *et al.* (1959) *Village Japan*, Chicago: University of Chicago Press.

Befu, Harumi (1962) 'Corporate Emphasis and Patterns of Descent in the Japanese Family', in R. J. Smith and R. K. Beardsley (eds) *Japanese Culture: Its Development and Characteristics*, Chicago: University of Chicago Press.

Berridge, D. and H. Cleaver (1987) *Foster Home Breakdown*, Oxford: Basil Blackwell.

Doi, Takeo (1973) *The Anatomy of Dependence* (trans by John Bester), Tokyo, London and New York: Kodansha International.

Goodman, Roger (1996) 'On introducing the UN Convention on the Rights of the Child into Japan', in Roger Goodman and Ian Neary (eds) *Case Studies on Human Rights in Japan*, Kent: Curzon Japan Library, pp. 109–40.

—— (forthcoming). 'The "Japanese-Style" Welfare State and the Delivery of Personal Social Services', in Roger Goodman, Gordon White and Huck-Ju Kwon (eds) *The East Asian Welfare Model: Welfare Orientalism and the State*, London: Routledge.

Goody, Esther (1982) *Parenthood and Social Reproduction: Fostering and Occupational Roles in West Africa*, Cambridge: Cambridge University Press.

Goody, Jack (1969) 'Adoption in Cross-Cultural Perspective', *Comparative Studies in Society and History*, vol. 11, pp. 55–78.

Hara, Yoshihisa (1995) *Kishi Nobusuke: Kensei no Seijika [Kishi Nobusuke: A Politician of Influence]*, Tokyo: Iwanami Shoten.

Hemphill, Elizabeth Anne (1980) *The Least of These: Miki Sawada and Her Children*, New York and Tokyo: Weatherhill.

Hendry, Joy (1986a) *Marriage in Changing Japan: Community and Society*, Tokyo: Tuttle.

162 *Roger Goodman*

—— (1986b) *Becoming Japanese: The World of the Pre-School Child*, London: Routledge.

Ishizaka, Fumiko (1990) 'Tokubetsu Yōshi Jishō Oboegaki' ['Notes on the Beginning of the Tokubetsu Yōshi system'], *Atarashii Kazoku* [*New Family*], no. 17, pp. 33–7.

Iwasaki, Mieko (1992) 'Zadankai [Discussion Meeting]', *Atarashii Kazoku* [*New Family*], no. 21, *Yōshi to Sato-oya o Kagaeru Kai*.

Keizai Kōhō Center (1995) *Japan 1995: An International Comparison*, Tokyo.

Kikuchi, Midori, (1991) 'Nihon no Sato-oya seido. Yōshi Seido o Kangaeru' ['Reflections on Japan's Adoption and Fostering Systems'], unpublished paper presented to the *Jidō Fukushihō Kenkyūkai* (Child Welfare Law Study Group), 22 October.

Komatsu, Ryuji (1992) 'The State and Social Welfare in Japan: Patterns and Developments', in Paul Close (ed.) *The State and Caring*, Basingstoke and London: Macmillan, pp. 128–47.

Kopytoff, Igor and Suzanne Miers (1977) 'African "Slavery" as an Institution of Marginality', in Igor Kopytoff and Suzanne Miers (eds) *Slavery in Africa: Historical and Anthropological Perspectives*, Wisconsin: University of Wisconsin Press.

Kōseitōkeikyōkai (ed.) (1992) *Kokumin no Fukushi no Dōkō* [*Trends in Public Welfare*], vol. 39, no. 12.

Lebra, Takie Sugiyama (1993) *Above the Clouds: Status Culture of the Modern Japanese Nobility*, Berkeley: University of California Press.

Ministry of Foreign Affairs, Japan (1996) *The First Report to the UN Committee on the Rights of the Child*, Gaimushō (Japanese language version), Tokyo.

Nakane, Chie (1967) *Kinship and Social Organisation in Rural Japan*, London: Athlone Press.

Nihon Shakai Minzokugaku Kyōkai (ed) (1954) *Nihon Shakai Minzoku Jiten* [*Dictionary of Japanese Folklore*], Tokyo: Seibundo Shinkōsha.

Nihon Sōgō Aiku Kenkyūjo (ed.) (1988) *Nihon Kodomo Shiryō Nenkan* [*Annual Statistical Review of Children in Japan*], *1988/89*, Nagoya: Chūō Shuppan.

Noguchi, Takenori (1988) 'Satogo' [Foster Child], *Kodansha Encyclopedia of Japan*, vol. 7, p. 26.

Nozawa, Masako (1991) *Jidō Yōgoron* [*The Theory of Child Care*], Tokyo: Minerva Shobō.

Ozawa, Martha N. (1991) 'Child Welfare Programmes in Japan', *Social Service Review*, March.

Saikō Saibansho Jimu Sōkyoku (ed.) (1988) *Yōshi Seido no kaisei ni kansuru System Shiryō* [*Documentation Concerning the Revision of the Adoption System*], Tokyo: Saikō Saibansho Jimu Sōkyoku.

Sato Oya Kai (ed.) (1990) 'Sato Oya Kenshūkai [Foster Parents' Symposium text]'.

Sekimoto, Teruo (1988) *Research Methods in Japanese Studies: Cultural Anthropology*, Office for the Japanese Studies Center, Tokyo: The Japan Foundation (Orientation Seminars on Japan, no. 31).

Shakai Fukushi Happyō, 1952–90.

Tabata, Hirokuni (1990) 'The Japanese Welfare State: Its Structure and Transformation', in *Annals of the Institute of Social Science* (Tokyo University), no. 32, pp. 1–29.

Takahashi, Toshikazu (1987) 'Japanese Children's Homes in Recent Years', *Child Welfare: Quarterly News from Japan*, vol. 7, no. 4, June, pp. 2–10.

Terrell, John and Judith Modell (1994) 'Anthropology and Adoption', *American Anthropologist*, vol. 96, no. 1, March, pp. 155–61.

Tokyo-to (1991) *Tōkyō no Sato-oya: Yōiku Katei Seido* [*Tokyo's Foster Parents*].

Tokyo–To Yōiku Katei Centre (1991) *Tōkyō-to Yōiku Katei Seido 17-nenkan no Hōkoku* [*Report on 17 years of the Tokyo City Adoption and Fostering System*], Tokyo: Tōkyō-to Yōiku Katei Centre.

Vogel, Ezra F. (1963) *Japan's New Middle Class: The Salary Man and his Family in a Tokyo Suburb*, Berkeley: University of California Press.

Yamamoto, Tamotsu (1988) 'Revision of the Foster Care System', *Child Welfare: Quarterly News from Japan*, vol. 8, no. 3, March, pp. 2–9.

Yonekura, Akira (1984) 'Problems Involved in the Child Adoption and Foster Parent Systems in Japan', *Child Welfare: Quarterly News from Japan*, vol. 4, no. 4, June, pp. 2–10.

Yuzawa, Kazuhiko (1983) 'Nihon ni okeru Yōshi Engumi no Tōkeiteki Ozei [Current Statistical Trends in Japanese Adoption]', *Atarashii Kazoku [New Family]*, no. 3, pp. 21–9.

Zadankai (1991) 'Yōgo Shisetsu no Genjō to Kadai' [Themes and the Current Position of Children's Homes]', *Kodomo to Katei: Tokushū Yōgo Shisetsu no Shōrai Tenbō [Family and Children: Special Issue on Future Perspectives for Children's Homes]*, vol. 28, no. 7, October, pp. 8–29.

Part III

Religion, science and cosmology

10 Gods, ancestors and mediators*

A cosmology from the South-western Archipelago of Japan

Teigo Yoshida

My aim in this article is to describe and analyse certain Japanese notions – such as that of the other world, ideas about the snake *habu* and about certain plants (pampas-grass and beans), and the image of a supernatural monster – current among the inhabitants of the Nansei Shotō (South-western Archipelago), particularly of the Amami Islands. While the notion of the other world has been investigated in Okinawa (see, for example, Ogo 1966; Origuchi 1975a, 1975b, 1976), its status in Tokunoshima, one of the Amami Islands, has been hardly documented – although Kreiner has reported (1971) with regard to the idea of the other world in Kakeroma, another of the Amami Islands. Native ideas of *habu*, of supernatural monsters and of plants have been given least attention by previous scholars. While my own emphasis here is placed upon the native point of view, interpretations independent of the people's own explanations are also attempted for certain phenomena.

THE NOTION OF *NEIRA*: THE WORLD BEYOND THE SEA

Among the inhabitants of the Amami Islands the notion of a world located far beyond the sea, variously called *neriya*, *neira*, *niira* or *nera* (*nirai* or *nirai-kanai* in Okinawa), exists even today.

It is in a ritual called *hamaori* (descent to the beach), annually performed in the island of Tokunoshima, that this notion of *neira* is most clearly revealed. The ritual is performed in almost every village on the island, and as in most other festivals and rituals in the Amami and Okinawa Islands, it is performed according to the old (lunar) calendar. It takes place on three days after *bon* (the festival honouring the ancestors) – namely, *hinoe* (elder of fire), *hinoto* (younger of fire) and *tsuchinoe* (elder of the earth).[1] On the first day several groups of patrilineally related families construct their own hut in which they place three stones in the shape of a 'U' to make a *kama*, or oven. It is said that this first day of the ritual is devoted to inviting ancestors to the beach to make them feel comfortable. On the second day the members of each group gather in their own hut to eat and drink together after offering food on the *kama* to their ancestors. Although several years ago the actual construction of huts ceased, they still gather on the beach and build the oven on the day of *hinoto*. On this day they perform a rite called *miibama kumashi* (*niibama fumashi* in standard Japanese, i.e., stepping on the new beach). The rite consists of taking to the beach babies that have been born since the last *hamaori* of the previous year to make them take their first steps on the sand of the beach. People say that this is done in order to inform the ancestors of the arrival of the babies to their descendants, and to obtain protection from them. The people then enter the sea and splash water three times towards the god of the sea. They then purify themselves by splashing water over themselves, with the prayer 'We came here today for the ritual of *hamaori*. Please accept our offerings.' On the third day sumo wrestling or bull-fights are performed on the beach.

Several notions are involved in the ritual of *hamaori*. With regard to its purpose, old informants in Tokunoshima state that it is performed once a year for the purpose of praying to the ancestors for a good harvest through pleasing them on the beach. It is also said that *hamaori* is a ritual for the ancestors who died more than thirty-three years ago. In many south-western parts of Japan the thirty-third anniversary is customarily the last occasion on which the Japanese honour their ancestors. However, in Amami this occasion is not the last, for those ancestors who died earlier are also remembered in this ritual of *hamaori*. It seems that they annually worship deceased relatives and ancestors who died during the period of thirty-three years on the occasion of the *bon* festival.

In the village of Kaneku in Tokunoshima there exists a legend concerning the origins of the *hamaori* ritual. It had been customary for the inhabitants to spread harvested ears of rice on the beach for two days before threshing. On one occasion a typhoon washed them all away. The villagers grieved at the loss of their rice. However, when they came to the beach afterwards, they found, to their surprise, that all the ears of rice had been returned to the beach, pushed back by the sea. Since then they began worshipping the god of the sea who, they thought, had been responsible for returning the rice to them – hence, according to the villagers, the beginning of the ritual of *hamaori*.

Thus the ritual of *hamaori* is practised to welcome the ancestors and to worship the god of the sea as the god of rice. The latter implies that a feature of the ritual is the celebration of a good harvest. Indeed, some informants from the island said that those ancestors who are prayed to during the ritual of *hamaori* would come from the other world of abundance called *neira* or *neriya*. The offering of food above an oven made of three stones on the beach is said to be for the purpose of expressing gratitude to the ancestors for a good harvest, and of praying for another good harvest the following year.

The *hamaori* ritual is thus directed towards the ancestors in order to secure a good harvest as well as the protection of their descendants, and to express gratitude to the god of the sea and to the gods of *neira*, as the god of rice. Praying in front of the stone oven is directed not only to the ancestors but also to the god of fire.

In villages on the island of Iheya in Okinawa, when a wife dies, the oven-hearth (*kamado*) of her house is destroyed and abandoned. After the *shōkō* (incense burning), on the forty-ninth day which follows the death, an auspicious day is chosen to go to the beach to look for three proper stones to worship as sacred objects of the god of the oven or god of fire. In all the houses in Iheya, the god of the oven called *okama-ganashi* is worshipped in the kitchen located in the north-western part of the house. The three stones are sacred objects which are said to come from *nirai-kanai*, equivalent to *neira* in Tokunoshima, located far beyond the sea. For this reason beach sand – sometimes seaweed – is scattered around the stones.

Accordingly, *neira* or *nirai-kanai* is, on the one hand, conceived by the inhabitants of Amami and Okinawa as the world of their ancestors; on the other hand, it is the world from which rice and fire are brought to people (Mabuchi 1980).

Moreover, evil things such as illness and misfortune are also thought to be brought from *nirai*. Some scholars think that *nirai* as a source of misfortune is older and has been transformed into a world of happiness; other scholars argue, on the contrary, that *nirai* was a paradise which in turn became a world of evil. In both cases a linear development is presupposed, but with little evidence. It seems that *nirai* is rather to be regarded as a world possessing the ambiguous characteristics of evil as well as of good, of misfortune as well as happiness.

Yet in the island of Tokunoshima the tendency exists to think of the *neira* rather as a paradise, where there live those ancestors who passed away more than thirty-three years ago, than as an evil world. In the village of Inokawa, located on the east coast of the island, they burn the leaves of a tree called *shii* (*Shiia sieboldii*) on the thirty-third anniversary of a death, and the spirit of the dead is then supposed to ascend to the sky along with the smoke from the leaves, to join the ancestors in the world of *neira* beyond the sea. In the village of Matsubara, located on the west coast of the island, they have a similar custom, following the same idea, where the soul is conceived of as making a journey along the line of a parabola.

The notion of *neira* seems to be closely connected with the idea that a man or certain creatures (such as dolphins or whales) or objects floating in from the sea are regarded as sacred things which can bring about happiness. This idea can be seen in a legend told by contemporary inhabitants of the village of Inokawa concerning a shrine called Ibiganashi. As I have noted elsewhere (Yoshida 1981), the motif in this legend – namely, that a man who treats a stranger with warm hospitality will gain happiness – can be found in several ancient folk tales in Japan. For example, a rich man who refuses to allow a beggar-priest to stay in his house becomes poor, whereas a poor man who offers lodging to the priest becomes wealthy. Such a motif can be found in the folk tales concerning Kōbō Daishi. A similar notion with regard to the stranger is also found in ancient Greece, where there existed a belief that the gods often visit cities in the guise of strangers from afar. Mystical notions about strangers can also be found in Africa and elsewhere (Fortes 1975; Maloney 1976).

It is illustrated clearly in the legend of Ibiganashi that objects from the sea (associated with *neira* or *nirai*) may be regarded as sacred things. This notion is also found in ideas about *yorimono* (*yurimun* in Okinawa; literally, 'objects which arrived'); the custom of collecting things which came from the sea in order to worship them is widely distributed among the coastal areas of the Japanese islands, and these objects are often worshipped as the god Ebisu.

In addition to what can be called the horizontal movement of the divinities deriving from *neira* or *nirai-kanai* located in the remote sea, below the sea, or in the bottom of the earth, we should also recognize the vertical movement of the celestial divinities associated with the cult of *utaki* (a cult dedicated to the mountains or the forests considered sacred).

THE SNAKE *HABU*, MESSENGER OF THE OTHER WORLD

According to folk notions in Amami and Okinawa, certain animals and plants are intermediaries between this world of reality and the other, supernatural world. In this region in general the *habu* (*Trimeresurus flavoridis*) is considered a messenger of the gods and the ancestors. The snake is feared as it is poisonous, and unless its bite is immediately treated with a serum injection, it will normally cause death. To dream about a *habu* is considered a sign that someone will die in the near future. Being bitten by a *habu* is believed to be a mystical punishment (*habu atari*) by some supernatural being, such as an ancestor or other deity. The punishment occurs because one has neglected ancestor worship, defiled certain sacred things or done some other thing to invoke the anger of the gods.

Since a bite by a *habu* implies some mystical involvement, people consult a *yuta* (shaman or medium) to discover the reason for the bite, and act according to the instructions given by the *yuta*. Several years ago Mr Matsuyama Mitsuhide in Tokunoshima was bitten on the heel by a *habu* in his garden and had to be hospitalized (Matsuyama 1967). One old woman from his village visited him in the hospital and told him that she could not understand why a good man like him had been bitten by a *habu*. However, his mother immediately went to consult a *yuta*, who told her that the bite was caused because her son had defiled something sacred. According to her report, her son soon realized that he had unwittingly moved a stone to use as part of a hand-basin for a toilet, but the stone had formerly been brought into the garden from the sea by one of his ancestors (as described above, a stone from the sea is considered sacred because of its association with the *neira*).

The *habu* also possesses positive attributes. If one saves the life of a *habu* instead of killing it, one will be protected from accidents involving fire.

The times when a *habu* is believed to appear are fixed, and they are liminal in character: viz., in the *āyone* (twilight), at the *yuna-asa* (midnight) and in the *akatoki* (dawn). Twilight and dawn are both liminal hours between day and night, and midnight is the turning-point of one day to the next.

The *habu* is not only a messenger of the other world, but a deity of water and is often considered to be the master of Mount Ude in Tokunoshima. In this mountain villagers refrain from killing *habu*, because they are thought to be mystically punished if they kill one. People say that *habu* bite those who are impure – because of their attendance at funeral ceremonies or because of a death among their relatives – if they enter the mountain. This impurity due to death continues for seven days. *Habu* exist in other mountains or hills as well, and they do not permit such 'impure' people to enter. Neither do they like the menstrual pollution of women.

Because the *habu* transmits messages of the other world to human beings, it plays the role of mediator between this world and the other. One of the names given to the *habu* is *ayakubushu mēregua*. *Ayakubushu* means 'decorated with beautiful designs', and is an admirable quality of the skin of the *habu*, and *mēre* means 'beautiful girl' (Matsuyama 1967). This comparison of the *habu* with a young girl is possibly due to its role of mediator between this world and the other world, because such a role is often symbolically associated with women. In the Amami and Okinawan Islands most women are traditionally priestesses for public rituals. In assuming the role of mediator, the *habu* bites men in order to let them know that the worship addressed to the god of water is not sufficient, that the cult of the ancestors has been neglected, that a tree has been cut down in a sacred place, that a sacred stone has been defiled or polluted, or that a house has not been properly built according to the relevant directions.

Besides the *habu*, various other living beings may play the role of mediator – including birds, in particular crows and butterflies. In Izena Island, Okinawa, rats are considered messengers sent from the *nirai* world. Also a tree called *kuba* in Okinawa and Amami (*birō* in standard Japanese; *Livistona chinensis* var. *subglosa*) is believed to be a temporary residence of the gods, and similarly the *akō* (*Ficus wightiana*) and *gajumaru* (*Ficus retusa*) trees are inhabited by monsters called *kenmun* (see next section). The *susuki* (*Miscanthus sinensis*), the *yomogi* (*Artemisia vulgaris*), the *urajiro* (*Gleichenia glauca*), the *bashō* (*Musa basjoo*) and the *tobira* (*Pitlosporum tobira*) are also considered mystical plants. For example, in rituals such as the *maburi wāshi*, which will be described in a later section, the *yuta* (shaman) in Amami customarily put on a garment called *bashagin*, made of the *bashō*.

THE MONSTER *KENMUN*

Beliefs in various kinds of supernatural monsters used to be widespread among villagers in Japan. For instance, the red bean (*azuki*) is associated with one such supernatural being, who was supposed to produce noises by washing these beans in hollows in the countryside. It is said that when strange noises like the washing of beans are heard as one passes a stream or dale in mountainous areas at dusk, the noises are made by an old 'red bean' woman (*azuki baba*). In Sakugun, Nagano Prefecture, she was also believed to live in an empty house and sing a song which ran, 'Shall I wash red beans or eat a man?'

In the Amami Islands a belief in the supernatural monster called *kenmun* has survived to this day. In the mainland of Amami, as well as in Tokunoshima, this monster, conceived of as being male, is said to be covered with red hair, short like a child, with a long trunk, and short legs, and to salivate; while elsewhere it is also said that the *kenmun* has legs longer than his trunk when squatting. In Omonawa, in Tokunoshima, it is said that the *kenmun* wears leaves of a tree and for this reason he looks as if he is wearing a kimono of *kasuri* (splashed patterns). According to traditional beliefs, the *kenmun* sleeps in the hollow of a dead tree, and is often found on the banks of rivers, on the boundaries between the village and the beach, in caves on the beach, in shallows, in *akō* or *gajumaru* trees, in the bush, and at crossroads; he is also said to walk around at night in the shallows at low tide, carrying a lamp.

A man who happens to look at a *kenmun* is said to get a fever. He then gets lost in the mountains and cannot find his way home; his eyes become bloodshot and he sometimes falls unconscious. According to an informant from the village of Kinen, Tokunoshima, when a girl disappeared years ago, villagers searched for her for three days until they found her unconscious in the mountains; they beat her with bark from a tree to bring her back to consciousness. She then told the villagers that she had been deceived by a *kenmun*, and vomited what she had eaten; it all consisted of snails, which traditionally were not considered food for human beings. It is said that what a *kenmun* offers to men appears to be delicious, but in reality it is nothing but horse dung or snails.

According to the folklorists Ebara Yoshimori in Nase and Matsuyama Mitsuhide in Tokunoshima, the *kenmun* is not 'a monster of hairs' (*ke no mono*) but 'a monster of trees' (*ki no mono*), where *mun* is a dialect version of *mono* in standard Japanese referring to a spirit or supernatural being (personal communication). This monster corresponds to the *kijimun* of villages in Iheya, the northernmost island of Okinawa. The *kijimun* is also believed to be a spirit of trees, and is called *akakanaza* because his body is covered with red hair (Moromi 1981: 69).

In spite of the notion of the *kenmun* and the *kijimun* as spirits of trees, they are also believed to walk in the shallow waters of the sea at night, carrying a lamp. It is said that if fishermen in the shallows find their lamp going out and unwittingly ask a *kenmun* or *kijimun* for a light, they may get drowned by the monsters. On the island of Iheya the *kijimun* is believed to dislike and fear octopuses. An informant told me of an instance in which a man who was frightened by a *kijimun* in the shallow water at night threw an octopus at him. In anger, the *kijimun* tried to kill him, but the man narrowly escaped.

Inhabitants of the west coast of the mainland of Amami say that the body of the *kenmun* is covered with red hair, but the hair on his head is grey, and his face has neither eyes, ears nor eyebrows. According to a local published report, one man saw two *kenmun* with hanging testicles and with plates on their heads; he told villagers later that when the *kenmun* squatted, their legs appeared so long that their knees were over their heads. The man died afterwards because, it is said, he was mysteriously 'defeated' by the *kenmun* just by looking at them (Setouchi-chō Editorial Committee 1977: 394–498).

However, while *kenmun* often harm people, they have benevolent aspects as well. In Kasaricho on the main island of Amami, and elsewhere, it is said that fishermen have a good catch in the sea when they become friends of *kenmun*; they also say that the fish a *kenmun* catches for his friends in this way have only one eye because he eats the other eye of the fish but does not eat the meat.

The *kenmun*, who has thus an amphibious character, is sometimes identified with the *kappa*, a monster legendary in the mainland of Japan, a spirit of the waters, who is said to drown people swimming in rivers by pulling at their legs. In Kikaijima, the northernmost island of the Amami chain, I found that the word *kenmun* is known, but is usually referred to locally by the term *gaorō*. It is said that they live in a freshwater pond connected with the sea. Unlike the *kappa* on the mainland, the *gaorō* shares characteristics with the *kenmun* in living also in the *gajumaru* trees.

Like other supernatural monsters in Japan, such as *oni* (half-man/half-beast) and *tengu* (half-man/half-bird), *kenmun* is said to be like a human child, yet a half-beast covered with red hair.

Many peoples in the world attribute mystical qualities to certain animals. One of the explanations why certain animals are endowed with mystical features is that they seem to have anomalous characteristics to the people concerned: for example, the pangolin in Lele culture (Douglas 1966), the cassowary in Karam (Bulmer 1967), the cuscus in Nuaulu (Ellen 1972), etc. Furthermore, people tend to create imaginary monsters such as the unilateral figure (Needham 1980) and the Japanese monsters discussed above. In this context then, it is interesting to note the deformity associated with the *kenmun*; in one oral tradition, as mentioned above, he has neither eyes nor brows nor ears. Also, the *kenmun* eats only one eye of a fish but leaves the meat intact. The *kenmun* is not explicitly said to be left-handed but it is associated with left-handedness. In Tokunoshima they say that one should bite the forefinger of one's left hand in order to escape from the *kenmun*, because he is said to carry away a man or woman by pulling his or her left hand, and he would then let it go. Moreover, in order to cure the victims of *kenmun*, they tie a 'left rope' (*hidari-nawa*) – that is, a rope made by twisting strands in the opposite way to usual – to an *akō* tree, in which the *kenmun* is supposed to live. Similarly, when an eye disease is attributed to a *kenmun*, they stretch a 'left rope' around a *gajumaru* tree – a tree in which a *kenmun* is also believed to live.

The magical power of the 'left rope' is used by villagers in Tokunoshima also for other purposes: for example, at a funeral those who carry the coffin from a house to the village graveyard customarily protect themselves from the spirit of the dead by tucking up their sleeves with a 'left rope'. Also, when domestic animals become ill, a 'left rope' is tied round the cowshed to prevent evil spirits from entering. Formerly, when it thundered, people tried to protect themselves by hanging a 'left rope' made of pieces of clothes under the eaves of the house. On a day designated for 'destroying insects' the owners of rice-fields used to place a 'left knot' made of *susuki* (*Miscanthus sinensis*) in the opening of the irrigation channel for the fields. It is also said in Tokunoshima that one can defeat a *kenmun* in sumo wrestling if one 'wrestles with the left' (left hand under the enemy's armpit) (Ogawa 1970: 583–4).

Thus, it seems that the left principle is endowed with the magical power to drive out the *kenmun* just as the 'left rope' and the *susuki*, or pieces of cloth tied in a 'left knot', are used to expel the spirits of the dead or evil spirits. It is also often found in other cultures that the left hand is used for some magico-religious purposes (Needham 1960, 1973; Goody 1962: 111; Vogt 1969: 419; and see also Matsunaga, in this volume).

Symbolic reversals are often considered effective in driving out evil. Thus in Omonawa, Tokunoshima, in order to avoid harm from the *kenmun*, men take off their loin-cloths and tie them around their heads.

The hypothesis that animals which violate spatial boundaries tend to be endowed with mystical powers (Douglas 1966; Tambiah 1969) is also relevant here because of the 'amphibious' character of the *kenmun*, in as much as they wander around in the sea as well as in the trees and mountains, and the way the supernatural monster is associated with both spatial and temporal boundaries. It will be recalled that the places where the *kenmun* is likely to appear include village boundaries, crossroads, and a freshwater pond where the sea-water comes in at high tide. Furthermore, just as the 'red bean' woman and other monsters are believed to appear in the evening dusk, the *kenmun* is said to be most likely to appear at twilight. In Matsubara, Tokunoshima, people say that it is most likely to be about in the twilight of rainy days.

Similar notions associating the dusk of the evening with supernatural monsters or evil spirits exist in Bali and Malaysia. The dusk of the evening is called in Bali *sandi kala*, *sandi* meaning 'joint' or 'knot' and *kala* meaning evil spirits or 'time' (Howe 1981). Possibly it refers to the time between day and night. In the Amami Islands twilight or dusk is called *santuke* (*yūgata* in standard Japanese). People there say that during this time one should not visit tombs, nor weave or cut clothes, and that childbirth at this time of the day is detested. They also say that it is at this time that the human soul (*maburi*) is likely to go out, so that it is better not to walk on the street at twilight. It is also advised that young girls should not go out at this time of day because they are particularly likely to encounter *mainamun* (supernatural monsters) and *minkirawa* (pig monsters without ears) during twilight.

As mentioned earlier, *kenmun* is a red monster; *kijimun* in Okinawa is called *akakanaza*, in which *aka* denotes 'red', because his body is covered with red hair. While the colour red in the Japanese mainland is used as a good, auspicious colour, in both Okinawa and Amami, however, red is not a good colour. According to Tsunemi Jūn'ichi, in Okinawa, while the colour blue is a symbol of life, red expresses ageing, old age and death. Thus it is no surprise that the colour of the *kenmun*'s body is red.

THE *SUSUKI* AND THE BEAN[2]

The *susuki* is called *zukki*, *azaha* or *adaha* in Amami. The *susuki* generally plays an important ritual role in the south-western archipelago. For example, in Amami, for the sake of an easy childbirth, a *susuki* used to be placed underneath the bed of a woman during her confinement. In Tokunoshima, in the ritual described earlier for expelling insects, a knot of 'left-tied' *susuki* is placed on the edge of an irrigation ditch. Its effectiveness may be attributed to the 'left tie' used, but the *susuki* itself is also supposed to have mystical powers.

Among the rites still performed today in Kikaijima there is a ritual called *shichami*, in which people pray for the health and growth of children of one to twelve years. It is performed in August on a prescribed day of the lunar calendar. Five *susuki* are prepared for boys of 5, seven for the girl of 7 and so on. Early in the morning their parents or grandparents take them to a pond or well, dip the *susuki* in the water, and shake the drops extracted over the children, saying 'Get bigger quickly!' (*Okiku nare nare*). After this, a number of stones equal to the age of the child is collected from the pond, wrapped in the *susuki*, and brought home. The stones are later placed in the domestic shrine (*kamidana*).

In Kikaijima there is another ritual in August called *shibasashi*. This involves ancestor worship in which flowers are placed on the surface of the tombstones, swept beforehand by some *susuki*, and then *susuki* are placed in the four corners of the house, on both sides of the gate, and beside the well, for the purpose of expelling evil spirits.

In Setouchi-chō, Amami Ōshima, on the day of the *shibasashi*, the *susuki* is first placed on the four corners of the roof and also of the rice-fields. The purpose of this is said to be to purify the houses and fields and to expel evil spirits. The day of *shibasashi* is also the day when people receive *kōsoganashi* or *kosuganashi*, 'ancestors of the old time'. They are undoubtedly the ancestors who died more than thirty-three years ago. On this day straw and grasses are burnt so as to make the smoke by which the ancestors are supposed to come down from the sky. The ancestors are said initially to have come from the *neira*, far beyond the sea, so that they are said to be wet and cold, and need to be made dry and warm by the fire. The *susuki* are put together with the flowers in a vase in front of the ancestral tablets moved from their usual place to a room on the east side of the house (*omote*).

In Okinawa, on the day of *shibasashi*, rice mixed with *azuki* (red beans) is offered at the family altar, and the *susuki* tied with branches of mulberry are planted in the eaves to expel evil spirits. As Yanagita Kunio has remarked (1951: 451), 'just like the *shichoku* (*Aucuba japonica*), the *susuki* . . . is liked by gods'.

On the one hand, the *susuki* is used to expel evil spirits; on the other hand, it is used to invite or summon up a spirit or soul of the dead. For example, there is a ritual in the Amami Islands called *maburiwaashi*, performed by the *yuta* (shaman). Generally, it is practised within the period of forty-nine days after a death – in general the nineteenth, twenty-ninth or thirty-ninth day – but certain shamans refuse to practise the rite before the seventh day, because during the period of seven days after a death the pollution caused by the death is said to be too strong. The ritual begins with the summoning of the soul (*maburi*) of the deceased. The shaman calls the soul by reciting certain formulae, while holding the *susuki* with a fan, then moving them in a circular fashion around his or her mouth. The *yuta* thus invites the soul to inform its living relatives through his or her mouth of anything that it might have failed to say when it was alive. The soul is supposed to possess the shaman, who then announces its wishes etc. as if the soul of the deceased itself were speaking.

After the departure of the soul which was possessing the *yuta* another rite takes place to expel the soul of the deceased. This consists of the symbolic act of cutting the air with a sword both inside and outside the house. Then the *yuta* scatters roasted soya beans (*Glycine max soybean*) which have thus become black. They say that just as the roasted beans will not germinate again, they throw them in order that the soul will never return.

Since it is believed that the souls of the living are inclined to leave with the soul of the dead, the *yuta* lightly strikes the head and shoulders of those present with the *susuki*, in order to make the soul of the living stay firmly inside the body.

The *susuki* is used to call up not only the souls of the dead, but also the souls of the living. It is believed in the Amami and Okinawa Islands that the souls of the living may escape when a man is surprised or falls out of a tree. In Nase city, Amami, the ritual performed by the *yuta* to call back the lost soul to its body is called *maburimuke* (to invite a soul), while in Okinawa this is called *maburigumi*. In this ritual the role of *susuki* is again important. In Okinawa the *yuta* holds the blades of *susuki* to call back the lost soul. She moves the *gen* (ring of *susuki*) three times over the head of the patient whose soul is missing. Then the *gen* is hung on the wall of the room for a week. In Nase, while the soul of a patient is absent, the *yuta* places the *susuki* beside the pillow of the patient, with the root directed towards the outside of the house and the leaves towards the inside. She also strokes the body of the patient with the *susuki* while reciting formulae.

Thus in the case of the ritual of calling up a soul of the dead, the *susuki* is first used to summon the soul of the deceased and is also used to hold the souls of the living at the time of expelling the soul of the dead. In the case of the *maburimuke* ritual, the *susuki* is again used to bring back the soul of a living being who is suffering from absence of the soul. In the context of the *shichami*, the *susuki* is used to pray for the health and growth of children. In the Amami and Okinawa Islands, the *susuki* is placed or planted not only in the ritual of *shibasashi*, but also in a new house, in a vacant house from which a family has moved out, and beside a new well for the purpose of expelling evil spirits. At funerals the *susuki* is placed on a coffin also to expel evil spirits.

In the last phase of the ritual of *maburiwaashi*, while roasted soya beans are thrown – with the idea that, since the roasted black soya will never germinate, the soul of the dead will never return – the *susuki* is used to hold in the souls of the living. Thus the roasted soya may be opposed to the *susuki* in this context, so that if the soya beans are situated on the side of the dead, the *susuki* can be placed on the side of the living (cf. Lévi-Strauss 1979, 1983: 271).

The *susuki* is thus used not only to invite back the souls of the dead, but to help growing children, to call back the souls of the living, and to expel evil spirits. Why is this so? As Lévi-Strauss noted in his recent book (1983: 271–2), the mystical nature of the *susuki* may stem from its enormous strength of growth in a wilderness. Note that in festivals in the Japanese archipelago the *susuki* is often used in place of the rice plant – a fact which may be related to the resemblance between the two plants; certainly the *susuki* belongs to the rice family.

Whereas the *susuki* was originally confined to the Far East, the geographical distribution of beans is very wide. The soya bean seems to have originated in northern China, but was already cultivated in Japan in the Yayoi period (300 BC to AD 300). The custom of expelling evil spirits on the day of *setsubun* (the eve of the beginning of spring) by throwing out roasted soya beans and reciting 'happiness be inside, demons be out!' still persists to this day. In some places in north Kyushu fishermen throw roasted soya beans into the sea to calm a storm.

Besides the soya bean, magical and mystical powers are attributed to the red bean (*Azukia angularis Ohwi*). Archaeological evidence indicates that the red bean was eaten in the early period of the Jōmon Culture (4800–300 BC). It is customary in Japan to cook rice with red beans on days of happy events. On 15 January Japanese eat a gruel of rice mixed with red beans. On the occasion of childbirth it is customary in certain places to eat *mochi* (pounded rice) with a paste of sweet red beans. In certain areas people cook rice or rice gruel with red beans at the time of starting on a journey or moving into a new house.

However, red beans are eaten not only on happy occasions, but also on unfortunate occasions: at funerals, for example, at the moment of placing a corpse in the coffin, the close relatives eat rice gruel and red beans, and again after the burial, (sweet) red beans.

It can probably be concluded then that the red bean is eaten at a time of transition from one state to another: New Year, childbirth, departure on a journey, moving in and out, death. Moreover, the red bean was used because of its mystical powers to expel evil beings, the god of leprosy, foxes, rabbits, and wolves, by feeding them with it. Some scholars contend that the mystical nature of the red bean stems from its red colour, but taking into account the mystical power attributed to the soya bean itself, it is not the colour that should be treated as the main reason.

The Japanese thus customarily treat beans in notable ways, but the attribution of mystical powers to beans is not unique to Japanese culture. In ancient Greece, for example, the broad bean was either prohibited food among certain groups or else considered sacred. According to Detienne (1972: 96–100), in ancient Greece the bean was considered a mediator between this world and the other. Among northern and central American Indians a certain mystical nature is also attributed to the bean (Lévi-Strauss 1983: 263–75). Of the Zinacantan Indians of Highland Chiapas, Mexico, Laughlin reports that 'if beans are mistreated their soul will cry and complain to the earth lord and to the gods in heaven, thus calling down famine upon mankind' (1975: 112).

In Japanese mythology the beans (soya and red beans) emerged from the genitalia of the goddess Ukemochi. According to one Japanese dictionary, the Japanese word for bean, *mame*, also in fact means genitalia, clitoris and woman. The symbolic association of the bean with woman is also found in other cultures. For example, the resemblance of the bean to the female sexual organ was also recognized in ancient Greece (Detienne 1972: 97). Gossen notes that in the mythology of the Chamula, Tzotzil-speaking Maya Indians of the Central Chiapas Highlands of Mexico, maize came from a piece of the (male) sun's groin and included a part of his pubic hair, which is the silk of the ear of maize, but the (female) moon gave potatoes (her breast milk) and beans (her necklace) (Gossen 1972: 143).

It seems clear then that the mystical notions associated with the bean – its ambiguous position as an intermediary between this world and the other, and its symbolic association with woman – are not unique to Japan. Yet the interrelation between these notions may have stronger force in the Japanese context, since, as Yanagita argued (1962: 14), it was customarily ordinary women in villages who played the magico-religious role of performing rituals as intermediaries between this world and the other.

In the Amami and Okinawa Islands, these women worked as farmers and housewives in daily life but performed various rituals as priestesses, clothed in white, for the welfare of their village. This pattern still persists to this day in certain villages in these islands. In the village of Tokuwase in Tokunoshima the highest priestess amongst these 'divine women' (*kaminchu*) used to live in a house called *agere* (related to the word *agari*, meaning the sunrise or east). The *agere* house is located on the eastern side of the *nēma* house in which the founder of the village and his successors lived. The *agere* and *nēma* are situated in the highest place on the mountain side of the village, which is considered to be superior to the sea or lower side. The presence of these two houses illustrates the traditional political structure of the village, though it has ceased to operate at present. Formerly, the village was politically controlled from generation to generation by the head of the *nēma* house, whereas one of his sisters who lived in the *agere* house acted as the highest priestess, conducting the rituals and other religious affairs of the village. Theoretically, the position of secular leader was inherited by his son, while the status of the priestess passed to one of the daughters of her brother, the leader of the village. The priestess never married and her successor was chosen from among the daughters of the secular leader. The political leader was called *iiri* (meaning 'brother'), and the priestess *unari* (meaning 'sister'). The *iiri* was in charge of village politics, but he discharged his duties according to oracles interpreted by the *unari* (Matsuyama 1970). While in secular life the *unari* was under the protection of the *iiri*, they had a complementary relationship (Mabuchi 1964). Dual sovereignty of this sort has also been found in Okinawa, well described by Torikoshi Kenzaburō in 1944.

Dual sovereignty is not practised any more in these villages. However, notions underlying it still persist today. It was customary, for example, for Okinawan men, when leaving for a distant fishing trip or long journey, to take along with them a towel of their sister as an amulet. During the Second World War soldiers took along with them to the battlefield a 'thousand stitch-belt' (*sennin-bari*), towels or hair of their sister as amulets. It was believed that brothers protect their sisters in secular life, while sisters extend their spiritual powers to protect their brothers (Mabuchi 1964).

CONCLUDING REMARKS

An analysis of the *hamaori* ritual performed in Tokunoshima reveals that the notion of ancestors is divided into two kinds: those ancestors who died more than thirty-three years ago and are supposed to live in the *neira* located far beyond the sea, and those who died during the period of thirty-three years. This division of the dead is clearly reflected in the plan of the house in the Okinawa Islands. In all houses on the island of Iheya it is always in the 'first' room on the east side of the house that more distant ancestors – identified with gods – are worshipped, while more recent ancestors are worshipped in the 'second' room, located on the western side of (and next to) the 'first' room. The distant ancestors are enshrined in an altar (*kamidana*) constructed on the northern side of the 'first' room, whereas the more recently deceased ancestors are represented by the *ihai* (ancestral tablets) placed in a small altar (*butsudan*) situated on the northern side of the 'second' room.

It is the *yuta* who are believed to transmit messages from the ancestors to human beings. It is also the *yuta* who serve as mediators between the living and other, supernatural beings. Moreover, there exist certain animals and plants which are conceived to mediate between this world of reality and the other. We have seen that the *habu* snake, the *susuki* and the bean are regarded as intermediaries between the two worlds, and that in a certain ritual context the *susuki* are situated rather on the side of life, whereas roasted soya beans are more on the side of the dead. A female *yuta* states that in the ritual of summoning a soul of the dead, roasted soya beans are scattered both inside and outside the entrance to a house in order to help the soul or ghost enter the house more easily because it has no legs with which to walk. It is assumed here that a soul or ghost comes in sliding on the beans. As for the red bean, in so far as it is eaten in Japan at the times of New Year, departure on a journey, moving house, childbirth and death, one can probably safely state that it is connected with transition.

The notion of the *kenmun* or *kijimun* can only be understood in relation to the symbolic structures of the inhabitants of the Amami and Okinawa Islands.

While there exist cultural peculiarities in the ideas and practices associated with dual sovereignty in these islands, dual sovereignty of a similar kind is described in detail by Georges Dumézil for the ancient Indo-European peoples. He has shown that the gods Mitra and Varuna in India were the cosmological projection of the dual sovereignty which existed there: Mitra as legislator and Varuna as priest. Mitra represents this world and Varuna the other world (Dumézil 1948). Rodney Needham has shown the existence of a dual sovereignty among the Meru in East Africa in which the 'elder' corresponds to Mitra and the Mugwe, high priest, is essentially equivalent to Varuna in ancient India (Needham 1960). Considering such comparative material, as Needham put it, 'complementary governance is not peculiar to any particular tradition . . . but is a fundamental and global instance of an elementary classification of powers' (Needham 1980: 88). Thus, the dual sovereignty and complementary protection between brothers and sisters found in the Amami and Okinawa Islands can be regarded as an example of such a classification of powers.

What seems to be the most important of all is the possibility of a synthesis between a regional detailed study of the collective notions of a particular society and a global point of view covering vastly different areas (cf. Geertz 1976). It is essential to study the peculiarities and uniqueness of a culture. But at the same time we should not lose sight of the similarities between cultures.

NOTES

* This paper is a modified English version of one that I originally published in Japanese, entitled 'Notes on the Symbolic Interpretation of Cosmology: Folk Ideas in the Amami Islands', in the *Research Bulletin of Liberal Arts* (University of Tokyo, Faculty of General Education), vol. XV (1983), pp. 1–21. I wish to thank Joy Hendry for her invitation to the Conference on the Social Anthropology of Japan, held in Oxford in 1984. I am also grateful to her for revising the English style and supplying helpful comments which are incorporated in this paper. A summarized English version of the original paper was presented in a seminar at the Nissan Institute of Japanese Studies, Oxford, in January 1984. I also wish to thank Itabashi Sakumi, Namihira Emiko, Shirakawa Takuma and Kanda Yoriko, with whom fieldwork was often jointly undertaken. Fieldwork was funded by the Scientific Research Fund of the Ministry of Education in Japan as part of a joint research programme on Japanese shamanism, whose representative was Professor Oguchi Iichi, and of my own research project in 1978, 1979 and 1981.
1 Five natural elements – wood, fire, earth, water and metal – are divided respectively into the elder and the younger, and then applied to days. For example, 6 and 7 August 1983 were *hinoe* (elder of fire) and *hinoto* (younger of fire).
2 This section has particularly benefited from Lévi-Strauss (1979).

REFERENCES

Bulmer, R. N. H. (1967) 'Why is the Cassowary not a Bird?', *Man* n.s., vol. II, pp. 5–25.
Detienne, Marcel (1972) *Les Jardins d'Adonis*, Paris: Gallimard.
Douglas, Mary (1966) *Purity and Danger*, Harmondsworth: Penguin Books.
Dumézil, Georges (1948) *Mitra–Varuna: Essai sur deux représentations indo-européennes de la souveraineté*, Paris: Gallimard.
Ellen, Roy F. (1972) 'The Marsupial in Nuaulu Ritual Behaviour', *Man* n.s., vol. VII, pp. 223–38.
Fortes, M. (1975) 'Strangers', in M. Fortes and S. Patterson (eds) *Studies in African Social Anthropology*, London and New York: Academic Press, pp. 229–53.
Geertz, Clifford (1976) 'From the Native's Point of View', in K. H. Basso and H. A. Selby (eds) *Meaning in Anthropology*, Albuquerque: University of New Mexico Press, pp. 221–37.
Goody, Jack (1962) *Death, Property and the Ancestors*, Stanford: Stanford University Press.
Gossen, G. H. (1972) 'Temporal and Spatial Equivalents in Chamula Ritual Symbolism', in W. A. Lessa and E. Z. Vogt (eds) *Reader in Comparative Religion*, New York: Harper & Row, pp. 135–49.
Howe, L. E. A. (1981) 'The Social Determination of Knowledge: Maurice Bloch and Balinese Time', *Man* n.s., vol. XVI, pp. 120–34.
Kreiner, J. (1971) 'Nansei Shotō ni okeru kami-kannen takaikan no ichi kōsotsu [A Study of the Notions of God and of the Other World in the Southwestern Archipelago]', in Tokihiko Omoni and Tōru Ogawa (eds) *Okinawa bunka ronsō [Discussions of Okinawan Culture]*, Tokyo: Heibonsha.
Laughlin, R. M. (1975) *The Great Tzotzil Dictionary of San Lorenzo Zinacantan*, Washington, DC: Smithsonian Contributions to Anthropology, no. 19.
Lévi-Strauss, Claude (1979) 'Pythagoras in America', in R.H. Hook (ed.) *Fantasy and*

Symbol: Studies in Anthropological Interpretation, London and New York: Academic Press, pp. 33–41.

—— (1983) *Le Regard éloigné*, Paris: Plon.

Mabuchi, Tōichi (1964) 'Spiritual Predominance of the Sister', in Alan H. Smith (ed.) *Ryukyuan Culture and Society*, Honolulu: University of Hawaii Press, pp. 79–91.

—— (1980) 'Onari-gami Kenkyū wo Meguru Kaikō to Tenbō [Recollections and Reconnaisances on Studies on Onari-gami]', Research Bulletin of the Research Institute for Studies of Japanese Folklore, Seijō University, vol. 4, Seijō University.

Maloney, C. (ed.) (1976) *The Evil Eye*, New York: Columbia University Press.

Matsuyama, Mitsuhide (1967) 'Habu kōshō ni matsuwaru zokushin to sono ryōhō [Folk Beliefs and Healing Methods with Respect to the Bite by the Snake *Habu*]', *Report of the Studies on Tokunoshima*, no. 1.

—— (1970) 'Sonraku kyōdōtai no kōzō [Structure of Village Community]', in Committee of Tokunoshima-chō (ed.) *Tokunoshima-shi [Description of Tokunoshima Town]*, Kametsu-shi: Tokunoshima Yakuba (Office of Tokunoshima Town), pp. 458–91.

Moromi, Seikichi (ed.) (1981) *Iheya son-shi [A History of Iheya Village]*, Naha: Committee for Publications of the History of Iheya Village.

Needham, Rodney (1960) 'The Left Hand of the Mugwe: An Analytical Note on the Structure of Meru Symbolism', *Africa*, vol. XXX, pp. 20–33.

—— (ed.) (1973) *Right and Left: Essays on Dual Symbolic Classification*, Chicago: University of Chicago Press.

—— (1980) *Reconnaissances*, Toronto: University of Toronto Press.

Ogawa, Gakuo (1970) 'Shinkō to seikatsu [Beliefs and Life]', in *Tokunoshima Chō Shi [Description of Tokunoshima Town]*, pp. 569–88.

Ōgo, Kin'ichi (1966) 'Hokubu Okinawa no soreikan to saishi [Ancestor Worship and Rituals in North Okinawa]', *Seikei ronsō [Discussions of Politics and Economics]*, vol. 35, no. 1, Tokyo: Meiji Daigaku Seikei Kenkyū Sho (Research Institute of Politics and Economics), Meiji University. Reprinted in *Gendai no esupuri – Okinawa no dentō bunka [Contemporary esprit: Traditional Culture of Okinawa]*, Tokyo: Dentō to Gendai, pp. 121–37.

Origuchi, Shinobu (1975a) *Origuchi Shinobu zenshū [The Complete Works of Origuchi Shinobu]*, vol. 1, Tokyo: Chūōkōronsha.

—— (1975b) *Origuchi Shinobu zenshū [The Complete Works of Origuchi Shinobu]*, vol. 2, Tokyo: Chūōkōronsha.

—— (1976) *Origuchi Shinobu zenshu [The Complete Works of Origuchi Shinobu]*, vol. 16, Tokyo: Chūōkōronsha.

Setouchi-chō-shi Henshū Iinkai Hen (Editorial Committee of the Description of Setouchi Town) (ed.) (1977) *Setouchi-chō-shi [Description of Setouchi Town]*, Setouchi-chō: Setouchi-chō Henshū Iinkai (Editorial Committee of Setouchi Town).

Tambiah, S. J. (1969) 'Animals are Good to Think and Good to Prohibit', *Ethnology*, vol. VIII, pp. 423–59.

Torikoshi, Kenzaburō (1944) *Ryūkyū kodai shakai no kenkyū – Seiji to shūkyō [A Study of Ancient Society of Ryūkyū: Politics and Religion]*, Tokyo: Sanichi Shobo.

Vogt, Evon Z. (1969) *Zinacantan: A Maya Community in the Highlands of Chiapas*, Cambridge, MA: Harvard University Press.

Yanagita, Kunio (ed.) (1951) *Nihon minzoku gaku jiten [Encyclopedia of Japanese Folklore]*, Tokyo: Tōkyō dō.

—— (1962) *Yanagita Kunio Zenshū [Collected Works of Yanagita Kunio]*, vol. 9, Tokyo: Chikuma Shobo.

Yoshida, Teigo (1981) 'The Stranger as God: The Place of the Outsider in Japanese Folk Religion', *Ethnology*, vol. XX, pp. 87–99.

11 The importance of the left hand in two types of ritual activity in Japanese villages

Kazuto Matsunaga

INTRODUCTION

The purpose of this chapter is to present and interpret certain findings concerning the left hand[1] in the context of worship at a Japanese village Shinto shrine and in funeral practices. I have found that the use of the left hand is significant in rituals at a Shinto shrine and also in Buddhist funeral practices at a village near Yame City in Fukuoka prefecture. Rituals performed at the shrine are considered pure by the villagers (who are all Buddhists), while the funeral practices are considered impure and polluting. In this sense, the two contradict each other. This is illustrated by the fact that members of a family in which a death has occurred neither visit the village shrine nor participate in any of its rituals for a year, because of the pollution caused by the death of the family member. In the first part of this chapter, I will describe the use of the left hand, and in the second part I will offer an interpretation. This chapter deals mainly with findings made at the village mentioned, but I will occasionally refer to data from other villages.

The main agricultural products of the village have traditionally been rice (rice cultivation begins in May or June and ends in October or November) and wheat (cultivated between November and May), although horticulture has recently been introduced also. There are ninety-eight households in the village, with a population of 548 (1984). About two-thirds of the inhabitants were born in the village, while the rest are newcomers from the nearby city, but both groups jointly maintain the annual rituals of the village shrine.

The three main rituals of the year are held at the beginning of the summer and in the autumn. There are two rituals at the beginning of the summer. One is called Manjū-Komori, thanking the *kami* (gods) for the good harvest of wheat in which villagers offer the *kami* cake (*manjū*) made of newly harvested wheat, and during which they confine themselves for half a day in the shrine (this ritual confinement is called *komori*). The other is Gan-Tate – praying to the *kami* for a good harvest of rice – practised a week after the ritual of Manjū-Komori. *Gan* means 'prayer', and *tate* 'to make a petition'. Subsequently, the ritual in the autumn (in the latter part of November) thanks the *kami* for the good harvest of rice; it is called Nigirimeshi-Komori (viz. the *nigirimeshi* confinement; *nigirimeshi* means 'rice-balls' made of newly harvested rice): the villagers offer the *kami* rice-balls and they confine themselves for half a day in the shrine in order to thank the *kami* for the good harvest of rice. In the first ten days of August, i.e., between these summer and autumn festivals, the villagers practise a ritual called Sendo-Mairi, which literally means 'to worship the *kami* a thousand times'. In this ritual, the villagers pray to the *kami* for good health in the hot summer by offering a thousand leaves of the sacred *sakaki* tree (*Cleyera ochnacea*); all the villagers, including the children, offer *sakaki* leaves until they have thus worshipped the *kami* a thousand times. In all these three main annual rituals, as well as in the smaller rituals practised during the course of the year, the left hand is often used.

THE LEFT HAND IN RITUALS

The left hand in the village Shinto shrine

The *haiden*, or hall of worship of the shrine, and the *torii*, or shrine gate, are always decorated with *shimenawa* (a sacred rope made with tufts of straw). The villagers do this cooperatively and exchange an old *shimenawa* for a new one twice a year, that is, before the summer rituals of Manjū-Komori and Gan-Tate and again before the autumn ritual of Nigirimeshi-Komori. The *shimenawa* is a 'left-handed' rope, that is, twisted from the left-hand side; moreover, it should be installed from the left side to the right side, viewed from the seat of the *kami* – in other words, the 'root' or the 'beginning' of the *shimenawa* should be put on the left side, as seen from the *kami*.

Before any ritual is carried out – such as worshipping the *kami* and making offerings, but certainly at every annual ritual – the Shinto priest and the villagers wash their hands at a special hand-washing place in front of the *haiden*. According to the Shinto priest, they must wash the left hand first, then the right, and finally the left hand a second time (although I did notice that some villagers washed the left hand only once, and sometimes even after having begun the washing with the right hand).

After washing their hands, the villagers worship the *kami* at four points surrounding the shrine, as shown in Figure 11.1. They move anti-clockwise (*hidari-mawari* in Japanese, or moving round to the left). After this, they ascend the *haiden* and make offerings as a preparatory act for the ritual.

Kome (rice) is offered first, directly in front of the *kami*, this being the most important offering at every ritual. At the ritual of Manjū-Komori they also offer *manjū* (the cake made of wheat), *sake*, salt and holy water, fish, vegetables, fruit and other items – all from the left side to the right side in the correct order. At the ritual of Nigirimeshi-Komori, rice-balls are offered instead of *manjū*. With regard to fish, vegetables and fruit, fish is, generally speaking, considered the most important, followed by vegetables and then fruit, in that order. In other words, villagers say that the sea is more important than fields and mountains, and that fields are more important than mountains. When offering two kinds of fish, they put a superior fish, such as a red snapper (called *tai* in Japanese, and used on most

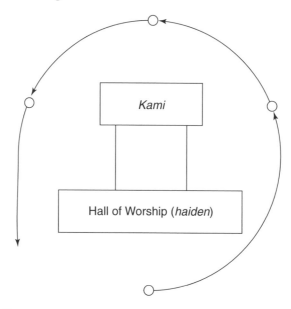

Figure 11.1 Four points of worship at the village shrine

happy occasions, such as weddings, childbirth, naming, etc.) at the left-hand side, and an inferior fish, such as blue mackerel (*saba*), at the right.

According to the Shinto priest, when either he or the villagers touch the ritual instruments on which the offerings to the *kami* are placed, they should do so with the left hand first and then with the right. When they need to carry them, they are not supposed to touch them with both hands at the same time, although in fact many villagers do so none the less.

After the ritual preparations, the priest and the villagers sit in front of the *kami*; the former sits on the left-hand side (viewed from the *kami*), and the villagers on the right. The priest then stands up and goes directly in front of the *kami*, stepping towards it carrying a *gohei* or *haraigushi* (a sacred staff with hanging paper strips) in order to recite ritual Shinto prayers. He steps forward with his left[2] foot first and then with his right, and then steps back with his right foot first. This means that his left foot is closer to the *kami* than his right foot for a longer period of time, and that he remains with his left foot in front of the *kami*. This practice is called *shinsa-taiu* (literally, 'step forward left, step backward right'), and it shows how the left foot is considered more important than the right.

The priest holds the *gohei* or *haraigushi* with both hands, but his left hand is kept in a higher position, and he moves it quickly to the left side first, then to the right, and finally to the left side again. Thus the left is again given primary importance. After various recitations by the priest, representatives of the villagers step forward to the *kami* in order to offer *tamagushi* (a sprig of the sacred tree *Cleyera ochnacea*). The way that the villagers step forward and hold the *tamagushi* follows the same method as that in which the priest steps forward and holds the *gohei* or *haraigushi*, i.e. forward with the left foot first and then backwards with the right foot first; the *tamagushi* is held with both hands, but the left hand is kept higher. After these movements, the priest and the villagers dine together and finish the ritual.

The description above applies to all rituals. However, two further points should be noted. First, the Japanese round cushion made of straw on which the priest and villagers squat in the *haiden* is woven anti-clockwise. Second, there are many instances of *chigaya-kuguri* in Shinto shrines in the northern part of Kyushu Island, viz. the practice of passing through a big ring made of *chigaya* in front of the *kami* (*chigaya* is a species of reed, *Phragmites communis*;[3] *kuguri* means 'to pass through'). Villagers practise the *chigaya-kuguri* in order to pray to the *kami* for their health in a hot summer. The way they do it is to pass through the big ring first anti-clockwise, then clockwise, then anti-clockwise again – so that, once more, the left side is given primary importance (see Figure 11.2).

The left hand in funeral practices

When a man dies, a vigil called *tsuya* is held at night before the funeral. Relatives and villagers gather at the vigil, a bag of sweets or biscuits being distributed to all visitors in the left hand of a family member of the deceased, and received in the visitor's left hand. Nowadays, it should be said, villagers do not follow this practice strictly.

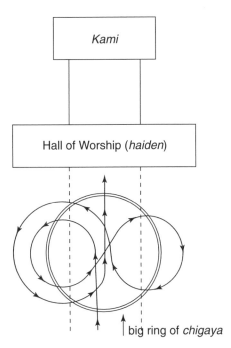

Figure 11.2 Passing through the ring of *chigaya*

On the morning of the funeral, householders and housewives of the neighbourhood to which the family of the deceased belongs divide up the preparations for the funeral, such as setting up the altar, making contact with Buddhist priests and cooking meals for visitors. The funeral is usually held in the afternoon, at the house.

In the past, when burial was the norm, villagers used to bind the coffin with a 'left-handed' rope, that is, one twisted by the left hand (like the 'left-handed' *shimenawa* rope mentioned above); this is not done nowadays, viz. since the introduction of cremation about twenty years ago. Formerly, the villagers carried the coffin to the graveyard on the hill near the village (nowadays it is carried to a crematorium by a motor-driven hearse); they wore *waraji* (straw sandals) and wound a rope round their waists. The thong of the *waraji* and the rope were also 'left-handed'; nowadays villagers wear shoes and no longer encircle their waists. Furthermore, two elders, respectively 78 and 81 years old, say that they used to carry a coffin on their left shoulders – in contrast to the carrying of farm tools on their right shoulders during the pursuit of daily agricultural activities.

On the day of the funeral, the chief mourner borrows from other villagers such things as dining tables, tableware, etc. and obtains foodstuffs from a shop for which he will pay later. Old informants say that in the past, the chief mourner recorded the various transactions made for a funeral in a special notebook with a left-hand margin or seam – as opposed to the use of a notebook with a right-hand margin or seam on other occasions, such as a wedding ceremony or in ordinary daily life (see Figure 11.3). This special notebook was called by villagers a *hidari-toji* (literally, 'left binding'); nowadays, however, any sort of notebook will be used.

Visitors to funerals are served with a cake and tea. On this occasion, it is considered proper that the paper serviette on which villagers put the cake they offer the visitors should be folded in such a way that the edge of the folded paper on the left side is uppermost, as shown in Figure 11.4. Again, this is in contrast to the method of folding used in daily life or on auspicious occasions such as weddings, when the fold should be such that the right-hand side is uppermost.

The corpse is dressed in a shroud in a manner called *hidari-mune* (literally, 'left-breast'), before being put into the coffin. The normal way of wearing a kimono in Japan presupposes the right side of the garment being placed underneath the left. A corpse, however, must be dressed in a kimono *hidari-mune*, that is, where the left side is placed underneath the right. Moreover, it is also said by villagers that the belt of the kimono used for a corpse, together with the *tekko* string (a covering for the back of the hand) and the *kyahan* (leggings), both worn by the dead, must all be of 'left-handed' rope.

After these preparations, the funeral ceremony itself is held. Buddhist priests step forward to the altar with their left feet first and chant a sutra. After they have finished chanting, first the family members of the deceased, then relatives and villagers, pay their respects to the deceased and burn incense powder, using their left hands for the purpose. Then the deceased is carried to the crematorium. After cremating the corpse, members of the family and other relatives put the bones into

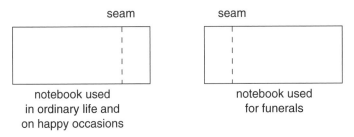

Figure 11.3 Use of notebook on auspicious and inauspicious occasions

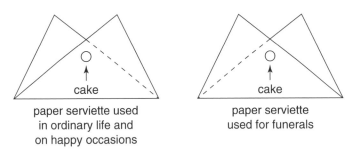

Figure 11.4 Use of serviette on auspicious and inauspicious occasions

a special urn, using chopsticks held with their left hands. Some villagers use their left hands throughout, while others use the left hand only at first, and thereafter use the right hand. The bones are brought to the house after the cremation and kept at the household Buddhist altar, or *butsudan*, for forty-nine days, after which they are transferred permanently to an ossuary in the village.

After the funeral ceremony, visitors are served dishes arranged in a fashion known as *hidari-zen* (*hidari* means 'left'; *zen* is a portable small dining-table). The villagers say that the arrangement of dishes at a funeral must be reversed (as shown in Figure 11.5) from their arrangement on an auspicious occasion and in ordinary daily life,[4] and this same arrangement is used at several memorial services held after the funeral. Thus, the principle of reversal or inversion – a concept that is critical in the interpretation of left-handed behaviour in general (cf.

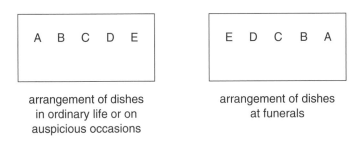

Figure 11.5 Arrangement of dishes on auspicious and inauspicious occasions

Needham 1973) – can be recognized in comparing practices at funeral ceremonies and those of other occasions. The subject has also been observed elsewhere in Japan: Yoshida (in this volume) has drawn attention to the importance of the left principle in the cosmology of the Ryūkyū Islanders.

Finally, it should be noted that according to village elders it was formerly the custom that when relatives and villagers visit the family of the deceased to offer worship and present incense sticks at memorial services, the incense sticks would be extinguished with the left hand. Young people today, however, no longer behave in this manner.

TWO PRINCIPLES OF THE LEFT HAND

As indicated in the foregoing description, the left hand is connected not only with the rituals of the village Shinto shrine but also with funeral practices – both in the village where I conducted fieldwork and in other villages as well – even though worship at the former is conceived of as pure and funerals as impure or polluting. In this respect, then, they appear to be contradictory to each other, and to involve two different principles and meanings.

My hypothesis is as follows. In the first place, the use of the left hand in funeral practices indicates the principle of reversal or inversion, namely, it is opposed to the use of the right hand, which is seen mainly on auspicious occasions or day-to-day activities. 'Right-handed' rope, for example, was used by villagers in binding rice-sheaves at harvest in the autumn, in binding straw on the roof of their houses, and in controlling their horses or cows in cultivating their fields (though some of these practices have lapsed nowadays). 'Left-handed' rope, however, was used when they bound a coffin. This kind of reversal (*sakasa*) is found in other funeral practices, such as *sakasa-hishaku* (using a ladle in a reverse way), *sakasa-kimono* (wearing a kimono in a reverse way), *sakasa-byōbu* (erecting a folding screen upside-down, i.e., an 'inverted' screen), and so on. The practice of *sakasa-hishaku*, also known as *sakasa-mizu* (literally, 'reverse water'), refers to the ladle (*hishaku*) which villagers use with their left hands when they pour hot water into cold water to make it lukewarm for the purpose of washing a corpse – whereas they would normally use the right hand and, in addition, would pour cold water into hot (rather than the other way round) when preparing lukewarm water in ordinary secular daily life. The principle of reversal, contrasting funeral practices with daily activities, extends, as has been indicated, to the use of the left hand (*hidari*), such as *hidari-zen* (the inversion of dishes), *hidari-mune* (the inversion of the right under the left in the normal way of wearing a kimono), *hidari-usu* (the practice of specially turning a hand-mill anti-clockwise to make the flour for the noodles used at funerals – though nowadays ordinary factory-made flour is commonly used), and so on.

However, it seems impossible to interpret the use of the left hand observed in the rituals of the village shrine only from the viewpoint of the principle of reversal; no such principle seems to operate in such contexts. My fieldwork enquiries lead me to propose here quite a different solution for the use of the left hand in such rituals, that is, in an acknowledgement of the cardinal directions of the east and the south, to both of which villagers attach importance in their agricultural activities, especially in rice cultivation. Temperature, represented by the south (the principal direction of sunshine), is an important factor at every stage of rice cultivation, since, as a tropical plant, rice needs a great deal of sunshine. For this reason, the south is regarded as the most important direction in agricultural activities, followed by the east, where the sun rises. Houses are constructed facing south, terrain permitting, in order to facilitate the drying of rice, wheat, etc., in the yard in front. Moreover, the Shinto priest prefers the village shrine itself to face south if possible, because the main purpose of worship there is to pray for success in agriculture, and in particular for a good harvest of rice. The east, as the direction of sunrise, has come to be regarded by the villagers as the root or beginning of all things. As they put it, 'at the village Shinto shrine, we install *shimenawa*, putting the "root" or the "beginning" of it in the east – in other words, at the left hand viewed from the *kami* – because when we face south, the east corresponds to our left hand.' It is at this point that a fresh interpretation can be proposed concerning the use of the left hand in the worship of the village shrine – namely, that since the left coincides with the east, it is symbolically related to it.[5] This is also expressed in the movements of the village priest when he ascends the stairway and makes offerings to the *kami*: keeping his left foot, facing east, closer to it than his right.

In summing up, therefore, it seems to me that the meanings of the left hand observed in the rituals of the village shrine on the one hand and in funeral practices on the other are different, although they are the *same* left hand in the *same* village. The use of the left hand observed in funeral practices is the opposite to the use of the right hand on auspicious occasions and in the ordinary secular activities of daily life, while the use of the left hand observed in the rituals of the village shrine may be connected with the relationship between the two directions of east and south, both very important for the villagers' agricultural activities. Hence my proposal to identify two principles of the left hand in the *same* village.

THE IMPORTANCE OF THE LEFT HAND IN THE JAPANESE FOLK BELIEF

One principle, not two principles, of the left is emphasized in Japanese folk beliefs. These are defined here as magico-religious practices which are not related to either Shintoism or Buddhism but are held by native people themselves, exclusive of Shinto priests and Buddhist monks.

I would like to present a few actual cases to illustrate the point. One of these is the ritual of the *ta no kami* which is practised in the southern part of Kyushu Island, especially Kagoshima prefecture, every spring. *Ta* means 'paddy field', *no* means 'of', and *kami* means 'god'. The villagers enshrine the statue of the *ta no kami*, which is made of stone, approximately 70 centimetres in height, in the centre of a paddy field and pray to the *ta no kami* for a good harvest in the autumn. They turn anti-clockwise (*hidari-mawari*) around the statue of the *ta no kami* and dance in special costumes with decorated tools. They clearly insist that they remove evil spirits and set up the sacred place in which they enshrine the statue of the *ta no kami* by turning anti-clockwise. This example indicates that the villagers consider turning anti-clockwise as a method of removing evil spirits and setting up a sacred place (see Figures 11.6 and 11.7).

In the village. the behaviour of turning anti-clockwise is also observed in funeral practices. The villagers explain that they used to remove evil spirits from the grave by turning anti-clockwise. Today, they cremate the dead. Accordingly, the practice of turning anti-clockwise around the grave is not seen. Even now, however, they turn the coffin anti-clockwise when they take it out of the house. In the past, before cremation was introduced, the villagers used to turn anti-clockwise around the grave when they buried the coffin.

In addition to this case found in agricultural villages, it is also observed in many fishing villages that fishermen turn their fishing boats anti-clockwise when they seek the gods' presence. They pray for a big catch, the safety of their boats and of themselves on the occasion of sailing out to go fishing. They explain that they remove evil spirits by turning anti-clockwise. Moreover, they also turn their fishing boats anti-clockwise when they launch new boats for the first time. This practice is observed not only in the sea but also in rivers. An example is found on the Gokase-gawa River running through the northern area of Miyazaki prefecture, Kyushu Island. The area is famous for sweetfish. Many inhabitants have their own boats and some order a shipbuilder to make new boats every year.

Figure 11.6 Villagers in southern Kyushu turn anti-clockwise at the *ta no kami* festival.
Photograph courtesy of Kazuto Matsunaga

Figure 11.7   Again the villagers turn anti-clockwise. Photograph courtesy of Kazuto Matsunaga

When a new boat is completed, the shipbuilder and the owner take it to the river. They pray to the god of the river for a big catch and the safety of the boat at the riverside before they launch it. The shipbuilder recites a special prayer for the god of the river. The Shinto priest does not appear. He has no role in this occasion, which is carried out by the shipbuilder and the owner of the boat. It is thus an example of folk beliefs. When they launch the boat, they turn it anti-clockwise three times and they pray to the god of the river again for a big catch and the safety of the boat.

In addition to these examples, the practice of turning anti-clockwise is observed in funeral practices. This has been explained so far as the left indicating the pollution of death. However, it must be noted that villagers see turning anti-clockwise in funeral practices as removing evil spirits. The same thing can be said about the sacred rope (*shimenawa*) at a small shrine in which the statue of the *ta no kami* is enshrined, and the rope with which people fastened the coffin on burial before cremation was introduced. Those ropes are both 'left-handed'. The villagers say that the left-handed ropes in both cases are for removing evil spirits from the sacred place where the god is enshrined, and from the dead person. Removing evil spirits is the common and key conception for left-handed ropes. In this way, one principle, not two principles, of the 'left' may be noted in Japanese folk beliefs.

This fact is also recognized in folk beliefs of the Southwestern Archipelago (Ryūkyū Islands) of Japan. For example, I observed this when I did fieldwork in Tokunoshima Island, Kagoshima prefecture, near Okinawa main island.

Tokunoshima Islanders turn anti-clockwise in a circle at the seaside when they thank their ancester gods, who come from the sea, for a good harvest of rice and when they pray to them for a good harvest next year. They also turn anti-clockwise when they celebrate their house warming and pray for peaceful and happy lives.

Moreover, the practice of turning anti-clockwise is observed in funerals. They turn the coffin anti-clockwise when they take it out of the house. They also used to turn anti-clockwise around the grave on burial. Buddhism has not been accepted in Tokunoshima Island. The funeral practices had been carried out by a kind of a native shaman and the people themselves until about fifty years ago, although the Shinto priest partly participates in a series of the practices nowaday.

The important thing is that they recognize turning anti-clockwise as removing evil spirits from the sacred place where they meet and worship their ancestor gods and from their new house and also from the grave.

In addition to turning anti-clockwise, they set up a sacred place by stretching left-handed rope and they also used to fasten a coffin with left-handed rope. Thus, one principle, not two, of the left may be pointed out in relation to worshipping gods and to funeral practices. This 'one principle' implies 'removing evil spirits'.

CONCLUSION

I would like to mention two things as the conclusion of this chapter. First, the left (left-handed rope, turning anti-clockwise) is recognized in opposition to the right in secular activities. For example, the rope used in agricultural activities is right-handed rope. Moreover, many villagers, especially older people, say that they used to turn clockwise when they cultivated their paddy fields with their cattle. This cannot be observed now because fields are cultivated by agricultural machines. Thus, turning anti-clockwise in religious activities can be seen in opposition to turning clockwise in secular (economic, social) ones. In this way, a dualistic opposition may be seen between magico-religious/secular: left/right in Japanese folk culture.

Second, it can be shown that three meanings of the left are recognized in Japanese culture. One of them is the importance of the left at Shinto shrines, understood in relation to the directions, east and south. Next, there is the left perceived as the expression of pollution of death in funeral practices. Finally, the left as the cultural meaning or the function of 'removing evil spirits' is recognized in folk beliefs. Now, the important thing is to understand how these three meanings are related in Japanese culture. This is a problem to be solved in the future.

NOTES

1 Left hand does not mean just 'hand' itself in this chapter but also foot, as shown by Hertz (1960). Hertz also refers to 'foot', despite the title of his paper. Thus, for example (p. 104), 'A holy place must be entered right foot first. Sacred offerings are presented to the gods with the right hand'.
2 Note that whereas the left position where the Shinto priest and villagers sit in front of the *kami* or where they put offerings is the left as viewed from the *kami*, the left concerning a person in motion (such as the priest here) is the left of the person in question (Jinja-Honchō 1975: 19). It is often said that the left is valued in Shintoism.
3 In former times, leaves of this reed were used by Japanese farmers to roof their houses with straw, and the root of this reed was used as medicine.
4 In another village, however, it is the placing of the pair of chopsticks on the left side of the *zen* at a funeral which is called *hidari-zen*. On auspicious occasions and in daily life, they are placed on the right side or in the middle of the *zen*.
5 The connection between left and east has also been pointed out by Professor Ōno (1974: 170).

REFERENCES

Hertz, Robert (1960 [1909]) 'The Pre-eminence of the Right Hand: A Study in Religious Polarity', in Robert Hertz, *Death and the Right Hand* (trans Rodney and Claudia Needham), London: Cohen & West.

Jinja-Honchō (1975) *Jinja saishiki gyōji sahō shidō yōkō* [*Guide Book on the Manners of Shinto Ceremonies*], Tokyo: Jinja-Honchō (Association of Shinto Shrines).

Matsunaga, Kazuto (1995) *Hidarite no Shinborizmu* [*The Symbolism of the Left Hand*], Fukuoka: Kyushu University Press.

Needham, Rodney (ed.) (1973) *Right and Left: Essays on Dual Symbolic Classification*, Chicago and London: University of Chicago Press.

Ōno, Susumu (1974) *Nihongo o sakanoboru* [*Going Back to the Past in the Japanese Language*], Tokyo: Iwanami Shoten.

12 'Years of calamity'

Yakudoshi observances in urban Japan

David C. Lewis

A formerly obscure Japanese religious cult became world headline news in the spring of 1995 when it was widely considered to have been responsible for the release of poison gas among travellers on the Tokyo subway system (Robinson 1995a; Shimazono 1995: 381–2; Reader 1996: 3–8). Suddenly the world media focused attention on the AUM Shinrikyō. Reports circulated about the manner in which adherents were brainwashed, malnourished and (among other ritual practices) were induced to drink the blood of the cult's founder, Asahara Shōkō, in order to obtain so-called spiritual 'power' (Robinson 1995b; Shimazōnō 1995: 405).

Adherents of AUM Shinrikyō were apparently motivated by teachings propounded by Asahara Shōkō that the world would soon be facing a 'doomsday' crisis, involving a collapse of present economic and political systems, world war, earthquakes and other disasters. The Kobe earthquake in January 1995 was apparently seen as one sign of this impending time of crisis. Cult members were also warned to prepare themselves to face the persecution and physical attacks which they expected from society at large (Reader 1996: 22–4, 54–74). In preparation for those anticipated attacks, they stored up gas masks and poison gas, for use both in defence and attack. Following the release of sarin gas on the Tokyo subway, a form of the 'persecution' anticipated by the cult's members took the form of a police enquiry, arrests and a strong public reaction against the cult. In fact, the 'persecution' became part of a self-fulfilling prophecy.

Just one week prior to the Tokyo gas attack, a legal case against AUM Shinrikyō had opened in the Ostankino district court of northern Moscow. The cult had about 30,000 members in Russia, as compared to an estimated 8,000 to 10,000 adherents in Japan itself. Already they had bought a helicopter in Russia, and some Russian journalists speculated whether or not they had set themselves up in Russia partly in order to buy nerve gas on the flourishing Russian black market (Corley 1995: 6–7).

AUM Shinrikyō posed a problem of interpretation, not only for politicians and journalists but also for religious commentators and for academic specialists on Japan.[1] The cult did not fall into the standard stereotypes expected of Japanese religious movements. Many other Japanese new religions had an emphasis on promoting 'world peace' or developing 'harmony' of some kind or other, but

AUM Shinrikyō was preparing itself for an expected violent conflict. A second peculiarity came from the cult's millenarian or 'doomsday' theology. For the most part, Japanese religious thought has tended to be characterized by a cyclical rather than a lineal view of history. Even among the many 'new religions', few 'Messianic' figures have emerged in the sense of leaders who are seen as themselves the bearers of salvation or harbingers of paradise. Shamanic figures have arisen, but they tend to offer a reconstruction of present circumstances or opportunities for communion with the spirit world, rather than being considered as saviours in themselves. Although aspects of a 'millenarian' theology had begun to emerge among some of Japan's so-called 'new new religions' like Agonshū (of which Asahara Shōkō himself had formerly been a member), in general there is a virtual absence of 'doomsday' concepts among Japanese religious movements. A few of the new religions have a notion of the end of the world which 'seems rather vague and does not signify the ultimate end', whilst religious cataclysms in Japanese folk religion 'are depicted not as final catastrophes but as natural disasters such as floods and earthquakes' (Kawanami 1995: 43). In the 'mainstream' Japanese religions, probably the nearest equivalent to any kind of apocalyptic teaching was the Buddhist idea of *mappō* – the third and last period of history characterized by a degeneration of moral standards, in which Buddhism would survive not as a way of life but merely as an abstract philosophy. This concept was important at the time of Hōnen (1133–1212) and Shinran (1173–1262), when the age of *mappō* was supposed to be dawning, but such teachings have not been at all important since then.

Instead, the nearest equivalents to the apocalyptic ideas of AUM Shinrikyō appear to be found either outside Japan or else within certain branches of Christianity. Certainly there is evidence that Asahara Shōkō was influenced by reading the biblical account of the coming battle of Armageddon in the book of Revelation (Reader 1996: 43, 55-7). However, I suspect that we do not have to search so widely in order to find 'under our noses' within most Japanese households the kind of religious concept which anticipates an impending time of calamity and misfortune. The only difference is that Asahara Shōkō applied this concept to society at large rather than to the individual's lifetime. In the course of their lives, the vast majority of Japanese people reach ages when they expect a whole year of potential misfortunes or disasters. These are called *yakudoshi* – 'years of calamity' – when one is thought to be particularly susceptible to illness or misfortune. Special religious rituals or the use of certain protective charms are considered necessary in order to avert the anticipated troubles of those years.

UNDERSTANDING PERCEPTIONS THROUGH ANTHROPOLOGICAL FIELDWORK

Time, space and eternity as *abstract concepts* are probably as important (or unimportant) to the average Japanese person as they are to the average Westerner: in everyday life, far more important than abstract concepts are the practical divisions of time and space into categories such as 'work' and 'home'. For many

Japanese, however, the life-cycle itself has several additional temporal divisions which have been introduced through the influence of so-called 'folk beliefs' such as *yakudoshi*.

Japanese writers have often classified *yakudoshi* as 'folk religion' (*minkan shinkō*) as distinct from Shinto.[2] However, even if some elements of the *yakudoshi* complex are derived from the Chinese divinatory system of Onmyōdō, nowadays in practice *yakudoshi* observances are inextricably fused with Shinto institutions. Their widespread persistence *in an industrial urban context* today indicates that it should not be taken for granted that such 'folk' beliefs necessarily decline in any of the three dimensions subsumed under the 'secularization' hypothesis – those of past/present, rural/urban and pre-industrial/industrial. Neither are *yakudoshi* observances necessarily static in rural areas; as Moon reports (in this volume), *yakudoshi* feasts have greatly increased in scale in recent years.

Apart from my own writings on *yakudoshi*, the other principal study available in English dealing with this belief is that by Norbeck (1955), who discusses how the *yakudoshi* complex might have developed and how there are many regional variations in it. However, he does not provide a detailed study of the extent to which people conform to the belief in practice or express either scepticism or belief in it. His comprehensive material on local variations in the complex is based almost entirely on *rural* sources, much of it secondhand data collected by Japanese folklorists and ethnographers. My own material complements Norbeck's by providing insights into contemporary practices and beliefs among residents of a modern Japanese city.

The fieldwork on which this chapter is based was conducted in a city with a population of over 230,000 in the Kansai region of Japan. Two urban neighbourhoods were selected for study, one of them the company housing of a large synthetic fibres firm which elsewhere (Lewis 1993a) I have called by a pseudonym. Therefore, both for the sake of consistency and also to protect the identities of people I interviewed, I am retaining the pseudonym of 'Ueno' for this city. In both neighbourhoods studied the majority of the residents are well-educated, white-collar salaried and professional people, plus a number of blue-collar and lower-middle-class families.[3] It will become clear from the following material that anthropological techniques of participant observation and detailed personal interviews shed considerably more light on actual attitudes towards such phenomena than do statistics from a questionnaire. However, I did use a questionnaire too, partly in order to establish my credentials as a researcher in the area, but also to gain an overall impression of the frequency of occurrence of various religious practices and beliefs.[4] Whereas the questionnaire gave some breadth to my data, the subsequent follow-up interviews provided a much greater depth of understanding.

Findings from any anthropological fieldwork are open to challenge on the grounds of representativeness, so it should be pointed out that five miles from the fieldwork area is a Shinto shrine which is famous for selling protective talismans (*mamori* or *fuda*) against the misfortunes which are thought to occur in a *yakudoshi* year. However, this shrine, which I am calling the 'Iwadani' shrine, is only one of several such shrines in the Kansai area and throughout Japan there are many other shrines also specializing in charms relating to *yakudoshi*. It is true that each year thousands of people visit the Iwadani shrine, especially between 15 and 17 January. During this peak visiting period the local Keihan bus company lays on a special shuttle service from the local railway station. Some visitors travel for an hour or two to get there from Kyoto or Osaka, but their choice of shrine is also influenced by tourist and convenience factors. The overt purpose of their pilgrimage is to pray for protection as they enter a *yakudoshi* year and to purchase a protective *mamori* or *fuda*.

However, even though Iwadani was the shrine most commonly visited by my informants who were in a *yakudoshi* year – largely because Iwadani happens to be conveniently near – it was only one of ten different shrines mentioned in this context. Most other Shinto shrines also offer for sale protective charms for those in a *yakudoshi* year. Such shrine visits had been conducted by thirty-four out of the forty-five people who said they 'paid attention to' *yakudoshi*, but others who had not gone personally had received a variety of charms from relatives who had gone vicariously on their behalf (ibid.: 151).[5]

Iwadani's *gomeinichi*, the special day in the month for worshipping its deity, falls on the 17th, so in January it is conveniently close to the 'Little New Year' of the 15th, when traditionally everyone in a community added a year to his or her age (Beardsley, Hall and Ward 1959: 295; Hanley and Yamamura 1977: 43, 209). This system has survived in the calculation of one's *yakudoshi*, whereby a newborn infant was counted as aged 1 at birth and 2 at the following New Year, so this *kazoe* system does not correspond with the 'Western' way of reckoning age which is nowadays used for most other purposes in Japan.

The ages counted as *yakudoshi* have varied both geographically (Norbeck 1955: 107–8) and historically (*Nihon Minzoku Jiten* 1971: 749), but all my informants in Ueno were aware of the ages of 33 for women and 41 or 42 for men as being *yakudoshi* years. Many people are also aware that the years preceding

	Men	Women
Principal *yakudoshi*	42	33
Major *yakudoshis*	25, 61	19, 37
Medium *yakudoshis*	24, 26 41, 43 60, 62	18, 20 32, 34 36, 38
Minor *yakudoshis* differentiated by sex	18, 19, 20 32, 33, 34 36, 37, 38	24, 25, 26 41, 42, 43 60, 61, 62
Minor *yakudoshis* undifferentiated by sex	1, 4, 7, 10, 13, 16, 22, 28, 40, 46, 49, 52, 55, 58	

Figure 12.1 Yakudoshi years for men and women

and following a major *yakudoshi* are *yakudoshi* years too. These years are called the *maeyaku* and *atoyaku* respectively, while the main *yakudoshi* year is called the *honyaku*. The *yakudoshi* ages listed at a large shrine in Ueno are as follows, but in Figure 12.1 I have taken the liberty of sub-dividing the 'major' *yakudoshi* years into 'principal' versus other 'major' *yakudoshi*s, and of sub-dividing the 'minor' *yakudoshi*s into those differentiated by sex versus those which are not so differentiated.[6]

POSSIBLE ORIGINS OF THE *YAKUDOSHI* COMPLEX

Norbeck (1955: 116–19) lists four possible reasons for the choice of these various ages as *yakudoshi*s, of which the fourth and to some extent the second are quite commonly reported by those whom I interviewed in Ueno. These reasons are as follows:

1 The Chinese calendar repeats the animal year of one's birth after every twelve-year cycle, and after every sixty years returns again to the same combination of element and animal (more technically called 'stem' and 'branch', respectively). Therefore, the repetition of one's 'year of birth' is a time of danger and uncertainty, especially the beginning of a completely fresh cycle after sixty years; so these ages in the life-cycle are times requiring particular caution and the use of special prayers or charms to avert danger. This theory accounts for the choice of the numbers 1, 13, 25, 37, 49 and 61, and for those 'medium' *yakudoshi*s associated with these numbers when these are 'major' *yakudoshi*s – i.e., the numbers 24, 26, 36, 38, 60 and 62. However, only three of these six numbers at twelve-year intervals are 'major' *yakudoshi*s, the other three being 'minor' ones – so the theory leaves un-explained many other *yakudoshi* years.

2 A few *yakudoshi*s may be explained by homonyms, considering the fondness which many Japanese have for such plays on words. This arises from the fact that most Chinese characters can be pronounced in more than one way, either by a Japanese rendering of the Chinese reading or by the use of a Japanese indigenous word of the same meaning. Therefore the number '4' can be read as the Japanese word *yon*[7] or as the Chinese-derived[8] reading of the character as *shi*. *Shi* is also the word for 'death', however, so the number 4 is often avoided in numbering rooms of buildings or houses in a block. Similarly, the number 9 can be pronounced as *ku*, with connotations of words such as *kurushimi*, suffering, or *kutsu*, pain, and may be avoided for similar reasons as those governing the use of 4, though avoidance of the number 4 seems to be commoner or stronger.

   Therefore the *yakudoshi* at the age of 42 is sometimes explained by saying that 42 can be pronounced *shi ni*, meaning 'to death', and is therefore to be feared. Moreover, 33 could be pronounced *sanzan*, a homonym for a word meaning 'hard', 'difficult' or 'troublesome'. It may also mean 'birth difficulty' (Bownas 1963: 152). While these two 'folk explanations' – as Norbeck (1955:

118) calls them – are those most commonly cited, the same reasonings might also be applied to the *yakudoshi*s at the ages of 4 and 49 (and perhaps some of the others containing the elements 4 or 9).

Norbeck (ibid.) considers this 'folk etymology' to be unlikely because it would depend upon a widespread knowledge of the alternative readings of numbers, which in turn would depend on a high degree of literacy among ordinary Japanese people during the Edo period or earlier. However, his reasoning can be challenged by the following considerations which would argue in favour of the 'folk etymology':

- Literacy was in fact fairly widespread by the end of the Edo period (mid-nineteenth century) among commoners as well as gentry, with about 40 per cent of the male population and 15 per cent of the women being literate – a figure higher than that of England and other countries at that time (Dore 1965: 100–1).
- 'Literacy' in Japan is not strictly a concept amenable to comparison with countries having a 'simple' alphabet system: two types of syllabaries (*kana*), each consisting of 52 'letters' (mainly representing syllables), form the level of literacy used in books for children of infant-school age. Gradually during primary school some of the most common or simpler Chinese characters (*kanji*) are introduced, among the first being the *kanji* for numbers. Therefore a knowledge of the variant readings of numbers does not require a high level of literacy to produce connotations of and word plays for the numbers 42 and 33.
- Even if the majority of the population were illiterate, a knowledge of such puns can be diffused from the literati into the general consciousness, perhaps forgetting the 'original' source of the idea in this process of diffusion – especially once the idea of *yakudoshi*s became widespread and practice took precedence over questions of origin.[9]
- If the numbers chosen as *yakudoshi*s are arranged in numerical order omitting the 'medium' *yakudoshi*s (which are dependent upon their proximity to the 'major' *yakudoshi*s), then almost all the *yakudoshi*s fall at intervals of three years. However, the marked exceptions are the *yakudoshi*s at the ages of 33 and 42 which are separated by intervals of five and four, and two and four years, respectively.[10] This produces a pattern of nineteen sets of (normally) three-year intervals between the ages of 1 and 61, which is distorted in order to incorporate the years 33 and 42. Such a pattern indicates that the choice of these years comes from a different source – most likely from the puns in the 'folk etymology'.

3 A third suggested origin of the *yakudoshi* complex is that these years mark times of critical change in the life-cycle. Norbeck (1953: 381; 1955: 114–17) has shown how some *yakudoshi* years marked the boundaries of formal age sets in traditional Japanese villages. It might be that such considerations influenced the attribution of sex distinctions to the 'major' *yakudoshi* years.

Either these differences by sex at the boundaries of major life-stages (such as retirement for men at the age of 61) were imposed upon the regular pattern of three-year stages outlined above, or else the major segments of the life-cycle according to age groups were then further subdivided into regular sub-sets of three years. Since detailed information on former age-grading practices in rural areas is rather fragmentary (cf. Norbeck 1953: 373),[11] it is impossible to decide which pattern preceded the other. According to this theory, the word *yakudoshi* is derived from another word for *yaku*, meaning 'responsibility', thus = rendering *yakudoshi*s as 'years of responsibility' (cf. also Bownas 1963: 173). However, as Norbeck (1955: 117) notes, the question then arises why the years of responsibility afterwards were not also feared, when some duties continued. Moreover, data on former demographic patterns are relatively scarce and will need further examination in relation to *yakudoshi*s, but what evidence there is shows that during the Edo period the age of marriage in Japan was relatively late – often well into the twenties for many women (Hanley and Yamamura 1977: 246–8). Therefore it is unlikely that the age of 19 was associated with a woman taking on the responsibilities of marriage, but there is evidence from the Edo period that the normal age for the cessation of childbearing was between the ages of 33 and 37 (ibid.: 216, 236, 241).

4 The most common reason for observing *yakudoshi*s reported by informants in Ueno is a theory that one's body changes at these critical points – in a way which, they claim, has been 'scientifically' demonstrated but which appears to have been a 'pseudo-scientific' gloss to validate a traditional belief.[12] Often informants would say they had 'heard' that it is 'scientific' that the body 'changes', 'deteriorates' or 'becomes tired' at the age of 42 for men and 33 for women, so that they are more susceptible to disease at these times – but these informants could not cite a scientific source for their ideas. Some were a little more precise in their affirmation that 'the hormone secretion levels of the body change' or that 'the incidence of cancer rises after these ages'. The most detailed exposition of such ideas came from a 49-year-old man who said, 'Past data shows that it is not superstition but scientific: at these ages parents receive a mental shock as they reach a crossroads in life when their children marry or leave home, and so on.' He, like the others, was unable to cite any specific 'past data' or 'scientific evidence' as such.

Those informants who assert that it is 'scientific' are mainly those without a high degree of specialization in medical or scientific fields of study. On the other hand, two men with such a background – one a dentist and the other a professor of pharmacology and biochemistry at a leading research institution – both dismissed such explanations about *yakudoshi*s and denied having any belief in *yakudoshi*s because they are 'not scientifically provable'. Nevertheless, this 'pseudo-scientific' theory about *yakudoshi*s provides a justification or validation of the belief in the minds of most informants. It is almost as if 'science' has taken the place once occupied by a religious literati – technical scientific language being like the use of Latin by medieval monks – so that the 'mystification' of 'science' in relation to ordinary people allows the possibility of 'science' being used to validate or provide a veneer of acceptability to folk concepts.[13]

PREVALENCE OF *YAKUDOSHI* BELIEFS AND PRACTICES

Statistics on the degree to which people pay attention to *yakudoshi*s are ambivalent because those who in early life say they do not pay attention to *yakudoshi*s may in fact do so when they encounter their own major (or 'principal') *yakudoshi*. However, the consciousness of *yakudoshi*s varies among different people, so that some women pay attention to their major *yakudoshi* at the age of 19 whereas the majority do not do anything about *yakudoshi*s until they are 32 or 33 years old. This ambivalence on account of whether or not a person has already experienced a 'major' or 'principal' *yakudoshi* partially accounts for those who are uncommitted in a questionnaire response and say that they 'neither do nor do not' pay attention to *yakudoshi*s. Out of 664 people who answered this question, 17.3 per cent were uncommitted in this way, but 48.5 per cent replied that they did pay attention to *yakudoshi*s and 34.2 per cent that they did not. Similar percentages were found in a nationwide survey in which 51 per cent replied 'yes' and 48 per cent 'no'.[14] This certainly indicates a high proportion of the population who do express some concern about reaching a 'major' or 'principal' *yakudoshi* age. A change in replies from 'no' to 'yes' is discernible among a few men in their early forties interviewed in 1984 who had bought special charms or visited particular shrines because of their entering a *yakudoshi* year but who in 1981 had replied on my questionnaire that they did not pay attention to *yakudoshi*s. This same change in attitudes probably accounts for the higher percentage of women who say they pay attention to them (55.5 per cent versus 44.1 per cent of the male respondents), because women reach their principal *yakudoshi* earlier in life.

However, these overall statistics are not amenable to finer correlations by age and sex because some people pay attention to 'non-principal' *yakudoshi*s (such as the minor *yakudoshi*s at the ages of 19, 25 or 61). A few are also aware of the minor *yakudoshi*s, and may or may not observe any ritual actions at such times. More informative findings come from reported behaviour as derived from my interviews. I questioned forty-five people who had reported that they 'paid attention to' *yakudoshi*s – including three men who had indicated a 'non-attention' to them in their initial responses to my questionnaire but had participated in *yakudoshi* rituals by the time I interviewed them two or three years later. Ten others who did not claim to believe were also questioned about their attitudes. It transpired that the formal questionnaire results were not always consistent with practice, largely owing to the ambiguity of the term 'pay attention to' used in the questionnaire. Most people interpreted this as intended, replying 'yes' if they had bought a special charm or visited a Shinto shrine especially because of their *yakudoshi*. Two people who had not done either of these nevertheless said that they 'took care' during their *yakudoshi*s, going to their doctors sooner than otherwise if they felt unwell, because they subscribed to the idea that the body deteriorates at that time.

Among the ten interviewed who had originally denied any concern with *yakudoshi*s were three men already past their principal *yakudoshi* who remained sceptical on scientific grounds and three other men not yet at that age who claimed to be sceptical but whose scepticism could not yet be checked with their practice. Two of these men, however, seemed to have a 'passive' rather than 'active' scepticism – in that one of them, aged 40, mentioned how many of his colleagues attribute illnesses to their *yakudoshi* and say he ought to visit a shrine in his coming *yakudoshi*; so he thinks he may go 'to be on the safe side'. The other man is in his mid-thirties but at new year went with his brother-in-law to a shrine in Wakayama prefecture for a 'purification' or 'exorcism' (*yakubarai*) against the latter's *yakudoshi*. He did not realize at the time that his wife was entering her *yakudoshi* year: otherwise, he says, he would have bought a charm for her at the same time – thereby indicating that in a few years he is likely to buy one for himself despite his present denial of any concern with *yakudoshi*s.

All four women interviewed who denied any concern with *yakudoshi*s had already experienced their main one (that of 33 years of age) by the time they were interviewed. The practice of only one of these was consistent with her 'disbelief', but she had also kept quiet to her husband about her approaching *yakudoshi* so that he would not feel pressurized into going to a shrine or buying a charm. Another denied a belief in *yakudoshi* on the grounds that 'it is just from a word play on *shi ni* and *sanzan* so is all nonsense', but she nevertheless accompanied her older brother and his wife to the Iwadani shrine for the sister-in-law's *yakudoshi* and bought a charm herself because the sister-in-law said she should, both of them being the same age. This informant described her purchase as 'a problem of human relations and obligations' (*giri-ninjō no mondai*) which forced her into purchasing the charm in spite of her scepticism. Several other informants mentioned the influence of social pressure from colleagues or relatives in their decision to visit a shrine or to buy a charm (Lewis 1993a: 152–4).

The two other women who said they did not pay attention to *yakudoshi*s had been pregnant at the time: both had girls that year. There is an idea prevalent among many Japanese women (though not all had heard of it) that the effects of a woman's *yakudoshi* are nullified if she bears a child in that year: the joy or happiness of motherhood cancels out the 'calamity' expected in a *yakudoshi*. Those mothers who had borne a son during their *yakudoshi*s claimed that the calamity is averted only if the child is male, whereas those who had borne a daughter said that a child of either sex would cancel the *yakudoshi*, although one of them (who had three daughters and no son) did admit that a son 'would have been better'. As the sex of the unborn child is normally unknown when the mother enters her *yakudoshi* at the New Year, it is noticeable that all four women interviewed with male children born in their *yakudoshi* – one of them having been born in the 'medium' strength *maeyaku* – did go to pray for safety and protection in their *yakudoshi* and to buy protective *mamori* or *fuda*.[15] They could not guarantee the sex of their child to mitigate the *yakudoshi*, so it was a 'relief' (*anshin*) when the boy was born as an 'added bonus'. On the other hand, two women with daughters born in their *yakudoshi*s had not conducted special rites, partly because they were sceptical about *yakudoshi*s and partly because they had a convenient 'justification' (pregnancy) for not going. Even so, one of them admitted to doubts when she had worse morning sickness than had been the case for her two previous children, so she sometimes wondered if it were on account of her *yakudoshi*.

One other woman, Mrs Yamamoto, had a daughter born in her 37-year old major *yakudoshi*. She claimed that a child of either sex eliminates the evil and that the birth of their daughter did (retrospectively) take away the 'calamity' of the *yaku-doshi*. Nevertheless, she and her husband went in the previous year (*maeyaku*, before the child was conceived), main year (*honyaku*) and following year (*atoy-aku*) to a large shrine, the Ueno *jingū*, where they received a special 'exorcism' or 'purification' (*yakubarai*) and each year they bought charms which they each wore around their necks for the whole year. This behaviour was rather extreme or unusual but it is understandable in the light of a confluence of influences:

- Both had *yakudoshi*s at the same time, when Mr Yamamoto was aged 42 and his wife 37.
- Mrs Yamamoto had already had one miscarriage and so they wanted to take special care this time; and
- Both parents were relatively old at the time of their first (and, it turned out, only) child's birth, so 'it would have been a shame (*kawaisō*) if anything were to happen to us while the baby was so young'.

Therefore pregnancy during a *yakudoshi* does not in itself prevent a mother from taking special precautions against her *yakudoshi*, and in cases like that of the Yamamotos' it might increase anxiety to some extent. Whether or not a mother thinks that only a male child or a child of either sex removes the 'calamity' can also exert an influence, but in cases like that of one woman whose boy was born in her *maeyaku* and theoretically took away the 'calamity' of the *honyaku* and *atoyaku* too, shrine visits may be continued in these subsequent *yakudoshi* years 'to be on the safe side'.

THE INTERPRETATION OF MISFORTUNES IN A *YAKUDOSHI* YEAR

During a *yakudoshi* year any ailments or injuries are easily attributable to the influence of *yakudoshi*s by people who in other years would regard such events as part of the normal circumstances of life. This psychological process was recognized by one of those interviewed, who gave it as the reason for his scepticism. Others with some openness to the idea of *yakudoshi*s would say about such illnesses, when talking with friends, 'I wonder if it could be anything to do with my *yakudoshi*?' – but would mention it in a tentative and unsure manner. Such was the case with Mrs Kimura, who after a major row with her husband was very tense for a few days, one symptom of which was a stomach ache. During that time she speculated about her *yakudoshi* – but after the ache was gone she abandoned the idea that it could have had any connection with her *yakudoshi*.

Those with a more 'active' belief more readily attribute such illnesses to the influence of *yakudoshi*s. An example of such a woman is Mrs Ikeda, aged 26 at the time of my interviewing her, so she was in a 'minor' *yakudoshi*:

> You're always told about people getting illnesses to an unbelievable extent in their *yakudoshi*s, and it's been just like that for me this year. I've had nothing but illnesses: my eyes have been aching recently and my child went down with chicken pox. It's been like that all the time this year.

Despite the fact that several informants mentioned hearsay cases of misfortunes happening in a *yakudoshi*, few could provide specific examples of such misfortunes happening to themselves. The few instances are as follows:

> I lost a tooth this year, my main *yakudoshi*, which is the first sign that one's getting old: the second is loss of eyesight and the third is loss of sexual appetite!
>
> (man, aged 41)

> In my *maeyaku* things did not go smoothly at work for several months.
>
> (man, aged 43)

> Though I agree with my husband that *yakudoshi*s are not scientifically provable, nevertheless when I was 19 I was ill in hospital for three months and when I was 32 I broke a leg and had to use crutches while it was in plaster.
>
> (woman, aged 33)

All these examples involve people who were relatively close to the time of their own *yakudoshi*s and could remember the incidents well, with the exception of the woman whose misfortunes occurred at the ages of both 19 and 32. By contrast, three men in their forties who had previously experienced more serious illnesses (meningitis, a heart operation and a stomach illness) while in their late thirties were all convinced that their illnesses had 'no connection' with their principal *yakudoshi*s, which occurred later. The more minor illnesses detailed above which did occur in a *yakudoshi* were emphasized as having a connection with the 'calamitous year': such observations further indicate a subjective element of interpretation in the management of illness, as some people use *yakudoshi*s as convenient scapegoats for any ailments occurring that year.

Such personal illnesses are the type which would be expected from the widespread 'folk' interpretation of *yakudoshi*s as times when the body is said to deteriorate and degenerative diseases to become more prevalent. However, breaking a leg or uneasy relationships at work do not fall into this category. Neither do the majority of other misfortunes which informants attributed to *yakudoshi*s, all of which involved a third party. Six such cases were reported to me, as follows:

Female informants
My husband's mother died young, when my husband was forty-one and in his *maeyaku*.

My father died when I was 33.

My younger sister died when my husband was aged 42.

My older sister's child became ill and died when my sister was 33 years old.

My mother died when I was 32.

Male informant

My wife had an accident when she was 19 and one of the children also had an accident when my wife was 33.[16]

While all of these involve 'calamities' (*yaku*), they do not conform to the common 'pseudo-scientific' rationalization for *yakudoshi*s according to which illnesses result from changes in the state of the person's own body. However, these kinds of 'dramatic' events involving a death are often those which circulate by hearsay and become distorted in the re-telling. In this way, a popular image is built up according to which such events commonly occur in a *yakudoshi*. Many of those who said they had a 'belief' in the occurrence of misfortune during *yakudoshi* years, but were unable to give any definite instances from their own experience, said that they had heard of such tales from 'acquaintances', 'my grandmother', or 'other people'. Some simply said it was 'ancient wisdom', 'said from of old'. These tales are then amalgamated with the 'pseudo-scientific' concept of degenerative diseases increasing from the time of a *yakudoshi* onwards, to form a 'folk mythology' of verbal traditions related to the *yakudoshi* cycle.

However, an element of circularity is introduced into people's thinking by their use of prayer and charms. Such circularity is particularly apparent in 'negative' prayers for protection and safety, as compared with 'positive' prayers for a definite, specific goal.[17] It is the former type which characterizes most Japanese prayer, of which *yakudoshi*s are a clear example. If one expects misfortune to occur and it does occur, then it can be attributed to one's *yakudoshi* and the 'belief' is reinforced. On the other hand, if one prays or buys a charm in order to counteract the *yakudoshi* and then no misfortune occurs, the 'belief' in the need for such prayers or charms is reinforced. Such 'belief' might still be mingled with scepticism, as in the common attitude that 'because nothing disastrous happened to me, I suppose the charm might have had some effect'. Others take a more cautious view and say that the charm's 'effect' is more psychological than technical: it gives 'reassurance' (*anshin*) or a 'sense of security' (*anshinkan*). It is noticeable that the three people cited earlier who attributed some personal misfortune in their own lives to the influence of a *yakudoshi* all hold attitudes of this kind, since all of them had taken the ritual precautions.[18]

It is difficult to assess the extent to which professed belief or scepticism concerning *yakudoshi*s is relevant until the time when a person actually encounters his or her principal *yakudoshi*. Even if a person does visit a shrine or buy a charm on account of social pressures, some inner scepticism about the 'truth' of the *yakudoshi* beliefs might remain. For other people, the very act of conforming to social pressures possibly helps to induce a certain suspension of disbelief and perhaps a willingness to regard the beliefs as in some sense 'true' during the *yakudoshi* period itself. Some experiences of life during that *yakudoshi* time might then be interpreted as confirming the idea that misfortunes do occur especially in *yakudoshi* years, whereas other experiences might provide reassurance (*anshin*) that one had taken the proper precautions. If those precautions had been taken but still a misfortune occurred, some attitudes towards the charms might undergo a shift in interpretation.[19] However, in my limited sample I came across no cases of *yakudoshi* charms being rejected on account of contradictory experiences.[20]

THE BAMBOO TREE OF LIFE

A few individuals mentioned certain restrictions on movement which they observed during their *yakudoshi*s (in addition to the more usual practices of shrine visits and special attention to diet or exercise). These restrictions are:

- One should not change one's position at work.[21]
- One should take special care of one's body in a *yakudoshi* year if one is in a different environment, such as on a business trip.
- One should not build or repair a house or change its structure too much (mentioned by two people).

All of these involve a change in location – becoming 'out of place' while one adjusts to the new and altered conditions. As such it might be useful to apply to *yakudoshi* concepts the framework of analysis developed by Douglas (1966) for purity and pollution concepts, in which she argued that 'dirt' can be defined as 'matter out of place'. Both Douglas and Leach (1976: 33–6) further argue that what does not fit into a clear category but is marginal and ambiguous is often regarded as 'dangerous' in some way. Ambiguous marginal states are seen in most cultures as sources of danger and taboo, according to this framework of analysis, and in Japan this applies not only to the changes in location listed above but also to the *yakudoshi*s themselves. We might graft this framework of analysis onto the common Japanese metaphor which describes *yakudoshi* years as like the nodes (*fushi*) of a bamboo tree: this indigenous metaphor focuses attention on the boundaries between compartments and relates them to critical or 'dangerous' transitional periods between one stage of life and the next. The bamboo tree symbolizes the human life-cycle in which critical junctures occur at regular intervals (about every three years for 'minor' *yakudoshi*s) and form crucial boundary markers in the life-cycle. At such important junctures one should take special ritual precautions to avert possible misfortunes, and some people also pay attention to the physical or social dimensions of location by avoiding, if possible, moving house or changing one's job in a *yakudoshi*. However, as many company employees have relatively little control over such aspects of their lives, it appears as if this particular element of the *yakudoshi* complex is less widely emphasized than perhaps it might have been at one time.

On the other hand, a possible decline in one element might be matched by a corresponding rise in another while the *yakudoshi* practices and beliefs as a whole remain relatively strong in an industrial, urban context. While specific rules about changes in location might be de-emphasized, it seems that paying attention to one's health at these ages is becoming increasingly emphasized. To some extent this is actually a by-product of modernization in so far as an increasing suspicion of Western, cosmopolitan medicine – which is alleged to produce many more side-effects than herbal medicine as well as to be responsible for some serious iatrogenic illnesses – has been partially responsible for a popular resurgence of interest in East Asian medicine (Lock 1980: 152). This is particularly concentrated among those over the age of 40 (ibid.: 99–100). For men at least this might be partially triggered off by their principal *yakudoshi*, which by Western reckoning falls at the age of 41, and its *maeyaku* at the age of 40. It is true that chronic illnesses of the kind less amenable to treatment by cosmopolitan synthetic drugs are likely to be more widespread once one reaches middle age, but the social awareness of one's state of health triggered off by a *yakudoshi* – in which one's family and friends often admonish one to 'take care' – is probably another major influence in Japanese attitudes to medicine. Lock (ibid.: 141) mentions the idea of bodily deterioration in the context of East Asian medical therapy rather than that of *yakudoshi*s, but a close link between the two is seen in the case of Mrs Kimura, mentioned earlier, who, the year after her principal *yakudoshi*, began to attend a class to learn *shiatsu*, a traditional type of 'pressure massage' – 'because', she said, 'my illness last year made me more aware of my health so I joined a keep-fit class and chose this one as it was the least expensive of those available'. A number of other informants were questioned about their use of East Asian medicine, and it appears that particularly for men some connection with passing their principal *yakudoshi* is discernible, as indicated by Figure 12.2.[22]

Younger generations have been affected in general by the popular interest in *kanpō*, but the greater use of East Asian medicine among women is attributable partly to their being responsible for the general health of their families, and partly to the fact that some of them use East Asian therapies during pregnancy or (in two cases cited) on behalf of a child.

A further consistency between attitudes towards *yakudoshi*s and East Asian medicine is their common emphasis on prevention rather than cure. Traditional medical systems emphasize preventive medicine through the regular use of herbal remedies, massage or other treatments (ibid.: 204, 245–6). A similar psychology might be expressed in Japanese business contexts by the encouragement for workers to do group exercises before and during the course of their work. In the same way, a Japanese emphasis on being 'forewarned and forearmed' (cf. Benedict 1946: 22–4) leads to *yakudoshi* charms being bought and prayers said during shrine visits in January in order to prevent imagined misfortunes from occurring in the *yakudoshi* years. Similarly, prayers at both Buddhist and Shinto household altars (*butsudan* and *kamidana*) are often prophylactic prayers (asking for a safe and healthy day, etc.), while a common attitude towards keeping *mamori* charms for traffic safety is 'if I didn't have one, something might go wrong, or I might have an accident' (Lewis 1993a: 34).

The close similarities in the motivations of those taking East Asian medicine,

			Men	Women
ACUPUNCTURE				
After *yakudoshi*		Used:	4	4
		Never used:	8	3
Before *yakudoshi*		Used:	0	3
		Never used:	8	6
SHIATSU (PRESSURE MASSAGE)				
After *yakudoshi*		Used:	2	4
		Never used:	10	3
Before *yakudoshi*		Used:	0	1
		Never used:	8	8
KANPŌ (HERBAL MEDICINE)				
After *yakudoshi*		Used:	10	2
		Never used:	2	5
Before *yakudoshi*		Used:	4	5
		Never used:	4	4

Figure 12.2 The use of East Asian medicine before and after a principal *yakudoshi*

paying attention to 'biorhythms', possessing *mamori* safety charms or taking care during a *yakudoshi* year point to some of the reasons why *yakudoshi* beliefs and practices appear to be deeply rooted and widespread in contemporary Japanese culture. The *yakudoshi* complex also displays structural links with deeply rooted Japanese values, such as concepts of purity and pollution – as discussed above – and the cultural emphasis on age (Norbeck 1955: 106–7). These are cultural values and emphases which are widely recognized as pervading Japanese daily life in both rural and urban areas (Ohnuki-Tierney 1984: 21–31, 34–5, 47–9; Norbeck 1953; Nakane 1970: 26–30, 128; Lewis 1993a: 120–36, 98–115). It is not unlikely that the persistence of *yakudoshi* observances in contemporary urban and industrialized Japan is partly attributable to their links with these two other cultural value-orientations which appear to have been little affected by the Japanese transition to an industrialized economy.

FACING THE FUTURE

Elsewhere I have argued that a substantial proportion of Japanese religious action is motivated by feelings of insecurity or fears about the future (Lewis 1993a: 22–34, 42–4, 84–93, 99–101, etc.). *Yakudoshi* beliefs focus this fear onto specific periods of time. To some extent, a possible stimulus towards the development of fresh religious movements through the teachings of Hōnen and Shinran was a feeling that the coming age of *mappō* would be a kind of society-wide or even global *yakudoshi*.

Are elements of this kind of religiosity re-emerging today? The AUM Shinrikyō provides one of the more conspicuous expressions of such a religious movement, but I would not be surprised if in the near future other 'millenarian' movements were to emerge too. My surmise is based on two observations: first, the recognition that several Japanese 'new religions' have already drawn on aspects of Christianity, and, second, the widespread knowledge of the Christian calendar in Japan – despite the fact that for most everyday purposes the years are reckoned from the beginning of the current emperor's reign. Moreover, concerns with *yakudoshi* are merely one facet of a common fascination with numbers (Crump 1992) which is likely to be fed by the fact that about 2,000 years have elapsed since the birth of Jesus Christ. Probably of more significance, however, is the fact that Jesus predicted the occurrence of major wars and earthquakes among some of the signs of his return. In a nation which became the 'guinea pig' for real-life atomic bomb experiments, which in other ways was devastated by the Second World War, and which just recently has been reminded of its vulnerability to earthquakes, it would not be surprising if certain religious movements were to draw more upon Christian apocalyptic elements. Japanese people who expect to encounter troubles in their *yakudoshi* years take precautions which they consider to be appropriate: in the same way, religious movements expecting the imminent return of their Messiah are usually warned to be prepared. For AUM Shinrikyō, the preparations involved the production and stockpiling of poison gas, but we can hope that other emerging movements will focus their preparations more on the kinds of armour described in the Bible as, for example, the 'helmet of salvation' or the 'breastplate of righteousness' (Isaiah 59: 17; Ephesians 6: 10–18).

NOTES

1   It was permissible for the secular media to describe the cult as corrupt or evil, but the word 'demonic' was reserved for Christian religious commentators. A further Christian religious interpretation came from a Christian in Toronto named Mark DuPont. He regarded both the Kobe earthquake and the Tokyo gas attack as fulfilments of a prophecy he had given in 1994 to the effect that the Almighty God would be allowing Japan to be shaken because most Japanese people were putting their security in material prosperity and not in spiritual values (DuPont 1995).

2   See, for example, the Agency for Cultural Affairs (1972: 133), Inokuchi (1983) or the *Nihon Minzoku Jiten* (1971: 749), the latter using the term *zokushin*, 'popular belief', a term also used by Hōri (1968: 44, 46) to refer to lucky and unlucky years (*toshi-mawari*), a concept akin to that of *yakudoshi*.

3   Those in the company housing range from departmental managers (*buchō*) down to blue-collar workers (though suitably differentiated by types and size of accommodation), while those in an adjacent estate of owner-occupied houses consist of white-collar employees of large firms, a number of professionals such as a lawyer, a dentist, two university lecturers, and some lower-middle-class people such as a professional bicycle racer, the local shopkeeper and the foreman/manager of a local garage who rents both the garage and his home.

4   I am grateful to Dr Fukui Katsuyoshi and Dr Nakamaki Hirochika of the National

Museum of Ethnology, Osaka, for enabling the questionnaire to be processed by the Museum's computers: the tape was made available for comparative research by other scholars wishing to have access to the statistics. My thanks are due also to the British Economic and Social Science Research Council and to the Japan Foundation, the organizations which funded my two periods of fieldwork in Japan.

5 A few had received 'substitute charms' which had not been bought from a shrine but were still held to be efficacious in protecting against evil. Examples include a pair of chopsticks made from *nanten* wood – since *nanten* can be written with characters meaning 'avoidance of disaster' (難転) or a kimono sash containing five different colours and said to be a protection against evil. One informant had been given by his mother a pair of decorative iron 'cooking chopsticks', about a foot long, bought from a shop in Himeji: a leaflet enclosed in the box explained that, according to a local legend from the Himeji district, such chopsticks expel evil (Lewis 1993a: 152).

6 Although Japanese lacks a plural form for the word *yakudoshi*, I have taken the liberty of adding a final 's' in places for the sake of clarity and English style.

7 Depending on the context, the Japanese reading can also be *yotsu*, in which case the character is read *yo*, plus a suffix for *tsu*.

8 The Japanese readings lack the Chinese intonation markers and are usually derived from ancient rather than modern Chinese forms. The lack of intonation also produces homonyms in Japanese among words distinguished by intonation in Chinese.

9 Compare the similar taboos on the number 13 in the West, which is said to have been derived from the fact that thirteen people were seated around the table at the Last Supper: if this is so, then the 'origin' in a literate tradition – in this case read and taught in churches and heard by those who were illiterate – is generally unknown, whereas the practice of avoiding the number 13 has continued.

10 The numbers so arranged are: 1, 4, 7, 10, 13, 16, 19, 22, 25, 28, 33, 37, 40, 42, 46, 49, 52, 55, 58 and 61.

11 On *a priori* grounds one might assume that the more complex *yakudoshi* structure was built upon the simpler structure of the age-grades, but I have my doubts about this too, because the 'simpler' can also be a 'degenerate' form of the more complex.

12 On a general level it is obvious that one's health does tend to decline as one reaches middle age, but it is not 'scientific' to assert that this process accelerates or begins at a fixed age such as 42 for men and another age for women. Rather, the fixing of such an age is a socially decided demarcation of boundaries in a continuous process of ageing occurring at varying rates of intensity for different individuals.

13 An extension of the idea that one's body changes and is more susceptible to illness during a *yakudoshi* might be the emphasis put upon 'bio-rhythms' in some Japanese factories, as mentioned by Kamata (1982: 121, 124). Although it would be less risky for me officially to withhold judgement about whether or not such ideas are 'scientific', I suspect that 'bio-rhythms' too are largely 'pseudo-scientific' but gain their popular appeal in the same way as *yakudoshi*s – namely, through a desire to predict times of misfortune and thereby to gain control over one's own personal destiny by taking precautions in order to avert the anticipated adversity.

14 The other 1 per cent are recorded as 'others'. Details of this survey were published in the *Asahi Shinbun*, morning edition, 5 May 1981.

15 One of them did not buy a *mamori* or *fuda* but instead went to the Iwadani shrine, prayed and bought a towel – as the cheapest available 'dedication gift' (*hōnō*) – on which she wrote her date of birth and name, leaving the towel as a kind of votive offering at the shrine.

16 The first part of this statement does involve an accident to the person during a *yakudoshi* year, but it was not included in the few cited earlier because this unspecified accident was reported at second hand.

17 There can be an element of circularity in both types of prayer if one allows for escape clauses such as 'if God wills'. Such escape clauses are very common in most religions

throughout the world, although a recent trend in some Christian circles has been to emphasize that one can expect very specific answers to prayer (such as healings) provided a few basic conditions are fulfilled. However, in practice even the more dramatic and medically verifiable cases of healing are still subject to controversies over the interpretation of the data, as I discuss elsewhere (Lewis 1989; cf. also Gardner 1983 and 1986). In general, I would argue that statistical probability can be used to test whether such 'answers to prayer' are possibly the result of 'chance' or are more likely to be the result of a significant relationship between prayer and the medically unexpected outcome (Lewis 1993b: 325–7, 334–9).

18 For example, the man who had lost a tooth in his *yakudoshi* says that the *mamori* charm which he wears next to his skin each day has some 'effect' only in a 'mysterious' rather than 'visible' manner. He says, 'If it gives relief of heart, it is efficacious' (*anshin dekireba, goriyaku ga aru*), so that 'to believe is to be saved/reassured' (*shinjiru koto wa sukuwareru/anshin sareru*).

19 An instance from a different context concerns a man who initially expressed a belief in the efficacy of prayers at his company's Shinto shrine but two years later revised this to saying that the prayers 'had no technical effect'. It appeared that a major influence on his change of attitude was his experience of returning from the prayers at the shrine to find that one of his men had just cut off a finger on a piece of equipment (see Lewis 1993a: 47). Perhaps this is an example of what Southwold (1979: 635–6) calls a shift from belief in something as 'factually' true to one of 'symbolic truth'. For *yakudoshi*s, however, the 'truth value' does not seem to be particularly categorized into either 'factual' or 'symbolic' truth until the time of the principal *yakudoshi* itself, but even at that time some scepticism can remain mixed in with a readiness to observe the expected rituals 'in order to be on the safe side'.

20 One case related to me in a different context concerns a man who threw away a charm for traffic safety when his car crashed and overturned on his way back from the shrine where he had bought the charm.

21 This was mentioned by the man who reported having problems at work in his *maeyaku*.

22 See Lewis (1993a: 155–6) for more detail on the medical conditions for which treatment was sought in these cases.

REFERENCES

Agency for Cultural Affairs (1972) *Japanese Religion*, Tokyo: Kodansha.

Beardsley, R.K., J.W. Hall and R.E. Ward (1959) *Village Japan*, Chicago: University of Chicago Press.

Benedict, Ruth (1946) *The Chrysanthemum and the Sword*, Boston: Houghton Mifflin.

Bownas, Geoffrey (1963) *Japanese Rainmaking and Other Folk Practices*, London: George Allen & Unwin.

Corley, Felix (1995) 'AUM Cult Fights Back', *Frontier*, June–August 1995, pp. 6–7.

Crump, Thomas (1992) *The Japanese Numbers Game: The Use and Understanding of Numbers in Modern Japan*, London and New York: Routledge.

Dore, Ronald P. (1965) 'The Legacy of Tokugawa Education', in Marius B. Jansen (ed.), *Changing Japanese Attitudes Towards Modernization*, Princeton, NJ: Princeton University Press, pp. 99–131.

Douglas, Mary (1966) *Purity and Danger*, London: Routledge & Kegan Paul.

DuPont, Mark (1995) Seminar on *Prophecy* during the New Wine Christian convention held at the Bath and West Country Showground in August 1995.

Gardner, Rex (1983) 'Miracles of Healing in Anglo-Celtic Northumbria as Recorded by the Venerable Bede and his Contemporaries: A Reappraisal in the light of twentieth-century experience', *British Medical Journal*, vol. 287, 24–31 December, pp. 1927–33.

212 *David C. Lewis*

—— (1986) *Healing Miracles: A Doctor Investigates*, London: Darton, Longman & Todd.

Hanley, Susan and Yamamura Kōzō (1977) *Economic and Demographic Change in Preindustrial Japan, 1600–1868*, Princeton, NJ: Princeton University Press.

Hōri, Ichiro (1968) *Folk Religion in Japan: Continuity and Change*, Chicago: University of Chicago Press.

Inokuchi, Shōji (1983) 'Yakudoshi', in *Kodansha Encyclopedia of Japan*, Tokyo: Kodansha International, vol. 8, p. 285.

Kamata, Satoshi (1982) *Japan in the Passing Lane*, New York: Pantheon Books.

Kawanami, Hiroko (1995) 'Waiting for Doomsday: The Rise and Rise of the Japanese Cult', *Demos*, vol. 6, pp. 42–3.

Leach, Edmund (1976) *Culture and Communication*, Cambridge: Cambridge University Press.

Lewis, David C. (1989) *Healing: Fiction, Fantasy or Fact?*, London: Hodder & Stoughton.

—— (1993a) *The Unseen Face of Japan*, Crowborough/Tunbridge Wells: Monarch.

—— (1993b) 'A Social Anthropologist's Analysis of Contemporary Healing', in Gary S. Greig and Kevin N. Springer (eds) *The Kingdom and the Power*, Ventura, California: Regal Books, pp. 321–43.

Lock, Margaret (1980) *East Asian Medicine in Urban Japan*, Berkeley: University of California Press.

Nakane, Chie (1970) *Japanese Society*, London: Weidenfeld & Nicolson.

Nihon Minzoku Jiten [*Encyclopedia of Japanese Folklore*] (1971), Tokyo: Seibundō.

Norbeck, Edward (1953) 'Age-grading in Japan', *American Anthropologist*, vol. LV, pp. 373–84.

—— (1955) '*Yakudoshi*: A Japanese Complex of Supernaturalistic Beliefs', *Southwestern Journal of Anthropology*, vol. XI, pp. 105–20.

Ohnuki-Tierney, Emiko (1984) *Illness and Culture in Contemporary Japan*, Cambridge: Cambridge University Press.

Reader, Ian (1996) *A Poisonous Cocktail? Aum Shinrikyō's Path to Violence*, Copenhagen: Nordic Institute of Asian Studies, NIAS Publications

Robinson, Gwen (1995a) 'Religious Cult suspected of gas attacks' *The Times*, Tuesday 21 March 1995, p. 1.

—— (1995b) 'Guru fed followers blood and mysticism' *The Times*, Thursday 23 March 1995, p. 10.

Shimazono, Susumu (1995) 'In the Wake of Aum: The Formation and Transformation of a Universe of Belief', *Japanese Journal of Religious Studies*, vol. 22, nos 3-4, pp. 381–415.

Southwold, Martin (1979) 'Religious Belief', *Man*, n.s. vol. XIV, no. 4, pp. 628–44.

13 Redefining Kuzaki

Ritual, belief and *chō* boundaries

D. P. Martinez

INTRODUCTION

The former fishing and diving village of Kuzaki had been incorporated into Toba city for several decades when I did my fieldwork in 1984–6. Yet the *chō* (ward) retained its distance from the city and other nearby *chō* (which had also been distinct villages in the past), both politically and geographically. In fact, on my return from the field, when I began to organize the material I had gathered, I realized that Kuzaki reinforced its spatial distance from other places through the yearly enactment of a series of rituals linked to the eastern, southern, western and northern boundaries of the village. The question is: why did I not spot this while I was doing fieldwork, since the material on 'folk' religion in Japan is full of examples of what might be termed 'boundary protection' (cf. Hendry 1984; Ohnuki-Tierney 1984 among others)?

The answer is simply that when I asked for explanations of the various rituals (monthly worship at Mount Sengen on the western side of Kuzaki; the Nifune *matsuri* (festival) on the eastern and southern sides; the *bon* festival on the eastern side; Hachiman-san *matsuri* on the northern side) the explanations I was given ranged from the functional to that of 'invented tradition'.

In this chapter I want to juxtapose the traditional explanations given about one such ritual (Nifune *matsuri*) with what I was told by various informants during fieldwork. In doing this I am not pointing to a 'problem' with the various explanations I was offered, but I would like to consider, yet again, the issue of 'belief' and 'practice' in Japanese religion (cf. Reader 1991; van Bremen 1995).

One way to re-explore the question of belief and religious practices is to compare the Japanese case more widely with religious practice in other parts of Asia (Southwold 1983) and the Pacific (Bloch 1986) and to reconsider the problem of belief (Needham 1972) as well as symbols which change through time (Ohnuki-Tierney 1990).

A BRIEF DESCRIPTION OF NIFUNE *MATSURI*

The festival of Nifune ('two boats') takes place over several days in November (15–19) and resembles other boat rituals in Japan as described by Davis (1977) and Bernier (1970). Descriptions of the Kuzaki ritual also occur in Nomura (1978) and Nakata (1979). The festival is composed of several elements which include a visit to Ise Shrine; the making of sacred implements for the main deity in whose honour the festival is held;[1] various feasts for different village age-grades (*dōkyūsei*); as well as the most picturesque and central act of the festival: the 'race' between two boats which represent the two main halves of the village.[2] I will limit this chapter's analysis to the race which occurs on the penultimate day of the festival.

The ceremony of 18 November starts on Yoriozaki beach which is on the eastern side of the village.[3] Early in the morning the representatives from the Kuzaki cooperative take out the two canoe-like boats which the young men of the village have to row. One boat is loaded with sacred implements which will be left at the small shrine on the island of Kaminoshima; the other boat must start out at the same time, but take a different direction in order to fool any demons. The sacred objects include a *gohei* (a sacred staff), a *shimenawa* (sacred rope), two wooden swords and sake which has been donated by Ise Shrine; all the objects have been purified in a ceremony at the village shrine.

At 1 p.m. the wives' club holds a banquet in the village hall for the ten young men who will row the two boats. The men have to be in the under-25 *dōkyūsei* of the Seinendan (young men's club) and must be unmarried. The two boat crews represent the two main village geographical divisions (Sato-naka and Kai-naka) and must sit facing each other during the feast. The Sato-naka men sit on the left and the Kai-naka men on the right, corresponding to the village division.

Slowly, after drinking a great deal of sake for courage, the young men head for Yoriozaki. Waiting for them are their grandmothers and a few married young men who have rowed in previous years. These are the people who will help dress the rowers in the sacred white clothing which they don after a naked jump into the cold November sea to purify themselves. The first and second oarsmen of the Sato-naka crew must dress first and, carrying their oars over their shoulders, go to the Shinto shrine to collect the deity's objects. At this point, one of the grandmothers told me that it was good luck for an unmarried man to row during Nifune: it meant that he would find a wife within the year. One young man kept telling his grandmother that surely, after this year '*yome-san motte iru*' (I will have a wife). Another man told me that these boats, the deity's boats, were the only ones in which women could not ride; the only instance of a taboo against women on boats in Kuzaki.[4]

Once the oarsmen have returned with the deity's sacred objects, the Sato-naka boat starts out for Kaminoshima. With a slight delay, the decoy Kai-naka boat follows and rows to Ōtsu harbour on the south side of the village. By the time the Sato-naka boat reaches Kaminoshima, the sea is full of fishermen's boats which follow the men to the island. The first rower must jump from the boat to the island, remove the previous year's offerings to the *kami*, and replace them with the new objects. The old offerings are carried back to the boat and the rowers then take them to be burnt on Kaminoshima beach (i.e., the beach which faces the island) where some of the village older men have been waiting. Meanwhile the Kai-naka crew docks in Ōtsu harbour where another crowd of men start a warming fire and share sake with the rowers. While this is occurring the village grandfathers are distributing the sacred *shige* (the Kuzaki term for sacred objects that resemble small arrows and which are made by the grandfathers on 17 November) throughout the village. It was also at this point that I discovered that the men in their forties and fifties had already spent part of the afternoon, dressed in their ceremonial kimono, meeting and drinking.

When the Sato-naka crew feels energetic enough to row again, and before dusk, the rowers get back into the boat and begin the return journey. When the waiting Kai-naka crew sees the other boat approaching Ōtsu, they climb back into their boat and row out to meet it. The two boats must return at the same time. On Yoriozaki beach the grandmothers are cleaning up and building a third fire. All the married village men, children, women and young girls begin to gather on the beach, everyone bringing old rice straw which is added to the bonfire until it grows large enough to be seen by the boat crews. The mothers of the rowers bring large buckets full of hot water and barrels of *amazake* (sweet sake) for everyone to drink.

The boats must try to land at the same time, so it often takes several attempts for the rowers to get in. One grandmother told me: 'It is bad luck for one side of the village if its boat lands after the other. For both Sato-naka and Kai-naka to have good luck and a prosperous year, the boats must land together.' The next day a grandfather explained this differently, claiming that if the Sato-naka boat had landed first, the next year would be a good one for *bora* (a type of young tuna) catches; if the Kai-naka boat landed first it would mean good sardine catches. The decrease in fishing in the village appeared to mean that it was less important for one side to land before the other and more important that both halves of the village have good luck. In 1984 it took six attempts to land the boats and once on shore, the young men washed, changed clothing, drank *amazake* and, eventually, made their way to a celebration held by the Seinendan. The older men often return to their group drinking in village pubs, and the women and children go home.

AN ANALYSIS OF NIFUNE *MATSURI*

One of my sources of frustration during fieldwork was that I often received fairly simplistic answers to my questions about ritual. In attempts to understand Nifune *matsuri* I steered many conversions during the festival around to the meaning of the ritual. The answers I received tended to be very practical: the food consumed by the grandfathers and rowers in various feasts throughout the five days was just the food which historically was available in the past; the meaning of the two boats was linked to the village's 'warrior past', perhaps a past more accurately represented by the fishermen's coast guard duty done for the local *daimyō*; and, as I noted above (see note 1), the central deity of the ritual was generally referred to as the 'young god' (the older deity having been destroyed in a typhoon in 1935) rather than as Haku-hatsu-daimyō. Various elements of the festival are common to all Japanese *matsuri* which are generally concerned with purification (the purification of the objects and the young men); the cosmological year (Nifune is one of several boundary-creating rituals in Kuzaki; see also Caillet in this volume); re-creating the cosmic circle to ensure prosperity for the living (the emphasis on good luck during the boats' landing); as well as stressing the importance of the cardinal directions, the two halves of a village and the symbolic struggle between them.

In a longer analysis of Kuzaki rituals (Martinez 1988) I emphasized that the following concepts also underlay large village rituals:

1   a large village ceremony requires that the whole village be represented by the members of the various village age-grades;
2   each age-grade has a separate and well-defined role in the ceremony;
3   the ceremony often re-enacts the sealing of an abstract/symbolic contract.

Nifune *matsuri* is best understood as one of several such contractual rituals which take place in Kuzaki and is most closely linked, I believe, with the January Hachiman-san festival. Both festivals seem to be concerned with the welfare of the village as a whole and of fishermen in particular. The January Hachiman-san *matsuri* is the symbolic re-enactment of the village's contract with a feudal lord, while Nifune is the symbolic renewal of the contract with the 'young deity' (who might well have been a feudal lord) who protects the ocean around the village. These two rituals begin and end the most intensive of fishing seasons for men in the village.

Women have a very small role in the January festival, and in Nifune only one evening of the five-day festival is given over to a celebration for the women who dive. Yet, like all large village rituals, Nifune *matsuri* is only possible with the cooperation of all the village age-grades. An informant once told me to live in Kuzaki meant to take part in all its public rituals, a villager could not 'believe in' a new religion, for example, which might preach that Shinto or Buddhist practices could not also be followed. To do so would be to be excluded from village social life; not to take part in the practices of all the village is not to be a member of the village. In short, large village rituals are symbolic renewals not just of cosmic contracts (with the deities), but of the social contract which binds villagers together.

However, when I asked people to explain ritual to me the answers I received ranged from the functional (as noted above with the example of why certain food was eaten); to the conflicting almost personal explanations (to get a wife, for good luck, for good fish catches); and to the far more common: 'don't ask me, read the following by so-and-so'. Occasionally people would offer standard interpretations about purification; appeasing, casting out or fooling evil spirits; and asking for good luck, health and safety for family. Implicit in such explanations are the concepts of protecting or re-creating boundaries (both personal and social); the ideas of *uchi* and *soto*; and the power of strangers – all the traditional stuff of Japanese folk religion. But while these concepts might be said to form the deep structure of Japanese religion, it was never clearly stated to me that the people of Kuzaki 'believed in' the deities they worshipped, nor was a clearly conceptualized unitary religious vision offered. This clearly posed a problem for a Westerner like me who arrived in the field with deeply embedded notions about belief and practice.

This issue is not a new one in the field of anthropology: the problem of belief, statements of disbelief and actual practice is an old chestnut. However, it is one which anthropologists of Japan (as opposed to religious specialists) seem to consider very rarely. Anthropological analyses of religion in Japan tend to range from the structural functionalist (especially on ancestor worship, cf. Plath 1964; Smith 1974); to the structuralist (cf. Ooms 1976; Matsunaga and Yoshida in this volume); to theories of social charter (cf. Bernier 1970; Moon 1984) as well as to ideas of creating a sense of tradition (Bestor 1990) and identity (Robertson 1991). The analysis of religious specialists on Japan often revolve around the concepts of purity and pollution (cf. Namihira 1977), the juxtaposition of Taoist, folk, Buddhist and Shintoist symbolism and practice (cf. Hōri 1968; Earhart 1982; Kitagawa 1987); or the history of particular deities, practices or events.

A particular problem has also arisen around the issue of belief: the Japanese are said to be less religious than in the past because when asked if they *believe* in Buddhism or Shintoism they reply 'no', but, as Reader points out, if asked whether they *practise* religion the answer is very different (1991: 12–15). As members of a modern, or even postmodern, society, the Japanese are aware that they often interact with people who label the religious practices of other societies as superstitious.[5] Thus, young people in Kuzaki would qualify statements of belief in demons or other supernatural creatures by telling me that only 'old people or children' believed such things but, of course, they themselves did not. So how is an anthropologist to proceed amongst this morass of competing discourses on religion, ritual and belief in Japan? How are we not only to offer an interpretation of a ritual like Nifune but to also say something general about the place of religion in Japanese life?

TOWARDS A CONCLUSION: REDEFINING VILLAGE RITUAL

What I have written above might be taken to imply that *none* of the above approaches to Japanese religion and ritual is correct. In fact, I believe that we need to consider most of these approaches in order to understand not only what Nifune *matsuri* was about in 1984, but also what it represents historically. Grasping both these aspects (the synchronic and the diachronic) is essential if we are to understand, in turn, the construction of Kuzaki as a place.

Furthermore, in giving primacy to practice over statements of belief (Reader 1991), Japanese religion is like many other religions (see especially Southwold 1983 on Sinhalese Buddhism). As in other religions, this emphasis on practice allows for the meaning of rituals to be both various and to change over time (Bloch 1986).[6]

Thus, the missing dimension in understanding Kuzaki ritual, I would argue, is the history of the village and of religion in Japan. The most important point to make here is that until the 1947 Constitution's attempts to depoliticize religion by allowing religious freedom, religion in Japan was always political. Even Tokugawa attempts to keep Buddhists from meddling in politics by bringing them under government control (cf. Nosco 1996), only succeeded in changing the nature of Buddhism's political involvement. In the seventeenth century all villages had to have a village temple, and it was during this era that Kuzaki gained its first *Sōtō* Zen Buddhist priest (in 1661). This sect was not the village's choice, their practices could be best described as Amida Buddhist, as well as what might be termed folk religion. The long line of priests in the village during the Tokugawa period appear to have overseen all Buddhist and Shinto rituals (a distinction that was not so very clear before the Meiji Restoration); and the village Shinto priest only appeared as a village office during Meiji.

The Buddhist temple in Kuzaki, like most villages temples before Meiji, was the centre of village life. Not just the ritual centre, but also the social and familial, as the priest kept family records and, in some way, was seen to represent the power of the Toba clan who ruled that area. The emphasis on Shintoism which grew up during the Meiji Restoration was not a huge problem for Kuzaki; it had, for several centuries, been a *kambe* (sacred guild) of the Ise Shrine, making the *noshi awabi* (dried strips of abalone) which were offered daily to the deities worshipped at Ise. However, the village did have to split the Buddhist and Shinto areas of worship during early Shōwa. Thus, the village shrine, which had for centuries been on the point overlooking Yoriozaki Bay, was moved to the northern boundary of the village. There, the 1926-constructed shrine overlooks the path up to the sacred Mount Sengen where the village women worship monthly.

Political changes in the nineteenth and twentieth centuries affected not only the religious structure of the village but the political hierarchy as well. From the 1870s Kuzaki suffered the same fate as many villages in Japan, ceasing to be part of the Toba clan and becoming part of Toba prefecture. In 1877 Toba prefecture became Toba city and was incorporated into Mie prefecture. Kuzaki was joined with its northern neighbour, Ijika, to be administered as one village. In 1890, the village became part of another *mura* (village) made up of five neighbouring villages and called Nagaoka (Kuzaki n.d.: 67). Kuzaki's neighbour and rival Ōsatsu was made the head of this administrative unit and continued to be part of the local government hierarchy above Kuzaki even after the 1955/6 incorporation of all the villages as wards (*chō*) of Toba city. So it is that Kuzaki's distinctive religious identity has been undercut in the last century both by the lost of status of Shinto at the end of the Second World War and by the changes in political structure throughout Japan. As a place, it is only one ward of many in Toba city and, as a tourist resort, it was much smaller and less developed than Ōsatsu in the 1980s.

In short, the former village was no longer an important place, although it still continued its yearly tribute of *noshi awabi* to Ise Shrine. The connection of fascism with State Shinto and Ise was still so powerful, however, that villagers did not talk in great detail about this part of their identity. Making *noshi awabi* made them unique, but whatever Ise or the goddess Amaterasu might represent, on that villagers would not comment.

Silence then about rituals and their meanings cannot be attributed solely to the fact that practice is more important than belief in Japan. Rather, the history both of Kuzaki and of religion in Japan is such that there is an inherent danger in trying to contextualize and explain rituals. For example, the only way to describe the continued Amida worship of village ancestors with a Sōtō Zen Buddhist temple and a strong Shinto presence in the village is by reference to historical events.

These events, well documented by religious historians of Japan, are often ignored by anthropologists. Thus, the fact that rituals might appear to be solely about creating the community is often the argument given in anthropological works on Japan. Community-wide rituals have certainly taken to emphasizing this aspect of their power and worshippers have taken to adding (or perhaps they always have added) personal meaning to the rituals. Hardacre has argued that this trend in new religions in Japan signals a shift in the balance between the needs of the individual and the demands of society (1986); but the trend is there in established religions as well. Given Japanese religion's long association with the larger political whole, and the changes in the balance of power between Buddhism and Shinto, as well as amongst different Buddhist sects, it is clear that the meaning of rituals in Japan has often shifted depending on the prevailing norm. Rituals may have stayed the same, but time and politics might well have affected their meaning.

In modern Japan, the association of politics with religion in pre-war times is seen to be a 'bad' aspect of religion, and much of what a ritual might mean – the defining of a place, the feudal history and religious background of a place – is not clearly articulated because silence about religion has always seemed the best tack to take. Religious experts (in the past, Buddhist priests, today anthropologists and folklorists) are the people to ask about what a ritual means – or so I was often told in the field. This sort of silence, in relation to belief and what it constitutes, might not then be about not-knowing or not-believing as much as it is about it being dangerous to know too much or of finding that there is a new, scholarly or political, interpretation of what has always been done. Centuries of leaving the theory to the experts and the practice to the worshippers means that the people of Kuzaki were rather annoyed by my insistence that they tell me what they believed their rituals meant. As one grandfather once told me:

> Don't ask me what the meaning of this is. I don't know. There have been some very wise professors from Japanese universities here to watch this and to watch me making *noshi awabi* with the other grandfathers. I always tell them: I don't know the meaning of this. I just do it.

There may well be an element of resistance in all this silence as well. As long as the rituals work, however they might be interpreted by others, whatever the meaning the current political world might give to them, it does not matter. The rituals are, in the end, about the definition of village space and about continuity of Kuzaki and its people, living and dead. Other meanings are valid, but not as important, and all meanings could well change over time, as the village has changed and as its people have changed. To charge them with too much meaning might well allow the rituals to become outmoded and useless. For the villagers, it is far better to keep on celebrating life and death and to leave the intellectual hairsplitting to others.

NOTES

1 This deity was referred to as the young deity (*wakai kamisama*); according to other sources [Sakai n.d.] his name was Haku-hatsu-daimyō.
2 For a complete description of the five days of the ritual see Martinez (1988).
3 This beach, the headland and its waters are the most sacred areas of Kuzaki. Both the village Buddhist temple and the original Shinto shrine were located here (the Shinto shrine was moved in 1926 to a new location) and the main rituals for the *bon* festival take place on this area as well. One of the village's most important myths, the visit of Princess Yamato to Kuzaki (in some versions it is a visit by Haku-hatsu-daimyō), revolves around the Yoriozaki location. In short, this area might be seen as a clear example of the importance of the east in Japanese folk religion (see Matsunaga in this volume).
4 In generally allowing women on boats, the villagers of Kuzaki differed from other fisherfolk in Japan (see Kalland 1980 for a discussion of this taboo).
5 Emiko Namihara (1977), who has written an important thesis on the concepts of purity and pollution in Japan, prefaces her thesis with reference to her own 'superstitious' beliefs.
6 I use the very general term 'religion' rather than a particular term such as 'world religion' or 'animistic religion', etc. because I agree with Rhum (1993) that dichotomizing the differences between a Judeo-Christian concept of 'belief in' over a non-Western concept of 'practice of' is not useful. In fact, he argues that 'What is needed is not simply a rejection of "belief" in understanding non-western cultures but a more thorough analysis of belief, even in the West' (ibid.: 802).

REFERENCES

Bernier, Bernard (1970) *Breaking the Cosmic Circle: Religion in a Japanese Village*, (Cornell University East Asia Papers, No. 5), Ithaca, New York: Cornell University.
Bestor, Theodore C. (1990) *Neighborhood Tokyo*. Stanford: Stanford University Press.
Bloch, Maurice (1986) *From Blessing to Violence: History and Ideology in the Circumcision Ritual of the Merina of Madagascar*, Cambridge: Cambridge University Press.
van Bremen, Jan (1995) 'Introduction', in J. van Bremen and D.P. Martinez (eds) *Ceremony and Ritual in Japan*, London: Routledge.
Davis, Winston (1977) 'The Miyaza and the Fisherman: Ritual Status in Coastal Villages of Wakayama Prefecture', *Asian Folklore Studies*, vol. 36, no. 2, pp. 3–29.
Earhart, H. Byron (1982) *Japanese Religion, Unity and Diversity*, Belmont: Wadsworth Publishing.
Hardacre, Helen (1986) Kurozumikyō *and the New Religions of Japan*, Princeton, NJ: Princeton University Press.
Hendry, Joy (1984) 'Shoes, the Early Learning of an Important Distinction in Japanese Society', in Gordon Daniels (ed.) *Europe Interprets Japan*, Tenterden: Paul Norbury.
Hōri, Ichirō (1968) *Folk Religion in Japan: Continuity and Change* (ed. J. Kitagawa and A.L. Miller), Chicago: The University of Chicago Press.
Kalland, Arne (1980) Shingū, *A Japanese Fishing Community*, London and Malmö: Curzon Press.

Kitagawa, Joseph M. (1987) *On Understanding Japanese Religion*, Princeton, NJ: Princeton University Press.

Kuzaki (n.d.) 'Kuzaki kambeshi [Records of the Sacred Guild Kuzaki]', unpublished historical records of Kuzaki ward, Toba City.

Martinez, D.P. (1988) 'The *Ama*: Tradition and Change in a Japanese Diving Village', unpublished dissertation, Oxford University.

Moon Ok-pyo, (1984) 'Economic Development and Social Change in a Japanese Village', unpublished dissertation, Oxford University.

Nakata, Shiro (1979) 'Kinsei no Shima ni okeru ama to Ise no oshi [The Ama and Ise Priests in Contemporary Shima]', in *Umi to Ningen* [*Ocean and People*], vol. 4.

Namihaira, Emiko (1977) *'Hare, Ke and Kegare*: The Structure of Japanese Folk Belief', unpublished dissertation, the University of Texas at Austin.

Needham, Rodney (1972) *Belief, Language, and Experience*, Oxford: Basil Blackwell.

Nomura, C. (1978) 'Kuzaki no nenchū gyōji [Annual Rituals of Kuzaki]', in *Umi to Ningen* [*Ocean and People*], vol. 6.

Nosco, Peter (1996) 'Keeping the Faith: *Bakuhan* Policy Towards Religions in Seventeenth-century Japan', in P.F. Kornicki and I.J. McMullen (eds) *Religion in Japan: Arrows to Heaven and Earth*, Cambridge: Cambridge University Press (University of Cambridge Oriental Publications no. 50).

Ohnuki-Tierney, Emiko (1984) *Illness and Culture in Contemporary Japan*, Cambridge: Cambridge University Press.

—— (1990) 'Introduction: The Historicization of Anthropology', in Emiko Ohnuki-Tierney (ed.) *Culture through Time*, Stanford: Stanford University Press.

Ooms, Hermann (1976) 'A Structural Analysis of Japanese Ancestral Rites and Beliefs', in W.H. Newell (ed.) *Ancestors*, The Hague and Paris: Mouton.

Plath, David (1964) 'Where the Family of God is the Family: The Role of the Dead in Japanese Households', *American Anthropologist*, vol. 66, no. 2.

Reader, Ian (1991) *Religion in Contemporary Japan*, Basingstoke and London: Macmillan.

Rhum, Michael R. (1993) 'Understanding "Belief"', *Man*, vol. 28, no. 4.

Robertson, Jennifer (1991) *Native and Newcomer: Making and Remaking a Japanese City*, Berkeley: University of California Press.

Sakai, Teikichirū (n.d.) *Kyōdoshi, Nagaoka mura ōaza Kuzaki* [*The Village Land Records of Kuzaki, a Major Section of Nagaoka Village*].

Smith, Robert J. (1974) *Ancestor Worship in Contemporary Japan*, Stanford: Stanford University Press.

Southwold, Martin (1983) *Buddhism in Life: The Anthropological Study of Religion and the Sinhalese Practice of Buddhism*, Manchester: Manchester University Press.

14 Science and religious movements in Japan
Hi-tech healers and computerized cults

Mary Picone

When the imperial government introduced Western science at the beginning of the Meiji period, it did not import an undifferentiated body of opinion, a consensus established by unadventurous positivists. In 1866, Alfred Russell Wallace, co-founder with Darwin of the theory of evolution, published an article on spiritualism called 'The Scientific Aspect of the Supernatural'. In 1882 the Society for Psychical Research was founded in London. Only four years later two young psychologists at Tokyo University, Inoue Enryō and Minosaku Genpara, founded the Fushigi Kenkyūkai (Mystery Research Group), for the rational investigation of mysterious phenomena (Tanaka 1974: 53). In later life Inoue became famous as the inventor of *yokaigaku*, the science of 'monstrology'. As G. Figal has described in his excellent dissertation (Figal 1992), Inoue's subsequent career was devoted to the 'eradication of superstitions', but in the process he gathered some 2,000 pages of material on the supernatural, often anticipating techniques used by Yanagita Kunio decades later. Paradoxically, Inoue's attempts to do away with invisible phenomena, showing them to be merely perceptual mistakes, actually served to perpetuate them, in the form of statues in the Tetsugakukan. The latter was a 'philosophical theme park' (ibid.) he built on the site of what is now Tōyō University.

Other scientific investigators at this period were wholeheartedly on the side of the paranormal. By the first years of the new century several types of ray invisible to the human eye had been discovered by physicists, and various distinguished scientists were attempting to use the same methods to investigate clairvoyance or spiritualism. In 1910 Japanese scientific journals published several articles on these subjects. The physicist Yamagawa Kenjirō tried to study the effects produced by Nagao Ikuko, the wife of a judge, who claimed to be able to sensitize a photographic plate at will. Two psychologists also participated in this experiment, one of whom, Miura Kinnosuke became a respected member of his profession. The other, Fukurai Tomokichi, was later forced to resign from Tokyo University when he devoted himself completely to 'thoughtography', as he called the new procedure (Watanabe 1976: 15–17). Various bodies dedicated to the study of the occult came into being in the Taishō period, but to my knowledge, the 'Japan Psychic Science Association', founded in 1946, and the IARP (International Association for Religious Psychology), dating from 1972, are probably the closest surviving equivalents to the British Society for Psychical Research.

Since 1980 I have visited both institutes in Tokyo several times and have found that they also carry out various types of 'alternative' or spiritual healing. I have selected the most technologically oriented healers, that is those using the most 'up-to-date' methods, among my informants. Religious practitioners include not only leaders of the new, or of the 'new-new' religions, but also independent practitioners of various sorts, whom we may call generically *shūkyōsha* or *machi-gyōja* or, in more popular terms, *ogami-ya*. Some of these healers I found through an unusual source, a handbook entitled '*Nihon no reinōryokusha*', first published in 1982. An idiomatic English translation of this title would be 'psychic specialists of Japan' – a more literal one 'Japanese possessing spiritual abilities'. The book lists nineteen specialists, gives their addresses and details their particular skills, and cites cases of clients they have cured. The author, Oishi Ryūichi, is a television journalist who first saw some of these healers on a *waido shō* (variety show), deciding on the spot that they were 'more effective than modern medicine' (1982: 4). He later decided to present the data he had collected in book form.

Instead of using 'traditional' names such as *dōjō* or *in* to designate their workplace, these practitioners associate themselves with the lay academic world, operating from a 'Research Institute for the Study of Religious Psychology' (*Shūkyōshinrigaku kenkyū-jo*), or 'Japanese Association for the Study of Divine Spiritology' (*Nihonshinreigaku kenkyūkai*), or the above-mentioned 'Scientific Spirit Association of Japan' (*Nihon shinrei kagaku kenkyūkai*). All are based in Tokyo. Eight of the practitioners have branch offices in other cities. I will describe the first of these institutes in greater detail. It possesses what Pierre Bourdieu (1984) would call 'cultural capital' and, without being an independent, legally recognized religious body, is well known and clearly a success in commercial terms. The head has opened a branch in California. The second smaller group, which I shall mention only briefly, is in a state of transition, but has survived the death of its founder, a charismatic healer. My third example is that of an individual healer who, after a period of prosperity, has lost most of his clients and greatly reduced his activities. I have met both leaders and several clients of these groups.

To return to the first case: The 'Research Institute' was founded by Dr Motoyama Hiroshi. He was born in 1925 and, according to materials given out at the centre has a PhD in philosophy either from the Tokyo University of Education and/or from a German university. His dissertation was entitled 'The Mystical Experience and the Absolute Nothingness of God, Spirit and Nature'. It is published, along with more than thirty other books by his own publishing house. In the newsletter of the Institute it is described as 'A logical-philosophical . . . system for categorizing different kinds of mystical experiences, drawing on sources from religious scriptures, as well as Dr Motoyama's and his mother's personal experiences'. He also lists a degree in physiological psychology. He is now head priest of the Tamamitsu Shrine, which was founded by his 'spiritual mother', now known to members as '*Myoko no kami*', in 1932. She was a successful practitioner in her own right using traditional Shinto-inspired methods.

Dr Motoyama's multiple interests and accomplishments are reflected in the buildings erected in the compound around the Institute. Since 1972 these include a research laboratory, an acupuncture clinic and a yoga retreat centre. In 1982 he hoped to start building an 'International University for Religion and Parapsychology'. Dr Motoyama, along with the other practitioners mentioned above, was greatly influenced by Professor J. Rhine of Duke University, who carried out parapsychological experiments in the 1950s and 1960s. The United States has been perhaps a bit more receptive than European countries to this kind of unaffiliated knowledge. NASA has funded experiments in the field and, in 1969, Margaret Mead (who was being treated by a healer at the time) managed to have parapsychology accepted by the American Association for the Advancement of Science.

In Japan I have never seen a religious practitioner use what Evans-Pritchard called a 'closed system' (Horton 1982). In all cases the healer will draw on a variety of causes and methods to effect a diagnosis and a cure. Dr Motoyama is no exception. Sometimes his cases (as reported in his newsletter or as recalled verbatim) are entirely 'traditional' in respect of etiology. For example, he describes a case of 'karma of place' having bad effect on the health of its inhabitants.

He has related cases of asthma, tuberculosis or heart disease to the karma of the water of wells filled in by the family of the women who consulted him. In illustrating his own faculties of 'retro-cognition' (a type of parapsychological ability) he tells the story of a Minamoto warrior who was killed in battle mistakenly by his own men, because he could not speak at the crucial moment due to an asthma attack. For these souls and entities Dr Motoyama recommends the traditional folk–Buddhist remedy: prayer so that 'their attachments to negative emotions be severed' and 'they can understand that they have died'.

In other issues of the newsletter, however, cases are described in a modern and scientific idiom. Acting as an acupuncturist, Dr Motoyama attempted to cure Mrs Y., who suffered from severe mental illness. He measured her *ki* condition in the whole body and in each meridian, which corresponds, according to a system he has perfected, to one of the *chakras* (centres of spiritual energy) in yogic doctrines. The machine which accomplishes this is also his own invention. The client's overall values were low and abnormal functioning was concentrated in the meridian connected with the *anahata chakra* and the cardiovascular system. Dr Motoyama explained the above by means of extrasensory vision. When looking at Mrs Y. he saw the the face of an old man 'who could have been her father'. He 'intuitively felt' that both Mrs Y.'s and her father's spirits are worrying about one another. The father had died of a heart attack. The cure consisted in prayer by the surviving relative in order 'to direct the father's mind to other worlds'. Mrs Y. was too ill to pray at this time. After less than a year, however, she found a job as an accountant.

To jump ahead for a moment, in this case we have a coincentric or Chinese-boxes type of etiological legitimation. Electrical measurements verify the existence and functioning of *ki*; *ki* verifies or is verified by *chakra* measurements, while extrasensory vision verifies in moral terms the imbalance reported in a particular group of meridians (that is, channels for the circulation of *ki* in Chinese medicine). Finally, changes in the emotional attitude of the spirit of a potential ancestor, the client herself and her surviving relatives bring about the desired cure. Numerical imbalance is corrected – actually and symbolically – in the end when Mrs Y. becomes an accountant.

The Japanese Association for the Study of Divine Spiritology was headed by a healer and a medium who died about fifteen years ago. The Association's library includes books on parapsychology (such as *Stalking the Wild Pendulum*) in Japanese and other languages, works describing Indian medicine, simplified versions of Tibetan Buddhism, and so on. Meetings are attended by regular members who perform hour-long 'Zen meditation' of a sort. A female medium walks around the room taking notes. At the end of the seance she gives general advice about health, describes the spirits she sees hovering behind some of the members, and warns others of illness to come. Particularly stubborn diseases and/or cases of possession will be treated in private sessions. The spirits identified tend to be as eclectic as the terminology of the association (foxes, mermaids, spirits of aborted foetuses, etc.).

The third healer I have mentioned works on his own. He lives in a dingy one-room apartment (*danchi*). He recalls his very successful television appearances in 1967 as the high point of his carreer. In the handbook he briefly describes one of his cases: a young girl in middle school is brought to him after a diagnosis of collagenosis. He sees with 'spirit sight' that there is a link with the *kami* Inari and perceives a fox spirit which he immediately exorcizes. His main activity, however, is *mushi fuji* (literally 'to close off insects'). He explains that it derives from Taoism and is a technique developed 3,000 years ago. After the healer recites an esoteric Buddhist formula, the *mushi* appear at the client's fingertips. Under strong magnification, he explains, they look like long white threads. He writes *mushi* with the Japanese sign for inverted commas. I asked him what they were, expecting either an explanation of the complexities of Taoist internal medicine or rich Japanese folk classification. Instead, he thought for a moment and answered 'It must be cholesterol'. It seemed to me that, now that his clients are few and far between, the double visual reproduction by magnifying glass and television camera of the *mushi* at people's fingertips was what made this uncertainly defined entity 'real' for him.

CONCLUSION

The more theoretical aspect of this chapter is the problem of legitimation or authority. I have asked a number of French theoretical physicists to define science, and none gave me the sort of positivistic answer often attributed to scientists by anthropologists or sociologists. S. Tambiah has lucidly presented these issues in *Magic, Science, Religion and the Scope of Rationality* (1990). In the new sociology of science (Latour and Woolgar 1979; see also Reyna 1996), there is an attempt to treat the construction of the boundary between true (or generally accepted) science and false science as the topic instead of the starting-point of debate. Among the types of legitimation used by the healers there is the notion of 'proof', either an actual event, particularly a cure, or confirmation of the causes of illness and misfortune identified by the healer. Here the notion of measurement is particularly important, like Dr Motoyama's *Chakra* machine for his measurement of '*psi*' energy and the lead-lined room in one of the buidings of his Institute which is used for carrying out telepathic experiments without interference from cosmic rays. Most healers have made 'spirit photographs', a proof of the existence of the entities said to be responsible for many illnesses. However, the pictures, taken at the time of appearance, paradoxically document the fact that the client does not perceive these entities. Only the healer sees what 'objectively' exists and is recorded impersonally by lenses and chemicals. This is an update of the premodern Buddhist idea of levels of perception related to spiritual achievement.

To return to modern notions of proof: it must be remembered in the context of proof based on experiment that, if all propositions based on experiments (accepted at a given moment) can be revised, it is not because of an inherent internal truth but because they correspond to currently accepted criteria of rigorous experimentations. These criteria depend on the state of knowledge and evolve with it. They also vary from one field to another. However, in contrast to extreme relativism, such as that of Latour, most scientists hold, I think rightly, the view that as the control (not in a mechanistic sense) of experiments becomes more effective, so the progress in empirical fields becomes more systematic and guides its own growth.

Another form of legitimation – personal testimony – is the opposite of the objective criterion outlined above. It is an important feature of all religious groups, particularly new charismatic movements. In the case of independent practitioners, a transcription of dialogues between healer and client propagated by widely selling handbooks or videos will take the place of witnessing enacted before a group of devotees.

Legitimation by affiliation with fully established scientific, academic or religious bodies is also common in the new religions and among individual healers. In Japan, as elsewhere, such movements (e.g. Mahikari or its offshoot Jōreikyō) often claim that modern biomedicine, chemistry, nuclear power, etc. are ineffective and/or evil. Minamata disease, various cases of iatrogenic damage, such as infected blood transfusions, and recent accidents on the sites of nuclear reactors have obviously greatly increased public concern with the misuse of science, but reaction often takes the form of citizens' movements. Scientism, however, is sometimes part of the legitimation process used by contemporary practitioners. Some hypermodern healers claim to have anticipated medical discoveries, and they seek recognition by physicians or other scientists, often in fields very far from their own. The limits of biomedicine are constantly emphasized. Medical cures, it is suggested, will not be permanent – a telling point, as many of us know to our cost – or it is pointed out that medicine does not explain why a person becomes ill or who they suffer from a particular illness. Japanese law, however, allows the prosecution of illegal practitioners of medicine. The founder of AUM Shinrikyō was found guilty of this charge years before he organized his cult.

Legitimation by descent or inheritance is also widespread. There are established 'medical dynasties' in Japan as well as in Europe, although, in modern times, each member must qualify at medical school before practising. Religious leaders instead often inherit a form of spiritual power (cf. Dr Motoyama's description of his childhood with his 'spiritual mother'). This form of legitimation was adopted even by the *rangaku* (Western-learning school) of physicians in the eighteenth century, when they chose Hippocrates as a tutelary deity in place of Shinnyō, the patron of *kanpō* (Chinese-medicine school) doctors.

Legitimation by means of imported knowledge has long been a feature of established as well as marginal scientific practices. Some Japanese social scientists have maintained that local religious healing methods are unique, along with almost everything else in Japanese culture. This seems to me to be a false dichotomy: all countries have imported large amounts of religious and scientific knowledge. The source of prestigious foreign theories and methods varies over time. If, in the past, science learnt by the elite, including the *kokugakusha* (native-learning) scholars, was legitimized by reference to the Chinese classics, more recently Indian (mostly yoga) or Anglo-American parapsychology or fashionable medical and psychiatric theories have been imported by the healers.

In the nineteenth century the Theosophist Mme Blavatsky introduced a number of Hindu and Buddhist notions to a European audience. Today Western healers or cult leaders draw on vague 'Eastern' ideas and refer to 'acupuncture without needles', to 'bio energy' and to karma.

The legitimation of religious healers is cumulative and non-exclusive; the 'secondary rationalizations' considered essential by Evans-Pritchard to preserve the survival of ritual and magical procedures coexist, at least in Japan, with an open system which is in constant expansion. The last word about contemporary therapeutic legitimation, however, may rest with Jacques Lacan, a founder of what some observers have called a Parisian 'new religion'. The *maître* apparently once remarked, with magnificent insouciance: *'le psychoanaliste s'authorise de lui-même'* (the psychoanalyst constitutes his own authority).

REFERENCES

Bourdieu, Pierre (1984) *Distinctions: A Social Critique of the Judgement of Taste*, Cambridge, MA: Harvard University Press.

Figal, Gerald (1992) 'The Folk and the Fantastic in Japanese Modernity', unpublished dissertation, University of Chicago.

Horton, Robin (1982) 'Tradition and Modernity Revisited', in M. Hollis and Stephen Lukes (eds) *Rationality and Relativism*, Oxford: Blackwell.

Latour, Bruno and Steven Woolgar (1979) *Laboratory Life: The Social Content of Scientific Facts*, Beverley Hills: Sage.

Miyata, Noboru (1988) *Yōkai no minzokugaku* [*The Folklore of Apparitions*], Tokyo: Iwanami Shoten.

Motoyama, Hiroshi (1982–6) *'IARP nyūsurēta* [*Newsletter of the International Association for Religious Psychology*].

Oishi, Ryūichi (1982) *Nihon no reinōryokusha* [*Psychic Specialists of Japan*], Tokyo: Nihon Bungeisha.

Reyna, S.P. (1996) 'Literary Anthropology and the Case against Science', *Man*, n.s., vol. 29, no. 3.

Tambiah, S. (1990) *Magic, Science, Religion and the Scope of Rationality*, Cambridge: Cambridge University Press.

Tanaka, Chiyomatsu (1974) *Nihon shinrei kagaku kenkyūkai* [*Japan Psychic Science Association Report*], no. 1, Tokyo.

Watanabe, Masao (1976) *The Japanese and Western Science*, Philadelphia: Pennsylvania University Press.

Part IV

Leisure: its impact and significance

15 *Sakariba*

Zone of 'evaporation' between work and home?

Sepp Linhart

GENERAL CHARACTERISTICS

It is, perhaps, surprising that in the Japanese literature on leisure behaviour almost no attention has been paid to what is – in Western eyes at least – one of the most conspicuous kinds of leisure and to the behaviour connected with it – namely, the amusement quarters or *sakariba*.[1]

Sakariba is defined by a widely used Japanese dictionary as *hito no ōku yoriatsumaru basho* or *hankagai*, 'a place where many people come together' or 'a busy street' (Shinmura 1969: 871). *Ba* is 'place' and *sakaru* means 'to prosper' or 'flourish'. The noun form *sakari*, then, is 'height', 'peak', 'prime', 'bloom' (as well as 'heat' of animals), so that a direct translation would be 'a flourishing place', 'a prospering place' or simply 'a top place'. *Sakariba* is not necessarily an amusement quarter, since it can also refer to a shopping centre; but here I will confine myself to the treatment of those places full of neon lights, bustling with people, where many small drinking-places line the streets. In a typical *sakariba* one will find *akachōchin* (red lantern pubs), cabarets, bars, discos, *no pantsu kissa* (literally, 'no-pants coffee-shops'), *pachinko* parlours, cinemas, strip shows, and many other kinds of places.

These *sakariba* nowadays exist in every large town and, on a smaller scale, in the smaller provincial towns as well. The names of the famous *sakariba* of the ten big cities with more than a million inhabitants are known practically all over Japan. Sapporo's Susukino, Nagoya's Sakae, Osaka's Minami, Fukuoka's Nakasu – not to mention Tokyo's Shinjuku, Roppongi or Akasaka – are only a few of the many place-names which can be heard time and again in the Japanese popular songs called *enka*. '*Sakariba* Blues', by the popular singer Shinichi Mori, is a simple enumeration of the better-known places from northern to southern Japan, starting with Ginza and ending with Ikebukuro. It would not, perhaps, be going too far to suggest that the *sakariba*, to a certain extent, are substitutes for other sightseeing places, with which Japanese cities are often rather poorly endowed. If one buys a travel guide written for Japanese men, there is usually an extensive treatment of these attractions of modern cities – where to dine, where to drink, and so on.

One important characteristic of the *sakariba* is that such a place always has to be crowded and noisy. Lots of people are coming and going or just strolling about, because they cannot decide which shop they should enter. There is music in the air, there are the '*Irasshai!*' yells of welcome from the boys – and the more polite '*Irasshaimase!*' greetings from the girls – to tempt customers to visit their establishments; there is the noise and the smell of fried delicacies and the laughter of drunken men everywhere. For the sociologist Ikei this overcrowding is the main characteristic of a *sakariba*, and he speaks of *zattō no miryoku*, 'fascination of the crowd', which pulls many men to the amusement quarters at night (Ikei 1973b: 22). Japanese festivals and holidays are usually marked by enormous crowds, a feature journalists commonly like to describe, for example in reporting on Golden Week at the beginning of May. In the *sakariba* at night the crowd is omnipresent in the narrow streets as well as in the little restaurants or drinking-places. What for many Europeans may be something quite unpleasant seems to be for Japanese an enjoyable setting. Many Japanese seem thoroughly to enjoy their daily ride to their workplace on crowded railways and underground trains; they simply cannot fall into a relaxed, leisurely mood if a *sakariba* is not full of people. They are disappointed if too few people are there – an empty place is not the right atmosphere for drinking.

Nowadays, every small provincial town tries to provide a kind of *sakariba* with a handful of drinking-places – but there is no crowd, so these places tend to look rather odd to an inhabitant of a large town. There is no sight as sad as an empty *sakariba* during the morning hours, with all the glitter gone, and only the dirt left behind. Ikei even links the definition of a 'big city' to the existence of a *sakariba*. For him, people who go to a *sakariba* enjoy an almost religious feeling among the crowd there, comparable to a traditional festival, as one of the reasons for coming to a *sakariba* is, for many men, not only to get drunk with alcohol but to do so in the company of crowds of people (ibid.: 28).

HISTORICAL DEVELOPMENT

According to the *Nihon Kokugo Daijiten* (dictionary), *sakariba* is an expression that was already in use during the Tokugawa period, and it cites the *kokkeibon*, or humorous work, *Ukiyoburo* [*Bathhouse of the Floating World*] (1809–13) of Sanba Shikitei as the earliest literary source (1974: 649). But Miyao tells us (1979) that the *sakariba* in the big towns of the Edo period had a meaning different from that of today. Open places which served as places of refuge in times of fire were used by various people to offer attractions, and this drew the masses to those *sakariba*. Such places were sometimes called 'broad roads' (*hirokōji*) or 'river banks' (*kawara*). Famous examples in Edo include Ryōkoku, Asakusa Okuyama and Ueno Hirokoji, and in Kyoto Shijō Kawaramachi. The kinds of attractions offered at the *sakariba* of the Edo period have nowadays largely disappeared, although traces can still be found in the *yose* plays (music-hall or vaudeville).

Another origin of the modern *sakariba* can be found in the amusement quarters next to religious centres in the temple towns (*monzenmachi*). Since ancient times, when people came to a religious place from far away, they have wanted to amuse themselves after offering their prayers and buying their amulets. Tokyo's main *sakariba* before the Second World War, Asakusa, was built around the famous Kannon temple, and there are many other examples.

Modern *sakariba* can, third, be seen as having developed out of former red-light districts (*yūkaku*). Many modern *sakariba* have in fact been built up out of places which formerly served as quarters licensed for this purpose. Besides this spatial continuity there is a certain behavioural continuity also. According to Ikei, the sort of poorly regarded leisure pattern which is typical for the modern *sakariba* – drinking alcoholic beverages, playing *pachinko*, mahjong gambling, looking at naked women – is often left out of account in descriptions of Japanese *rejā* (leisure), because *rejā* as a loan-word from English denotes only noble actions or behaviour that is well thought of, rather than more basic human desires. At any rate, this kind of amusement dates back to the second half of the Edo period (Ikei 1973a: 15).

Other elements that added to the development of modern *sakariba* were local shopping centres, which included small restaurants and drinking-places, and which sometimes developed into substantial amusement centres. The urban sociologist Okui states in his description of life in Meiji Tokyo that at that time every urban neighbourhood (*chō, machi*) within Tokyo had its own neighbour-hood *sakariba* (*chōnai sakariba*), with a shopping street, amusement and recreational facilities, shops open in the evening, and traditional festival days called *ennichi*. The most representative amusement facility was a simple *yose* theatre, which in this century, at the end of the Meiji period and the beginning of the Taishō, was often transformed into a cinema called *katsudō shashin koya* (moving-picture hut), a denomination which is a good linguistic example of the difference between the small neighbourhood *sakariba* and the luxurious *sakariba* in the town centres, where cinemas were more likely to be given names such as 'Cinema Palace'. When people had ended a day's work, they would change their clothes and take a stroll in a relaxed mood to the *sakariba* nearest to their home (Okui 1975: 406–7).

With the development of the inner Tokyo railways there began a new developmental stage of the *sakariba*. When the stations of the Yamanote circle line were opened, at least a small *sakariba* developed around almost every station. On the other hand, previously prospering *sakariba* within the Yamanote district which had no direct access to the railway, such as Shibajinmei or Azabujūban, lost a great deal of their former importance. With the growing orientation of Tokyo to the west, and the establishment of new private lines from Shinjuku and Shibuya stations, inner-Tokyo *sakariba* such as Yotsuya, Ushigome, Kagurasaka and Shiomachi lost a great deal of their night population to the new centres (ibid.: 194).

People who chose to live in the suburbs differed from the traditional town inhabitants, and so did the new centres from the old *sakariba*. Katō Hidetoshi, who uses the phrase 'terminal culture' to denote those urban developments that occurred in the Taishō and early Shōwa period in Osaka as well as in Tokyo, states that the 'banish-one's-worries' sub-centres of Sennichimae in Osaka and Asakusa in Tokyo were old middle-class, while Umeda and Shinjuku or Shibuya were new middle-class centres for the petty bourgeoisie (Katō 1972: 381). But the new centres had only local importance before the war, compared to Tokyo's two big amusement areas of Ginza and Asakusa. The *yose* theatres were no longer representative: cinemas and *kafē*, the predecessors of the modern bars, had taken their place, and *shamisen* music was replaced by foreign-influenced music from the radio or from records.

After the Second World War the devastation of the big towns also resulted in a restructuring of the amusement districts. Some amusement centres, like the red-light district of Tamanoi, masterly portrayed by Nagai Kafū in his novel *Bokutō kidon* [*A Strange Tale from East of the River*] (1937), were never to be rebuilt for the same function. The trend to sub-centres at the starting-points of the suburban railway lines and to the development of big *sakariba* then continued, while on the other hand the old centres lost even more importance. When prostitution was officially abolished in 1958, the red-light districts were often transformed into *sakariba* – though in effect the *sakariba* now also performed the functions of those former pleasure quarters.

Some modern *sakariba* owe their existence and development purely to fashion, which is especially true for places which are dominated by youth culture such as Roppongi or Harajuku in Tokyo. This is also partially true of Kichijōji, which at the same time fulfils the functions of a suburban centre.

THE ACTIVITIES

There are different names for the activities people engage in at the *sakariba*. One author speaks of *naito rejā* (night leisure) or of *sakariba rejā* (Saitō 1976: 153ff.), another of *taun rejā* (town leisure) (Ujigawa and Uemura 1970: 103ff.), but most Japanese go there simply to play, *asobu*, or to relax, *kutsurogu*. *Asobu*, for many Japanese men, can be divided into three activities: *nomu, utsu, kau* (drinking, gambling and buying women), all of which are representative of *sakariba* leisure behaviour.

Drinking can have many different aspects. Takada (1980: 130) has offered a typology of Japanese drinking-places (*nomiya*) and has divided them into six different kinds according to the main function which they perform:

1 The prototype of a *nomiya* consists of five elements: a place, the alcoholic drink, something to eat with the drink (*tsumami*), a person who serves the drink, and the guest. *Tachinomi, nawanoren*, and *akachōchin* are examples of this category.[2]

2 The second kind is a place where one goes to eat and drink, e.g., a sushi shop or a *sukiyaki* restaurant.

3 Specialized drinking-places include beer halls, Western bars with male bartenders, pubs, etc.

4 A variety of erotic drinking-places, using names such as bar, club, salon, cabaret, etc.

5 Many drinking-places specialize in information exchange. Typical are the so-called *sunakku* (snack), which have shown a tremendous increase during the last two decades.
6 Many drinking-places specialize in music. Examples of this kind include discos, jazz pubs, and *utagoe* pubs.[3] The *karaoke sunakku*, which is very popular at present, falls in-between categories five and six.[4]

There are primarily two kinds of gambling at the *sakariba*: *pachinko* and *mājan* (mahjong). These two games can be interpreted as a good imitation of blue-collar work and white-collar work respectively. *Pachinko*, slot-machine games, remind one of the monotonous, repetitive work at a factory assembly line, while *mājan* recalls the duties of an office worker or a company employee – 'the complicated addition of numbers, calculating the probability, the busy exchange of information, and the decision-making process' (Inoue 1973: 94), all well known from such a person's daily experience. When I undertook research into the differences in lifestyle of white-collar and blue-collar workers in Tokyo and its vicinity in 1972/3, I found that among twenty-seven given activities *mājan* occupied rank eight in frequency among the white-collar workers and *pachinko* ranked twenty-three, while with the blue-collar workers it was the other way round: *pachinko* thirteen and *mājan* twenty (Linhart 1976: 221). Other activities which might be included in this category are playing *gō* and *shōgi* (Japanese chess) or hard-core gambling, usually with gangsters, in the form of the card game *hanafuda*, etc. Bowling, which has enjoyed several booms during the last decades, could also be included here, although its gambling character is less pronounced. Recently, darts has also been enjoying a boom at the *sakariba*.

The third category of activities, *kau* (buying sex), belongs to the realm of the so-called soaplands and pink saloons. The most famous chains of the latter kind are called Monroe and London. It is little wonder that the soaplands are often located at the same places where brothels stood until 1958, as is the case in Yoshiwara. There is not only spatial continuity, but also continuity with regard to the activities engaged in.

To the three activities mentioned – drinking, gambling and sex – at least a fourth can be added: visiting cinemas, theatres and shows of all kinds.

It is very difficult to obtain reliable figures about these various activities, because many people prefer not to speak about their *sakariba* leisure. The 1973 time-management survey organized by NHK (Nippon Hōsō Kyōkai, the Japan Broadcasting Corporation) discovered that on a normal day 26 per cent of the male white-collar workers go for a drink after work, compared with 20 per cent of all blue-collar workers and 17 per cent of the self-employed. For women the figures in the same occupations were lower: 17 per cent, 7 per cent, and 3 per cent, respectively (Furukawa 1974: 39). Another investigation produced the result that roughly 30 per cent of all male company employees interviewed very often do not return straight home after work, 45 per cent of them usually go for a drink, and 27 per cent play mahjong. Asked with whom they usually go, 70 per cent said 'with other people from their company' (Ishikawa 1972: 55–6).[5] More important than the figures, which can never be exact, is the fact that so many people go to visit the various *sakariba* every evening after work. Takada has calculated that the Japanese drank 2.5 times more alcoholic beverages per head in 1977 than they did in 1935 (1980: 132). Shikata Hisao reports that in 1970 there were 12,241 pubs in Nagoya, of which 939 belonged to Sakae, the town's biggest *sakariba* (1973: 147–8). These figures and the actual crowds seem more convincing than those found through interviews in leisure studies carried out by sociologists.

SEX ROLES

As should be clear by now, the *sakariba* is predominantly a place for men. Men take the active role; they are the guests who pay for amusement, while women's role is mainly to serve the men and earn money. Women add an erotic touch to the place and give lonely, motherless men a feeling of belonging. In performing these roles, the 'water trade' (*mizu shōbai*) women, as they are called, behave very conservatively and traditionally, as the men expect them to. This role behaviour is musically expressed in the *enka*. But on the other hand, the *sakariba* women are, out of pure necessity, among the most emancipated of women. Many of them mothers who have to care for one or more children after an unsuccessful marriage, they go to the *sakariba* every night to work, not to play as men do. For women who strive for liberty from their husbands or families, the *sakariba* is often the only refuge.

Of the younger unmarried generation, both sexes amuse themselves in coffee-shops, pubs or discos. This holds true for teenagers, students, young *OL* ('office ladies') or *BG* ('business girls'), and is no new trend either. As long ago as the late 1920s, *moga* and *mobo* ('modern girl', 'modern boy') used to stroll around the Ginza hand in hand.

So-called *kyariā uman* ('career women'), such as female university teachers, sometimes drop in for a drink with their male colleagues, but usually even they attend only more official parties like *bōnenkai* (party at the end of the year) or *shinnenkai* (party at the beginning of the year). On such occasions they usually return home after the official party is finished and before the more interesting part of the evening begins – in the form of a *nijikai* or *sanjikai*, a 'second' or 'third party'. Some of the *kyariā uman* in their middle years, unmarried and without children, have adopted a more or less male life- and leisure-style. Like their male colleagues, they go out frequently in the evening, have their favourite pub, which they visit several times a month, and even copy men in their relations with the opposite sex by visiting 'host clubs', where they can enjoy being entertained by men and, if they wish to do so, can buy the male hosts, often students, as sexual partners.[6]

In spite of such exceptions, the *sakariba* by and large is a place for the male sex, and for every host club there exist dozens of soaplands and hundreds of clubs, bars and cabarets catering to a male clientele. According to prevalent thinking, the *sakariba* is no place for a married middle-class wife or mother to visit.

THE TIME FOR A VISIT

As already mentioned, evening is the proper time to stroll around a *sakariba*. Although some restaurants and *pachinko* saloons are also open in the daytime, a *sakariba* at noon is a rather sad sight. Five o'clock in the afternoon is the time when the work officially ends in many companies, and it is after this hour that most places at the *sakariba* open their doors. It has to be dark if one is to enjoy the right atmosphere of a *sakariba* – hence the expression 'night leisure' which Saitō uses interchangeably with '*sakariba* leisure' (1976: 153ff.).

In Japanese society drinking in the daytime is generally frowned upon and, in contrast to Europe, no Japanese worker can be found drinking beer at his workplace: '*Konna ni akarukucha yoe ga shinai*' ('I can't get drunk, when it is still so bright'), '*Asa kara sake o nomu no wa dōmo ki ga hikeru*' ('I feel bad if I start to drink already in the morning') (Watanabe 1975: 3), '*You ni wa dōmo akarukusugiru*' ('It is still too bright to get drunk'), or '*Aitsu hiruma kara sake o nonde iyagaru*' ('I hate him because he starts to drink in the daytime') (ibid.: 43) are typical Japanese expressions frequently heard in this connection. *Sakariba* leisure always starts after work, and it must never conflict with work obligations.

Words about the time of day that one would normally find in the *enka* are all associated with evening or night: *yoru* (evening), *akari* (light), *neon* (neon), *hoshi* (star), *yogiri* (night fog), *yozora* (night sky), *tsuki* (moon), *kurai* (dark), *konya* (tonight), *tsukiyo* (moonlit night) are only a small sample of the many words connected with evening which can be heard in almost every *enka*.

There seems to be a certain weekly rhythm at the *sakariba*. Since Saturday ceased to be a normal working day for Japanese office workers, the crowds at the *sakariba* – according to Japanese sociologists – reach their peak on Friday and Monday. On Friday groups of employees hold their weekly farewell parties, and on Monday they go out to celebrate their reunion after having had to spend a weekend as strangers together with their families, cut off from the company. According to Tada Michitarō, on Monday Japanese men can finally feel like human beings again ('*Hisashiburi ni shokuba de atte, yatto ningenteki na kibun ni nareru no da sō desu*', Kawazoe *et al.* 1980: 113). Sunday is a rest day for many pubs and bars, because their regular visitors, the company employees, are busy with their families performing 'family service' (*katei sābisu*) and cannot come.

At the seasonal level, little variation is to be noted except that on the days around important festivals like the *bon* festival in summer or New Year the *sakariba* are rather empty. The same is true for the weeks during the rainy period in July. There are generally more visitors in autumn and winter than in summer, although modern air-conditioning tends to minimize this difference.

THE FUNCTIONS OF THE *SAKARIBA*

The most typical *sakariba* nowadays are located near the stations of the suburban railway lines. In Tokyo, the stations of Ikebukuro, Shinjuku and Shibuya, for example, from where the suburban lines to the Tama region and Kanagawa prefecture start out, have shown a substantial development over the last three decades or so. Uncontrolled growth of Japanese cities has resulted in rather long daily trips to work and back; it is at these stations that the company employees have to change trains, and so these places are best suited for an interruption of the long journey home after work. It is understandable that many people break their journey at a *sakariba*, in order to reduce the accumulated feeling of stress after a long working day. Since many people need take only one more train from the big stations at the periphery in order to get home, it is convenient to visit a *sakariba* on the way, even if only for a couple of drinks.

For Saitō Seiichirō the *sakariba* constitute a 'space of evaporation' (*jōhatsu kūkan*) for the office worker (1976: 155). '*Jōhatsu*', a word fashionable in the 1970s, designates people who suddenly disappear – because they can no longer bear the strain of work at the company or of discord within the family. But unlike the many thousands of people who disappear every year, never to return, disappearing at a *sakariba* is only temporary, as expressed in the phrase '*Chotto jōhatsu shite mairimasu*' ('I am going to disappear and shall come back again') (Morris 1973: 121). Disappearing at a *sakariba* is by no means complete. Although there exist discreet 'love-hotels' – and similar places at pubs, bars and snack-bars – the Japanese custom of exchanging visiting-cards is as valid there as in any other context in Japanese society. A good *mama-san* (the term used for the manageress of such establishments) will always try to uphold a certain standard among her guests – there are bars or snack-bars for employees of big companies, for university professors, for small entrepreneurs, and so on, and the identity of at least the regular customers is no secret. The *mama-san* knows who her guests are and where they are from – which means that certain social norms are functioning even in these amusement quarters; 'evaporation', therefore, is nothing more than an illusion. Furthermore, the male guests feel safe only if they can make a personal relationship with the people who work at these bars or pubs; if they succeed in doing so, they affectionately call the place which they visit most frequently 'my nest' (*watashi no su*). It has to be added that many company employees spend several years away from their families when they may be temporarily transferred to some other town. In such cases a *sunakku* or a *bā* at a *sakariba* for these men can really become their second home.

Modern Japanese company-men have few opportunities to act as free individuals. Group pressures are at work in the company and in the family, the latter often being based on an arranged marriage and concluded by giving way to social pressures for the single aim of producing children so as to guarantee the family line. So the *sakariba* in the world-order of Japanese company-men constitutes a zone of liberty (*kaihō kūkan*), often the only one they have. When a man is visiting a modern *sakariba*, he is on a journey, and for the Japanese 'on a journey shame can be thrown away!' ('*tabi no haji wa kakisute*'). The *sakariba* is the only place where the organization-man, a 'correct person' (*majime ningen*) – necessarily 'correct' because he has a lifetime commitment to both his firm and his family – can act *fumajime* or 'incorrectly' (Ikei 1973b: 36). Here he can drink, gamble, sing and make love with women other than his wife. Of course a *sakariba* is not a good place according to general opinion, and therefore people go there with a bad conscience. The degree of bad conscience depends on the particular kind of place where one goes, but the feeling of doing something which is not accepted by society, by the firm, by one's wife, will always be present.[7] So people who visit a *sakariba* without companions are usually very bashful when they meet acquaintances, while on the other hand there can develop a certain kind of solidarity between strangers. Ikei speaks of the 'sympathy of wrongdoers' (*hanzaisha no kyōkan*) (ibid.: 37). Another proverb about travelling is worth mentioning here: 'On a journey your fellow travellers will help you, but in the world nobody but God!' (*'Tabi wa michizure, yo wa nasake'*). The sympathetic manner in which drunken men are treated in Japan, compared to the somewhat rougher reaction Western drunkards can expect, well illustrates the full meaning of this saying.

The *sakariba* with its various forms of amusement offers wide scope for self-expression and self-fulfilment. Best known in recent years is karaoke singing, which need not be discussed here.[8] The *karaoke* bars and snack-bars promise their guests that they will become star singers (*'Anata o sutā ni!'*). This act of becoming a star singer, be it only in karaoke bars, is a kind of temporary metamorphosis (*henshin*). This change of roles is a form of behaviour which can also be observed in most traditional festivals, which no longer have any meaning for the modern city-dweller.

> Farmers took the role of gods in the plays and rituals; ordinary people had a chance to be special. It was a release from farming, a let-up of rules, an 'orgy after abstinence'. *Hare* functioned to renew and refresh for the next season of work.
>
> (Murray 1975: 92)

Modern men need not wait for special holy occasions (times of *hare*) to change their appearance. In the big cities they can undergo a metamorphosis daily by going to the *sakariba* – they can become an Elvis Presley, a seductive Casanova, or a daring gambler. The anthropologist Ishige Naomichi has noted with regard to Japanese eating and drinking habits that special food and drink in the course of Japan's modernization have become a daily affair (1982: 26ff.). The same phenomenon can be seen in *henshin*. But of course nowadays those 'dreams of becoming someone else or of doing something other than what we do' are stage-managed. It is the producers of hit songs and of *karaoke* sets, of whisky and beer, who create those dreams and dream figures; they may function as outlets for societal pressure, but they are created for their own commercial profits.

A special kind of escapism is the so-called *bureikō* or Japanese psychotherapy. When, for example, people of the same company go out together, it is permissible to get drunk rapidly, and the drunken man is allowed to complain about everything and to make all kinds of accusations. As long as everyone agrees that the *bureikō* continues, such behaviour is tolerated and even encouraged, but it is expected that the man who has found relief at the *bureikō* will return to his usual behaviour the following morning.

To sum up: the *sakariba* constitutes a third zone between company and home, complementary to these other two spheres. It is not, according to Japanese thinking, a real leisure sphere as such. Leisure is something connected with Sundays and hobbies, more removed from the daily routine. Using the scheme of Japanese leisure concepts which I have introduced elsewhere (Linhart 1984), going to a *sakariba* belongs to *ikoi* (resting, relaxing) rather than to *yasumi* (holiday).

Japanese critics have explained the existence of the many huge *sakariba* as a result of the bad housing situation (Kawazoe *et al.* 1980: 113). For me, the continuing popularity of *sakariba* leisure is rather to be connected with the stress put upon the company employee at his workplace and with Japanese family organization. Whereas in most European cultures the conjugal family relationship fulfils the function of offering relief from the stress which has accumulated over the day at the workplace, in Japan there typically exist two separate worlds of men and women, with the effect that the *sakariba* institution functions to refresh and revitalize the male labour force for the next working day.[9]

NOTES

1 In Confucian terminology a *sakariba* and its predecessors in the Edo period are *akusho*, 'bad places'; this Confucian tradition might be partly responsible for the neglect of research into *sakariba* leisure behaviour. Typically, one of the most extensive treatments of *sakariba* in the sense in which I use this term here is a moralistic article in a series on urban social pathology (see Shikata 1973).

2 *Tachinomi* is a place where one stands while drinking, *nawanoren* is a drinking-place with a rope curtain, and *akachōchin* is a drinking-place with a red paper lantern (the cheapest kind of drinking-place).

3 *Utagoe* pubs are places where people sing folk-songs, often Russian folk-songs, with guitar or accordion accompaniment. They used to be popular after the Second World War in student circles and among leftist intellectuals, who formed something like an *utagoe* movement. Nowadays *utagoe* pubs have almost completely disappeared.

4 *Karaoke*, literally 'empty orchestra', is a device which provides backing music and a microphone so that customers can have automatic accompaniment to their singing (for a detailed description see Stroman 1983).

5 It is difficult to distinguish between visiting the *sakariba* for one's own pleasure, for relief of stress, as a kind of obligation as in business meetings, or when drinking with people from the same workplace (*tsukiai*). For the latter kind see Atsumi (1979).

6 Ms Yoko Fujita Hirose has told me (personal communication) that it is well known among Japanese historians that high-ranking female attendants of the women's quarters of the *shōgun*'s palace in the Edo period used to buy actors as sexual partners (*yakusha-gai*), so that it can be said that there exists a certain tradition of this behaviour in Japan.

7 One example to illustrate this bad conscience is that when Tamanoi still served as a pleasure quarter before the war, people had to go there by train from Asakusa. But almost nobody bought a ticket to Tamanoi itself. One usually asked for a ticket to Kanegafuchi, the next station, at the same price, so as to conceal where one was in fact going (Asahi Shinbun Tōkyō Honsha Shakaibu 1978: 56).

8 See note 4.

9 Since *sakariba* behaviour as described above is not normally available to the average housewife, it is little wonder that many housewives nowadays tend to drink at home. The increase of female alcoholism has become a topic of considerable interest to the Japanese mass media during the last decade.

REFERENCES

Asahi Shinbun Tōkyō Honsha Shakaibu (1978) *Shitamachi* [*Downtown*], Tokyo, Nagoya, Osaka, Kitakyūshū: Asahi Shinbunsha.

Atsumi, Reiko (1979) '*Tsukiai*: Obligatory Personal Relationships of Japanese White-collar Employees', *Human Organization*, vol. XXXVIII, no. 1, pp. 63–70.

Furukawa, Masayuki (1974) 'Nihonjin no yoka seikatsu no ba – Shōwa 48-nen kokumin seikatsu jikan chōsa kara [Places for the Leisure Life of the Japanese: From the 1973 National Time Budget Survey]', *Bunken geppō*, vol. 10, pp. 37–46.

Ikei, Nozomu (1973a) 'Gendai to goraku [Amusement and the Present Age]', in Nakamura Shōichi (ed.) *Gendai goraku no kōzō* [*The Structure of Contemporary Amusement*], Tokyo: Bunwa Shobō, pp. 9–16.

—— (1973b) 'Sakariba kōdō-ron – kūkan to goraku [A Theory of Action at the *Sakariba*: Place and Amusement]', in Nakamura Shōichi (ed.) *Gendai goraku no kōzō* [*The Structure of Contemporary Amusement*], Tokyo: Bunwa Shobō, pp. 17–45.

Inoue, Shun (1973) 'Gēmu-ron – gūzen to goraku [A Theory of Games: Chance and Amusement]', in Nakamura Shōichi (ed.) *Gendai goraku no kōzō* [*The Structure of Contemporary Amusement*], Tokyo: Bunwa Shobō, pp. 75–103.

Ishige, Naomichi (1982) *Shokuji no bunmei-ron* [*A Theory of the Civilisation of Meals*], Tokyo: Chūō kōronsha (Chūkō shinsho 640).

Ishikawa, Hiroyoshi (1972) *Ningenha sararīman – ikigai, asobigai no saihakken* [*Company Employees as Human Beings: A Rediscovery of the Fun of Living and Playing*], Tokyo: Diamondosha.

Katō, Hidetoshi (1972) 'The Growth and Development of "Terminal Culture"', *The Japan Interpreter*, vol. VII, nos 3–4, pp. 376–82.

Kawazoe, Noboru, Kusaka, Kimindo and Tada, Michitarō (1980) 'Teidan: taishū bunka to nihonjin [A Three-Man Talk: Mass Culture and the Japanese]', *Jūrisuto zōkan sōgō tokushū* [*The Mass Culture of Japan*], vol. 20, pp. 99–114.

Linhart, Sepp (1976) *Arbeit, Freizeit und Familie in Japan: Eine Untersuchung der Lebensweise von Arbeitern und Angestellten in Grossbetrieben* Wiesbaden: Harrassowitz (Schriften des Instituts für Asienkunde in Hamburg, no. 43).

—— (1984) 'Some Observations on the Development of "Typical" Japanese Attitudes towards Working Hours and Leisure', in Gordon Daniels (ed.) *Europe Interprets Japan*, Tenterden: Paul Norbury Publications, pp. 207–14, 269–70.

Miyao, Shigeo (1979) 'Sakariba', in Nihon Fūzoki-shi Gakkai (ed.) *Nihon fūzoku-shi jiten* [*Historical Dictionary of Japanese Manners and Customs*], Tokyo: Kōbundō, pp. 252–3.

Morris, V. Dixon (1973) 'The Idioms of Contemporary Japan IV (*jōhatsu*)', *The Japan Interpreter*, vol. VIII, no. 1, pp. 121–36.

Murray, Patricia (1975) 'The Idioms of Contemporary Japan XII (*henshin*)', *The Japan Interpreter*, vol. X, no. 1, pp. 90–5.

Nagai, Kafū (1972) *A Strange Tale from East of the River* (trans. Edward Seidensticker), Tokyo: Tuttle.

NKD (1974) *Nihon kokugo daijiten* [*Large Dictionary of the Japanese Language*], vol. 8, Tokyo: Shōgakkan.

Okui, Fukutarō and Nihon Toshi Gakkai (eds) (1975) *Toshi no seishin – Seikatsu-ronteki bunseki* [*The Urban Spirit: A Life-theory Analysis*], Tokyo: Nihon Hōsō Shuppan Kyōkai.

Saitō, Seiichirō (1976) 'Goraku to supōtsu [Amusement and Sports]', in Umesao Tadao (ed.) *Kōza hikaku bunka 4 – nihonjin no seikatsu* [*Lectures on Comparative Culture, 4: The Life of the Japanese*], Tokyo: Kenkyūsha, pp. 127–56.

Shikata, Hisao (1973) 'Sakariba', in Nasu Sōichi *et al.* (eds) *Toshi byōri kōza 3 – toshi chiiki no byōri* [*Lectures on Urban Anomie 3: Anomie of the Urban Region*], Tokyo: Seishin Shobō, pp. 151–61.

Shinmura, Izuru (1969) *Kōjien* [*The Wide Garden of Words*] (second edition), Tokyo: Iwanami Shoten.

Stroman, John (1983) 'Boom with a Beat', *PHP (Peace Happiness Prosperity, Matsushita Electric/National Panasonic)*, vol. XIV, no. 6, pp. 42–9.

Takada, Yasutaka (1980) 'Bunka to shite no sake [Alcoholic Drinks as a Form of Culture]', *Jūrisuto zōkan sōgō tokushū – nihon no taishū bunka* [*The Mass Culture of Japan*], vol. 20, pp. 127–33.

Takeuchi, Dōkei (1969) 'Sakariba' in *Dainihon hyakka jiten* [*Great Encyclopedia of Japan*], Tokyo: Shōgakkan, pp. 49–50.

Ujigawa, Makoto and Uemura, Tadashi (1970) *Sararīman kakumei – shisutemu jidai no erīto no jōken* [*The Salaryman Revolution: Conditions of an Elite in the Systems Era*], Tokyo: Nihon Seisansei Honbu.

Watanabe, Yoshio (1975) 'Utage no shōchōteki sekai [The Symbolic World of Banquets]', in Itō Mikiharu and Watanabe Yoshio (eds) *Foruko sōsho 6 – Utage* [*Folk Series 6: Banquets*], Tokyo: Kōbundō, pp. 1–117.

16 One over the seven

Sake drinking in a Japanese pottery community

Brian Moeran

INTRODUCTION

Anyone who spends any length of time in Japan soon discovers that drinking is an indispensable social activity. It is almost as if two worlds exist side by side in Japan's cities – one with its department stores and office blocks, peopled by housewives and 'salarymen'; the other with its less permanent buildings in which these same businessmen carouse away the hours of darkness, soothed by the murmured sweet nothings and occasional caresses of attractive hostesses who pour their drinks. There is a world of light and a world of darkness (known as *mizu shōbai*, or the 'water trade'), the Siamese twins of Japanese industrial capitalism. Foreign businessmen recount (not without a trace of nostalgia) tales of how they have been taken to expensive bars by their Japanese hosts and of how it is in the friendly, informal and sexually suggestive atmosphere of these bars that they have been able to conclude many a business deal.[1]

When I went to do fieldwork for the first time in Sarayama, a community of potters in Kyushu, I soon discovered that people drink more seriously in the country than they do, perhaps, in cities.[2] As a newcomer to a rural community, I was feted at first almost every night as the local inhabitants began checking out my weaknesses. Could I hold my liquor? Was I able to sing and dance? Was I really what I pretended to be – an anthropologist – or was I, perhaps, a government spy or local tax inspector in disguise? Above all, was I a good drinking companion?

Before describing these drinking sessions, I wish to make two points by way of introduction, both of them concerning a person's behaviour while 'under the influence'. It has often been suggested that, in Japan, what is said during the course of a drinking session is soon forgiven and forgotten. Drinking acts as an outlet for repressed feelings, seen to be brought on by the way in which the individual is expected to subordinate his own interests to those of the group in Japanese society. It is only while drinking that a junior may forcefully criticize a senior to his (or her) face, and only while drinking that a senior will accept such open criticism. Drinking is seen to break down all social barriers. It is a 'frame' (see Nakane 1970) for egalitarian relations which nicely counterbalances the hierarchy of everyday life.

In the valley in which I lived and studied for four years between 1977 and 1982, I soon discovered that this was not exactly the case. Of course, people occasionally said that it did not matter what you told them while you were yourself under the influence of drink, but this was just an ideology designed to pull the wool over the eyes of an unsuspecting anthropologist. In fact, local residents not only remembered what was said during drinking sessions; they stored this information away, to use for their own political ends. Nothing was forgotten, since anything said under the influence of alcohol might, at some time or other, prove useful to people involved in the competitive reality of community life.

This disparity between ideals and reality became more obvious when I considered the way in which people would speak to one another while drinking together. The Japanese in general make a vital distinction between what they call *tatemae* and *honne*, or *honshin*. *Tatemae* refers to the language which is used in public as a matter of 'principle'; *honne* to words that 'come from the heart' and express an individual's innermost, private feelings. It is this distinction which ultimately clarifies the relationship between group and individual in Japanese society, for *tatemae* is the language of out-group, and *honne* that of in-group, communication.

I soon discovered that it was during drinking sessions that my informants shifted from *tatemae* to *honne*, from – to use Bernstein's distinction (1971) – 'public' to 'private' language. There appeared to be no taboos concerning subject-matter and, as the evenings wore on and the sake flowed faster, so I found myself listening to men talking about subjects which, during daylight hours, they had either refused to discuss or had evaded with an embarrassed laugh. At the same time, I discovered that some of the answers which I had received during the normal course of interviews were directly contradicted by these same informants as we drank together. As a result, I soon found myself paying frequent visits to the lavatory so that I could jot down in my notebook revelations which oncoming alcoholic inebriation threatened to – and sometimes did – erase.[3]

THE POTTERY COMMUNITY OF SARAYAMA

Sarayama is a small community (*buraku*) of fourteen households, of which ten make and fire a form of stoneware pottery known as *Ontayaki*, or Onta ware. Situated at the top of a narrow valley in the mountains to the north-west of the town of Hita, in central Kyushu, the community has become famous over the past three decades for a style of pottery which closely accords with the ideals of *mingei*, or folk craft, put forward by a scholar-critic, Yanagi Muneyoshi, from the late 1920s (cf. Moeran 1981a, 1981b). Sarayama's potters have been praised in particular because they have steadfastly kept to traditional techniques of production – digging their own clay and glaze materials locally, using kick wheels to throw their functional wares, decorating the finished forms with certain old Korean techniques, and firing their pots in a wood-fired cooperative climbing kiln. In 1975, these techniques were designated an Intangible Cultural Property (*mukei bunkazai*) by the Japanese government's Agency for Cultural Affairs (*Bunkachō*).

Sarayama's fourteen households consist of four name groups (Kurogi, Yanase, Sakamoto and Kobukuro) and are organized along the customary lines of main-house/branch-house relations. Cross-cutting ties between name groups have been established through marriage, residential and cooperative labour groupings, together with a seniority system of age-grades whereby the oldest men have generally been in charge of community affairs (see Moeran 1984a).

Until approximately 1960, there was little demand for Onta ware; the potters were primarily farmers who turned to pottery in their spare time or when the weather was too bad for them to work in the fields. In the 1960s, however, there began what came to be called the 'folk craft boom' (*mingei būmu*). Potters found that, for the first time ever, they could sell whatever they made. This increase in market demand happened to coincide with a government policy curtailing the production of rice (*gentan seisaku*) and, during the next fifteen years, potting households began one by one to give up farming entirely. By 1979, ten of Sarayama's households were specializing full-time in pottery production, while the other four pursued such occupations as carpentry, plastering, rice-farming, the cultivation of oak mushrooms (*shiitake*), running a noodle-shop, a sake shop and a family inn (*minshuku*).

Occupational specialization has been accompanied by a considerable disparity of incomes between potting and non-potting households. Prior to the folk craft boom there was not that great a difference in the incomes of all households in Sarayama. Because they shared a cooperative kiln, potters fired and marketed approximately the same number of pots and earned more or less the same amount of money from them. Twenty years later, however, potting households were earning on average almost twice as much as non-potting households (¥8 million as opposed to ¥4 million). This disparity was accompanied by an ever-widening income gap among potting households, for increased demand led to some potters leaving the cooperative kiln and setting up private kilns which they could fire as and when they pleased (household incomes ranged from ¥16 to ¥5.5 million in 1979).

Every rural Japanese community is ideally organized in such a way that the individual subordinates his or her interests to those of the household to which s/he belongs, and each household in turn subordinates its interests to those of the community as a whole. A set of historical incidents has led to the Japanese rural community forming a closed social group whose inhabitants tend to see the outside world as starting a few hundred yards down the road. Sarayama is no exception to this ideal, but the recent development of the Japanese market economy has led to a number of strains in the residents' notion of community solidarity. In particular, we find that the hitherto accepted division between elders and younger men is being challenged, while the emerging economic differentiation between potting and non-potting households has further upset the much-valued emphasis placed on harmony. It is when Sarayama's men start drinking that these strains tend to break out into the open. At the same time, it is through drinking that they try to patch up their differences and recreate a feeling of 'togetherness'.

SAKE DRINKING PARTIES

Drinking in Sarayama occurs on any number of pretexts and may in some exceptional circumstances start from as early as 9 o'clock in the morning. A pottery dealer, for example, may visit a potter's workshop after a kiln firing and be invited into the house for 'refreshments' at the conclusion of business. Alternatively, a forester from a nearby hamlet may drop by on his way home from work and invite one of Sarayama's inhabitants down to the local sake shop for a few bottles of beer. A potter may have to discuss firing schedules with other potters sharing the cooperative kiln, and they may decide to share a few drinks together at the home of one of the potters, in the community noodle-shop, or even down in one of the bars of the local town, 17 kilometres away. Here, however, I wish to discuss formal drinking encounters, when either the community as a whole, or the ten households forming the potters' cooperative, gather together to celebrate Sarayama's ceremonial occasions. Some of these ceremonies involve fixed amounts of sake: the Mountain God festival (*Yama no kami*), for example, is limited to one *go* of sweet sake (*amazake*) per household; on New Year's Day, only one *shō* of sake is drunk at the villagers' annual greeting. Most ceremonies, however, do not limit the amount of alcohol to be consumed, and it is these which I shall discuss here.

Such ceremonial occasions tend to follow a general pattern. Community gatherings rotate among households and are usually attended by one man (and sometimes one woman) from each household in Sarayama, the time of day being announced over the community's loudspeaker system. Special ceremonies, such as the potters' celebration of *Ebisu-sama* (God of Trade), held only once a year, are initiated by the sound of a conch shell, blown by the 'duty officer' (*sewa motokata*), whose job it is to look after community affairs for the year. At the appointed hour, representatives from each household gather at the place where the ceremony is to be held. On arriving, each representative takes off his shoes and steps up into the hallway, before making his way to the *nando*, or *kotatsu* room, an informal living-room where the household's family gathers to eat, socialize and watch television. There he will be served green tea and be asked to help himself from a tray of candies or bowl of fruit. Idle conversation will ensue, centring mainly on the host's family, with comments on how big the children are growing, how well they are getting on at school, and so on. The emphasis here is on household members, or on events occurring in the outside world. Community affairs as such are not discussed.[4]

Once everyone is assembled, the host will ask people to move into the main guest room (*zashiki*), where low tables have been laid out in an inverted U-shape. The *zashiki* in fact often comprises two rooms, separated by sliding screens which can be removed when many visitors are present. Tables are lined down each side of these rooms as well as across the top. I say 'down' and 'top' and 'inverted' U-shape for a reason. Behind the lateral row of tables is to be found the *tokonoma*, a slightly raised 'sacred dais' which is built into every country house. The *tokonoma* is considered to be the most important part of the whole building and so only the most important people are placed with their backs to it along the top row of tables. In the event of casual visiting, a guest will always be placed with his back to the *tokonoma*, while the host will sit opposite him in an inferior position. On community occasions, the eldest household representative present is placed at the centre of the top table, the second-eldest is placed to his right, the third to his left, the fourth-eldest to the second-eldest's right, and so on right down the two lines of tables to the most junior men present. When women participate, they are placed below the men and adopt a similar order of seating by seniority. Younger women, however, seem to be less particular about the seating order and occasionally younger housewives find themselves 'above' somebody who is their senior by a year or so. In general, it can be said that the older a man or woman becomes, the more strictly he or she adheres to seating by age seniority, and that men tend to be stricter than women about seating order.

Once everyone is settled and kneeling formally in front of his or her place (each place being marked by a side saucer, chopsticks and empty sake cup, together with a small covered lacquer bowl of clear fish soup, a porcelain bowl of boiled vegetables or *niimono* and a side dish of raw fish), the host, who is not included in the age seniority seating order but kneels at the bottom of the room, formally greets and welcomes his guests. The most senior member of those present then replies in a speech which is highly formalized, consisting of a number of set phrases thanking everyone for taking the trouble to gather together at such a busy time, and praising the elements for being so kind as to favour the occasion with good weather (this bit may be dropped when the weather is not so benign, or substituted by comments on how people must be suffering from the cold, snow, rain, wind, or whatever).

Having made these initial comments in reply to the host's greeting, the eldest man proceeds to blur the in-group/out-group distinction hitherto present by informing everyone about why they have gathered together on this particular occasion. The rarer the occasion, the more detailed this information is likely to be and the more the occasion stressed. The host household will then be thanked for providing a place for everyone to gather. Everyone is thanked again for taking the trouble to come, and a toast is proposed. At this point, the women will get up and move away from their places at the bottom of the room to fill everyone's sake cup from the bottles of heated alcohol that stand already on the tables. The speaker raises his voice: '*Kanpai!*' ('Glasses dry!') – or, on less formal occasions, '*itadakimasu*' ('for what we humbly receive'). The cry is taken up by all present as they, too, raise their cups and drink. For a few seconds there is silence as everyone drinks together. The contents of each cup are downed. There is a sudden exhalation of breath as people express their satisfaction with the sake.

This marks the end of the initial stage of the ceremonial gathering, and participants now find themselves slipping into informality as they shift from a kneeling to a cross-legged position and refill their cups. They will start sipping soup and eating some of the food spread before them, but not too much, for drinking is the important activity, and it is a man's capacity to drink and talk which in the end marks him out from among his fellows. The first cup or two of sake is poured out for him by those sitting on either side and he in turn will fill his neighbours' cups, since it is considered impolite to serve oneself. Frequently, the women will remain on the inner side of the inverted U-shape of tables and serve the men with rice wine as they join in the casual conversation. This starts with somewhat formalized exclamations on the weather, food and other people's business, before shifting to more informal gossip and a discussion of recent community events. It is at this stage that a man proceeds to exchange cups with his neighbours.

What does an exchange of sake cups consist of?[5] When his cup is empty, a man will pick it up and, holding it by the foot rim balanced between the tips of his fingers, he will present it to someone sitting nearby. As he presents the cup, he will call the other person's name and raise the hand with which he is holding the cup very slightly once or twice, in order to attract the other person's attention. This gesture is at the same time a sign of humility from a man offering a gift. The receiver will take the cup – usually with an exclamation of slightly feigned surprise – bow his head slightly, again raise the cup in his hand in a gesture of humble acceptance, and allow the donor to fill it for him from one of the bottles on the table between them. The receiver then downs the sake and almost immediately returns the cup with a similar set of formal expressions and gestures.

When a man exchanges cups with his immediate neighbours, the flow of conversation is not immediately affected in any appreciable way. However, the first exchange is a signal for those concerned to shift from informal gossip to somewhat more intimate conversation about how events, previously touched upon, affect those concerned. When a man has exchanged cups with those sitting immediately next to him, he will proceed to pass cups to others sitting further away. Each time, the same formalities are gone through, but here the purpose of the exchanges is for the donor to take the opportunity to initiate a conversation with someone else (or, possibly, to draw him into a continuing conversation). A man may well have to go through a preliminary round of formal pleasantries but will, with a second exchange of cups with the same person, proceed to informal and more intimate conversation.

Provided that the people with whom he is exchanging cups are within arm's reach, a man will tend to remain seated in his initial position according to age. However, as the gathering gains a certain alcoholic momentum, men will find themselves exchanging cups with others several feet away, since it is considered rude to drink on one's own without exchanging cups and since every man wants to spread and reinforce his web of contacts as widely as possible. In this case, a man may have to pass a cup along the table via his neighbours; or he may prefer to get up and walk along behind where everyone is sitting in order to exchange cups. Sometimes, he may step across the low table in front of him into the middle of the room and proceed to exchange cups with a fellow drinker from the inside of the inverted U-shape (previously occupied only by the women). This point in the cup exchanges can be said to mark the third stage of the ceremonial gathering, and it is usually by this time that the women will have withdrawn to talk, drink and eat among themselves at the bottom of the room.

This third stage usually begins within ten to fifteen minutes after the proposal of the formal toast, and it is from this time that the gathering starts to become a 'serious' drinking session. It is marked by complete informality of speech, with virtually no restrictions on who says what to whom. Whereas the initial formal opening was probably conducted in standard Japanese (or as closely approximating the standard as local elders can manage), both the second and third stages are characterized by use of dialect. Potters and other residents of Sarayama speak in their own language, not in some idiom imposed on them by ephemeral outsiders in Tokyo or wherever.

It is said that in the past (a vague term which can refer to any time between ten and fifty years previously, depending on the speaker's age), a man could exchange sake cups only with someone sitting below him. He was strictly prohibited from passing his cup up the table to anyone older than himself (cf. Befu 1974: 200). This meant that, to some extent, the shift from the second to the third stage of the gathering was determined by the elders, since it was they who made the first move in getting up to exchange cups with others junior to them who were sitting out of arm's reach lower down the tables. It was, of course, possible for a certain amount of lateral movement to occur, since people of very similar ages found themselves on opposite sides of the room as a result of formal seating arrangements, and they were permitted to cross over to exchange cups with one another. Nowadays, however, it is possible for a man to pass his cup 'up' the table to someone his senior, although it would still be slightly presumptuous for a man of – say – 30 to exchange cups with his neighbours and then step across the table, walk up to the top of the room and present his sake cup to one of the elders at the top table. He would be expected first to present cups to at least one or two of the older men sitting between him and those at the top. Once the third stage has begun, however, and has been continuing for five or ten minutes, a young person can suddenly break away from his drinking group and walk straight up to the top of the tables to exchange cups with men there. The breakdown of formality permits this. At the same time, many of the oldest men will have 'come down' to sit in the middle of the room, so that a younger person can join and exchange cups with an elder much more unobtrusively by first presenting his cup to – say – a 40-year-old man and talking with him (although codes of politeness presuppose an elder to be accorded first cup when he is talking in a small group).

I have used the word 'unobtrusively' here for a reason. People do not just exchange cups during these drinking sessions; they talk. And they do not talk just about local gossip and other trivia. As the sake flows, they tend to talk about those affairs which are closest to their hearts and which rankle in their minds. Hence, conversation is political in the context of the community, and a man is constantly alert during the course of drinking, weighing up who is talking to whom, putting two and two together from his background knowledge of local affairs, and frequently using the custom of cup exchanges to join a conversation in which he feels that he might well have a vested interest. To a certain extent, those who really wish to make use of the gathering to further their intra-community political interests will do their best to move about unobtrusively and to make their membership of certain drinking groups seem as casual as possible. They will decide what they want to talk about and who the best person would be to talk over the matter. They then proceed to plan a route towards drinking with that person in as 'natural' a manner as possible, so that when they do meet, their conversation will not attract the attention of others. This may prove difficult, especially when both men concerned are moving about the room independently, perhaps with completely different strategies, but during the course of the third stage (which can last for an hour or more) they are bound to get together sometime and the matter in hand will be discussed. There are, after all, only fourteen households in the community and, even when both father and son attend a drinking session, there are rarely more than twenty-five men present at any gathering.

As I mentioned earlier, so far as the formal organization of Sarayama is concerned, it is the elders who officially hold the reins of authority in the community. It is the men over 60 years of age whose opinions are publicly respected and whose commands are generally obeyed. These men still remain heads of their households, even though they may have sons living and working with them who are in their mid-thirties and in the prime of life so far as their physical strength is concerned. The point of interest about drinking sessions, therefore, is that when the third informal stage is reached, it is not the elders but the middle-aged men who are the most active in the exchange of sake cups. The first to get up from their seats and move about the room are almost invariably younger heads of households, aged between 40 and 60. Some men are slower to get up than others, perhaps, but in the end it is the middle-aged group of men who are talking, arguing and consuming the most sake. The oldest men remain more or less rooted to the top tables with their temporary visitors seated before them.

In the meantime, potters up to their mid-thirties generally form their own drinking groups at the far end of the room, very often sitting with the women. This means that the centre of the *zashiki* becomes completely empty, so that the third stage in the drinking session is marked by a complete separation of participants into two groups. Those at the bottom of the room keep their conversation light and trivial; they discuss such things as local and professional baseball games, fishing, popular music and their occasional outings to bars in Hita (and appraise the hostesses working there). Those at the top of the room generally discuss community affairs, local valley politics, problems surrounding Sarayama's pottery production and other matters seen to be important for the community as a whole (see Figures 16.1, 16.2 and 16.3).

By this time the women will have begun clearing some of the unoccupied tables of dishes, and use kitchen work as an excuse to retire from the main room to the back of the house (where they indulge just as earnestly in their own gossip and political manoeuvring). A number of men will be getting very drunk. (The only thing that prevents them from getting drunk sooner is the fact that they are provided with large ashtrays, into which a man will tip out much of the sake poured for him when his interlocutor is not looking. Although frowned upon by those who can hold their drink, this 'bad' habit is generally accepted since complete drunkenness is not thought to be conducive to a good party.) There is a

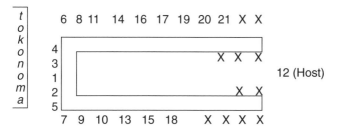

Figure 16.1 Informal seating arrangement (stage 1)

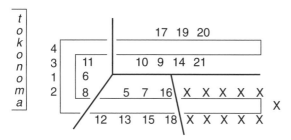

Figure 16.2 Informal seating arrangement (stage 2)

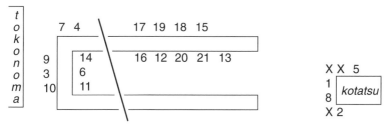

Figure 16.3 Informal seating arrangement (stage 3)

Key	Households	Potting		Non-potting	
1–4 = 60 + years		Kaneichi	1, 19	Yamamaru	2, 9
5–7 = 50 + years		Yamani	3, 14	Kaneyo	18
8–11 = 40 + years		Yamasai	15	Maruta	8
12–16 = 30 + years		Irisai	10	Yamamasu	16
17–21 = 20 + years		Kanemaru	7, 21		
		Yamasan	6, 20		
X = women		Irisan	5, 13		
		Yamaichi	11		
		Iriichi	12		
		Yamako	4, 17		

tendency at this point for many of the eldest men to retire quietly (frequently by way of the lavatory) to the *kotatsu* room. There they will sit and watch television over a cup of tea, talking once more in restrained voices about the nothing-in-particulars of life in a country valley. One of their peers or juniors may stagger in and make an attempt to drag them back into the main room and then use their refusal as an excuse for himself to stay in the *kotatsu* room and drop out of the drinking. It is generally at this point that the gathering enters its fourth stage.

This stage is marked, then, by the departure of the elders and by the introduction of singing, and sometimes dancing. Singing is important, for it enables one man to claim the attention of others. This means two things: not only do men break off their conversations in order to listen to one man singing, but a man's ability to attract attention by standing up and singing may well stand him in good stead later on during his own political arguments with others. Singing in itself livens up the party. A successful singer will find himself at the centre of attention, and he may well be able to turn this attention into support in order to help him present, and win, an argument at a later stage when a quarrel breaks out.

In general, people tend to listen to the first songs that are sung, but to ignore later singers and continue their conversations uninterrupted. This means that it is to one's own advantage to initiate the fourth stage of the gathering by being the first to sing. The problem, though, is gauging when people are likely to want to listen to a song and timing one's own exuberation to coincide with the general mood of the gathering, for once a man has drunk too much he tends not to sing well, and if he has not drunk enough he may well be too self-conscious to put over his song effectively. The precise point when a man gambles on singing is a matter of delicate political finesse. Sometimes someone will suddenly decide to start singing, raise his voice in the hope of catching the attention of everyone present, and find that in fact people are not yet ready for a song and ignore him entirely. The man who can stand up, claim the attention of one and all in a loud voice, and then keep that attention focused on himself right to the end of his song, is also likely to be able to claim their attention when it comes to arguing community affairs. An effective singing voice is in some respects essential to winning an argument, and winning an argument is the prerequisite for a community leader.

Here we should note that it is the men in the middle age-group, and not the elders, who generally initiate the singing successfully. If a younger man starts singing, he is almost certain to be ignored. This is partly, perhaps, because younger men tend to sing popular songs, rather than the more 'classical' and accepted forms of *utai*, *shigin* or *minyō* folk-songs favoured by the older men. Men from the middle age-group have come to be known for their singing prowess: Shigeki (11) for his Shimazaki Tōson songs, Moriyuki (9) for his *minyō*, and Toshiyasu (7) for his *utai*. Those who want to get ahead in community life have a tendency to perfect a certain style of singing which is acceptable to, and praised by, other villagers.

As the singing gathers atonal momentum, so conversations among drinkers become more earnest. Men will by now have downed their quota of seven *gō* of sake (the amount considered equivalent to our eight pints of beer), and their speech will be slurred as they no longer hold back on topics which they hold most dear to their hearts. One potter will accuse another of selling his tea bowls at five times the agreed retail price; another will upbraid a neighbour for maltreating his daughter-in-law and forcing her back to work immediately after a miscarriage; a group of potters will get at one of their number who has arbitrarily had a woodshed built on a piece of land over which the bulldozer must pass to dig out all the potters' clay. It is at this point that major arguments, quarrels, even fights occur. Almost invariably, it is those in the middle age-group (nos 5 to 11 in the Figures) who are the most voluble, particularly potters, who are jostling for position as next leader of the cooperative and hence, in time, of the community as a whole. Frequently they fight amongst themselves and it is the junior age-groups or those who (like 9) are not potters who act as intermediaries and try to stop the men concerned from coming to blows.[6]

It is about this time that most men make up their minds about whether they are really going to make a night of it, or whether they will slip away. Younger men in particular tend to leave now, and soon there is only a handful of men left in the *zashiki*. By common consent, they may all move to the *kotatsu* room, where they will continue to drink sake or turn to tea. One or two men who, like the dormouse at Alice's tea party, have fallen asleep, may well be roused and made to join in what is left of the party. This is the fifth and final stage of the drinking session, and can be marked by more anger and quarrelling, or by a general sobering up of all concerned. Sometimes, when everyone is feeling in a particularly good mood, someone will telephone for a taxi and the men will go down to Hita for further, more expensive, frolicking in the town's bars.

CONCLUSION

I have shown here that sake-drinking parties in the community of Sarayama follow much the same pattern as that described for drinking among the Subanun (see Frake 1964). Drinking sessions can be divided into five discourse stages, each of which has a separate focus of speech act and separate language-type (see Table 16.1). Among both the Subanun and the residents of Sarayama, drinking talk takes on importance in the context of the assumption of authority. Among the Subanun, verbal skills during drinking encounters enable a man to act as legislator in disputes and thereby to gain status in the eyes of his fellow men. Among the potters of Sarayama, the ability to talk and sing well ensures a man a position of power in community affairs. The more mobile a man and the better able he is to talk to all, the more likely he is to assume authority. Drinking is thus a political activity.

The point to be made about the community of Sarayama is that drinking encounters would appear to reflect the growing loss of power of the elders and the increasing influence of the middle-aged group of men in community affairs. What should be stressed here is that, although on formal occasions the eldest men assume authority through formal speeches and through such overt marks of deference as being seated at the head of the table at drinking parties, informally it

Table 16.1 Analysis of drinking parties

Encounter stages	Discourse stages	Focus of speech acts	Language types
1. Formal gathering	Formal opening speech and toast	Role expression	Standard
2. Immobile cup exchange	Semi-formal introductory talk	Context definition	Dialect
	Local gossip; intimate level discussion	Topic (household)	Dialect
3. Mobile cup exchange	Intimate level discussion	Topic (community affairs)	Dialect
4. Song drinking	Singing as verbal art;	Stylistic	Dialect/Standard
	Discussions and quarrels	Topic (community affairs)	Dialect
5. Informal separation	Incoherence (?)	Context closure	Dialect

is the group of men below them who wield most power. It is those between the ages of 40 and 60 who manipulate to their own ends the conversations which occur during drinking sessions, and who argue out vital community matters. I would suggest that it is this middle age-group – in particular two or three articulate men – who covertly influence formal decisions overtly made by the elders. The loss of power of the latter can be seen in the fact that, first, the elders no longer determine the overall pattern of a drinking encounter, because they no longer have the prerogative to dictate the course of sake cup exchanges; and second, the elders cannot sing well and tend to remove themselves somewhat rapidly from major drinking encounters, leaving their immediate juniors to discuss and virtually to decide important community matters. Elders retain their authority in official ex cathedra statements, but in practice these comments are influenced by those junior to them.

Of course, it could be argued that the elders are able to leave sake parties early precisely because their sons are often present as well. They remain secure in the knowledge that information will be relayed to them from a trustworthy source. The trouble with this argument is that there are several drinking encounters where only one member from each household is present and yet the elders still leave early. In such cases, there is no guarantee that they will learn, let alone be able to influence indirectly, what happens in their absence.

Another criticism might take the line that, in fact, it is usually the middle-aged who are the most influential in any small-scale society, and that the notion that the elders used to be in control of community matters is a typical idealization of a state of affairs which has never in fact existed. This is possible. After all, the elders have never been able to sing well, so did they leave drinking sessions early in the past? I cannot be sure about this, of course, but potters in Sarayama used to stress that in the past the main activity of the elders was drinking (*hikari*) and that they would frequently gather over a few bottles of home-made sake and come to decisions about community affairs without bothering to consult the younger household heads. It is claimed that one reason for this was that younger men were too busy farming to be able to get together very much. It is here, perhaps, that the farmers' conversion to full-time pottery may have affected drinking habits, for the middle age-group of men are now always at home in their workshops, rather than scattered in distant fields up to three kilometres from Sarayama, and can gather at a few minutes' notice. Not only this, but the development of a market for folk-craft pottery, together with the emergence of a notion of 'artistic talent' as a result of the external criticism of Onta ware, has enabled younger potters to have more say in the running of the potters' cooperative.[7] All in all, therefore, it would seem that the pattern of drinking parties described here reflects fairly the general pattern of the erosion of the power of the elders over the past quarter of a century.

A second point to be made in this connection is that drinking *per se* is not what really counts. By this I mean that it does not matter if a man is too old, or not physically strong enough, to hold his alcohol. Provided that he is prepared to stay with his drinking companions and not go home early, a man can still wield a lot of influence. In other words, drinking in itself is a desirable, but not essential, prerequisite for power. This point is best illustrated by one potter, Shigeki (11), who at one stage during fieldwork was suffering from a bad liver and had been advised by his doctor to stop drinking sake for a few months. This he did. But rather than delegate his wife or even son to go along to community sake parties, Shigeki himself attended them (complete with a supply of tomato juice). Not only this, but he used to stay until the fifth and final stage of almost every drinking session, and so participated in all the major discussions that took place. He even went so far as to feign a certain drunkenness and exclaim that tomato juice made him 'happy' because he drank it out of used sake cups. What I wish to stress is that Shigeki had no need to attend these gatherings in the first place; alternatively, he could have put in an appearance and left early at about the third stage (this is precisely what another man from a non-potting household, Osamu (8), who complained of a bad liver, used to do – a fact which illustrates, I think, the way in which potters are more concerned with power than are non-potters). The fact that Shigeki chose to remain to the bitter end shows the importance he attached to the way in which community affairs were discussed during these gatherings. To have missed them would have meant a considerable weakening of his own position of power within the community. Drinking is thus the idiom in which decisions are made, and not necessarily their cause.

Which brings me back to my original point about drinking acting as a licensed outlet for repressed frustration. When insulted on such an occasion, a man is supposed to behave the next day as if nothing had happened. All is forgiven and forgotten, it is said. But to suggest this is, in my opinion, to take an extremely naive view of Japanese (or indeed any) society. It is clear from my fieldwork in Sarayama that people were offended by quarrels picked during the course of drinking sessions and that, although they did their best to pretend that they had not been offended, the old adage that what is said under the influence of alcohol is always forgotten was simply not true. I soon learned that people in Sarayama, even people who appeared at the time to be very drunk, remembered very clearly who had said what to whom and why during drinking parties. Not only this, but these discussions and disputes, which were not openly discussed during the course of everyday activities, were weighed and used in further arguments. Drinking arguments thus formed a covert discourse which people proceeded to draw on for the advance of their own political interests. There were, in other words, two discourses in action in Sarayama. One was the overt daytime discourse, conducted mainly by the elders and in fairly formal situations. The other was a covert night-time discourse entered into by the middle-aged group of men, mainly under the informal influence of sake. It was vital for any man who wished to gain access to authority and power to be aware of the night-time discourse and to make use of it as and when appropriate. In other words, if he was to gain any position of authority in the community, a man was bound to drink, or at least keep company with drinkers.

Much of the discussion of drinking parties in Sarayama ties in with work done on political oratory in traditional societies. The way in which potters use informal occasions such as those described here to hammer out community problems is paralleled, for example, by the Maori in New Zealand, who make use of informal meetings to decide local and inter-tribal matters. In each of the two societies we find that some questions are perennial favourites for debate – the arguments about the production, marketing and aesthetic appraisal of Onta ware in Sarayama, the teaching of the Maori language and preservation of Maori culture in New Zealand *marae* – and also that these questions are never really settled, because none of the participants wants to settle them. We find, too, that the distinction between *tatemae* and *honne* is similar to the distinction made by Salmond (1975: 62–3) between 'tight' oratory and 'loose' plain speaking, and to that made by Rosaldo (1973) between 'crooked' and 'straight' speech. Indeed, it ties in with the more generalized distinction made by Bloch (1975: 13) between 'formalized' and 'everyday' speech.

Bloch's notion that there is a correlation to be made between types of political oratory and types of political system has been shown to be wrong, and it has recently been reformulated by Borgström (1982), who has suggested that the mode of political address correlates with the type of power relationship pertaining between speaker and audience. In general, types of speech have been seen to reflect power relations between superior and inferior, and in this respect, perhaps, *tatemae* and *honne* are not so different. But they also encompass a second, frequently perceived distinction between *omote*, the 'open' where surprises should not occur, and *ura*, the 'back' which shrouds the wheeling and dealing which lead up to decision-making (see Johnson 1980). What goes on in the Japanese Diet, for example, is *omote*; the real political bargaining amongst factions is all *ura*. This makes oratory as such unnecessary.

The fact that *tatemae* is linked with *omote* also ties in with the Japanese sociological idea that the individual should subordinate his interests to those of the group (cf. Moeran 1984b), for *tatemae* is the expression of group ideology. In this respect, then, it is not simply a form of 'authority' speech, but a means by which an in-group shuts itself off from the outside world. *Tatemae* and *honne* represent both authority and power, public and private, politeness and intimacy, form and content, out-group and in-group. In other words, Japanese data suggest that we should not see relations of authority and power only in terms of a hierarchical structure, but also as a function of social distance (cf. politeness forms and Bernstein's restricted and elaborated codes) which extends horizontally between in-groups and out-groups.

NOTES

1 For the record, we might note Sir William Harcourt's words in 1872: 'As much of the history of England has been brought about in public ale-houses as in the House of Commons.'
2 I would like to thank the Social Science Research Council and the Japan Foundation for funding these two periods of fieldwork in Japan.
3 It would, perhaps, be tempting providence to declare that the whole of my PhD thesis (and the book which derived from it) were written on the basis of information given under the benign influence of sake. I would, however, be attempting to delude all and sundry were I to suggest that I could have begun to write a thesis without participating regularly in the sake parties held so frequently in Sarayama. Those interested in the general topic of anthropologists doing fieldwork might like to glance at my *Ōkubo Diary: Portrait of a Japanese Valley* (1985).
4 This format of conversational niceties is, of course, not limited to a remote Japanese valley community. I have noticed that English suburban dinner parties tend to go through a similar shift in conversational style as guests proceed from cocktails to food.
5 Harumi Befu has recently brought to my attention an article which he published in *Arctic Anthropology* on after-dinner entertainment in general. In this he outlines a number of 'elementary rules of the sake party' which are mentioned here, and talks of the 'socially defined rules of drunken behaviour'. Although I read much of this article with a certain sense of *déjà vu*, I feel that my own work retains some value for its analysis of a specific ethnographic community.
6 It should be pointed out here that there are some songs which are consciously sung in order to avoid or stifle quarrels and that these are folk songs, like the *Tankō bushi* or *Kuroda bushi*, which immediately create a sense of community and harmony. It is not surprising, therefore, to find that it is frequently the man who is good at singing these folk songs (Moriyuki [9]) who acts as mediator in arguments which get out of control.
7 I have discussed, at some length, the way in which younger potters have gained control in the running of community affairs in my monograph *Lost Innocence* (Moeran 1984a: 150–81).

REFERENCES

Befu, H. (1974) 'An Ethnography of Dinner Entertainment in Japan', *Arctic Anthropology*, vol. XI (supplement), pp. 196–203.

Bernstein, B. (1971) *Class, Codes and Control*, New York: Schocken Books.

Bloch, M. (1975) 'Introduction', in M. Bloch (ed.) *Political Language and Oratory in Traditional Society*, London: Academic Press, pp. 1–28.

Borgström, B.-E. (1982) 'Power Structure and Political Speech', *Man*, n.s., vol. XVII, no. 2, pp. 313–27.

Frake, C. (1964) 'How to Ask for a Drink in Subanun', *American Anthropologist*, vol. LXVI, no. 6 (part. 2, special publication), pp. 127–32.

Johnson, C. (1980) '*Omote* (Explicit) and *Ura* (Implicit): Translating Japanese Political Terms', *Journal of Japanese Studies*, vol. VI, no. 1, pp. 89–115.

Moeran, B. (1981a) 'Yanagi Muneyoshi and the Japanese Folk Craft Movement', *Asian Folklore Studies*, vol. XL, no. 1, pp. 87–99.

—— (1981b) 'Japanese Social Organization and the Mingei Movement', *Pacific Affairs*, vol. LIV, no. 1, pp. 42–56.

—— (1984a) *Lost Innocence: Folk Craft Potters of Onta, Japan*, Berkeley: University of California Press.

—— (1984b) 'Individual, Group and *Seishin*: Japan's Internal Cultural Debate', *Man*, n.s., vol. XIX, no. 2, pp. 252–66.

—— (1985) *Ōkubo Diary: Portrait of a Japanese Valley*, Stanford: Stanford University Press.

Nakane, C. (1970) *Japanese Society*, Berkeley: University of California Press.

Rosaldo, M. (1973) 'I Have Nothing to Hide: The Language of Ilongot Oratory', *Language in Society*, vol. II, no. 2, pp. 193–223.

Salmond, A. (1975) 'Mana Makes the Man: A Look at Maori Oratory and Politics', in M. Bloch (ed.) *Political Language and Oratory in Traditional Society*, London: Academic Press, pp. 45–63.

17 Models of performance*

Space, time and social organization in Japanese dance

James Valentine

Cultural performances such as dance provide participants and observers with exemplary models that embody significant aspects of the wider culture and society. While the focus here will be on spatial and temporal aspects together with the social organization of performance, methodological questions must be addressed in conjunction with the interpretative and institutional analysis.

Research on dance in Japan has to confront the initial question of definition, whose resolution depends partly on a broader characterization of dance for anthropological purposes. Of the few general texts devoted to the anthropology of dance, most include at least one chapter on the question of definition, coming up with their own criteria for what counts as dance. Aspects of both movement and motive tend to be included, so that common to the definitions is an emphasis on non-verbal body movements deliberately patterned or fashioned in a way that transcends utility.[1] This 'patterning' involves the organization of movement in time and space, as noted by several writers. Royce, for example, in reviewing various methods of dance notation, observes that Labanotation includes reference to both the time value and the direction of movement, and Effort–Shape notation indicates both exertion of the body in time and position of the body in space (1977: 45, 50). Lange similarly argues that form in dance is composed of the spatial properties of movement together with the rhythmic pattern that shapes the flow of movement in time (1975: 36–7).

Anthropologists of dance may be agreed on some basic defining properties of dance, but they vary in the degree to which they would take account of participants' categories. For example, Kaeppler argues that we must take account of native dance classification (1978: 37, 46–7), while Hanna emphasizes that we must put forward a definition of dance that transcends participants' concepts (1979: 18). These positions are of course not contradictory, and both writers would probably concur with Royce that we should decide on a minimal definition of dance, so that native terms can be preserved within this (1977: 7–8).

Whether we give emphasis to outsider or insider categories, there seem to be considerable problems in deciding what constitutes dance in Japan. Certainly, if we sustain a Western preconception of dance, focusing on so-called 'pure dance' as a rather abstract art form, we are likely either to recognize very little dance in Japan, or to misinterpret it as abstract when it is not. Indeed pure dance, as conceived in Indian classical dance under the Sanskrit term *nritta*, is rarely found in Japan. Most dance in Japan is combined with religious ritual and/or narrative and mime. Japanese dance is claimed to have its origins in mime (Gunji 1981), and in much contemporary Japanese classical and folk dance the mimetic aspect is predominant. Moreover, the assumption that dance engages the whole body must be abandoned in the Japanese context. For instance, drum dance (*taiko odori*) which focuses on skilful, sometimes rapid and generally exaggerated drumming gestures, would not normally be recognized as dance in the West; nor perhaps would some items of Japanese classical dance in which the performer kneels on the floor and uses only the upper part of the body to make largely mimetic gestures. Japanese dance typically relates closely to the ground, with movements directed towards it rather than away from it, and thus contrasts sharply with ballet, which emphasizes lightness of step and removal from the ground. Dance envisaged as the execution of steps is likely to overlook or misconstrue classical Japanese dance, which is neither conceived nor learned in terms of discrete steps: whole sections are imitated from the teacher.

An evident way of skirting problems in the identification of dance is to have recourse to Japanese concepts. This seems legitimate in terms of the anthropological definitions already mentioned, as all Japanese dance identified as such by participants would fall within the general definition of dance outlined above. The two basic terms used for dance in Japan are mai (舞) and odori (踊り), with an apparent distinction between the two along the lines of classical versus folk, a freer versus more regular rhythmic structure, slow versus quick tempo, gliding rather than leaping, and movements by the upper rather than the lower half of the body. However, in practice the distinction is less clear, with considerable overlap, as in *kagura*,[2] and realignment, as in the legitimation of classical dance. While dance in *nō* is recognized as *mai*, the classical status of *nihon buyō* is a more recent achievement.

Labels such as 'classical' and 'traditional', which are carefully distinguished for dance in India, are not clearly differentiated for Japanese dance. A variety of epithets is applied to different types of dance, and the labels may lack demarcation in terms of more abstract criteria, but because discussion of dance in Japan tends to remain on the particular level, overlap is not noticed or not deemed significant: it is just considered important to know the discrete category into which the dance form fits. Attempts at abstract systematization of dance forms are thus rare in Japan. One such attempt, made by Honda (n.d.), presents a typology that is claimed to be constructed in terms of the motive for dancing: in practice the classification appears to be based on several implicit criteria, including (in addition to motive) the types of movement and props used, the number of participants, the degree of refinement and status, and whether native Japanese or of foreign origin.

Some Japanese dance terms are of rather recent origin, for example *nihon buyō*. This means literally 'Japanese dance', and refers to *kabuki* dance and the styles of dance derived therefrom, including the classical dances performed by *maiko* (dancing-girls) of Kyoto, and more austere and sophisticated forms such as *zashiki mai* and *jiuta mai* that were originally developed to be performed on *tatami* mats in restricted space, and are less spectacular and more restrained than *kabuki* dance. The term *nihon buyō* was coined only in the Meiji era, when contact with the West brought the need to distinguish Japanese dance from Western dance (*seiyō buyō*). Western-style dance performed in Japan today tends to be called *dansu*, and a sharp distinction is made between this and Japanese dance categories.[3]

The difficulty of deciding what constitutes dance in Japan arises, as already mentioned, partly because dance is so often a component of a wider cultural performance. This difficulty brings with it certain advantages, however: dance, if integrated with other elements of Japanese culture, is likely to be a more significant indicator of key cultural characteristics, and thus can be treated as a cultural document.

PERFORMANCES AS CULTURAL DOCUMENTS

Interpreting cultural documents is an essential feature of the construction of cultural models. Singer advocates a focus on dance and other 'cultural performances' as 'the elementary constituents of the culture and the ultimate units of observation' (1972: 71). Geertz takes up this concept of cultural performances in his research in Indonesia, and develops the notion of cultural document and the metaphor of a manuscript to apply to a whole range of verbal and non-verbal behaviour which the anthropologist tries to interpret: culture is seen as an acted document, and its interpretation is 'like trying to read (in the sense of "construct a reading of") a manuscript – foreign, faded, full of ellipses, incoherences, suspicious emendations and tendentious commentaries, but written not in conventionalized graphs of sound but in transient examples of shaped behaviour' (1975: 10). A further argument for using non-verbal performances as cultural documents is that one is less likely to take the text out of context:[4] with a performance it is less easy to overlook contextual aspects, such as where and when it takes place, by whom and for whom.

Along with social anthropologists, sociologists too have emphasized the importance of non-verbal documents for the study of the wider culture. An early advocate of this approach was Karl Mannheim, who suggested the documentary interpretation of cultural objectifications as a means of understanding the '*Weltanschauung*, the global outlook behind these objectifications' (1952: 42). He also argued that the most revealing documents, those richest in documentary meaning for the interpretation of *Weltanschauung*, would be a-theoretical (ibid.: 38). This approach has gained prominence in cultural studies, notably in the work on youth subcultures carried out in the tradition of the Centre for Contemporary Cultural Studies at Birmingham, where the emphasis is on 'reading' or decoding non-verbal documents such as dress, music and movement, whose stylistic features may be related to the values and social location of the subcultures.[5] Non-verbal documents could be argued to be particularly appropriate for the study of Japan where, even in speech, the *how*, the style or manner of communication, may be more significant than the *what*, the manifest content. The meaning is to be found in the wrapping (Hendry 1993: 64–5).

Dance then, as a non-verbal cultural performance, may provide documentary evidence of more general cultural characteristics, especially where, as in Japan, it is integrated with other cultural forms. From a Western standpoint, it would be easy to assume a sharp division between the religious and aesthetic spheres, but in Japan it is worth remembering Geertz's suggestion that the line between 'religious performances and artistic, or even political, ones is often not so easy to draw in practice, for, like social forms, symbolic forms can serve multiple purposes' (1975: 113). Singer similarly notes the mistake of assuming that artistic performances represent 'a secular, aesthetic culture distinct from the ritual and religious culture' (1972: 148). Thus Japanese dance may integrate aesthetic and religious orientations, as in *kagura*, by definition, and *bugaku*, with its dual role as artistic entertainment and sacred ritual (Inoura and Kawatake 1981: 35). Most folk dance in Japan has religious origins, and retains religious significance, especially in rural areas; in urban areas the religious aspect may be less apparent or less well integrated.[6] Along with the dance itself, the occasion of performance has traditionally defied categorization as exclusively religious or artistic: for example, *matsuri* (festivals) tend to combine entertainment and religious functions (see Figure 17.1), as may performers.[7]

Apart from integrating religious and aesthetic orientations, dance by its very nature integrates different art forms or acts as a link between them or focus for them, as in the dramatic, musical and costume-design aspects of dance performance.[8] In so far as dance acts in this way as a point of integration for different art forms, it may provide a useful document of aesthetic values common to several Japanese arts. Their spatial and temporal aspects in particular may be indicated by dance, given that it involves, as noted above, the organization of movement in space and time. The following discussion will thus deal in turn with spatial and temporal aspects of dance performance.

SPATIAL ASPECTS OF PERFORMANCE

Two recurring spatial emphases are common to many Japanese dance performances: rather static pictorial presentation, and asymmetrical posture.

(i) Pictorial presentation

In much Japanese dance, the visual aspect predominates: aural and kinetic senses are less intensely called upon in the dance perception. Even in *kabuki*, where narrative is a major component, it is said that visual presentation is considered more important than the words (Kawatake 1981). In *kabuki* and many forms of *nihon buyō* the spectacular may thus be the main focus of attention, with gorgeous costumes (and costume changes) being a principal feature, together with characteristic make-up and wigs, magnificent scenery and frequent use of special effects. At public performances audience appreciation of these spectacular aspects is particularly noticeable.

Figure 17.1 Komachi odori danced at the *tanabata* festival. Photograph courtesy of James Valentine

Attention to costume may thus outweigh interest in dance movements. While this may be the case even in folk dance, it is more likely in staged folk dance (increasingly common in urban areas), where dances are deliberately selected because of their visual impact on stage, as in the use of impressive costumes, masks or props, or where dances are adapted to enhance the spectacular aspect. Apart from the attraction of strange or lavish costumes, striking dance formation patterns are often used in folk dance to add to the visual effect. Such dance formations are especially likely where each individual's movements are limited, for example where leg movements are simple and a fan or parasol is held.

These points – the attraction of extravagant costumes and the emphasis on dance formations where individual dance movements are limited – seem equally applicable to a famous example of contemporary youth dance in Japan: the Takenoko-zoku (bamboo-shoot tribe). Practice and performance of dance and music can be seen each Sunday on a pedestrianized urban highway by Yoyogi

Figure 17.2 Rock 'n' roll at Harajuku: youths dancing in a circle. Photograph courtesy of James Valentine

Park at Harajuku in Tokyo. In the early 1980s two dance styles were in evidence at Harajuku: one was performed by the Takenoko-zoku, who attracted the most attention from spectators and the media, and the other was based on 1950s' rock-'n'roll (see Figure 17.2): dancers of this latter style could still be seen at Harajuku in the 1990s, but in fewer numbers, having given way to amateur rock bands.

The dance movements of the Takenoko-zoku consisted mostly of gentle and uncomplicated arm movements while standing in a circle. Leg movements tended to be confined to a few steps forward towards the centre of the circle, or turning on the spot, or knee-bending in time with the beat. Both participants and spectators paid more attention to clothing and make-up than to dance, so that the dance seemed to be a pretext for exhibition and spectacle. Adjustment of costume and make-up preoccupied participants for much of the time, and the youth magazines that frequently reported the happenings at Harajuku focused on the fashion aspect, which in 1981 included the long colourful robes and trouser-suits described as Chinese style.

Emphasis on the visual aspect is not confined to contemporary dance, folk dance and *nihon buyō*, but may also be noted in current performances of ancient dance. One of the main features of *bugaku* is its colourful costumes. *Gigaku*, though described as a 'comical dance and ballad drama',[9] has now become primarily a spectacular procession, which would link it with many of the *matsuri* processions that combine historical re-enactment with costume spectacle to provide a pageant well suited to photographic recording. In these events, indeed, as in some folk dance performances, posing in costume for photographs may seem more significant than any dance or processional movement. Such precedence given to the camera may indicate that an emphasis on the visual extends beyond the arts understood in a narrow sense. A further example would be the observations often made on the importance of visual presentation in a Japanese meal and in gift-giving: again there is the suggestion that how one presents, the visual style of presentation, is as significant as the content of one's offerings.[10]

It may be noted that in some of the dance forms already mentioned there is an emphasis not just on the visual aspect, but on periodically static presentation, as in posing in dance costume. Striking a pose may indeed be an integral part of the dance performance, most famously in the *mie* in *kabuki*, in which the action is frozen in a theatrical pose that condenses the emotional expression. Not surprisingly, the use of a static pose is also a characteristic feature of *nihon buyō* more generally. In some of the *maiko* dances (and even some folk dances) presented at festivals such as Gion Matsuri, whole sequences may be made up of successive poses reminiscent of semaphore. In *kabuki* and *nihon buyō*, posing often takes the form of a spectacular tableau wherein several dancers strike poses in gorgeous costumes amidst stunning scenery or visual effects.[11]

That such periodically static presentations are an important part of *kabuki* and *nihon buyō* is confirmed by Kawatake (1981), noting that the ideal is for every moment on the stage to resemble a beautiful painting. Within such tableaux a characteristic feature of individual and group poses is asymmetry, which constitutes the second spatial feature notable in many Japanese dance presentations.

(ii) Asymmetry

Asymmetry is especially apparent in *nihon buyō*: in some performances individual poses are reminiscent of the curving asymmetry of Japanese flower arrangements,[12] suggesting a further link between some Japanese dance forms and the visual arts more widely, including painting and gardening.

Asymmetrical posture may also be found in some folk dance, especially where learnt by middle-aged urban women as a hobby, or by young girls for public presentation at a major festival. In more traditional folk dance, however, most dance movements involve symmetrical repetitions, such as a step with one leg repeated by the other, or arm movements to one side and then likewise to the other. Such symmetry is also characteristic of the ancient *bugaku* dance, and suggests caution in generalizing about the degree of asymmetry in Japanese dance. Similar aesthetic divisions can be seen in the temporal aspects of Japanese dance.

TEMPORAL ASPECTS OF PERFORMANCE

The first temporal aspect to be discussed parallels asymmetry of posture: in classical Japanese dance one might refer to asymmetry of rhythm, in the sense of the avoidance of strict rhythm, the extensive use of melisma, and the general emphasis on movement flow in contrast to following a regular metric beat.

(i) Avoidance of strict rhythm

It is perhaps significant that 'rhythm' is a rare concept in Japanese, whether in the term *onritsu* used for poetry and music, or *ritsudō* for dance: when the concept is needed the imported word *rizumu* is usually employed.[13] *Nihon buyō* in particular exhibits relative freedom from rhythmic constraints, and is thereby able both to incorporate longer set poses (as already mentioned) and to flow more smoothly, thus more effectively expressing elegance, refinement and controlled emotion. Lack of fixed rhythm not only allows the flow to be interrupted by poses, but also facilitates variations in speed as an expressive device, as where faster movement is used to indicate passionate feelings. Flow in the temporal sense of uninterrupted movement is often combined in *nihon buyō* with movements suggesting spatial flow, as of a stream: for example, a fan may be manipulated in a smooth undulating fashion like gently flowing water.

Not all Japanese dance flows in this way: avoidance of strict rhythm seems to be a characteristic of *nihon buyō* rather than of folk dance, and rhythm may thus be a way in which *mai* and *odori* are distinguished. Fujii[14] argues for the inclusion of *nihon buyō* in the *mai* category, largely because of its freer, less clearly defined and regulated rhythm. He sees *mai* as being less concerned with metric beat and more varied in the speed and frequency of movement in relation to any discernible beat. In contrast *odori*, primarily folk dance (*minzoku buyō*), tends to involve a simple and direct relationship of each movement to regular musical beat. Most folk dance is indeed framed within a strict and simple rhythmic structure appropriate to the jaunty style that characterizes, for example, much of *bon odori*, that is danced at the time of the *bon* summer festival when ancestral spirits return to their families. The distinction between *mai* and *odori* is less easy to uphold in relation to *kagura*, where the musical rhythm may be fast and regular, yet the dance may still avoid a strict movement-to-beat regularity, and may at times make use of continuous twirling movements.

Modern dance in the West often demonstrates free flow rather than strict rhythm. In Japan this means that *modan dansu* is able more readily to borrow or blend traditional dance styles, especially the classical emphasis on slowly flowing movement. The classical styles of *nō* and *nihon buyō* may thus lend themselves with surprising ease to an adaptation to or synthesis with *modan dansu*, as certain elements are already held in common: in comparison with classical ballet, there is less emphasis on plot development, less emphasis on technical brilliance, and greater flow and serenity of movement rather than discrete steps rapidly executed. These characteristics, and the influence of Japanese dance traditions, are also apparent in another form of contemporary Japanese dance: *butō.*

Butō is an avant-garde dance form that has its origins in the dancers Hijikata Tatsumi and Ōno Kazuo, who collaborated in 1959 and thereafter developed distinct styles of *butō* (Kuniyoshi 1985). In contrast to the rhythm and balance of ballet, *butō* emphasizes discontinuity and imbalance, bends the body into strange and awkward postures, and avoids the imposition of fixed technique. Yet *butō* demonstrates certain continuities with classical Japanese dance: slowly flowing ground-related movement, asymmetry of poses and avoidance of strict rhythm. Without fixed rhythm, the flow of movement is readily suspended by statuesque or static presentation, which has already been noted in the use of the pause that is a feature of other forms of Japanese dance.

(ii) The pause

As we have seen in considering the periodically static presentation in Japanese dance poses, the pause (*ma* 間) is a device that extends beyond classical dance (where most notably it provides the opportunity for the *mie* in *kabuki*), and may be found to a greater or lesser extent in all Japanese dance forms.[15]

In folk dance the pause, as an aesthetic device to heighten effect, is most evident in the staged folk dance that emphasizes the spectacular, and in recently choreographed folk dance. In performances of such dance (no longer strictly 'folk' yet still referred to as *minzoku buyō*) a common feature is for each movement to the beat to be followed by a regular pause to hold a pose. Such poses, held at intervals throughout, are likely to be sustained for a longer period in a concluding tableau. Recently choreographed folk dance, in particular, is likely to resemble *nihon buyō* in this and other respects.

Regular interruption of movement to strike a pose is even a feature of the rock'n'roll dancing at Harajuku: the youths dancing in this style would often display a succession of poses to the beat of the music, to a greater extent than was apparent in the original American style.

The temporal aspects characteristic of Japanese classical dance – flow relatively unconstrained by regular metric beat yet interrupted by occasional pauses – might be taken as a document of a more general Japanese orientation to time. It has often been remarked that the Japanese traditional arts focus upon the fleeting moment, and this has sometimes been interpreted in terms of a high evaluation of transient phenomena. This, however, is to confuse the acknowledgement of transience with its positive evaluation: on closer analysis, temporal aspects of Japanese dance suggest a more complex attitude towards the passing of time. Japanese concern with the fleeting moment is often concern *about*, and regret for, the passing show: its fleeting aspect is regarded not only as especially worthy of attention and as contributing to its beauty, but also as a cause for sorrow. The acknowledgement of transience in Japanese poetry, for example, is often accompanied by a sense of melancholy concerning the passing of the seasons and the brevity of human and other life. Furthermore, the recognition of transience should not be taken to imply the lack of desire for permanence:[16] one may at the same time appreciate transient phenomena and yet wish to make them, or one's experience of them, last as long as possible. In the case of Japanese dance, the fleeting moment may be extended to savour it at length. A brief episode may be dwelt upon in the flow of slowly developing movements, or the moment may even be frozen, as seen most obviously in the *mie* and less dramatically in the poses struck where pauses intersperse Japanese dance forms, both classical and non-classical.

DOCUMENTARY INTERPRETATION AND THE COMPARTMENTALIZATION OF PERFORMANCE

Although aspects of Japanese dance styles may be considered to indicate more general Japanese aesthetic concerns, or even wider Japanese orientations beyond the confines of the arts, we have already seen that Japanese dance forms do not always provide consistent documentary evidence for generalization. Discrepancies on the degree of symmetry, and on the extent of regularity in rhythmic structure and of employment of the aesthetic pause, all counsel caution in the interpretation of Japanese dance as a cultural document. We may attempt to account for discrepancies in the characteristics of Japanese dance forms by bearing in mind several interrelated factors that contribute to the differentiation of Japanese dance.

(i) Preservation

In Japan there is great concern to preserve certain performance styles from the past, constituting a kind of living museum. *Bugaku* provides a good example of the retention of past dance forms. *Bugaku* (literally 'dance music') is the dance part of *gagaku* (literally 'refined music'), the ancient court music and dance of Japan. Originating in dances mainly introduced from the Asian continent from the seventh century onwards, *bugaku* was codified at the height of its social significance at the Heian court. Thereafter its history is primarily one of preservation (Wolz 1971: 10), though with significant loss of individual dances (Inoura and Kawatake 1981: 34). What remains is fixed in form, preserved by a few families at the Imperial court. The foreign and ancient derivation of *bugaku*, with its history of preservation, renders its use as a document of modern Japanese culture problematic. More generally this warns us not to assume that the arts are culturally integrated in Japan: they may in some cases be culturally compartmentalized, thus being of limited value as documents of the wider culture. Kimura[17] contends that classical dance is especially likely to be compartmentalized in this way, through preservation of past forms, accompaniment in old linguistic styles, and use of complicated vocabulary of gestures. Folk dance, he suggests, is more integrated with its local context, and is thus more subject to alteration with changes in lifestyle.

(ii) Legitimation and codification

Classical Japanese dance, legitimated by a cultural elite, emphasizes the traditional aesthetics of refinement (*miyabi*), including a restrained elegance that since the Heian court has been seen as a criterion of elite art (Varley 1974: 43).

The predominance of such aesthetics has meant that when subsequent dance forms have aspired to legitimate status as high or classical art, they either have had to be already in compliance with the traditional canons of elite taste, or have had to adapt to these canons through stylistic modification. The complex codes of elite tradition preclude a simple reading of dance as a cultural document. While complexity of aesthetic codes is a characteristic of elite art in Japan, as in most societies, popularity, often resting on simplicity of codes, is inversely correlated with legitimacy. Folk dance functions through more readily accessible codes of comprehension, and indeed of performance. Where transmission of the form is more open, less deliberately organized and less the prerogative of experts guaranteeing legitimacy, the codes of performance will tend to be characterized by ease of cultural access and of mnemonic retention: symmetrical dance movements to regular beat satisfy both these requirements for simplicity. Here one should avoid reading too much into stylistic features which derive from the practical needs of transmission rather than from the expression of cultural values.

(iii) Access and exclusion

Questions of access already arise when considering legitimacy and codes. Complexity of codes may limit *cultural* access in terms of competence (interpretation) and performance. Whereas elaborated codes 'require an audience experienced in decoding, a subculture of taste defined by its decoding ability' (Fiske and Hartley 1993: 46), more restricted codes allow wider participation. Apart from barriers to cultural access, *social* access may be limited to those occupying a particular status. Certain dance forms thus become social preserves, as for example in exclusive rights to performance by men: this will be considered in the discussion of gender stratification. Exclusive participation may be further upheld through barriers to material access. This is most obvious in the costs incurred in *nihon buyō*, said to be the world's most expensive art form to learn (Havens 1982: 227).

Differential access to various dance forms reminds us that they may be too exclusive to constitute a reliable document of the wider culture. Special care must be taken not to overgeneralize from examples of elite dance forms: the limited social context of their significance must be borne in mind. Dance forms may be compartmentalized rather than integrated with the life of most members of the society. Nevertheless, although degrees of preservation, legitimation and codification, access and exclusion may differentiate Japanese dance, hindering or at least complicating the attempt to treat dance as a cultural document, it should be noted that the divisions within Japanese dance, and the processes contributing to such differentiation, may themselves be indicative of wider structures and processes in Japanese society. Compartmentalization can itself act as a document.[18]

To treat such organizational features of dance as documenting the wider society is to bridge the normal division between documentary-interpretative and organizational-institutional approaches to the social scientific study of the arts.

Viewing art as a social institution is often contrasted with an interpretative approach to art as a cultural document: the two alternatives may even be taken to be irreconcilable. Yet, as already noted, features of dance organization involved in the compartmentalization of dance must be taken into account when attempting to generalize on a performance's social and cultural significance, and such organizational features may themselves function as documents, in that they are both derivative and indicative of the wider social structure (Valentine 1982: 17). Rather than giving a general account of Japanese dance organization and its documentary significance, the focus here will be on those organizational aspects which augment the documentary evidence from stylistic features, whether spatial or temporal.[19]

PERFORMING SOCIAL ORGANIZATION

Before turning to certain wider aspects of Japanese social organization documented by both dance organization and spatial aspects of dance style, it is worth following up the theme of Japanese attitudes to time, and especially transience, as documented by *temporal* aspects of Japanese dance style.

The acknowledgement of transience in Japanese dance style, along with the attempt to prolong or preserve the moment, is paralleled in the organization of Japanese dance by the attempt to fix the transient through institutional conventions and traditions. The passing beauty of a Japanese dance performance, and the common thematic focus of the fleeting moment, are held within an enduring social network of conventions and their supporting human relationships, as in the *iemoto* system that organizes the transmission of classical dance: the system persists despite the transience of the individual *iemoto*'s life. The artist of genius with no followers, a unique and new bloom destined to vanish after brief glory, is not a characteristic of Japanese aesthetic organization, which typically emphasizes the continuing family line.

A further, though arguably far-fetched, example of the attempt to prolong or circumvent transience might be seen in the honouring of a renowned performer as a 'living national treasure' (*ningen kokuhō*).[20] This might be interpreted simply as indicating a special Japanese conception of treasure: unlike the Western notion, which refers to relatively permanent objects, a Japanese perspective might be construed as placing highest value on the impermanent. I would favour an alternative interpretation, according to which the bestowal of the title 'treasure' on a living human being is an attempt to render as permanent as possible the impermanent: to give the label 'worthy of careful preservation' to that which will inevitably perish.

It is not just the carriers of the conventions who are, at least through their descendants, enduring: the conventions themselves may be preserved through codification, with rigid and detailed rules ensuring continuity over the centuries. This is most obvious in the oldest forms of classical dance, such as *bugaku* and *nō*, but is also evident in *nihon buyō* and *kabuki*, where prescribed forms or models (*kata*) are handed down through the *iemoto* system.[21] It is found more widely in

Japanese arts, for instance in tea ceremony, where the *kata* are strictly observed by practitioners under the ultimate authority of the *iemoto* (Kumakura 1981: 5). Thus, while the art itself, or what it represents, may be transient, the organization within which it is transmitted and presented is hedged around by strict and enduring conventions. The same ambivalent attitude to transience may thus be seen in the organizational as in the stylistic features of Japanese dance.

In looking at the *spatial* aspects of Japanese dance, certain features, such as static visual presentation and asymmetry, were seen to be characteristic of a wider or narrower range of the Japanese arts. Spatial aspects of style may, however, along with modes of organization of Japanese dance, document characteristics of wider social organization in Japan, most clearly in the emphasis on collectivity and in restrictions on women.

In the organization of Japanese dance the collective nature of transmission and performance is especially noteworthy in folk dance. This in itself is hardly unexpected: a collective emphasis is probably characteristic of folk dance in most societies. Stylistic features may here be more revealing: undifferentiated collective space may be arranged through dancing in a large circle, as so often in *bon odori*. More surprisingly, this is also found in contemporary youth dance, as in Harajuku, where the Takenoko-zoku dancers would form a large circle, making hand or arm gestures reminiscent of *te odori* (hand/arm dance), as seen for instance in Hachijōjima folk dance. However, in Harajuku, as indeed in some folk dance, collective space has its contrast: the dance would be led from the centre by a few individuals, notably older and male, unlike the majority of those in the circle. In rock'n'roll, the other style danced at Harajuku, the organization of dance transmission is collective (and, by girls especially, in a circle), and while there is more room for individuality and improvisation in performance, even here the majority of the dancing is in groups. This may indicate the adaptation of an American style to a more collective Japanese orientation.

The most striking example of Japanese adaptation of a Western style in this way may be seen in *modan dansu*. Individualistic expression is greatly outweighed by patterns of group formation, though sometimes a collective shape is contrasted with a lone individual, who may be an older dancer and bear the family name of the dance school. Spatial patterns reproduce patterns of hierarchy in the dance organization and beyond.

The adaptation of modern dance in Japan thus involves not merely an emphasis on collectivity, on group formations, but also the creation of certain dance roles for the less nimble older performer. These roles, emphasizing subtlety and grace rather than agility and brilliance, favour length of experience over youthful vigour, thus preserving the prestige and authority of the older dancer, and ensuring the survival of a traditional principle of Japanese social organization whereby status is conferred by age.

Patterns of social stratification are thus reproduced in dance style and organization. Stratification by gender is documented in a similar way. In dance organization this can be seen in terms of exclusion and authority. While some *kagura* dances are reserved for *miko* (shrine maidens), in certain other religious dances, such as *rokusai nenbutsu odori*, women are excluded for reasons of ritual impurity. In some cases only young boys are qualified to dance, by virtue of their special purity prior to their *genpuku*, the ritual attainment of adulthood. *Bugaku* and *kabuki* have also traditionally excluded women from public performance, thus denying women an important means of claiming professional legitimacy in these styles. This is especially significant in *nihon buyō*: female *nihon buyō* dancers are at an inevitable disadvantage where some of their male colleagues can demonstrate their authenticity in the male preserve of *kabuki*. Although most of the students of *nihon buyō* are women, progression up the pyramid of the dance school towards the *iemoto* reveals an increase in the proportion of men. As we have seen, such a pattern is not confined to classical dance: young women were observed to constitute the great majority of dancers among the Takenoko-zoku, with their leaders and teachers tending to be male.

Gender differentiation is further documented by the spatial aspects of Japanese dance style, most obviously in *nihon buyō*. Here the style depends of course on the role danced, not on the actual sex of the dancer: whether the dancer be male or female s/he may perform both feminine and masculine dance roles, though feminine dance roles are more popular and considered to be more fundamental to the practice of this dance form.[22]

The feminine style in *nihon buyō* emphasizes constraint and humility: movements are directed downwards, backwards and especially inwards. A shy or coy impression is conveyed with eyes downcast. Retreating from the front of the stage the dancer will tend to make inward-directed movements. The direction inwards is emphasized by protective movements against the outer world: the arm, or a prop such as a fan or parasol, may be held up in front of the performer as a shield from public attention and embarrassment, a common theme of the dance. Where props are held and gently waved, they tend eventually to close in again on the body. Movements of legs and feet are dainty and again inward-turning: this restraint may be seen as conditioned by female costumes, yet costume can itself be viewed as a further document. Costume is indeed an important part of *nihon buyō* performance (as already noted above), and the long sleeves characteristically worn for female dance roles are used to reinforce the image of inwardness and passivity: the sleeves may be closed in on the body like a screen, and they extend the slack passivity of the gently swaying arm, giving an impression of elegance and frailty.

In contrast, male roles in *nihon buyō* suggest preparedness for action, rather than withdrawal from action into an elegant pose to be appreciated by others. Arm movements are firmer and more outward-directed; the hand may be held in a fist or a rigid open-palm position. The body commonly stands stiffly upright rather than curved and swaying. Leg movements are much wider, and feet are turned outwards.

In *nihon buyō* the delimited physical space drawn by women's movements symbolizes restricted cultural space.[23] Women's retreat into private space here is not just a model *of* women's social role in exaggerated form: it also acts as a model *for* women, reinforcing social restraint and self-control. Geertz argues that cultural patterns have this intrinsic double aspect, as both models *of* and models *for* reality: 'they give meaning, that is, objective conceptual form, to social and psychological reality by shaping themselves to it and by shaping it to themselves' (1975: 93). Dance may thus provide not only a model that performs (stands for, embodies, enacts) social organization and cultural values, but also a model that through performance instructs, induces and reproduces further enactment beyond its compartmentalized sphere.[24] Indeed, *nihon buyō* may be recommended for and undertaken by women precisely for its corrective and refining qualities, to engender restraint and control of both body and emotions for the sake of an elegant humility. Thus, *nihon buyō* is a favoured amateur accomplishment amongst women of a certain social status: not the highest (as this dance form still suffers from its association with the popular and morally dubious *kabuki* of former times) and not of course amongst poorer women who cannot afford the expenses.

Although *nihon buyō* provides the clearest example of stylistic differentiation by gender, the performance of gender may be found in almost all Japanese dance, involving many of the elements noted above. For example both *bugaku* (danced only by men) and male roles in folk dance are characterized by widely spaced leg movements, while leg and foot movements in female folk dance are inward-directed: again costume restrictions must be taken into account. Staged folk dance also tends to have inward-directed arm movements for women as in *nihon buyō*, and male and female dance styles remain sharply contrasted.[25]

In contemporary youth dance, stylistic differentiation by gender is no less in evidence. This is the case even where the exemplary models are treated as negative rather than positive, counter-models or models *against* (see figure 17.3) rather than models *for*, contra-cultural examples of ritualized rebellion (Littleton 1987), that none the less reveal conformity to gender conventions (Valentine 1997). In Harajuku, among the rock'n'roll dancers there is a clear gender distinction in movement, the feminine style being more restrained and the masculine style more ambitious and dramatic: women here largely focus on hand/arm movements while men tend to dance with the whole body. This latter contrast could also be seen between the circle of Takenoko-zoku dancers, largely female, and the few male dancers in the centre of the circle. Again the dancers act as models for the performance of gender beyond the sphere of dance.

More plausible counter-models are provided by *butō*. *Butō* presents challenges to rationality, conventional aesthetics and social norms: it portrays eroticism and violence, the embarrassing and the ugly, wasteland and alien worlds. Some *butō* performers work with disabled people and in mental hospitals, appropriating unconventional movements for the dance. The white face paint used in *kabuki* is often used over almost naked bodies in *butō*. Visual images are paramount, typically portraying agony and ecstasy, distortion and the grotesque.[26] There is exploration of the boundaries between life and death, human and animal, male and female (Valentine 1994: 135). Dwelling on these boundaries, however, confirms their significance: the juxtaposition of multiple transgressions may ironically, in Durkheimian style, reinforce the normality operative beyond the compartmentalized sphere of art.

Figure 17.3 A young man supervises the dancing at Harajuku. Photograph courtesy of
James Valentine

Other forms of contemporary dance are manifestly less challenging to
convention, especially with respect to gender. In *modan dansu*, classes are usually
directed towards women, with appropriate invitations to new students: for
example, 'modern dance is now awaiting the will and enthusiasm of young to
middle-aged women who like to live creatively'.[27] This means that modern dance
from the West is often adapted, not only to a more collective orientation as noted
above, but also to what are assumed to be natural female styles and capacities.
Where men participate in *modan dansu* they tend to dance apart from the group,
or to play less passively appealing roles and to include more active leaping
movements in their dance. This form of gender differentiation, however, is also
typical of much modern dance in the West, warning us against the temptation to

characterize Japan in isolation. Indeed certain models of Japanese culture that appear to be constructed in isolation turn out to be set up in implicit opposition, as uniquely other to Western models.[28] Such cultural models are reciprocally constructed, revolving around each other.

THE SPIRAL DANCE OF MODELS

The preceding analysis has concentrated on how spatial and temporal aspects of Japanese dance style may, along with organizational features of practice and performance, document wider characteristics of Japanese culture and society. There remains however the question of how researchers know how to read these documents, and whether they are 'reading in' what they already suspect is there from a wider knowledge of the culture and its formulation in interpretative models. These are significant methodological problems. The first revolves around dance codes and their interpretation. It is very easy to make gross errors here: for example, where a Japanese performance operates with a complex code for the expression of emotion, as in *nō*, outsiders may interpret according to the only code at their disposal which seems to fit, categorizing the movements as 'abstract dance'.[29] Similarly, in *nihon buyō* a common mistake of non-Japanese is to view the dance as a freely flowing improvisation, as they are unaware of the constraints of a complex stylistic code and of the social organization of its transmission through strict imitation of the teacher.

The only solution to this problem of unfamiliar codes is the usual one of increasing familiarity, whilst retaining maximum possible awareness of one's own preconceptions, thus remaining open but without the dishonest and unworkable assumption of a blank mind. This honest but messy solution is the one advocated by hermeneutics: a circular movement, perhaps better represented as a reflexive spiral, between researcher and object of interpretation, with awareness of one's own viewpoints but openness to their transformation through progressive involvement with the 'text', thus changing self and interpreted object in a constant interaction conceived as dialectical or as a hermeneutic circle.[30]

A further version of this circle underlies the problem and solution involved in relating a document to its wider cultural context.[31] The difficulty consists in finding a starting-point for the interpretative process, and in ascertaining how much is being read into the part from knowledge of the whole. Again the honest answer recognizes the circularity of this process: document and culture have to be viewed in relation to each other. Models of performance and of the wider culture are dialectically constructed. The one that acts as starting-point will and should be reinterpreted in the light of the other, and so on in a developing spiral of interpretation of part and whole. Where discrepancies block the smooth progression of this spiral, they do not have to be seen as unfortunate and annoying hitches: first, they indicate a degree of openness whereby not all the evidence is being forced into a preconceived mould; and second, they can reveal significant divisions within the culture. Such divisions are not always sufficiently acknowledged by approaches that emphasize 'totality' of interpretation:[32] not only may the whole be compartmentalized into cultural divisions, but the part, the particular range of documents to be interpreted, may be internally differentiated (as in diverse dance forms), which may prevent generalization to a 'whole' culture, and yet reveal structural divisions and their generative processes extending beyond the part itself. Thus, while recognizing the doubly circular process of research into cultural documents, one must avoid the assumption of homogeneity whether in culture or document, whole or part.

Therefore, in the case of Japanese dance, generalization cannot be extended unequivocally to the whole culture: conclusions may instead be drawn on different levels of generality. On the more specific level, certain spatial and temporal aspects of Japanese dance were seen to have links with other Japanese arts, for example in the emphasis on asymmetry: here the danger of overgeneralization is clear, as not even all dance in Japan manifests such qualities. Certain orientations, however, appear to extend beyond what is normally conceived as the arts to a wider aesthetic preference, as in the emphasis on visual presentation, often in rather static form.

On a broader level, some of the orientations apparent in dance were seen to indicate more general orientations in Japanese culture, extending well beyond the aesthetic sphere. This is the case with the attitude to time in Japanese dance, combining acknowledgement of transience with the desire to prolong or freeze the passing moment. This attitude to time was found to be further documented by features of Japanese dance organization. Similarly, spatial aspects of Japanese dance style, when seen in conjunction with Japanese dance organization, document wider social structural principles, such as collective participation and stratification by age and gender.

This twofold reading of dance, in both stylistic and organizational terms, draws on a pair of theoretical approaches that are all too often disconnected in the social scientific study of the arts: art as a cultural document versus art as a social institution. When organizational features are themselves read interpretatively as documents, along with the styles they organize, this not only brings the benefit of further documentary evidence, but begins to break down the artificial division between institutional and interpretative approaches.

Interpretations themselves become institutionally effective: performance that appears to be a model *of* social reality turns out to act as a model *for* social reproduction. Furthermore, performing models, practically engaged in the dialectical process of (re)presentation and (re)production, are themselves interpreted in terms of researchers' models that develop through the doubly dialectical construction of whole and part, and of text and self. This double dialectic, involving two versions of the hermeneutic circle (better conceived as spiral), is not to be confused with the double (better conceived as multiple) hermeneutic of social scientific constructs of constructs. Schutz recognized that social scientists form model constructs of the constructs of everyday actors (1973: 6, 44). Giddens sees this as involving the social sciences in a double hermeneutic: 'Sociological knowledge spirals in and out of the universe of social life, reconstructing both itself and that universe as an integral part of that process' (1990: 15–16). Double may be an underestimation. When proceeding to the sociology of sociology, further hermeneutic reconstruction appears unavoidable (Alexander 1994: 182). Interpreters are inevitably caught up in the construction of models of models of models in recursive and reflexive fashion. Schehr, in his discussion of Proust, observes multiple orders of interpretation of interpretation as self-reflexive acts: a performance that 'interprets' a role, a narrative interpretation that undercuts the theatricality of the performance while proposing itself 'as the model of the revelation of truth' (1995: 50), and a critic's interpretation of the narrator's own acts of interpretation (ibid.: 39). The characterization of interpretation itself, as in the hermeneutic 'circle' of the analysis of 'texts' (Hekman 1986: 141), has to make use of models. Using spatial metaphors to plot temporal advance, the construction of models can be envisaged as moving beyond confirmatory circles to progressive spirals. Dance itself can supply a model of interpretation here: a spiral dance, such as that described by Starhawk (1989: 246–7), involves the interactive formation of alternating outward and inward spirals, extensive and intensive progression, unravelling and drawing together.

NOTES

* This paper is based on fieldwork in Japan during eight months from January to August 1981. Further fieldwork was carried out during a subsequent visit of four months in 1990. I am most grateful to the British Academy and the Japan Society for the Promotion of Science for supporting this research under the terms of their Exchange Agreement. I should also like to express my gratitude to the Bukkyō Bunka Kenkyūsho of Ryūkoku University and the Nihon Bunka Kenkyūsho of Kokugakuin University for accepting me as Visiting Research Fellow in 1981, and to Waseda University for accepting me as Exchange Researcher in 1990.

1 These aspects are especially emphasized in the definitions provided by Hanna (1979: 19) and Royce (1977: 8). Transcendence of utility is also stressed by Kurath (1960: 234) and Lange (1975: 57). Spencer argues against confining dance to non-utilitarian patterned movement, as dance often merges into other performances and wider contexts (1985: 1–2). As we shall see, the wider involvement of dance extends its significance as a cultural document.

2 Kagura (神楽), written with the *kanji* for god and music, refers to music and dance performed for the gods, and includes many popular festive dances as well as more formal ritual dances performed by Shinto priests or *miko* (shrine maidens).

3 The dance forms I observed included those loosely categorized as classical (*gigaku*, *bugaku*, *nō* and *nihon buyō*), *kagura* and several types of folk dance (*minzoku buyō*, including *dengaku*, *nenbutsu odori* and *bon odori*, along with particular dances of wide renown such as *shishi mai*, *sagi mai*, *awa odori*, *komachi odori* and *hanagasa odori*), and contemporary dance (including *butō*, the Takenoko-zoku and rock'n'roll dancers at Harajuku, and Western-style contemporary art dance that is designated *modan dansu*). Further details of dance classification can be found in Valentine (1994). In addition to observation of dance forms, interviews were held with dancers, dance teachers and students, organizers and critics.

4 As a corollary, to avoid taking texts out of context and to complement the view of performances as texts, texts can be regarded as performances. A set of verbal signs becomes a text 'when it is realized by a reader, who thus acts as a "performer"' (Martindale 1993: 18).

5 See for example Hall and Jefferson (1993) and Hebdige (1979). Dance, however, has

been marginalized by the rationalism that Ward finds in cultural analysis in sociology (1993: 18).

6 For example, at a performance of *komachi odori* at Shiramine Shrine in Kyoto on 7 July 1981, there were rites of purification at the beginning, but once underway the performance seemed aimed primarily at photographers and local and national television. Similar tendencies can be observed in rural festivals: for example, see the Foreword by Robert J. Smith to Yamamoto (1978).

7 For example, Yamaguchi points to the entertaining (including dancing), trading and ritual functions of itinerant priests in pre-Tokugawa Japan (1977: 156).

8 For example, the skilful integration of song and dance is suggested by the *kanji* that are now used to write *kabuki* (歌舞伎) (euphemistically wrapping its earlier sense of deviation).

9 From the programme notes for a performance of *gigaku* and *gagaku* by the Gagaku Department of Tenri Daigaku, 15 February 1981.

10 For example Allison, in her brilliant decoding of the Japanese lunchbox, notes that special attention must be given to its visual presentation (1991: 197).

11 For example, most performances included, and concluded with, such tableaux in the annual performance of the Nihon Buyō Kyōkai at the Kokuritsu Gekijō (National Theatre) in February 1981, part of the Tokyo Arts Festival.

12 Such asymmetry was apparent in performances by the Hanayagi School at the Kokuritsu Gekijō, 24 March 1981.

13 Contrast this with the systematic elaboration of concepts of rhythm in Indian music and dance.

14 Interview with Fujii Tomoaki at the National Museum of Ethnology, July 1981. It is interesting to note that *buyō* (舞踊) combines the *kanji* for *mai* and *odori*. *Nihon buyō*, formerly classified along with folk dance as *odori*, is now included by Fujii and others under *mai*. This may mark its achievement of classical legitimacy.

15 Lebra relates *ma* more widely to the cultivation of silence in Japanese culture (1987: 344).

16 In his history of feelings in modern Japan, Mita notes a feeling of impermanence coloured by emotional attachment (1992: 117). His analysis of Japanese popular songs reveals that, since the end of the nineteenth century, transience, both temporal (impermanence) and spatial (wandering), is a common motif, documented through a variety of 'emotional symbols' (ibid.: 132–5).

17 Interview with Kimura Hideo, Director-General of the International Artists Centre, Tokyo, February 1981.

18 Similarly, Thomas indicates how the sociological marginalization of dance can document modern Western conceptions of art, the body and femininity (1995: 9).

19 The *iemoto* system, for example, where operative in the organization of certain forms of Japanese dance, may be indicative of wider principles of Japanese social organization (as suggested by Hsu 1975: 62 ff., Kumakura 1981: 6, and Hendry 1995: 169-72), but will not be discussed here except in so far as it relates to spatial or temporal aspects of Japanese dance styles.

20 Similarly the title 'intangible cultural property' (*mukei bunka-zai*) may be given in recognition of a great traditional cultural performance.

21 Gunji comments that *kabuki* performance tends to consist of 'a string of different *kata* arranged so as to show all the different facets of the performer's ability' (1985: 18). Nakamura notes the continuing power of the *iemoto* system in *kabuki* and *nihon buyō* (1990: 37).

22 This reflects the focus on feminine dance roles in *kabuki*, where the *onnagata* (males playing women's roles) gradually took over the dance elements, resulting in 'the specialization in dancing that is a feature of the *onnagata*'s art to this day' (Gunji 1985: 23). Robertson notes that '*onnagata* were exemplary models (*kata*) of "female" (*onna*) gender for females offstage to approximate' (1991: 170). The centrality of

women's roles could also be argued for *nō*. As Inoura and Kawatake point out, the great *nō* dramatist Zeami considered the most important *nō* plays to be those in which the central roles are female (1981: 116–18). These 'woman pieces' are the most lyrical and expressive of *yūgen*, a profound, subtle and mysterious beauty.

23 For a perceptive examination of the restricted cultural space of youth subcultures in Britain, see Hall and Jefferson (1993).

24 Similarly, Adair argues that ballet in Britain upholds the dominant ideology 'by re-inforcing traditional sex roles and by the hierarchical structures of both the training institutions and the ballet companies' (Adair 1992: 88–9). Fiske and Hartley suggest that, even when we move away from the elaborated code of ballet to the restricted code of a spectacular show on British television, the spectacular dance 'differentiates sex roles and refers to the class system' (1993: 48).

25 An interesting example of this was a performance of *komachi odori* at Shiramine Shrine, Kyoto, 7 July 1981, for *Tanabata* (Star Festival: according to the Tanabata legend, the Cowherd Star is allowed to cross the Milky Way to meet his love the Weaver Star on only this night each year). Most of the performers of *komachi odori* were young girls, who danced in a circle, their movements inward-directed, coy and *kawaii* (sweet, cute). An adult woman, in the role of Ori-hime (the Weaver Princess), danced in the centre of this circle and later on a raised stage with a man performing the role of the Cowherd. Their dance styles were sharply contrasted in the ways described above, and the final pose was of the Cowherd standing proudly upright with the Weaver Princess kneeling by his side.

26 Raz suggests that the avant-garde here are following older traditions, as in the rituals of inversion evident in Japanese folk tradition (1988: 15).

27 Programme of the Kamizawa Modern Dance Institute at their performance of modern dance in Kyoto, 3 July 1981. Hirai similarly notes that 'jazz dance gives the impression of being an activity for young mothers and middle-aged women.' (1990: 211).

28 The group model, one of the models critically outlined by Befu (1990), is constructed in this way. An alternative model of individualistic calculation is sometimes presumed to be universally applicable, and may go unrecognized as a model (Valentine 1997).

29 In similar fashion Western modern dance may be interpreted in Japan according to an available code that makes sense of it as 'chaotic movement', which may then become a model not just *of* interpretation but *for* the creation of new pieces of *modan dansu*.

30 Hekman, discussing the work of Gadamer, notes that he 'emphasizes both sides of the dialectic of interpretation' (1986: 146), so that the circle is not 'vicious' (ibid.: 101). Moreover, the dialectic is not supposed to confirm both sides, but to move towards transcendence 'that goes beyond the insistence of the number two, of binary opposi-tions, and of shackled couples' (Schehr 1995: 24). Willis proposes 'a dialectical notion of *integral circuiting* between processes and structures of the self and elements of text which changes both' (1990: 154). For the interpretation of art, an admirably clear account of the hermeneutic approach is provided by Wolff (1975: 102ff.).

31 The circular or interactive process here was noted by Mannheim in his documentary interpretation of *Weltanschauung*: 'we understand the whole from the part, and the part from the whole. We derive the "spirit of the epoch" from its individual docu-mentary manifestations – and we interpret the individual documentary manifestations on the basis of what we know about the spirit of the epoch' (1952: 74). Interpretation depends on framing contexts that have to be constructed 'from other texts, which also have to be interpreted' (Martindale 1993: 13).

32 For example, where hermeneutics suggests proceeding towards a 'complete' or 'global' interpretation (Bleicher 1982: 141; Giddens 1976: 56).

REFERENCES

Adair, Christy (1992) *Women and Dance: Sylphs and Sirens*, Basingstoke: Macmillan.

Alexander, Jeffrey C. (1994) 'Modern, Anti, Post, and Neo: How Social Theories Have Tried to Understand the "New World" of "Our Time" ', *Zeitschrift für Soziologie*, vol. XXIII, no. 3, pp. 165–97.

Allison, Anne (1991) 'Japanese Mothers and *Obentōs*: The Lunch-box as Ideological State Apparatus', *Anthropological Quarterly*, vol. LXIV, no. 4, pp. 195–207.

Befu, Harumi (1990) 'Four Models of Japanese Society and Their Relevance to Conflict', in S.N. Eisenstadt and Eyal Ben-Ari (eds) *Japanese Models of Conflict Resolution*, London and New York: Kegan Paul International, pp. 21–38.

Bleicher, Josef (1982) *The Hermeneutic Imagination*, London: Routledge.

Fiske, John and John Hartley (1993) 'Dance as Light Entertainment', in Stephanie Jordan and Dave Allen (eds) *Parellel Lines: Media Representations of Dance*, London: John Libbey.

Geertz, Clifford (1975) *The Interpretation of Cultures*, London: Hutchinson.

Giddens, Anthony (1976) *New Rules of Sociological Method*, London: Hutchinson.

—— (1990) *The Consequences of Modernity*, Cambridge: Polity Press.

Gunji, Masakatsu (1981) 'Miburi to monomane [Gesture and Mime]', public lecture, Kokuritsu Gekijō, Tokyo, 13 March.

—— (1985) *Kabuki*, Tokyo: Kodansha.

Hall, Stuart and Tony Jefferson (eds) (1993) *Resistance Through Rituals: Youth Subcultures in Post-war Britain*, London: Routledge.

Hanna, Judith Lynne (1979) *To Dance is Human*, Austin: University of Texas Press.

Havens, Thomas R.H. (1982) *Artist and Patron in Postwar Japan*, Princeton, NJ: Princeton University Press.

Hebdige, Dick (1979) *Subcultures: The Meaning of Style*, London: Methuen.

Hekman, Susan J. (1986) *Hermeneutics and the Sociology of Knowledge*, Cambridge: Polity Press.

Hendry, Joy (1993) *Wrapping Culture*, Oxford: Clarendon Press.

—— (1995) *Understanding Japanese Society*, London and New York: Routledge.

Hirai, Takane (1990) 'External Influences in the Transformation of Japanese Dance', in Michael Moerman and Nomura Masaichi (eds) *Culture Embodied*, Osaka: National Museum of Ethnology (Senri Ethnological Studies, no. 27).

Honda, Yasuji (n.d.) *Nihon no minzoku geinō [Japanese Folk Performing Arts]*, Tokyo: Kokusai Geijutsuka Sentā.

Hsu, Francis L.K. (1975) *Iemoto: The Heart of Japan*, Cambridge, MA: Schenkman.

Inoura, Yoshinobu and Kawatake, Toshio (1981) *The Traditional Theater of Japan*, Tokyo: Weatherhill.

Kaeppler, Adrienne L. (1978) 'Dance in Anthropological Perspective', *Annual Review of Anthropology*, vol. VII, pp. 31–49.

Kawatake, Toshio (1981) 'Japanese Theatre', public lecture, Scottish Centre for Japanese Studies, University of Stirling, 9 October.

Kumakura, Isao (1981) 'The Iemoto System in Japanese Society', *Japan Foundation Newsletter*, vol. IX, no. 4, pp. 1–7.

Kuniyoshi, Kazuko (1985) 'An Overview of the Contemporary Japanese Dance Scene', *Orientation Seminars on Japan*, no. 19, Tokyo: The Japan Foundation.

Kurath, Gertrude Prokosch (1960) 'Panorama of Dance Ethnology', *Current Anthropology*, vol. I, no. 3, pp. 233–54.

Lange, Roderyk (1975) *The Nature of Dance: An Anthropological Perspective*, London: MacDonald and Evans.

Lebra, Takie Sugiyama (1987) 'The Cultural Significance of Silence in Japanese Communication', *Multilingua*, vol. VI, no. 4, pp. 343–57.

Littleton, C. Scott (1987) 'Rituals of Rebellion Among Contemporary Japanese Youth: The Outdoor Disco at Tokyo's Yoyogi Park', *Religion*, vol. XVII, pp. 119–31.

Mannheim, Karl (1952) *Essays on the Sociology of Knowledge*, London: Routledge.

Martindale, Charles (1993) *Redeeming the Text: Latin Poetry and the Hermeneutics of Reception*, Cambridge: Cambridge University Press.

Mita, Munesuke (1992) *Social Psychology of Modern Japan*, London: Kegan Paul International.

Nakamura, Matazō (1990) *Kabuki: Backstage, Onstage*, Tokyo: Kodansha.

Raz, Jacob (1988) 'Foreword: Turbulent Years', in Jean Viala and Nourit Masson-Sekine (eds) *Butoh: Shades of Darkness*, Tokyo: Shufunotomo.

Robertson, Jennifer (1991) 'Theatrical Resistance, Theatres of Restraint: The Takurazuka Revue and the "State Theatre" Movement in Japan', *Anthropological Quarterly*, vol. LXIV, no. 4, pp. 165–77.

Royce, Anya Peterson (1977) *The Anthropology of Dance*, Bloomington: Indiana University Press.

Schehr, Lawrence R. (1995) *The Shock of Men: Homosexual Hermeneutics in French Writing*, Stanford: Stanford University Press.

Schutz, Alfred (1973) *Collected Papers I: The Problem of Social Reality*, The Hague: Martinus Nijhoff.

Singer, Milton (1972) *When a Great Tradition Modernizes*, London: Pall Mall Press.

Spencer, Paul (1985) 'Introduction: Interpretations of the Dance in Anthropology', in Paul Spencer (ed.) *Society and the Dance: The Social Anthropology of Process and Performance*, Cambridge: Cambridge University Press.

Starhawk (1989) *The Spiral Dance*, San Francisco: Harper.

Thomas, Helen (1995) *Dance, Modernity and Culture: Explorations in the Sociology of Dance*, London and New York: Routledge.

Valentine, James (1982) 'The Anthropology of Cultural Performances in Japan: Dance as a Document of Japanese Culture', *Annual of Institute of Buddhist Cultural Studies* (Ryūkoku University), vol. V, pp. 15–18.

—— (1994) 'Danse', in Augustin Berque (ed.) *Dictionnaire de la Civilisation Japonnaise*, Paris: Hazan, pp. 132–8.

—— (1997) 'Conformity, Calculation, and Culture', in Donald Munro, John F. Schumaker and Stuart C. Carr (eds) *Motivation and Culture*, New York and London: Routledge.

Varley, H. Paul (1974) *Japanese Culture: A Short History*, Tokyo: Tuttle.

Ward, Andrew H. (1993) 'Dancing in the Dark: Rationalism and the Neglect of Social Dance', in Helen Thomas (ed.) *Dance, Gender and Culture*, Basingstoke: Macmillan.

Willis, Paul (1990) *Common Culture*, Milton Keynes: Open University Press.

Wolff, Janet (1975) *Hermeneutic Philosophy and the Sociology of Art*, London: Routledge.

Wolz, Carl (1971) *Bugaku: Japanese Court Dance*, Providence: Asian Music Publications.

Yamaguchi, Masao (1977) 'Kingship, Theatricality, and Marginal Reality in Japan', in R.K. Jain (ed.) *Text and Context: The Social Anthropology of Tradition*, Philadelphia: I.S.H.I.

Yamamoto, Yoshiko (1978) *The Namahage: A Festival in Northeast of Japan*, Philadelphia: I.S.H.I.

Name index

Subject index

abortion 136, 140–41, 153
access (to dance forms) 269–70
action, models of (place-making) 68–85
adoption 4, 10, 145–60
Africa 9
agricultural households 120–1
Akita prefecture 18, 19, 22
Amami Islands 8, 167–80
American Association for the
  Advancement of Science 224
amusement quarters (*sakariba*) 6,
  231–40
ancestors: 'career' of 33–5; gods and
  mediators 8, 167–80; *hamaori* ritual
  167–8, 178–9
'annual rites' 15–28
anthropology 69–70, 145; fieldwork 3,
  195–8; social 1–11
anthropomorphic hypothesis 25, 27
anti-clockwise turns 189–92
Aomori prefecture 136, 138
Aoyama Cemetery 135
asymmetrical posture (dance) 265
AUM Shinrikyō 5–6, 194–5, 208–9, 227
Azande people 9

bamboo tree of life 206–8
bean 167, 171; *susuki* and 174–8, 179
beliefs: ritual and *chō* boundaries (Kuzaki)
  3, 6, 213–20; *see also* religion
bipartition of ritual year 23–4
birth (in Ryūkyūan houses) 32–3
boat rituals 190–1, 213–17
bon festival 17, 19–20, 23, 24, 26, 213,
  237, 266, 271
Buddhism 64, 71, 82, 127, 134, 140, 217,
  226; Amida 218, 219; funeral practices
  182, 185–8, 192; *mappō* 195, 208;
  Pythagorean view 44–6, 47, 48; Risshō

Kōseikai sect 45, 48; rituals 19, 23,
  31; Tendai sect 72; Zen 218, 219,
  225
bugaku dance 262, 264, 265, 268, 272,
  273
Bunaze myth 37
bureikō 239
butō dance 266–7, 273
buying sex 235, 236, 238

calendar: lunar-solar 17–18; ritual year
  14, 15–28; zodiac signs 16, 17, 35, 198
cemeteries 135
Centre for Contemporary Cultural Studies
  261
chakras 224–5, 226
Chiba Memorial Parks 135
chigaya ring 185
Child Consultation Centre 146
Child Welfare Law (1947) 150, 155
children: adoption and fostering 4, 10,
  145–60; fetus cults 140–1; ghost
  marriages 4, 133–9; succession
  practices 35, 120–1, 147
chō boundaries (Kuzaki) 3, 213–20
codification of dance performance 268–9
commitment, politics and (Hieidaira)
  78–80
community 68–85, 216, 219, 243–57
companies, memorial cults in 140–1
compartmentalization of dance
  performance 268–70
computerized cults 222–7
Confucianism 83, 91, 96
contested identities (in discourses of
  place-making) 3, 6, 68–85
corporate functions of *ie* (past/present)
  119–20
cosmology: gods, ancestors and mediators